PHYSICIAN ASSISTANT LEGAL HANDBOOK

Aspen Health Law Center

Patricia Younger, J.D.
Cynthia Conner, LL.L.
Kara Kinney Cartwright, J.D.
Susan M. Kole, J.D.
Jennifer C. Forsyth, J.D., M.P.H.

AN ASPEN PUBLICATION®
Aspen Publishers, Inc.
Gaithersburg, Maryland
1997

Library of Congress Cataloging-in-Publication Data
Physician assistant legal handbook / Aspen Health Law Center;
Patricia Younger . . . [et al.].
p. cm.
Includes bibliographical references and index.
ISBN 0-8342-0925-X (hardcover)
1. Physician assistants—Legal status, laws, etc.—United States. I. Younger, Patricia A. II. Aspen Health Law Center.
KF2915.P45P49 1997
344.73′0412—dc21 97-16412
CIP

Orders: (800) 638-8437
Customer Service: (800) 234-1660

Editorial Resources: Marsha Davies
Library of Congress Catalog Card Number: 97-16412
ISBN: 0-8342-0925-X

Printed in the United States of America
1 2 3 4 5

Table of Contents

Editorial Board

Preface

Physician assistants (PAs) have become increasingly important to the practice of medicine in the past decade. Partly due to the growth of managed care and its reliance on nonphysician practitioners, the PA profession has gained increasing recognition, and PAs have experienced an increase in both practice opportunities and patient care responsibilities. Today, patients encounter PAs in nearly all practice settings, including physicians' offices, group practices, hospitals, health maintenance organizations, nursing homes and home health, and outpatient clinics. As a result of this growth, the legal issues with which PAs should be familiar have also broadened; laws addressing prescriptive privileges, for example, have proliferated as legislatures have become more familiar with the capabilities of PAs. The increasing scope of legal privileges and obligations, as well as restrictions, relevant to PA practice requires PAs and their supervising physicians and employers to educate themselves about the expanded legal implications of day-to-day clinical practice.

The *Physician Assistant Legal Handbook* is intended for PAs, supervising physicians, employers of PAs, PA educators, attorneys, health administrators, and policy makers who are interested in the legal and professional issues of significance to PA practice. In addition to offering a detailed account of the evolution of the PA profession, the book discusses future challenges and trends, including the continued expansion of PA education programs, the impact of managed care, and the latest developments in health care quality improvement and comparative performance measurement.

The book also serves as a comprehensive reference on the federal and state laws that impact upon PA practice. Federal laws, for example, concern health care financing and reimbursement, controlled substances, employment, and occupational health and safety. State PA practice laws cover licensure, scope of practice, and related regulation of PAs. Also important are issues relevant to health care practitioners generally, such as medical records, mandatory reporting requirements, and informed consent. Numerous other legal issues that touch PA practice are addressed in the book, including prescriptive authority, malpractice, risk management, peer review and credentialing, employment discrimination, and third-party reimbursement. Throughout the book, the reader will find useful information on how to play an active part in reducing liability risks, developing workplace policies for improving the quality of patient care, and participating in legislative and regulatory process.

Acknowledgments

The *Physician Assistant Legal Handbook* could not have been written without the assistance of the American Academy of Physician Assistants (AAPA), which provided access to current state PA practice laws and regulations, as well as current data and background information on the PA profession. Nicole Gara, Vice President of Government and Professional Affairs for the AAPA, reviewed a majority of the manuscript, and her thorough comments and support throughout the writing process deserve a special thanks. Other AAPA staff members—Michael Powe and Ellen Rathfon in particular—provided useful suggestions after reviewing sections of the manuscript. In addition, substantial comments and valuable insight into the issues discussed in this book, including the history of the profession, challenges for the future, and the practical application of laws that impact on PAs, were provided by each member of the editorial board

The Aspen Health Law Center is grateful to all of these reviewers, and also to every member of its staff, for the patience and dedication they brought to this project. The Center's staff attorneys, Patricia Younger, Cynthia Conner, Kara Kinney Cartwright, Susan Kole, and Jennifer Forsyth, each made significant contributions to the book through their writing and research efforts. Diane Marvin, the Center's librarian and paralegal, also provided valuable help in obtaining resources for this project. We also are grateful to Ruth Bloom and Marsha Davies, Managing Editors in Editorial Resources, for keeping us on schedule and producing the final printed product.

CHAPTER 1

Physician Assistants and the Law

INTRODUCTION

Physician assistants (PAs) are touched by sources of law as fundamental as the United States Constitution and as specific as state regulations detailing the procedures that a PA may perform with or without physician supervision. In addition, private individuals may sue PAs in state courts for violating legal duties created by statute, regulation, or case law. This chapter illustrates the broad spectrum of legal authority that affects PA practice.

This chapter also describes the variety of practice settings in which PAs are currently employed, and provides an overview of important legal requirements that PAs should consider an intrinsic part of medical practice. Decisions made by PAs every day have potential legal consequences. Because legal advice is not available at every turn, no PA should enter practice without understanding the legal implications of the patient care activities in his or her specialty.

SOURCES OF REGULATION

Physician assistants are governed by laws, regulations, and court decisions on both the federal and state level. Each of these forms of regulation differs in terms of enforcement and penalties.

Federal Laws and Regulations

A *law,* or *statute,* is enacted by the legislature, which on the federal level consists of the House of Representatives and the Senate. Ordinarily, federal legislation must also be approved by the President, although Congress can override a presidential veto with a two-thirds majority. Laws establish required, permissible, or prohibited conduct, and violating the law can lead to either civil or criminal penalties (discussed later).

A *regulation* also establishes the bounds of conduct, but is issued by a federal agency after public comment, rather than by the legislature. Regulations are intended to carry out laws by providing detailed guidance to members of the public governed by a law, as well as to agency employees responsible for enforcing the law. Although regulations do not officially carry the same legal force as statutes, there is little practical difference between the authoritativeness of laws and regulations. A statute may specifically state that a violation of the regulations interpreting it automatically constitutes a violation of the statute itself. Further, because the federal agency responsible for enforcing a law will rely on its regulations to determine whether the law has been broken, and because legal challenges to regulations rarely succeed, compliance is well advised under most circumstances.

A variety of penalties may result from violating federal regulations, including exclusion from federal programs such as Medicare, revocation of federal licenses, and fines. Although federal agencies can penalize individuals for violating either a regulation or a statute, a *criminal action* can only result from a statutory violation. A federal government prosecutor initiates a criminal action by charging the alleged violator with a crime, perhaps on the recommendation of an administrative agency. The violator, known as a *defendant,* is tried in federal court before a federal judge, and a finding of guilt may lead to criminal punishment, including monetary penalties or incarceration, if the statute allows.

Federal Administrative Agencies

The federal government regulates health professionals largely through its administrative agencies. Administrative agencies, which are part of the executive branch of the federal government, develop the regulations that implement federal laws. Varying aspects of PA practice are regulated to some degree by certain federal agencies, for example, the Health Care Financing Administration (HCFA) [discussed in Chapter 10: Third-Party Reimbursement], and federal drug enforcement agencies such as the Drug Enforcement Administration (DEA) and the Food and Drug Administration (FDA) [discussed in Chapter 4: Prescribing and Dispensing]. Federal employment and labor agencies such as the Equal Employment Opportunity Commission (EEOC) and the Occupational Safety and Health Administration (OSHA) also develop and enforce regulations of interest to PAs. [See Chapter 9: Employment Laws.]

Federal agencies often generate documents other than regulations that, while not binding on the public, offer additional guidance on what the laws and regulations require. For example, an agency might create "interpretive guidelines" to educate investigators concerning what conduct may constitute a regulatory violation. Letters between an agency and the public, or between one government agency or another, may also serve to establish the parameters of acceptable conduct.

Federal agencies also enforce laws and regulations by investigating violations and bringing administrative actions against the alleged violators. An *administrative action* can result from violation of either a statute or regulation, and typically begins with an agency investigation. If the agency concludes that a violation has occurred, it will formally notify the alleged violator, who may agree to enter into a *settlement,* which involves an agreement between the violator and agency officials as to the facts of the case and the appropriate penalty. If the violator does not settle, the agency will likely hold a hearing.

An administrative agency hearing does not take place in a court of law, but before an agency decision maker known as an administrative law judge. Such hearings are similar to court trials, however, in that both the agency and the alleged violator present evidence and arguments. If the agency decision maker concludes that a violation occurred, penalties such as fines or license revocation may be imposed. After exhausting administrative appeals within the agency, the violator may have the right to appeal to a court of law.

State Administrative Agencies

Like the federal government, states largely rely on administrative agencies to oversee the conduct of PAs. In many states, PAs are governed by the board of medicine, an administrative agency charged with policing physicians and physician assistants as directed by state laws. In other states, a separate PA licensing board, or a PA task force committee within the state medical board has been established to regulate the conduct of PAs. [See Chapter 11: Participation in Government Affairs, at PA Representation on Regulatory Boards.]

These regulatory entities have the authority to issue regulations establishing the scope of PA practice and to grant or revoke PA licenses. The state laws authorizing the PA licensing scheme are commonly known as PA practice acts. Except for Mississippi, every state has enacted a PA practice act. These statutes, and the regulations that implement them, can govern acceptable conduct for PAs very specifically. [See Chapter 3: Licensure and Scope of Practice.] Other state agencies, such as state Medicaid agencies and state food and drug or drug enforcement agencies, also impact the day-to-day practice of PAs.

Lawsuits

A *civil suit* is a lawsuit initiated by a private individual who sues to obtain compensation for an injury allegedly caused by another individual's wrongdoing. If a PA improperly prescribes medication, for example, and a patient is harmed as a result, the patient may sue the PA for medical malpractice. If the PA is found liable, the PA will be ordered to pay monetary damages to the patient. Typically, damages include past and future medical expenses, lost wages, and "pain and suffering" damages aimed at compensating the patient for emotional distress.

A civil action does not preclude other types of penalties, regardless of the lawsuit's outcome. Thus, if the PA in the previous example also violated state prescribing rules, the PA could be investigated by the state medical board and lose his or her prescribing privileges or license to practice, even if the PA was not found liable for medical malpractice.

Physician assistants should understand that courts play a crucial role in regulating PA conduct in two ways:

1. *Interpreting laws and regulations*. No law or regulation can be written so that everyone who reads it will agree on how it applies in every circumstance. Although regulations provide detailed guidance on what conduct is permissible or required under certain laws, even regulations do not anticipate every factual situation that can occur. Court decisions make finer distinctions than regulations and laws by determining whether a particular individual's conduct violated a law or regulation, and by establishing what conduct is required or prohibited by law.
2. *Developing and applying case law*. Not all law is found in statute books. Judicial decisions not only interpret statutes, but also create new law, known as common law or case law. Medical malpractice is a state common law theory, for example. A long history of cases has established the elements that a patient must prove to recover monetary damages in a malpractice action, as well as the level of proof that a patient must show for each element. The courts have also adopted tests, or standards of care, to determine whether a health care provider has provided adequate care to a patient. [Medical malpractice is discussed in Chapter 5: Liability.]

Private Organizations

Professional associations and accreditation bodies may also guide the conduct of PAs. The American Academy of Physician Assistants (AAPA), for example, has issued a code of ethics and numerous other guidelines and position papers to advise its members. The National Commission on the Certification of Physician Assistants (NCCPA) is responsible for administrating the certification exam for PAs, an important credential because it is required for licensure in most states. [For further discussion, see Chapter 2: Education and Certification.] From a clinical perspective, PAs' conduct may be informed or even directed by various medical practice organizations that generate clinical practice guidelines or treatment protocols. [Protocols and guidelines are discussed in Chapter 3: Licensure and

Scope of Practice, at Job Descriptions and at Protocols, and clinical practice guidelines are discussed in Chapter 6: Quality Review and Risk Management, at Clinical Practice Guidelines.]

PROFESSION PROFILE

Today's PAs are members of a growing profession. According to the AAPA, which represents PAs nationwide, approximately 25,700 PAs were in clinical practice as of January 1996. The Department of Labor Bureau of Labor Statistics projects PA job growth at 23 percent between 1994 and 2005—faster than the growth in total employment by 9 percentage points [AAPA, "Facts at a Glance," Nov. 5, 1996, http://www.aapa.org/glance.htm].

PAs practice in diverse specialties and practice in a wide array of practice settings. The range of specialties and settings is reflected in the data contained in the AAPA's annual census survey. The most recent survey elicited a response rate of roughly 56 percent of survey recipients consisting of 26,660 PAs (both members and nonmembers of the AAPA) [*1996 AAPA Physician Assistant Census Report* (Dec. 1996)]. Adjusting for nonrespondents, the report's data reveal that the majority of PAs are in clinical practice on a full-time basis, and that:

- 40 percent work in physician offices (solo or group practice)
- slightly more than 30 percent provided the majority of their services in a hospital
- more than 11 percent work in clinics (freestanding outpatient clinics, rural and inner city health clinics)
- roughly 7 percent work in HMO facilities
- nearly 3 percent work in nursing homes, home health, and correctional facilities
- 2 percent fall in a variety of "other" practice settings, including the military

While PAs practice in more than 60 specialty fields, the AAPA's 1996 survey revealed more than half of the respondents (53.8 percent) practice in primary care, including family/general medicine, general internal medicine, general pediatrics, and obstetrics/gynecology. The two most common specialties are family/general medicine (39.8 percent) and surgery (18.8 percent) [*1996 AAPA Physician Assistant Census Report* (Dec. 1996)].

PRACTICE SETTINGS AND SPECIAL LEGAL ISSUES

Although many legal issues (such as licensure and liability) are important to all PAs, in every practice setting PAs face legal issues of special importance to their particular circumstances. Certain practice settings, however, are beyond the scope of this book and are not included, such as PAs in the military or in correctional facilities. The following discussion is an introduction to the broad legal areas that are noteworthy in the practice settings where the majority of PAs currently practice; in the chapters to follow, these legal issues are discussed in greater detail.

Hospitals

In the hospital setting, PA duties vary widely in accordance with the arrangement, employment or otherwise, that the PA and the supervising physician(s) have set up with the hospital. A PA, for example, may be employed by a group practice and have clinical privileges at a hospital associated with following the medical care of patients admitted to the hospital by the group practice, or the PA may be employed by the hospital under the supervision of a hospital staff physician, making rounds in place of the physician and providing daily care to inpatients. In some hospitals, PAs may be among the first health care providers to evaluate a patient, taking detailed histories, performing examinations, and ordering tests in accordance with protocols. Also, PAs may play an important role in the patient discharge process, instructing patients about medications and home care. A significant number of PAs in hospital settings work in specialty areas such as surgery or emergency, and are credentialed to perform procedures particular to that service.

Physician assistants employed by hospitals, on hospital medical staffs, or exercising clinical privileges at hospitals must be aware of the legal issues surrounding credentialing and peer review [discussed in Chapter 8: Credentialing and Peer Review]. In addition, scope of practice laws may limit the services a PA may provide or require a specified degree of physician supervision in a hospital setting. [See Chapter 3: Licensure and Scope of Practice.] Quality improvement (QI) and risk management (RM) are also important parts of hospital practice, and PAs working in hospital settings should be familiar with QI/RM concepts and their implementation in the workplace. [See Chapter 6: Quality Review and Risk Management.]

Within specialized hospital settings, PAs may encounter legal concerns in addition to the clinical privileges process. Licensure and reimbursement rules, for example, may impact upon whether PAs can serve as assistants at surgery. [See Chapter 3: Licensure and Scope of Practice, and Chapter 10: Third-Party Reimbursement.] Although all PAs in hospitals should know about legal concerns related to advance directives, do not resuscitate (DNR) orders, competency, and informed consent to treatment, PAs practicing in emergency or psychiatric departments must be particularly familiar with these issues. [See Chapter 5: Liability, at Informed Consent and at Balancing Legal and Ethical Issues.]

Ambulatory Care

Ambulatory care refers to health care provided to patients who are not admitted to a hospital or other institution. Ambulatory care settings include medical clinics, physicians' offices (solo and group practices), ambulatory surgical centers, mental health centers, and urgent care centers. Primary care, which is essentially the first contact for patients entering the health care system, is provided in ambulatory care settings. The typical role of a PA in these settings is to examine patients, make diagnoses, and prescribe treatment in accordance with authority delegated by the supervising physician. If necessary, the PA also facilitates the referral process by directing the patient to the appropriate physician or specialist for handling the patient's medical problem. Because the focus of primary care is on prevention and health promotion, a crucial part of PA practice in ambulatory settings is patient education and counseling (i.e., explaining the patient's overall health problems and increasing the patient's awareness of the social and psychological elements of good health).

Physician assistants in ambulatory care settings may see patients seeking an appointment with a physician who is booked, may cover appointments for physicians called away for an emergency, or may follow their own patients. A PA who is privileged at nearby hospitals may follow patients during hospitalizations. Some PAs in ambulatory care practices may provide care in other settings, such as private homes for patients who are not able to make a trip into an office or clinic or nursing homes and mental health institutions for patients admitted to such facilities.

Because the types of care provided in the ambulatory care setting have dramatically expanded in recent years, and because managed care contracts may penalize providers for referring patients to specialty or hospital care, PAs must be closely familiar with legal limitations on the scope of PA practice. State PA practice rules or the job descriptions required under those rules, for example, may specify medical procedures that PAs are prohibited from performing, or, more commonly, may limit the type or scope of procedures (e.g., invasive procedures, prescribing) that a PA may perform without a physician's presence. [See Chapter 3: Licensure and Scope of Practice, and Chapter 4: Prescribing and Dispensing.]

In addition to scope of practice laws and regulations, the risk of medical malpractice liability also impacts the services PAs provide in ambulatory care settings. If the standard of care requires a referral to a specialist or consultation with a physician, a PA could face liability for failing to seek that assistance. [See Chapter 5: Liability, at Conduct That May Lead To Liability.] With respect to every patient encounter or referral, it is important for PAs in these settings to pay close attention to their performance in terms of the potential liability risks associated with clinical practice. [See Chapter 6: Quality Review and Risk

Management.] Moreover, PAs who practice in primary care and other ambulatory care settings should ensure that they are properly credentialed for following patients who are hospitalized or who are admitted for nursing home care. [See Chapter 8: Credentialing and Peer Review.] Finally, because many of the services provided by PAs in physician offices or clinics are an integral part of the physician's care, PAs should be familiar with Medicare coverage for PA-provided services "incident to" a physician's services. Medicare will cover some PA services at 100 percent of the physician's fee schedule amount if certain supervision, employment, and treatment conditions are met. [See Chapter 10: Third-Party Reimbursement.]

Medically Underserved Areas

Physician assistants who practice in medically underserved areas, such as rural health clinics and inner city clinics, face the same legal issues as PAs in other ambulatory care settings, along with some other concerns specific to remote practice and providing medical services to disadvantaged and poor populations.

Because PAs practicing in rural areas often provide a variety of care with limited supervision, they must take care to observe state scope-of-practice laws. [See Chapter 3: Licensure and Scope of Practice, at Scope of Practice under State PA Practice Laws.] The isolation of rural practice also makes it important for PAs to seek out continuing education and peer review opportunities, so that they remain familiar with the standard of care for rural medical practice and avoid liability. [See Chapter 5: Liability, at Negligence.] Very different concerns are of particular importance to PAs in inner city health clinics, where drug abuse, violence, sexually transmitted diseases (including human immunodeficiency virus (HIV)), and poverty are frequently the causes behind a patient's health problems. In these settings, PAs must be particularly careful about compliance with federal laws limiting maintenance prescribing of narcotics, as well as state law limits on PA prescribing. [See Chapter 4: Prescribing and Dispensing.] State laws also govern the reporting of possible domestic violence, child abuse, and sexual abuse; PAs who treat patients in these categories should be familiar with reporting requirements. [See Chapter 7: Medical Records.]

Medicare and Medicaid regulations impose special rules on medical practices in designated medically underserved areas and health professional shortage areas. In rural areas, PAs should be aware of the reimbursement policy under Medicare and Medicaid for services provided by PAs in certified rural health clinics, while PAs in inner city practice settings should understand Medicaid reimbursement rules, which generally cover reimbursement for health services provided to poor patients. [See Chapter 10: Third-Party Reimbursement.]

Managed Care

Contracting is a legal concern for PAs in practices that participate in managed care plans. A PA in a physician group practice or a single physician practice, for example, must ensure inclusion in managed care participation contracts signed by physicians. If a physician enters into a participation agreement without negotiating for PA participation, the managed care plan will not cover care provided to plan members by the PA.

Other managed care contracting clauses may place a PA in the position of choosing to violate the clause (and forfeit payment under the plan) or risk malpractice liability. Gag clauses that preclude providers from offering patients treatment alternatives not covered by the plan are an example. Capitation agreements and other contracts that reward providers for not referring patients for tests or specialty care may also create a risk of liability if the PA does not order the care that a patient needs. [See Chapter 5: Liability, at Balancing Legal and Ethical Issues.]

Risk management and quality assurance programs are an integral part of most managed care plans. Because compliance with established quality assurance procedures is required for continued participation in managed care plans, PAs should be familiar with the risk management and quality assurance concepts. [See Chapter 6: Quality Review and Risk Management.]

The integrated approach to health care emphasized by managed care plans has highlighted the legal issues related to medical records. The computerization of medical records, or allowing a variety of providers to access a patient's entire record, for example, raises confidentiality concerns. [See Chapter 7: Medical Records.]

Nursing Homes and Home Health Care

In nursing homes, the Medicare Conditions of Participation strictly regulate the care provided to patients. The regulations impose specific requirements such as the use of catheters and nasogastric tubes and the unnecessary use of drugs. Failure to follow these rules may result in the facility's loss of Medicare participation. Medicare reimbursement rules may also limit the amount of payment for services provided by PAs. [See Chapter 10: Third-Party Reimbursement.] As with PAs employed in other institutional settings, credentialing processes are an area of legal concern for PAs practicing in nursing homes. [See Chapter 8: Credentialing and Peer Review.]

The poor health of nursing home patients also leads to some special legal considerations for PAs. Because medication management is an important part of nursing home care, PAs must know and comply with state PA prescribing laws. [See

Chapter 4: Prescribing and Dispensing.] Physician assistants following nursing home patients must also be familiar with consent to treatment laws, as well as procedures for administering treatment to incompetent patients. Finally, understanding the implications of documents such as advance directives is an important part of administering nursing home care. [See Chapter 5: Liability, and Chapter 6: Quality Review and Risk Management.]

Home health care providers may be independent contractors or employees of a home health agency, hospital, clinic, or other type of provider, and thus PAs contemplating providing home health care should consider the implications of these different employment relationships. [See Chapter 9: Employment Laws, and Chapter 5: Liability.] State laws establishing the permissible scope of PA practice and the required level of physician supervision for PAs must be followed in home health care practice. [See Chapter 3: Licensure and Scope of Practice.] Medicare reimbursement rules also impact PA coverage policies in the home health arena. [See Chapter 10: Third-Party Reimbursement.]

CHAPTER 2

Education and Certification

INTRODUCTION

The comprehensive review of PA education and PA national certification provided in this chapter rarely touches upon the legal implications of PA practice. Nonetheless, it does provide important background on the PA profession, including PA education program development, program accreditation, curriculum, and the mandatory requirements for obtaining and maintaining national certification upon graduation. All PAs should be familiar with the evolution of PA education, and also the challenges facing today's PA education programs in their attempts to meet the growing demands for PAs in a health care system focused on cost-effectiveness and increasing access to primary care medicine. This chapter outlines important historical events, as well as current issues, in PA education and PA national certification.

HISTORICAL BACKGROUND

Physician assistants were introduced into medical practice in the United States in the early 1960s in response to generalist physician shortages and decreased health care access. The PA concept was first articulated by Charles L. Hudson in 1961, but his vision of producing a new type of medical generalist to extend physician services was not implemented into an actual PA educational program until 1965 when Dr. Eugene Stead, chairman of the Department of Medicine at Duke University, became director of the first PA program [*see* C.E. Fasser, "Historical Perspectives of PA Education," *Journal of American Academy of Physician Assistants* 663 (Oct. 1992)].

At that time, circumstances at Duke University Medical Center in Durham, North Carolina, were particularly appropriate for the initial attempt at creating an educational program to train PAs. The Medical Center had a shortage of both physicians and nurses, and the number of rural physicians in North Carolina was dwindling. Recognizing the changing medical service and personnel needs within the Medical Center and in surrounding communities, Dr. Stead sought to develop an educational program, including extensive training in clinical procedures, for a new class of "dependent" medical clinicians who could be trained in a relatively short period of time to assist physicians in a broad range of practice settings but with a special emphasis on practice locations in medically needy areas (i.e., rural counties with physician shortages).

Dr. Stead first pursued development of this concept through nursing channels, proposing an advanced medical education program for clinical nurses designed to expand their capabilities. The National League of Nursing, however, opposed the program based on its perception that the PA concept would divert nurses to a new profession based on the "medical" model, rather than the concept of advanced nursing. Consequently, Dr. Stead's initial program failed to develop beyond the proposal stage.

Unable to gain access to nurses for purposes of training a new midlevel practitioner, Stead focused his efforts on another source of personnel, ex-military corpsmen. During the early 1960s, Duke University had begun to train a group of ex-corpsmen and other noncollege graduates to fill service gaps resulting from personnel shortages at Duke University Hospital. In September 1965, the new Duke PA program enrolled four ex-Navy corpsmen in a two-year intensive medical education program under Stead's direction. The educational curriculum was divided; the first year consisted of accelerated studies in basic and preclinical science, followed by a second year of clinical rotations in inpatient, outpatient, and office settings. The final two months of the program were designated for completion of a preceptorship, usually with a physician or institution that was a potential employer.

Program Models

The Duke University program, a medical center model PA program, was quickly followed by a host of other PA programs at universities with affiliated medical centers. Universities that structured some of the earliest PA programs in accordance with the medical center model included Bowman Gray (Wake Forest University), Oklahoma, Yale, Alabama, George Washington, Emory, and Johns Hopkins. [For a full listing of physician assistant programs and their accreditation status, see Appendix 2-A.]

A significantly different educational model was followed in developing a PA program at the University of Washington in 1969. Dr. Richard Smith, then associate professor of preventive medicine at the university, established the Medical Extension (MEDEX) Program, which emphasized the deployment of PA students and graduates in community-based preceptorships with physicians practicing in medically underserved, primarily rural areas. Although the University of Washington MEDEX program initially enrolled only former military corpsmen as trainees, the applicant pool expanded beyond military personnel as MEDEX demonstration projects were developed at sites across the country. By the early 1970s, MEDEX model programs, with curriculums and deployment objectives similar to that of the original model, had been established at University of North Dakota School of Medicine, University of Alabama–Birmingham, University of Utah College of Medicine, Dartmouth Medical School, Howard University College of Medicine, Charles Drew Postgraduate Medical School, Pennsylvania State University College of Medicine, and Medical University of South Carolina. [Some of these programs subsequently closed due to lack of adequate funding, and today there exists only a few MEDEX PA programs. For a full listing of accredited physician assistant programs, see Appendix 2-A.]

Another early educational model for PA programs was derived from the concept of an advanced pediatric nursing program. In 1969, Dr. Henry Silver, a professor of pediatric medicine at the University of Colorado, founded the Child Health Associate Program, in which enrollees would receive academic instruction and clinical training in a three-year curriculum focused primarily on health care for children. The objective of the program was to increase the supply of pediatric health care services in underserved areas; thus, enrollees spent their third year in community-based internships at pediatricians' offices, usually located in rural areas. Perhaps the most innovative aspects of the program were its acceptance of applicants without any prior medical experience (but with at least two years of undergraduate coursework), and its offering of a master's degree upon completion of the graduate school requirements and the third-year internship. [For a related discussion on the range of academic degrees offered by PA programs, see Education Programs, at Academic Degree Options.]

The four-year undergraduate-level PA program was another educational model. The first of these programs was developed in 1969 by Dr. Hu Myers at Alderson Broaddus College (West Virginia). Because it offered two years of liberal arts education with a concentration in general science courses and two years of professional training as a PA, the program required no prior medical experience for admission. Students enrolled in the program received clinical training at a campus hospital and affiliated clinic, and attained a baccalaureate degree on graduation. Other colleges and universities, some affiliated with university medical centers, subsequently established similar programs, including the PA programs at St. Francis College (Loretto, PA), Gannon University (Erie, PA), and King's College (Wilkes-Barre, PA).

Specialty programs for PAs are another category of the PA educational model. The first specialty program was developed at the University of Alabama in 1967 and was designed to train surgeon assistants to serve in medically underserved areas. The two-year program offered didactic instruction similar to other PA programs, but the clinical training phase focused exclusively on surgery and surgical subspecialties. During the 1970s, additional entry-level PA education programs (i.e., programs at the undergraduate level) developed around other specialties including urology, orthopedics, and pathology, but all of these programs subsequently closed or converted to primary care PA programs.

For the most part, specialized training for graduate PAs has been replaced by PA postgraduate residency programs, which are usually based in teaching hospitals. In 1993, there existed only 11 such residency programs in the specialty areas of surgery, neonatology, pediatrics, emergency medicine, obstetrics/gynecology, and occupational medicine. Applicants are PA graduates seeking advanced clinical training, and these programs usually offer an intensive one-year clinical experience in a particular specialty area. Although predominantly focused on clinical skills, some of these residency programs also provide a didactic instruction phase of advanced-level courses. Only a small percentage of practicing PAs have formally completed a postgraduate residency program; collectively, the programs train approximately 75 PAs per year [*see* U.S. Department of Health and Human Services, *Physician Assistants in the Health Workforce 1994—Final Report of the Advisory Group on Physician Assistants and the Workforce* (1994), at 31 (hereinafter *"1994 AGPAW Report"*)]. Because of the small number of PA postgraduate residency programs, there is no formal accreditation mechanism in place. Nonetheless, PA postgraduate residencies are well-regarded within the profession, and well-organized through their national representative organization, the Association of Physician Assistant Postgraduate Residency Programs. [For a listing of Physician Assistant National and Specialty Organizations, see Appendix A.]

Another comparatively recent development in PA postgraduate education is programs that are more academically oriented, offering enrollees graduate coursework in research methods, health policy analysis, rural health, and public health education and practice. For example, graduate PA programs in rural health are offered at Alderson Broaddus College (West Virginia), and the University of Nebraska–Omaha. Additional graduate PA programs in occupational medicine, public health, and/or preventive medicine are offered at University of Oklahoma (Oklahoma City), George Washington University (Washington, DC), University of Iowa (Iowa City), and St. Francis College (Loretto, PA). PAs graduating from these programs typically receive a master of public health (MPH) degree or a master of medical science (MMSc) degree.

Program Expansion via Federal Funding

Funds underwriting the initial PA programs were provided by private sponsoring institutions and philanthropic organizations such as the Upjohn Company, the Commonwealth Fund, the Kellogg Foundation, and the Robert Wood Foundation. Also, in 1969, the National Center for Health Services Research undertook funding for a few MEDEX pilot programs. Although some federal funding for PA education programs was authorized under the Allied Health Professions Personnel Act of 1966 [Pub. L. No. 751] and the Health Manpower Act of 1968 [Pub. L. No. 90-490], the dramatic increase in federal grant support for such programs did not occur until the 1970s.

In the early 1970s, the Department of Health, Education, and Welfare, and other federal policymakers strongly supported the training and employment of PAs and nurse practitioners. Congress responded by enacting the 1970 Health Training Improvement Act, the Comprehensive Health Manpower Act of 1971 (CHMA), and the Nurse Training Act of 1971, which together authorized the appropriation of $14.5 million for PA and nurse practitioner education programs. [*See* C.E. Fasser, "Historical Perspectives of PA Education," *Journal of American Academy of Physician Assistants* 663, 666 (Oct. 1992)]. The CHMA was reauthorized in 1973 and became an even more significant federal endorsement of PA education programs because it included PA program-funding support programs under Title VII of the Public Health Service Act. From 1972 to 1976, funding from Health Manpower Educational Initiatives Awards and Public Health Service contracts totaled $32,669,565 for 43 programs. [*See, e.g.,* Health Resources and Services Administration, Bureau of Health Professions, *Annual Report* (Oct. 1990); J. Cawley, "Federal Health Policy and PAs," *Journal of American Academy of Physician Assistants* 679, 683 (Oct. 1992)].

Federal grant support for PA education was continued in 1976 in the Health Professions Educational Assistance Act [Pub. L. No. 94-484], now codified under Section VII of the Public Health Service Act, which authorized the categorical grants program administered by the U.S. Public Health Service, through its Health Resources and Services Administration (HRSA), Bureau of Health Professions, to include educational institutions sponsoring PA programs. As a result of its link to public health policy, federal grant support successfully influenced the rapidly expanding network of PA programs to maintain curricula focused on primary care and to continually develop strategies for utilization of

PAs in medically underserved areas. In this regard, another important federal legislative initiative was Congress's 1977 enactment of the Rural Health Clinic Services Act [Pub. L. No. 95-210], which authorized Medicare and Medicaid coverage of medical services provided by PAs in certified rural health clinics as a mechanism for sustaining the viability of these clinics and increasing access to health care in underserved rural areas. [For a more detailed discussion of the Rural Health Clinic Services Act, see Chapter 10: Third-Party Reimbursement, at Rural Health Clinics.]

Federal grant support for PA programs has been consistently authorized by Congress since the 1970s, but since grant funds must regularly be reauthorized and reappropriated, the funding is unpredictable. For example, total annual federal grant awards to PA programs from 1972 to 1978, the early years of the PA profession, ranged from $6 million to $8 million, and from 1978 through 1981 this amount remained fairly stable at approximately $8 million for about 40 programs. From 1982 through 1991, however, these funds were severely cut to approximately $4.8 million annually. Although federal grant awards have increased in the 1990s (ranging from approximately $5 million to $6.5 million), the number of PA programs has also increased, from 40 to nearly 70 programs eligible for funding [*see, e.g.,* Health Resources and Services Administration, Bureau of Health Professions, *Annual Report* (Oct. 1990); *1994 AGPAW Report,* at 26]. Statistics on grant funding over this period indicate that typically only half of the eligible PA programs applying for grant support receive HRSA grants [*see 1994 AGPAW Report,* at 26; for a more detailed discussion of sufficiency of funding for expanding PA programs, see Current Issues in Education, at Adequacy of Funding].

From 1972 to 1991, the federal grant awards under Title VII of the Public Health Service Act have totaled approximately $120 million, and during the 1990s that total amount has risen to approximately $140 million [*see* Health Resources and Services Administration, Bureau of Health Professions, *Annual Report* (Oct. 1990); J. Cawley, "The Evolution of New Health Professions," in *The U.S. Health Workforce: Power, Politics, and Policy* 189, 194 (1996)]. In 1995, however, the authorization for HRSA grant support technically expired when the Health Professions Educational Assistance Act was not reauthorized by Congress, but some form of reauthorization legislation is likely to be enacted in upcoming congressional sessions.

PROGRAM ACCREDITATION

Rapid proliferation of PA programs based on various educational models prompted PA educators and organized medicine to quickly become concerned about PA program accreditation. In 1969, the leading PA educators at Duke University, Dr. E. Harvey Estes, chairman of the Department of Community Health

Science, and Dr. D. Robert Howard, director of the PA program, requested from the American Medical Association (AMA) some educational guidelines for PA programs, with particular emphasis on the development of minimum standards to govern such programs. The Board of Medicine of the National Academy of Science was another early advocate of developing guidelines to ensure the quality of PA education programs [*see* C.E. Fasser, "Historical Perspectives of PA Education," *Journal of American Academy of Physician Assistants* 663, 666 (Oct. 1992)].

The AMA's Council on Medical Education responded to these recommendations by creating the *Essentials of an Approved Educational Program for the Assistant to the Primary Care Physician* (Essentials) for the accreditation of PA programs. The Council developed the Essentials with the assistance of various medical societies representing internists, family physicians, and pediatricians, as well as three leading PA educators (one from each of the three earliest PA program models: Duke Univerity, MEDEX–University of Washington, and the Child Health Associate Program–University of Colorado). In 1971, the AMA's House of Delegates approved the Essentials, and shortly thereafter, they were used by federal agencies as criteria for evaluating PA program applications for grant awards.

Under a contract with the National Institutes of Health, the AMA's Division on Medical Education began its accreditation activities in 1972, including initial consideration of applications for accreditation, conducting on-site evaluations, and approving or denying accreditation status. Accreditation responsibilities were transferred in 1977 to the AMA's Committee on Allied Health Education and Accreditation (CAHEA), which carried out most of its accreditation activities through the Accreditation Review Committee on Education for the Physician Assistant (ARC-PA). The ARC-PA continues to review PA programs today, but since 1994, CAHEA's successor, the Commission on Accreditation of Allied Health Education Programs (CAAHEP), makes the final accreditation decisions. [For a more detailed description of PA program accreditation entities, see the later discussion of CAAHEP and the ARC-PA.]

The number of accredited PA programs is rapidly increasing: in March 1996, there were 64 accredited PA programs in the United States, and after CAAHEP's formal accreditation decisions were issued in April 1996, that number jumped to 78. As of the end of 1996, under a fully operational provisional accreditation system, there are 87 accredited PA programs, with more programs up for review in April 1997. [See Provisional Accreditation.]

Accreditation Standards

Since the original version of the Essentials, the accreditation guidelines have been revised in 1978, 1985, 1990, and 1996. Although updated to reflect changes in PA educational programs over time, the current version of the Essentials [*see*

CAAHEP, *Standards and Guidelines for an Accredited Educational Program for the Physician Assistant* (1996) (hereinafter "Standards")] has the same objective as earlier versions—to outline the criteria on which PA program accreditation is based. The Standards provide that the PA program must submit timely self-study reports to document a process of continuous self-evaluation regarding the effectiveness of the education it provides, and must also agree to a comprehensive review by the ARC-PA, which usually includes a site visit. The ARC-PA relies upon the self-study reports and its own on-site evaluation in making recommendations to CAAHEP, which makes the ultimate decision to approve or withhold accreditation. The process is designed to encourage continual improvement of educational approaches as PA programs make modifications to maintain or exceed the accreditation standards.

The Standards guide PA programs in developing their educational objectives by setting out key requirements that must be met to receive CAAHEP accreditation. Specific aspects of PA education addressed in the Standards include:

- curriculum content (e.g., course objectives, clinical training affiliations, basic and clinical science offerings)
- faculty qualifications
- educational resources and facilities
- fiscal stability
- administration
- recordkeeping systems
- program support services in areas such as admissions, library facilities, publications, student scholarship and financial assistance, and institutional sponsorship

The Standards also provide a detailed description of the PA profession, which is necessary background for the development of a PA program curriculum.

The physician assistant is described in the Standards as an individual who is "academically and clinically prepared to provide health care services with the direction and responsible supervision of a doctor of medicine or osteopathy" and who has the capability within the physician-PA relationship to make clinical decisions and provide a broad range of diagnostic, therapeutic, preventive, and health maintenance services [CAAHEP, *Standards and Guidelines for an Accredited Educational Program for the Physician Assistant* (1996) at § II(A)]. Because PAs practice in such a wide variety of settings, the description of the profession does not delineate specific tasks that an individual PA typically performs, but provides that, at a minimum, PAs are educated in basic medical science and clinical disciplines, and discipline-specific problem solving.

The Standards also provide a list of clinical services typically performed by PAs while practicing with physician supervision; those five services are:

1. *evaluation:* eliciting a detailed and accurate patient history, performing an appropriate physical examination, ordering or performing appropriate diagnostic tests, delineating problems, and recording the data collected
2. *monitoring:* implementing patient management plans, recording progress notes, and participating in provision of continuous health care
3. *therapeutic:* performing therapeutic procedures and managing or assisting in the management of medical and surgical conditions, which may include assisting in surgical operations, and performing therapeutic procedures in life-threatening situations
4. *patient education:* counseling patients regarding issues such as complying with prescribed medications or other therapeutic regimens, normal growth patterns, family planning, and emotional problems of daily living
5. *referral:* assisting in the referral of patients to other health care providers or agencies as appropriate

[CAAHEP, *Standards and Guidelines for an Accredited Educational Program for the Physician Assistant* (1996), at § II (A) (1) through (5)].

In further describing PA practice settings, the Standards state that PA practice is characterized by clinical knowledge and skills in areas traditionally defined by family medicine, internal medicine, pediatrics, obstetrics/gynecology, surgery, and psychiatry/behavioral medicine and includes ambulatory, emergency, surgical, inpatient, and long-term care practice settings.

CAAHEP and the ARC-PA

Established in 1994, CAAHEP is one of the largest accreditation organizations in the United States, as well as the most active in terms of the number of programs falling under its accreditation system. From its offices in Chicago, it presides over the accreditation of educational programs in 19 allied health occupations and works in affiliation with over 50 national health professional organizations and medical specialty societies. No longer under the auspices of the AMA, CAAHEP is a freestanding accreditation organization that has approximately 25 review committees assisting in the evaluation of more than 2,500 accredited programs in roughly 1,500 colleges and universities across the United States. To ensure that the organization fulfills its responsibilities, CAAHEP must meet certain requirements to achieve and maintain recognition by the U.S. Department of Education.

CAAHEP relies on recommendations from the ARC-PA in making PA program accreditation decisions. The ARC-PA specifically monitors the accreditation status of PA programs, conducts on-site visits, and evaluates whether programs comply with the Standards. The current ARC-PA consists of representatives from the Association of Physician Assistant Programs (APAP), American Academy of Physician Assistants (AAPA), American Academy of Family Physicians, American Academy of Pediatrics, American College of Physicians, American College of Surgeons, and American Medical Association. The ARC-PA on-site evaluation is conducted by a team of volunteer on-site visitors consisting of ARC-PA members (PA and non-PA) and other educators and clinicians (i.e., PA and non-PA clinician educators and practicing clinicians).

Federal agencies and state licensing boards recognize CAAHEP as the accreditation agency for PA programs. For example, the Health Resources and Services Administration, an agency within the U.S. Public Health Service, will not consider a PA program for federal grant award eligibility unless it is CAAHEP-accredited [*see 1994 AGPAW Report,* at 24]. The medical or PA licensing boards in nearly all states require graduate PAs to pass the National Commission on Certification for Physician Assistants (NCCPA) exam to obtain state licensure, and all exam applicants must be graduates of a PA program accredited by CAAHEP, or its predecessor agency, the AMA's CAHEA. [See Chapter 3: Licensure and Scope of Practice, at Application for Licensure and License Maintenance.]

Accreditation Process

Although the Standards are broadly written, CAAHEP and the ARC-PA oversee and engage in a fairly strict accreditation process. After the ARC-PA receives an application for accreditation, usually from the chief executive officer (CEO) of the PA program's sponsoring institution, the PA program must complete a self-assessment culminating in the submission of a self-study report to the ARC-PA. The report includes the program's assessment of its curriculum, resources, the degree of sponsorship, and operational and student policies and practices.

Although discontinued in 1995 as a service provided by the ARC-PA, for many years the committee issued Letters of Review to PA programs interested in applying for accreditation. The ARC-PA's Letter of Review evaluated the degree to which the plans for a program in the very early stages of its operation were consistent with the goals of the Standards. Receiving a Letter of Review was not a step in the accreditation process, but it was often a precursor to that process.

After receiving the self-study report, the ARC-PA's on-site team visits the program and subsequently prepares a comprehensive evaluators' report discussing the program's relative compliance with the Standards. From the self-study report, the on-site review report, and all other related documentation, the ARC-PA develops its accreditation recommendations and forwards them to CAAHEP, which makes final accreditation decisions twice a year, in April and October. A formal notice of accreditation status is sent to the CEO of the sponsoring institution and to the PA program director.

Once a program is CAAHEP-accredited, periodic review, which may include on-site evaluation by the ARC-PA, is required to maintain accreditation status. The ARC-PA meets on a semiannual basis to consider applications for provisional, initial, and continuing accreditation. The Standards require that PA programs notify the ARC-PA of any changes in program director, medical director, or core program faculty and obtain advance approval by the ARC-PA for any substantive program changes, including degrees or certificates granted at program completion, curriculum, length of program, requirements for graduation, maximum class capacity, and creation of a satellite program.

Provisional Accreditation

Provisional accreditation is a new accreditation status awarded to PA programs that are in developmental stages and, ideally, have not yet accepted students. Under the provisional accreditation process, instituted in 1996, a PA program under development can apply for provisional accreditation as long as one year before enrolling its first class. However, provisionally accredited programs must apply for and receive initial accreditation no later than six months after graduation of the first class or lose their accredited status. If provisional accreditation is denied, the PA program is discouraged from accepting students until it is able to successfully pass the ARC-PA's accreditation review.

Prior to CAAHEP's recent approval of provisional accreditation, a new PA program could not apply for accreditation until students were enrolled. As a result, PA students enrolled at PA programs that were subsequently denied accreditation were ineligible for the NCCPA exam and for state licensure. One result of allowing new PA programs to enter the accreditation process at a much earlier stage of development is a higher level of compliance with the Standards. Moreover, students enrolling in provisionally accredited programs have some assurance that they will not encounter an obstacle when applying for the NCCPA exam [*see* The Education Council of the AAPA and APAP, "In a Growing Profession, Implications for PA Education," *Journal of American Academy of Physician Assistants* 84, 89 (May 1996)].

EDUCATION PROGRAMS

Some common characteristics of PA programs, including curriculum and academic degrees awarded at completion, are discussed in the following sections. Statistics regarding PA program applicant trends, educational costs, and composition of faculty and enrolled students are also provided prior to describing some of the current issues in PA education.

Curriculum

The Standards broadly require accredited PA programs to offer learning experiences and curriculum sequences that provide the PA graduate with the necessary knowledge and skills to perform accurately and reliably the functions set out in the Standards' description of the PA profession. More specifically, the Standards provide that PAs should receive instruction in the following five key areas:

1. basic medical sciences, including human anatomy, physiology, pharmacology, pharmacotherapeutics, and clinical laboratory medicine
2. applied behavioral sciences, including basic counseling skills necessary to assist patients in coping with illness and injury, following prescribed treatment regimens, and modifying unhealthy behavior patterns
3. clinical didactics, including courses with a focus on clinical medicine, clinical decision making, preparation for prescriptive privileges, evaluation of clinical research, and patient assessment techniques such as interviewing and eliciting a medical history, performing a physical exam, and presenting the data in oral and written form
4. the role of the PA in health care delivery and in relation to physicians and other health care providers, including a historical perspective of the PA profession, the political and legal factors affecting PA practice, biomedical ethics, and professional responsibility
5. supervised clinical experience such that the PA can function in medical and surgical settings and, at minimum, should include experiences in family medicine, general internal medicine, pediatrics, obstetrics and gynecology, general surgery, and emergency medicine

[CAAHEP, *Standards and Guidelines for an Accredited Educational Program for the Physician Assistant* (1996), at § II (B) (1)(a) through (e)].

Although the Standards are quite specific as to required curriculum content, they do not prescribe a specific configuration of course offerings and clinical experience that must be provided by the PA program. Rather than enforcing a single model for PA programs, the Standards allow for a wide variety of instructional approaches, providing PA programs the opportunity to develop unique and innovative education models, shaping the program in accordance with individual institutional resources.

The typical PA program admission criteria include a requirement that applicants have completed the equivalent of two years of undergraduate-level biological, social, and behavioral science prerequisites. The average PA program curriculum is 108 weeks, usually completed over a period of 24 to 27 continuous months; in contrast, the standard medical student completes medical school in 153 weeks, typically over a four-year period. The first 9 to 12 months of PA education are devoted to preclinical didactic studies. While courses in the basic medical sciences account for the most substantial portion of the didactic component of PA education, there is also significant emphasis on behavioral and social sciences (including courses in psychosocial dynamics, health promotion and disease prevention, health care organizations, human sexuality, death and dying, cross-cultural medicine, medical ethics, medical sociology, and professional issues). Technical skills developed during this didactic phase of PA education include cardiopulmonary resuscitation, assisted cardiopulmonary life support, casting, suturing, and injection.

Because eligibility for federal grant support is conditioned on offering a curriculum with a primary care focus and PA graduate placement in health professional shortage areas, most PA programs direct curriculum content toward primary care for medically needy populations. Course offerings, for example, include health care topics such as acquired immune deficiency syndrome (AIDS), substance abuse prevention and treatment, adolescent pregnancy, health care for the homeless, women's health, childhood immunizations, risks of cancer and heart disease, and reduction of infant mortality. More than half of all PA programs have developed specific educational content to address the health and medical problems of inner city populations. Most PA programs have also developed contacts and collaborative connections with area health education centers, community education centers, rural health clinics, community and migrant health centers, and other primary care providers.

Once didactic clinical instruction is completed, usually within the first year of a PA program (in conjunction with or following the completion of medical science courses), the PA student is prepared for the next phase of training, typically a 9- to 15-month period of a physician-supervised clinical rotation in internal medicine, family medicine, surgery, pediatrics, obstetrics and gynecology, emergency medicine, and geriatric medicine. The settings for the clinical rotation include hospitals, physicians' offices, clinics, or other institutions (nursing homes, mental health facilities) located in urban, rural, and inner city communities. In some PA programs, didactic PA education and medical student education is conducted with shared classes and resources, and it is in the second phase of the program that PA students are educated in a clinical setting by residents, attending physicians, and/or graduate PAs.

Most PA programs provide clinical rotations or preceptorships at locations that are separate from the sponsoring institution, even where the programs are affiliated with academic medical centers. Often these sites are distant from the sponsoring institution, sometimes across the country from their affiliated academic medical center or in remote areas where there is a shortage of health professionals. By removing PA students from the academic medical center for their clinical rotations, PA programs have been able to provide greater opportunities for the development of clinical skills because PA students have not been forced to compete with medical students, residents, and staff physicians for clinical and patient care experiences. [For a related discussion on the shortage of clinical sites for PA clinical rotations, see Current Issues in Education, at Sites for Preceptorships.]

Also, some PA programs have successfully placed PA graduates in medically underserved areas through community-based satellite clinical training programs. For example, the University of Washington–MEDEX Northwest PA program offers satellite education opportunities in rural practice locations in Washington, Idaho, Montana, Oregon, and Nevada. The programs enroll qualified applicants who might not otherwise be able to relocate to an urban area with an academic health center [*see* P.E. Jones and J. Cawley, "Physician Assistants and Health System Reform," *JAMA* 271, 1266, 1267 (1994)]. Similarly, the PA program at the University of Texas Medical Branch–Galveston offers a satellite program near the Texas–Mexico border in a geographic area predominantly comprised of Hispanic communities; one objective of the program is to encourage local residents who intend to remain in the region to consider PA education opportunities. Other PA programs that have developed satellite-model clinical training for the purpose of placing PA students and graduates in rural areas include the progams at the University of Nebraska and St. Louis University [*see 1994 AGPAW Report,* at 25].

Academic Degree Options

PA programs have developed under a philosophy that PA education is competency based, and that the central objective is to provide the curriculum and clinical training necessary to ensure that the PA graduate has the knowledge and skills required for competent clinical practice. As a result of this competency-based approach, PA programs are quite diverse, offering a wide array of PA training options and awarding a range of academic degrees (e.g., bachelor's degree from a four-year college, master's degree as part of a graduate program, and associate's degree or certificate of completion from a two-year PA program).

Flexibility in the academic degree awarded for PA education has allowed PA programs to develop unique and creative curricula that may not fit institutional requirements for awarding a specific academic degree, but nonetheless effectively prepare the PA graduate for clinical practice. Moreover, in not limiting the academic degree to any one type, PA programs have been able to draw on applicants from diverse ethnic and educational backgrounds. Opening the applicant pool to individuals from these backgrounds (i.e., racial and ethnic minorities, less financially advantaged) is important to many PA programs, especially those receiving federal grant award support, because these individuals have demonstrated the most proclivity for practicing in primary care roles in medically underserved areas [*see 1994 AGPAW Report,* at 85].

Currently, approximately 61 percent of all PA educational programs award a bachelor's degree, and the remaining programs offer a master's degree (nearly 19 percent), associate's degree (7.5 percent), or certificate of completion (12.5 percent). [A. Simon, M. Link, and A. Miko, *Twelfth Annual Report on Physician Assistant Educational Programs in the United States, 1995–1996* (APAP 1996), at 5]. Since the late 1980s, an increasing number of two-year PA programs are either commencing as graduate-level programs, or converting from a baccalaureate- to a graduate-level curriculum. Master's degree PA programs now include programs at Baylor College of Medicine, Duke University, Emory University, George Washington University, Northeastern University, University of Colorado, University of Detroit–Mercy, University of Iowa, and University of Nebraska. Several types of master's degrees, are awarded by these programs, such as the master of science (MS), the master of health science (MHS), the master of science in physician assistant (MS in PA), the master of medical science (MMS), and the master of physician assistant (MPA). [For a description of joint-degree graduate programs combining the standard PA curriculum with a graduate degree in a health-related field, see Program Models.]

Heading up to the year 2000, it is anticipated that additional programs will convert to a graduate-level curriculum. Although the graduate-degree, entry-level credentials for PA programs may become the norm in the future, whether to maintain flexibility in academic degree options is a current controversial issue in PA education. [See Current Issues in Education, at Academic Degree Requirements.]

Applicant Trends

In response to increased demand in the health care services market, PA educational programs have experienced significant growth in numbers as well as in student enrollment. Awareness of the PA profession has increased over the past decade, resulting in not only more job opportunities for PAs, but also higher salaries. These factors have generated a new interest in the profession, which is demonstrated, in part, by the dramatic increase in the number of PA program applicants. According to one estimate, between 1988 and 1992 the number of applicants per program increased by 136 percent. More specifically, in 1988, the mean number of applicants per program of standard class size (i.e., 25.9 enrolled students) was 86.1, while in 1992 the standard class size had increased to 35, and the mean number of applicants per program was 203 [*1994 AGPAW Report,* at 29]. Another estimate indicates that in 1995, the average annual number of applicants to a PA program was 419.5 for a standard class size of 42.9 students. [A. Simon, M. Link, and A. Miko, *Twelfth Annual Report on Physician Assistant Educational Programs in the United States, 1995–1996* (APAP 1996), at 38].

Since 1984, women have comprised a majority of all enrolled PA students, thus accounting for the rising percentage of women in the PA profession, who currently comprise nearly half of all practicing PAs. Approximately 20 percent of all enrolled PA students are ethnic and racial minorities, a percentage that has been fairly constant since 1987 [*see* P.E. Jones and J. Cawley, "Physician Assistants and Health System Reform," *JAMA* 271, 1266, 1268 (1994)]. With respect to educational background, most PA students have completed one to two years of coursework in premedical sciences on enrollment in a PA program. Most students admitted to PA programs also have received a baccalaureate or higher degree, and there appears to be an increasing number of applicants who hold master's or doctoral degrees. [See Current Issues in Education, at Academic Degree Requirements.] In addition, many students admitted to PA programs have previous health care experience; types of health care roles commonly encountered among PA program applicants include medical technologist, military medical corpsman, registered nurse, emergency medical technician, and orderly.

Educational Costs

The majority of PAs enter PA education programs with extensive science and health care backgrounds, and thus PAs generally can be trained more quickly and less expensively than physicians. The time needed for medical school education and residency is double that of PA academic and clinical training. Moreover, in comparison to medical student educational costs, the overall expense of PA education is relatively low. The average total cost for educating an allopathic medical student has been estimated to be over $92,000 per year, while the current average cost of PA education (based on nonresident tuition figures) is approximately $26,132 per student per two-year program or $13,000 per year [*see, e.g., 1994 AGPAW Report,* at 36; A. Simon, M. Link, and A. Miko, *Twelfth Annual Report on Physician Assistant Educational Programs in the United States, 1995–1996* (APAP 1996), at 11]. The substantial difference in the cost of educating a PA as compared to educating a physician is frequently highlighted for the purpose of seeking increased federal grant funding for PA educational programs. [See Current Issues in Education, at Adequacy of Funding.]

Current Issues in Education

Academic Degree Requirements

Physician assistant programs offer an array of credentials on completion of training—from certificate to baccalaureate degree to master's degree—and such diversity has allowed for a broader applicant pool. The merit of PA programs offering varying levels of credential, however, has been a continual subject of debate within the PA profession and among PA educators. In the past decade, that debate has revolved around whether it should be a requirement that all practicing PAs have attained at least a baccalaureate degree.

Supporters of a baccalaureate-degree requirement for entering the PA profession contend that without such a requirement, the profession itself loses credibility, and that the lack of such a requirement has been an obstacle to broader PA scope of practice in some states. Under this argument, a degree requirement would give PAs credibility in addition to that already provided by NCCPA certification. Moreover, according to degree-requirement advocates, such a requirement would eventually enhance opportunities for PAs in leadership roles within the federal government and academic systems [*see* R. Ballweg, "History of the Profession," in R. Ballweg, S. Stolberg, and E. Sullivan, eds., *Physician Assistant: A Guide to Clinical Practice* 1, 17 (1994)].

The main concern of those opposed to a degree requirement is that such a requirement may limit entry into the PA profession, especially for experienced health care workers who are interested in PA education but have little access to formal academic prerequisites (i.e., applicants from rural, inner city, ethnic minority, or financially disadvantaged backgrounds, or applicants working toward a "second career" transition to the PA profession). Opponents of the degree requirement highlight the fact that many other professions, including physicians, are credentialed the same way that PAs are currently credentialed—not by degree, but by competency-based training and a certification examination. Another argument posed by those opposing the degree requirement emphasizes the trend demonstrated by non-PA health care professionals with advanced degrees (e.g., nurse practitioners) to practice in areas other than primary care. Because the primary objective of the PA profession has always been the provision of primary care services to medically underserved populations, it is argued that a degree requirement counters the very core of that mission [*see* R. Ballweg, "History of the Profession," in R. Ballweg, S. Stolberg, and E. Sullivan, eds., *Physician Assistant: A Guide to Clinical Practice* 1, 17 (1994)].

The lines of this debate were drawn nearly 10 years ago; in 1987, the AAPA House of Delegates passed a resolution recommending that all PAs possess at least a baccalaureate degree. The APAP neither supported nor opposed the resolution at the delegate conference, but subsequently voiced several concerns about imposing a degree requirement, including:

- the extent of problems arising for practicing nonbaccalaureate-degree PAs who must obtain an academic degree to remain in practice
- the constraints that might be imposed on existing PA programs that do not offer baccalaureate degrees
- the extent to which a degree requirement would be a barrier to PA training for individuals and institutions at a time when demand for PAs still significantly exceeded supply

[*See* R. Ballweg, "History of the Profession," in R. Ballweg, S. Stolberg, and E. Sullivan, eds., *Physician Assistant: A Guide to Clinical Practice* 1, 17 (1994); for a more detailed description of APAP and its activities, see The Role of APAP.]

The emerging trend toward postgraduate degree PA programs [see Academic Degree Options] has added another layer to the controversy. This trend toward graduate-degree, entry-level credentials in PA programs has given rise to some of the same objections made in the earlier debate on degree requirements. If PA programs were predominantly at the postgraduate level, some commentators contend, a potentially adverse impact on the pool of applicants results when competent persons opt not to apply to programs because they have no desire or inadequate financial resources to attend graduate school. Moreover, as discussed in the context of the degree-requirement debate, increased employment opportunities for PAs with graduate-degree credentials may redirect PA graduates from primary care and practice in underserved communities to specialties, hospital settings, and other jobs at higher salary levels. On the other side, however, is the likelihood that graduate-degree credentials will increase opportunities for PAs in roles other than clinical practice, including education, administration, and research. A future trend in PA programs may be the development of academic tracks culminating in master's degrees for PAs who are interested in teaching, administration, or research as a career [*see* The Education Council of the AAPA and APAP, "In a Growing Profession, Implications for PA Education," *Journal of American Academy of Physician Assistants* 84, 95 (May 1996)].

Adequacy of Funding

Federal grant support for PA programs under Title VII of the Public Health Service Act has remained essentially level since 1981. Less than half of the 59 eligible PA educational programs received federal grant support of $5 million in fiscal year 1993. In fiscal year 1994, there was a modest increase in the level of funding to $6.53 million, of which only approximately $6.4 million went in direct support of PA training, with the remainder allocated for PA research projects and faculty development contracts by the Bureau of Health Professions [*see 1994 AGPAW Report,* at 26]. The increase in funding did not equal the sharp rise in the number of programs receiving federal grant support, from 33 to 46, including a number of new PA programs. In fiscal year 1995, despite the fact that the number of eligible PA programs rose to 64, federal grant support fell slightly to roughly $6 million; only half of those programs received a federal grant, which averaged $135,000, a decrease from the previous year's federal grant award program average of $143,500 [*see 1994 AGPAW Report,* at 26; *see also* The Education Council of the AAPA and APAP, "In a Growing Profession, Implications for PA Education," *Journal of American Academy of Physician Assistants* 84, 95 (May 1996)].

To convince the federal government to increase categorical grant funding for PA programs under Title VII of the Public Health Service Act, PA educators and others concerned about meeting the demands of continued PA program expansion often highlight the cost-effectiveness of supporting PA training programs, as compared to supporting physician-residency programs. In 1995, for example, the average federal grant award received by eligible PA programs was $135,000, amounting to a per-pupil federal support of approximately $1,928 (average class size: 70), as compared to Medicare graduate medical education (GME) payments to teaching hospitals, which amounted to an annual federal subsidy per medical resident ranging from $47,000 to $102,000 (in 1993 dollars) depending on the medical student's year of residency [*see* U.S. Congressional Budget Office, *A CBO Study: Medicare and Graduate Medical Education* (Sept. 1995)].

Given the continued increase in the number of PA programs, and the expansion of class size at many of the established programs, increased federal appropriations for PA training grant support is needed to maintain educational quality. [For a more detailed discussion of nongrant federal funding for PA educational programs, see Impact of GME Reform.] Increased funding would give needed start-up funds to the growing number of universities, academic health centers, and colleges seeking to establish new PA programs and would allow existing programs to accommodate greater annual enrollment. Moreover, new sources of funding need to be fostered; through state funding and increased internal support from sponsoring institutions, PA programs may be able to sustain operations and develop some measure of self-sufficiency when federal grant support is lacking. California, Kansas, and New York, for example, have adopted funding initiatives designed to expand PA educational program enrollment capacity and graduate output [*see 1994 AGPAW Report,* at 27].

Impact of GME Reform

The largest share of the federal government's financial support for health professions education is the approximately $6 billion Medicare GME subsidy [*see* U.S. Congressional Budget Office, *A CBO Study: Medicare and Graduate Medical Education* (Sept. 1995) (estimate for fiscal year 1995)]. Financial support through Medicare is provided directly to teaching hospitals sponsoring the clinical specialty training of physicians. The Medicare system of GME financing supports a large proportion of physician residency training. It pays for a portion of hospital educational costs by reimbursing hospital charges through a direct cost "pass through" mechanism and by allowing for an indirect cost educational adjustment for payments to hospitals eligible for reimbursement for educational activities under Medicare Part A diagnosis-related group (DRG) payments.

A variety of health professionals other than physician-residents also receive educational subsidies through GME financing. According to Health Care Financing Administration (HCFA) estimates and projections, teaching hospitals received approximately $248 million in GME funding support for nursing in 1994, which will rise to nearly $450 million by the year 2000. Graduate nursing programs, however, are not included in these estimates, as the current policy excludes graduate nursing education from receiving GME funding [*see* L. Aiken, "Medicare Funding of Nurse Education: The Case for Policy Change," *JAMA* 273, 1528, 1530]. In addition, 13 other health care provider training programs are eligible for GME funding under the collective title of paramedical or allied health personnel, including medical technology, medical records, X-ray technology, physical therapy, occupational therapy, pharmacy residencies, inhalation therapy, hospital administration, dietetic internships, cytotechnology, nongraduate level professional and practical nursing, and nurse anesthesia. Because the PA profession did not exist at the time Medicare and GME were created, PAs are the only primary care providers not eligible to receive GME subsidies, and thus PA educational programs do not benefit from these payments.

Currently facing cutbacks in Medicare subsidies for medical education, teaching hospitals have been compelled to decrease, or put some limitations on, the use of physician residents. The Physician Payment Review Commission (PPRC), the body that advises Congress on Medicare physician payment policy, has recognized that PAs are a viable alternative to replace physician resident and international medical graduate (IMG) positions that will likely be lost as a result of reduced GME funding [*see* PPRC, *Annual Report to Congress* (1994), projecting a loss of 11,000 residency positions within GME-sponsoring institutions over the next three to five years, and the creation of replacement slots for approximately 7,700 nonphysician providers, both PAs and nurse practitioners]. Concurrently, an increasing number of states have enacted laws or adopted regulations imposing limitations on the numbers of hours worked by physician residents.

Both developments have led teaching hospitals to use PAs and advanced nurse practitioners (NPs) to augment physician resident services, even though Medicare GME funding completely excludes the use of PAs or NPs in inpatient clinical services. According to a 1993 national survey of hospitals conducted by the Council of Teaching Hospitals (COTH), a majority of GME residency programs employ or plan to employ PAs and NPs, or both, to replace physician residents [*see* R. Riportella-Muller, D. Libby, and D.A. Kindig, "The Substitution of Physician Assistants and Nurse Practitioners for Physician Residents in Teaching Hospitals," *Health Affairs* 181 (Summer 1995)].

The prospect of continual reductions in GME funding has reinvigorated discussion as to the alternatives to current GME reimbursement methods. The current GME system limits subsidy payments to teaching hospitals for reimbursement of physician residents and, as such, essentially ignores current health care work force requirements, including the need for greater numbers of generalist health care providers. Reform proposals have recognized the need to shift GME subsidies to encourage an increase in the supply of generalist physicians; for example, restructuring the subsidy payments to increase primary care physicians and achieve a 50–50 percentage balance between generalist and specialist physicians in the health care work force. Some restructuring options under consideration are changing the current allocation of GME subsidies for residents' training experiences (e.g., away from teaching hospitals to outpatient/ambulatory care clinics), modifying financing mechanisms to facilitate teaching hospitals' substitution of PAs and other nonphysician providers in physician resident positions, and allowing a portion of GME subsidy payments to be designated for an all-payer funding pool from which funds could be channelled specifically for the support of PA and other advanced nursing educational programs [*see, e.g., 1994 AGPAW Report,* at 79; U.S. Congressional Budget Office, *A CBO Study: Medicare and Graduate Medical Education* (Sept. 1995)].

Recently, the PPRC recommended to Congress that PAs and advanced practice nurses be included in the GME funding stream currently available to diploma nursing and other allied health personnel [PPRC, *Annual Report to Congress* (1994); *see also* L. Aiken, "Medicare Funding of Nurse Education: The Case for Policy Change," *JAMA* 273, 1528, 1530]. The PPRC concluded that funding those professions through GME would achieve the objective of ensuring not only an adequate supply of health care providers in primary care, but also that a sufficient percentage of those providers would enter clinical practice in rural and other medically underserved areas [PPRC, *Annual Report to Congress* (1994)]. According to the AAPA, 85 percent of all PAs are in clinical practice, and when those practicing part-time are factored in, that estimate rises to 93 percent. Moreover, a higher percentage of PAs practice in rural and medically underserved areas (i.e., inner city or small towns) than any other primary care provider; under one estimate, roughly 30 percent of all PAs practice in communities of 50,000 or less [*AAPA Physician Assistant Census Report* (Dec. 1996)].

Another factor supporting the inclusion of PAs and PA education programs in future GME funding is the potential shortage of nonphysician primary care providers resulting from increased use of PAs in teaching hospitals. Taking into account that positions available for PAs in inpatient and specialty roles currently tend to be in greater supply and pay higher salaries than primary care positions in medically underserved areas, some policy analysts have predicted that PA substitution for physician residents lost as a result of GME funding cutbacks will give rise to a critical need for PAs in primary care and ambulatory health care settings [*see 1994 AGPAW Report,* at 70].

As yet, there are no definitive studies addressing the costs and medical aspects of PA substitution for residents, but the PPRC has countered concerns as to whether nonphysician providers are more expensive to hire than residents. In its 1994 report to Congress, the Commission revealed its research indicating that hiring PAs may be less costly than salary figures suggest because some hospitals have found that PAs require less faculty supervision and are equally or more efficient than residents [PPRC, *Annual Report to Congress* (1994); *see also* A. Schwartz, et al., "Reforming Graduate Medical Education," *JAMA* 270, 1079 (1993)].

Moreover, reimbursement for services provided by PAs under Medicare Part B could ease the financial burden of decreased GME funding. Even though inpatient services provided by PAs have been covered under Medicare Part B at 75 percent of the physician's fee schedule since 1986, many hospitals continue to operate as if Part B coverage for PAs did not exist; instead, they incorporate PA costs into per diem charges that are billed and reimbursed under Medicare Part A DRG-based payments. [For a more detailed discussion of reimbursement for PA services, see Chapter 10: Third-Party Reimbursement.] If teaching hospitals were to employ PAs in greater numbers, however, it is predicted that the hospitals would seek Medicare B reimbursement on a consistent basis, and thereby minimize the per resident loss of GME payments [*see 1994 AGPAW Report,* at 73].

Program Faculty

For the period from 1984 to 1995, the average faculty composition of PA educational programs included a program director (usually a PA who holds a master's degree), a medical director (a physician who serves part-time), 3.7 full-time employee personnel serving in various instructional roles, and 1.3 full-time employee noninstructional PA program personnel (average class size: 58) [*see* A. Simon, M. Link, and A. Miko, *Twelfth Annual Report on Physician Assistant Educational Programs in the United States, 1995–1996* (APAP 1996), at 15, 16, and 37]. Other health care professionals and educators used in PA programs include physicians, PAs, nurse practitioners, and doctoral-level instructors in the basic medical sciences, the behavioral and social sciences, and other disciplines.

In general, PA programs have encountered problems in identifying, recruiting, and retaining qualified faculty members. There is no formal training program for PA educators. Typically, a clinically experienced PA is self-referred or recruited into PA education, often with little or no training in educational theory, methods, and applications. Without any background in education methods, PAs recruited into faculty positions are often unaware of the difficult tasks of academic instruction, including the obligations of continual scholarly activity, preparation of lectures and coursework, and consistent attention to administrative tasks (i.e., preparation of course materials, exams, and grading). Some of the turnover in PA faculty positions has been linked to job dissatisfaction, perhaps derived from discovering the vast differences between the environments of academia and clinical practice [*see, e.g., 1994 AGPAW Report,* at 30; J.D. Blessing, "PA Education Is Everyone's Concern," *Journal of American Academy of Physician Assistants* 23, 24 (Aug. 1996)].

The insufficient supply of PA educators can be linked primarily to other factors, however, including an increasing number of both PA programs and enrolled students, and the growing availability of clinical positions at relatively high salary levels. As new PA programs develop and existing ones expand, the shortage of qualified faculty has become an increasingly worrisome concern for the PA profession. Existing PA programs have responded by encouraging students and graduates interested in education to pursue faculty positions, but also by devising strategies for facilitating PAs' adjustment to academia, such as expanding the responsibilities of administrative personnel to relieve faculty members of purely administrative functions.

For many PA programs, however, recruitment and retention of faculty members involves meeting the competition of higher paying clinical practice positions. Thus, an increasing number of PA programs offer joint teaching–clinical practice positions to those faculty members who wish to supplement their teaching income. According to one estimate, 59 percent of PA faculty are concurrently engaged in clinical practice on a part-time basis (an average of 10 hours per week), earning an average of $28.84 per hour [*see* A. Simon, M. Link, and A. Miko, *Twelfth Annual Report on Physician Assistant Educational Programs in the United States, 1995–1996* (APAP 1996), at 18].

Sites for Preceptorships

Several factors underlie the potential shortage of clinical sites for PA training rotations and preceptorships, including current redirection of medical student and resident training from teaching hospitals to ambulatory care settings. Such changes in medical schools' placement of physician residents demonstrate an increasing concern over statistics and reports indicating heightened demand for generalist primary care physicians to adequately meet the U.S. population's health care needs, but are also a reaction to the downsizing of GME funding and consequent loss of residency positions at teaching hospitals. The impact of redirecting medical students and residents to primary care clinical sites is increased competition for such sites, which now must accommodate a rapidly expanding number of PA programs, as well as nurse practitioner programs and an increasing number of residency programs that are starting to implement placements in ambulatory care settings [*see, e.g.,* P.E. Jones and J. Cawley, "Physician Assistants and Health Reform," *JAMA* 271, 1266, 1271 (1994); R. Ippolito, "Are PAs Prepared to Educate Their Colleagues of Tomorrow?" *Journal of American Academy of Physician Assistants* 268, 269–70 (Apr. 1994)].

Other economic incentives may result in reduced availability of clinical training sites for PAs. For example, some non-PA programs provide a stipend to clinical training sites, an incentive payment that many PA programs cannot feasibly include in their limited budgets [*see* The Education Council of the AAPA and APAP, "In a Growing Profession, Implications for PA Education," *Journal of American Academy of Physician Assistants* 90 (May 1996)]. Moreover, some potential clinical rotation sites have expressed a reluctance to participate in PA preceptorship programs based on concerns about whether cost-effectiveness will be hampered by placing the burden of educating precepting PAs on already busy staff physicians and nonphysician providers [*see* R. Ippolito, "Are PAs Prepared To Educate Their Colleagues of Tomorrow?" *Journal of American Academy of Physician Assistants* 268, 271 (Apr. 1994)].

Expansion of clinical rotation sites is essential for PA programs at a time of anticipated growth, and PAs can, and should, play an important part in developing such sites. Physician assistants in clinical practice can participate in one of many steps involved in the clinical rotation development process, including identifying potential clinical sites and making arrangements for the PA program's initial contact with the site, educating potential participants about the PA profession and clinical training arrangements, and volunteering to be the on-site clinical supervisor for a precepting PA's daily activities. Also, PAs should consider involvement in their state PA chapter's project on PA education issues. Some state chapters, for example, have assigned committees responsible for working with PA programs to expand rotation sites [*see* R. Ippolito, "Are PAs Prepared To Educate Their Colleagues of Tomorrow?" *Journal of American Academy of Physician Assistants* 268, 271–272 (Apr. 1994)].

The Role of APAP

The APAP is an organization involved in tracking developments in PA education and working to ensure the quality of PA education programs. Founded in 1972 by a group of program faculty concerned about the effect of PA program expansion on PA education, APAP's primary objective is to improve the quality and accessibility of health care through quality education of PAs. Currently, more than 70 accredited PA programs are members of APAP, which has a board of directors elected by member programs, and relies on the individuals from member programs to participate in the activities of its various committees.

In collaboration with its member programs, APAP strives to maintain quality PA education through its achievement of these goals:

- developing and implementing a wide range of services and opportunities for member programs, such as providing guidance on the maintenance of high professional standards and review processes for PA programs

- developing and monitoring research in areas of concern to the PA profession and to member programs, such as accreditation, certification, continuing education, evaluating core competency, and certain scope-of-practice issues
- identifying, establishing, and maintaining sources of support for PA programs, including review and development of position statements on behalf of member programs
- coordinating academic and other activities of member programs, and facilitating communication between programs, as well as between programs and health care providers
- planning, managing, and coordinating services in response to the collective needs of member programs, and ensuring wide and effective dissemination of information on the PA profession and the education provided by member programs

Aside from its own research and networking activities, APAP actively participates in certain activities of the NCCPA and PA program accrediting bodies. APAP has two representatives on the NCCPA board of directors and, as a sponsoring organization of the ARC-PA, it sends three representatives to serve as ARC-PA committee members and one representative to serve as a CAAHEP commissioner.

In response to the significant increase in new and proposed PA programs over the past few years, APAP also has developed a consultation service known as PATH (Program Assistance and Technical Help), which is a confidential fee-for-service program designed to assist established and developing PA training programs to achieve and maintain excellence in PA education. PATH consultation services are available on the request of existing PA programs or programs under development. A program director may choose from several types of consultations, including:

- *an initial informational consultation,* designed to provide basic information and perspectives on PA education to institutions considering the feasibility of developing a PA program
- *a general consultation for developing programs,* designed to assist developing programs to meet PATH standards for excellence
- *a general consultation for existing programs,* designed for programs seeking an objective external evaluation to complement their self-study, or for programs that have undergone substantial changes
- *a focused consultation,* designed to assist programs with a focal problem, such as admissions, minority recruitment or retention, research, resource procurement and utilization, or curriculum

The PATH services are based on written guidelines and are provided by a panel of experienced and specially trained consultants. After these consultants conduct an on-site evaluation, the program director receives an extensive postvisit report written in accordance with PATH guidelines.

CERTIFICATION

Certification is a regulatory process directed at limiting the use of a specific occupational title such as the designation "certified PA." To use that title, the PA program graduate or the practicing PA seeking recertification must submit to a process administered by the nongovernmental agency, the NCCPA, which evaluates whether individual applicants have met national qualification criteria for obtaining a certified status [see The Role of the NCCPA]. Although this form of regulation does not restrict any individual from entering the PA profession, it enables the public to identify those individuals who have met certain standards and provides physicians and other employers with some evidence of competency. Uncertified PAs may practice as long as they observe any restrictions imposed on that status by state laws or regulations. [See Temporary Certification and Recertification.]

Regardless of the form by which the state regulates PAs, two requirements for obtaining state licensure are consistently included in state PA licensing statutes or rules promulgated thereunder: (1) graduation from a PA program approved by CAAHEP or its predecessor agency, CAHEA, and (2) successful completion of the NCCPA certifying exam. [See Chapter 3: Licensure and Scope of Practice, at Application for Licensure and License Maintenance.] The following sections describe the process for obtaining and maintaining NCCPA certification and other current NCCPA developments.

The Role of the NCCPA

The PA national certifying examination is prepared by the National Board of Medical Examiners (NBME) and administered by the NCCPA. The examination was developed in the early 1970s by the NBME and the Council of Health Manpower of the AMA. NBME administered the exam in its first two years of existence (1973 and 1974) but then turned over the task to the NCCPA, which was established in 1974 by the AMA, the federal government, and several medical professional groups. Currently, the NCCPA's board of directors is composed of representatives from a host of medical and allied health professional associations, including the AMA, AAPA, and APAP, as well as American Academy of Family Physicians, American Academy of Pediatrics, American College of Physicians,

American College of Surgeons, American Hospital Association, Association of American Medical Colleges, Federation of U.S. State Medical Boards, and the U.S. Department of Defense.

NCCPA is active in many realms beyond mere administration of the certifying exam. In overseeing the entire national certification process for PAs, the Commission is engaged in multiple activities, including:

- determination of eligibility requirements for taking the exam
- review of applications to take the exam and registration of eligible PA graduates
- administration of the exam (under contract with NBME) and setting the standards for passing the exam
- issuance and verification of certificates to PA graduates who pass the exam
- reregistration of certificates every two years on proof of compliance with Continuing Medical Education (CME) requirements
- administration of recertification exams as necessary
- assistance to state medical boards that request information on national certification for the purpose of modifying or creating new PA practice legislation
- research subjects related to the responsibilities of PAs to government, medical or other professional groups, the public, and other health care providers, and dissemination of resulting information for the purpose of increasing awareness of the PA profession

[*See* D.M. Pederson, "Credentialing and Employment," in R. Ballweg, S. Stolberg, and E. Sullivan, eds., *Physician Assistant: A Guide to Clinical Practice*, at 627, 630–631 (1994).]

Physician Assistant National Certifying Exam

The two-day PA national certification exam (PANCE) for many years has consisted of three distinct parts:

1. the general functions component—a 3.5-hour, 250-question multiple-choice test designed to assess knowledge of clinical material
2. the extended core component—a 2.5-hour, 180-question multiple-choice test in either primary care or surgery
3. a clinical skills component—a one-hour test divided into three clinical vignettes designed to evaluate selection and performance of physical examination steps

To qualify for certification, PA graduates must take both the general multiple-choice and clinical skills sections, as well as one of the extended core sections (with an option to take both sections).

To attain certified status, test scores on the two required components must meet or exceed the minimum pass score as determined by NCCPA. If the PA graduate opts to take both extended core portions of the exam, a minimum score on only one of those components is necessary for certification. The PANCE, however, is currently under revision, and the revised version of the exam will likely not include the same clinical skills component; the new PANCE will be administered for the first time in October 1997. Also as of 1997, the PANCE will no longer be administered once a year, but twice—in April and October.

On passing the PANCE, a PA graduate uses the designation "C" for "certified" after the initials PA, or PA-C, to indicate passing the exam, but also prospective adherence to the NCCPA's requirements for continuing medical education: 100 hours every two years. Recertification by examination or by an alternative recertification process is required every six years [see Recertification].

Since 1985, only PA graduates of educational programs accredited by CAAHEP or CAHEA have been eligible for the PANCE. Prior to that year, nurse practitioners and informally trained health care professionals, including physicians unlicensed in the United States but possessing medical degrees from foreign medical schools, were allowed to sit for the exam. Without a formal PA educational background, the prospective examinee merely had to demonstrate experience as a primary care PA gained during the four consecutive years preceding application to take the exam. Although non-PAs who passed the NCCPA exam in the 1970s or early 1980s are eligible to sit for subsequent recertification exams, the initial certifying exam is now closed to individuals who have not graduated from an accredited PA program. Whether unlicensed physicians of foreign medical schools should be allowed to sit for the exam has been a controversial issue from the inception of this particular eligibility requirement and recently has been litigated before state courts in California and Florida. [See International Medical Graduates.]

Temporary Certification

Most states have statutes and/or regulations authorizing the issuance of a temporary certificate for PAs who have successfully completed an accredited PA program, but either are awaiting NCCPA exam results or have yet to take the exam. Typically, these temporary certificates are only valid for eight months to a year, and are rescinded on failure of the certification exam. Also, the PA's scope of practice under a temporary certificate is more restricted than under a permanent certificate; temporarily certified PAs are usually prohibited from prescribing or dispensing medication, practicing without direct on-site physician supervision, and practicing at a remote clinical site.

In many states, temporary licensure provisions were enacted because the NCCPA administered the PANCE only once a year, often creating frustration for the PA graduate eager to start practice, and sometimes resulting in a shortfall in the supply of certified PAs to meet the demands of physician employers. As of 1997, however, the PANCE will be offered twice a year, which may result in a substantial decrease in need for temporary certification of PAs.

Recertification

Once a PA attains permanent certification, the mandatory requirements for maintaining that status are registering the required number of CME hours (100 hours every two years with a minimum of 40 hours in Category 1) and taking the Physician Assistant Recertifying Exam (PANRE) every six years, or completing the officially recognized alternate recertification route, including a take-home exam [see Alternative Recertification Pathway]. The first PA recertification exam was given in 1981. It was instituted as part of the certification process as a quality assurance mechanism and to demonstrate a reliable system of certificate maintenance, thereby giving credibility to the PA profession in legislative and policy arenas. Although NCCPA and the AAPA worked together to successfully develop an alternative route to recertification other than taking the PANRE, an exam requirement for certificate maintenance remains an issue of debate within the PA profession. [See Alternative Recertification Pathway.]

Until recently, the certified PA who failed the PANRE could retake the exam an unlimited number of times, as long as those subsequent attempts were within consecutive administrations of the recertification exam. Starting in 1998, however, this policy will undergo a significant change and be replaced by a time frame "endpoint" system that will allow the certified PA only two chances to pass the PANRE, or an equal number of chances to fulfill the requirements of the alternative recertification pathway. PAs who fail to pass in both attempts will have to obtain a one-year extension of their NCCPA certificate and earn new NCCPA certification by passing the PANCE at its next available administration [*see* L. Alexander, "Preparing for the Recertification Exam," *Journal of American Academy of Physician Assistants* 73, 77 (Jan. 1997)].

Alternative Recertification Pathway

Although initial certification of PAs, which tests material taught in PA programs, is clearly an asset to the profession, the concept of recertification by examination remains controversial. From the initial years of the recertification exam requirement to the present, PAs and others have questioned whether the PANRE fairly tests a PA's knowledge, skills, and abilities in practice. Taking the PANRE at 6-year intervals, contend critics of the exam requirement, is an inadequate mechanism to evaluate the clinical knowledge of PAs, many of whom have been in specialty practice or not engaged in primary care practice for over 10 years.

On the other side, supporters point out that the PANRE is not intended to test all the knowledge related to the diverse primary care and specialty settings in which PAs function, but rather is designed to identify practicing PAs who do not meet a minimum level of core general medical knowledge to maintain certification. Supporters highlight research indicating that generalist medical knowledge provides the foundation necessary for the knowledge and skills needed for specialized practice [*see* J. DaVanzo, "The Role of National Skill Standards in the Design of Core Curriculum," in *Proceedings of the Workshop on Core Curricula in Allied Health,* Pew Commission Conference, San Francisco, 1995].

After considering and ultimately rejecting several alternatives, including the option of taking a recertifying exam geared for the PA in specialty practice, the AAPA House of Delegates approved an Alternative Pathway for Recertification in 1991. The Alternative Pathway was developed through negotiations with NCCPA, and provides a system designed to assess the PA's knowledge and skills by methods other than the traditional recertification exam. The alternative pathway option was first utilized by a group of PAs requiring recertification in 1993. In preparation for the PAs electing this option, NCCPA and the AAPA established Pathway II, a pilot study of the alternative means to maintain current certification. According to the AAPA, participants in that study reported that the process was a valuable learning experience, and was more relevant to their current professional practice than the traditional written exam [*see* AAPA, "Professional Competence," *1996–1997 Policy Manual* (1996) (position paper prepared by the AAPA Educational Council)].

After five successful administrations of the Pathway II option, the NCCPA Board of Directors approved it as a permanent avenue for recertification in May 1996. In its current form, Pathway II offers an opportunity to achieve recertification over the six-year NCCPA maintenance cycle through the completion of a self-directed education plan that includes a mandatory general take-home exam. The process consists of three elements, all of which must be completed to obtain recertification:

1. CME required for each two-year logging cycle within the current six-year NCCPA maintenance cycle must be completed; the CME requirement for recertification under Pathway II and PANRE is the same—100 hours every two years with a minimum of 40 hours in Category 1.
2. An elective component comprised of nine options—Category 1 CME, clinical skills training, medical teaching, publications, postgraduate coursework, professionally relevant postgraduate degree, formal clinical presentation, specialty review, and other activities resulting in the learning of relevant new skills— two of which must be chosen and fulfilled by com-

pleting 100 elective component points, which may not include activities previously logged for the two-year CME logging cycle required for maintaining NCCPA certification.

3. The Pathway II recertifying exam, which has the eligibility requirement of successfully completing the elective component requirement; the take-home exam assesses general medical knowledge and may be completed with the aid of reference materials.

The take-home exam portion differs from the sit-down examination in that the examinee is permitted to use any available resource to answer questions, including books, journals, colleagues, and online databases. Some participants in Pathway II pilot projects have noted that both the elective component and the take-home exam are more relevant to actual clinical practice than taking a written, proctored recertification exam because providing quality care for patients necessitates continual enhancement of medical knowledge, including the learning of new clinical skills, and the use of all available resources to resolve an uncertain clinical situation.

International Medical Graduates

During the 1970s, a number of states had provisions in their state PA statutes and/or regulations that essentially allowed unlicensed IMGs to qualify to practice as PAs. Such legislation, however, has consistently been repealed or withdrawn because state legislatures and professional licensing boards have often concluded that the applying IMGs need additional training to meet the standards for PA practice. Some examples of states' experiences with this issue include:

- *Illinois:* The state legislature passed a 1987 amendment to the definition of a PA in the PA practice law specifically excluding all medical school graduates.
- *Maryland:* In its 1994 legislative session, the state general assembly rejected a bill (H.B. No. 1039) that would have allowed unlicensed IMGs to qualify for practice as PAs by granting them an automatic exemption from the state certification process and assessing them by an examination specifically designated for IMGs. The state legislature had considered similar proposals in four previous years, despite firm opposition each year from the Governing Council of the Maryland Board of Physician Quality Assurance.
- *Michigan:* Initial PA practice laws allowed individuals from a variety of backgrounds to obtain PA licensure, provided that they could pass a certifying examination. Since only graduates of an accredited PA program are eligible to take the NCCPA exam, the legislature realized that unless they revised this provision of the PA law, the state would be responsible for providing two

separate exams, one for formally trained PAs and the other for IMGs. Accordingly, the PA law was amended in 1986 to standardize the educational prerequisite to permit only formally trained PAs to be eligible for state certification. The amendment prompted eight foreign-trained physicians who had been issued temporary PA certificates to sue the state, arguing the right to take the NCCPA exam. On reaching an agreement with the NCCPA, the state purchased an old NCCPA exam and administered it twice to the IMGs, none of whom passed on either occasion. The state PA law has since not been challenged for its certification eligibility criteria.

- *New York:* Prior to a 1992 amendment, passing the NCCPA exam was not a requirement for PA registration in the state, and the state education department had the authority to review the educational qualifications of applicants and to declare an applicant's training or experience equivalent to graduation from a PA program. Under current PA practice law, passage of the NCCPA exam is a prerequisite for practicing as a PA in that state. Because PAs must be graduates of an accredited PA education program to sit for the exam, IMGs are not eligible to take the exam; the Commissioner of Health, however, still has the authority to deem an IMG's educational qualifications equivalent to graduation from a PA program [N.Y. Educ. Law § 6541 (1)(d), and N.Y. Comp. Codes R. & Regs. tit. 8, § 60.8(b)(3)].

[Two articles provide excellent general summaries of state legislative activity involving the certification of IMGs: (1) AAPA Governmental Affairs Division, "A Challenge for the Physician Assistant Profession: Report of the AAPA Task Force on Unlicensed Medical Graduates," *Journal of American Academy of Physician Assistants* 65 (Jan. 1993), and (2) L. Howard, K. Garman, and R. McCann, "Another Go at the Experiment," 110 *Public Health Reports* 668 (1995).]

Whether IMGs should be allowed to sit for the NCCPA exam has also been the subject of recent litigation before the courts in Florida and California. In 1991, Florida's legislature passed a law requiring the Florida Board of Medical Examiners either to allow IMGs meeting specified criteria to take the NCCPA exam or to develop, in cooperation with the Department of Professional Regulation (DPR), a statewide exam that would permit IMGs to practice as PAs only in Florida [*see* Fla. Stat. § 458.347(6) and (7)]. In December 1994, after extensive negotiation between the DPR and NCCPA, the Commission decided not to sell a certifying exam to the state of Florida, and the DPR spent the next year developing a statewide exam modeled after the NCCPA exam.

Prior to thc scheduled October 1995 exam date, a professional IMG association filed suit against the DPR on behalf of 450 IMGs holding temporary state PA licenses, contending that they should be allowed to take the standardized NCCPA exam rather than the state-developed exam. Under a subsequent unpublished stipulation, the suit was dismissed by a circuit court just eight days prior to the scheduled exam date. The court ruled that the state exam would be given as planned, but that any of the IMG-plaintiffs could retain their temporary certificates and wait until the following October for the next exam administration. Only 24 of the 450 eligible IMG exam candidates opted to take the October 1995 exam; half of those candidates passed the written exam, but all failed the clinical skills portion.

Some of those candidates have requested that their exams be rescored, suggesting that the exam was graded unfairly by practicing PAs who may oppose certification of IMGs as PAs. In response, the Florida Academy of PAs has pointed to its careful efforts to ensure objective scoring of the exam, including videotaping of the clinical skills portion and grading by two examiners. Although none of the initial exam candidates passed, the certification of IMGS as PAs will continue to be the subject of controversy in Florida in upcoming years, especially in lieu of a recently passed law allowing IMGs who fail the state exam to apply for re-examination up to four times [FLA. STAT. § 458.347(7)(b)(1) through (3)].

In another case, 40 IMGs filed a complaint in 1996 against the California Physician Assistant Examining Committee (PAEC) and the NCCPA, seeking licensure as PAs without either passing the NCCPA exam or attending an accredited PA program. The IMGs argue that because California law has a provision allowing graduates of "medical schools approved by the Division of Licensing" to practice as PAs if they pass the NCCPA exam, the Commission should be required to permit them to take the exam. Moreover, the IMGs contend that, under that law, the PAEC should either pressure NCCPA to offer the exam to them or make some other arrangements, such as a state-developed exam, to enable them to obtain licenses as PAs.

The court dismissed the suit in parts: first dismissing on jurisidictional grounds the case against NCCPA, which has offices located primarily in Georgia, and then dropping the suit against the PAEC on grounds that the IMGs had failed to exhaust administrative remedies [*see, e.g., Carache v. California,* No. DC138 471 (Los Angeles Sup. Ct. May 6, 1996) (tentative ruling)]. According to California law, proceedings involving denial, suspension, or revocation of a PA license must be conducted in accordance with the California Administrative Procedure Act, under which the relevant agency must uphold a denial of a license before the applicant can appeal to the courts [*see, e.g.,* CAL. BUS. & PROF. CODE § 1670; CAL. GOV. CODE § 11500 *et seq.* (administrative procedure provisions)]. Since the IMGs in this case did not allege that they had applied for a license, or that they had requested approval for their foreign medical school degree for the purpose of applying, the court reasoned that the IMG's action against the PAEC was premature. Because the ruling does not preclude IMGs from bringing similar actions once thay have exhausted their administrative remedies, the certification of IMGs as PAs may come again before the California courts in the near future.

APPENDIX 2-A

Accredited Physician Assistant Programs

This appendix is a listing of physician assistant programs accredited by the American Medical Association's Committee on Allied Health Education and Accreditation (CAHEA), its predecessor (The AMA Council on Medical Education), or its successor agency, the Commission on Accreditation of Allied Health Education Programs (CAAHEP).

KEY:

- **This listing issued in November 1996.**
- ***Programs in italics have closed.***
- **Programs in bold face hold provisional accreditation, a time-limited accreditation status awarded to a new program that had not accepted students at the time of its application.**
- **Programs with provisional accreditation must apply for and receive initial accreditation no later than six months after graduation of their first class or lose their accredited status.**
- **Provisional accreditation status was first offered in April 1996.**

continues

Courtesy of American Academy of Physician Assistants, Alexandria, Virginia.

State	*Program Name and Institutional Sponsor*	*Month/Year Accredited*	*Closed or Transferred*
ALABAMA	Surgeon Assistant University of Alabama-Birmingham Birmingham, AL	9/75	
	Medex *University of Alabama-Birmingham*	*6/73*	*8/76*
	Physician Assistant **University of South Alabama** **Mobile, AL**	**4/96**	
ARIZONA	*Emergency Nurse Practitioner* *Maricopa County General Hospital* *Phoenix, AZ*	*10/80*	*4/82*
	Community Health Medic (Indian Hlth Srv) *Phoenix Indian Medical Center* *Phoenix, AZ*	*9/72*	*Consolidated with Gallup program 1977* *Discontinued in 1983*
	Physician Assistant Kirksville College of Osteopathic Medicine Phoenix, AZ	10/96	
CALIFORNIA	Physician Assistant Chas R Drew University of Medicine & Science Los Angeles, CA	9/72	
	Physician Assistant University of Southern California Los Angeles, CA	10/75	

CALIFORNIA, cont'd	Physician Assistant University of California-Davis Sacramento, CA	3/74	
	Primary Care Associate Stanford University School of Medicine Stanford, CA	3/76	
	Physician Assistant Western University of Health Sciences (formerly the College of Osteopathic Medicine of the Pacific) Pomona, CA	5/90	
	Physician Assistant *Loma Linda University* *Loma Linda, CA*	*10/79*	*10/81*
	Physician Assistant US Navy San Diego, CA	4/80; 5/91	8/82 (reopened 5/91)
COLORADO	Child Health Associate University of Colorado Health Science Center Denver, CO	2/73	
	Ob-Gyn Associate *University of Colorado* *Denver, CO*	*3/75*	*6/77*

continues

State	Program Name and Institutional Sponsor	Month/Year Accredited	Closed or Transferred
CONNECTICUT	Physician Associate Yale University School of Medicine New Haven, CT	3/75	
	Physician Assistant Quinnipiac College Hamden, CT	10/95	
DISTRICT OF COLUMBIA	Physician Assistant George Washington University Washington, DC	11/72	
	Physician Assistant Howard University Washington, DC	11/73	
FLORIDA	Physician Assistant Santa Fe Community College Gainesville, FL	6/73	1/78
	transferred to: University of Florida Gainesville, FL	1/78	
	Physician Assistant Nova Southeastern University North Miami Beach, FL	5/94	
GEORGIA	Physician Assistant Emory University Atlanta, GA	9/72	

GEORGIA, cont'd	Physician Assistant Medical College of Georgia Augusta, GA	11/73	
ILLINOIS	Physician Assistant Chicago CityWide College/Cook County Hospital <u>transferred to:</u> Malcolm X College Chicago, IL	10/88	10/92
	Physician Assistant Chicago Medical School/ Finch University of Health Sciences North Chicago, IL	5/93	
	Physician Assistant Midwestern University (formerly the Chicago College of Osteopathic Medicine) Downers Grove, IL	5/93	
INDIANA	*Physician Assistant* *Indiana University* *Ft Wayne, IN*	*11/73*	*8/77*
	Physician Assistant Butler University/Methodist Hospital Indianapolis, IN	4/96	
IOWA	Physician Assistant University of Iowa Iowa City, IA	2/73	

continues

State	*Program Name and Institutional Sponsor*	*Month/Year Accredited*	*Closed or Transferred*
IOWA, cont'd	Physician Assistant University of Osteopathic Medicine & Health Sciences Des Moines, IA	4/83	
KANSAS	Physician Assistant Wichita State University Wichita, KS	11/73	
KENTUCKY	Physician Assistant University of Kentucky Lexington, KY	11/74	
LOUISIANA	Physician Assistant Louisiana State University Medical Center Shreveport, LA	4/96	
MAINE	**Physician Assistant** **University of New England** **Biddeford, ME**	**4/96**	
MARYLAND	Physician Assistant Essex Community College Baltimore, MD	9/72	
	Health Associate *The Johns Hopkins University* *Baltimore, MD*	*11/74*	*6/79*

MARYLAND, cont'd	**Physician Assistant** **Anne Arundel Community College** **Arnold, MD**	**10/96**
MASSACHUSETTS	Physician Assistant Northeastern University Boston, MA	9/72
	Physician Assistant Springfield College/Baystate Health Systems Springfield, MA	4/96
MICHIGAN	Physician Assistant Mercy College (merged to become University of Detroit Mercy) Detroit, MI	9/72
	Physician Assistant Western Michigan University Kalamazoo, MI	9/72
	Physician Assistant **Central Michigan University** **Mount Pleasant, MI**	**4/96**
	Physician Assistant **Wayne State University** **Detroit, MI**	**4/96**
MINNESOTA	Physician Assistant Augsburg College Minneapolis, MN	10/96

continues

State	*Program Name and Institutional Sponsor*	*Month/Year Accredited*	*Closed or Transferred*
MISSISSIPPI	*Physician Assistant* *University of Mississippi* *Jackson, MS*	*9/72*	*1/75*
MISSOURI	Physician Assistant St Louis University St Louis, MO	6/73	
	Physician Assistant *Stephens College* *Columbia, MO*	*12/76*	*10/78*
MONTANA	**Physician Assistant** **Rocky Mountain College** **Billings, MT**	**4/96**	
NEBRASKA	Physician Assistant University of Nebraska Omaha, NE	11/74	
NEW HAMPSHIRE	*Medex* *Dartmouth Medical School* *Hanover, NH*	*2/73*	*1/76*
NEW JERSEY	Physician Assistant University of Medicine & Dentistry of NJ Piscataway, NJ	3/76	
NEW MEXICO	*Community Health Medic (Indian Hlth Srv)* *Gallup Indian Medical Center* *Gallup, NM*	*11/73*	*8/83*

NEW YORK	Physician Assistant	11/72	
	Albany Medical College & Hudson Valley		
	Community College		
	Troy, NY		
	Physician Assistant	9/72	
	The Brooklyn Hospital & Long Island Univ.		
	Brooklyn, NY		
	Physician Assistant	6/73	
	Touro College		
	Dix Hills, NY		
	Physician Assistant	2/73	7/76
	Antioch College (Ohio) & Harlem		
	Hospital Center		
	<u>transferred to:</u>		
	New School for Social Research &	7/76	1/78
	Harlem Hospital Center		
	<u>transferred to:</u>		
	City University of New York &	1/78	
	Harlem Hospital Center		
	Surgeon Assistant	3/75	
	<u>changed to</u>: Physician Assistant,		
	A Surgical Focus		
	Cornell University Medical College		
	New York, NY		
	Physician Assistant	11/72	11/81
	US Public Health Service Hospital		
	<u>all USPHS hospitals sold 1981:</u>	11/81	
	Bayley Seton Hospital		
	Staten Island, NY		

continues

State	*Program Name and Institutional Sponsor*	*Month/Year Accredited*	*Closed or Transferred*
NEW YORK, cont'd	Physician Assistant State University of New York Stony Brook, NY	9/72	
	Physician Assistant State University of New York Brooklyn, NY	10/92	
	Physician Assistant D'Youville College Buffalo, NY	10/94	
	Physician Assistant Rochester Institute of Technology Rochester, NY	10/94	
	Physician Assistant Catholic Medical Center of Brooklyn & Queens Woodhaven, NY	10/95	
	Physician Assistant Bronx Lebanon Hospital Bronx, NY	4/96	
	Physician Assistant **Wagner College/Staten Island University Hospital** **Staten Island, NY**	**4/96**	
	Physician Assistant **Le Moyne College** **Syracuse, NY**	**4/96**	

NORTH CAROLINA	Physician Assistant Duke University Durham, NC	9/72	
	Physician Assistant Bowman Gray School of Medicine Winston-Salem, NC	9/72	*11/80*
	Emergency Care Physician Assistant *Catawba Valley Technical College* *Hickory, NC*	*4/78*	*8/81*
	Surgeon Assistant *University of North Carolina* *Chapel Hill, NC*	*10/78*	
	Physician Assistant **Methodist College** **Fayetteville, NC**	**4/96**	
	Physician Assistant **East Carolina University** **Greenville, NC**	**10/96**	
NORTH DAKOTA	Family Nurse Practitioner (now Physician Assistant) University of North Dakota Minot, ND	12/74	
	Medex (for Native Americans) *University of North Dakota* *Grand Forks, ND*	*11/74*	*4/75*

continues

State	*Program Name and Institutional Sponsor*	*Month/Year Accredited*	*Closed or Transferred*
OHIO	Physician Assistant Kettering College of Medical Arts Kettering, OH	3/75	
	Physician Assistant Cuyahoga Community College Parma, OH	3/74	
	Surgeon Assistant Cuyahoga Community College Parma, OH	4/79	
	Physician Assistant *Cincinnati Technical College* *Cincinnati, OH*	*11/74*	*10/79*
	Physician Assistant *Lake Erie College* *Painesville, OH*	*3/77*	*7/87*
	Physician Assistant **Medical College of Ohio** **Toledo, OH**	**10/96**	
OKLAHOMA	Physician Associate University of Oklahoma Oklahoma City, OK	9/72	
OREGON	Physician Assistant Oregon Health Sciences University Portland, OR	10/96	

PENNSYLVANIA	Physician Assistant Gannon University Erie, PA	10/78	
	Physician Assistant St. Francis College Loretto, PA	9/80	
	Physician Assistant Allegheny University of Health Professions (formerly Hahnemann University) Philadelphia, PA	9/72	
	Physician Assistant King's College Wilkes-Barre, PA	4/79	
	Physician Assistant *Community College of Allegheny County* *Pittsburgh, PA*	*4/80*	*8/85*
	Physician Assistant *Pennsylvania State University* *Hershey, PA*	*3/74*	*9/86*
	Physician Assistant Duquesne University Pittsburgh, PA	10/93	
	Physician Assistant **Beaver College** **Glenside, PA**	**4/96**	

continues

State	Program Name and Institutional Sponsor	Month/Year Accredited	Closed or Transferred
PENNSYLVANIA, cont'd	Physician Assistant Philadelphia College of Textiles & Science Philadelphia, PA	10/96	
	Physician Assistant Pennsylvania College of Technology Williamsport, PA	**10/96**	
SOUTH CAROLINA	Physician Assistant Medical University of South Carolina Charleston, SC	11/73; 10/95	6/83 (reopened 1994)
SOUTH DAKOTA	Physician Assistant University of South Dakota School of Medicine Vermillion, SD	4/95	
TENNESSEE	Physician Assistant Trevecca Nazarene College Nashville, TN	10/78	
TEXAS	Physician Assistant Baylor College of Medicine Houston, TX	2/73	
	Physician Assistant University of Texas Southwestern Medical Ctr Dallas, TX	11/73	

TEXAS, cont'd	Physician Assistant University of Texas Medical Branch Galveston, TX	2/73	
	Physician Assistant US Army transferred to: Academy of Health Sciences AMEDDC&S Ft Sam Houston, TX	6/73 and 5/90 4/96	8/77
	Physician Assistant US Air Force Sheppard AFB, Wichita Falls, TX	9/72 and 10/91	6/85
UTAH	Medex (now Physician Assistant) University of Utah Salt Lake City, UT	11/72	
VIRGINIA	*Physician Assistant* *US Navy* *Portsmouth, VA*	*4/80*	*8/86*
WASHINGTON	Medex (now Physician Assistant) University of Washington Seattle, WA	2/73	
WEST VIRGINIA	Physician Assistant Alderson Broaddus College Philippi, WV	9/72 ***Provisional accreditation 10/96***	Withdrew from CAAHEP 4/95
	Physician Assistant The College of West Virginia Beckley, WV	4/96	

State	*Program Name and Institutional Sponsor*	*Month/Year Accredited*	*Closed or Transferred*
WISCONSIN	Physician Assistant University of Wisconsin Madison, WI	3/77	*10/81*
	Physician Assistant *Marshfield Clinic Foundation* *Marshfield, WI*	*3/74*	

CHAPTER 3

Licensure and Scope of Practice

INTRODUCTION

State regulation of PAs encompasses licensing statutes and administering regulatory board rules in which the state sets out its requirements for granting permission to individuals seeking to practice as PAs and the scope of permissible activities within such practice. Although state occupational regulation of PAs varies from state to state, all states (except Mississippi) have some form of regulatory system governing PAs. This chapter outlines state PA practice laws and their requirements (focusing primarily on provisions that are fairly uniform among state PA practice acts and accompanying regulations). Because state regulation of PA practice continues to undergo frequent change, however, this chapter should only be used for general reference purposes; the most current and up-to-date version of a particular state's PA practice statutes and regulations should be obtained from the state's PA regulatory board. [See Appendix B for a state-by-state list of citations and contact information for the regulatory board.]

HISTORICAL BACKGROUND

During the early years of the PA profession, there was much uncertainty surrounding the question of whether physicians could legally make use of "paramedicals," especially given existing legislation in many states that criminalized the provision of health care services by anyone not licensed to provide such services [*see* C.E. Fasser, P. Andrus, and Q. Smith, "Certification, Registration and Licensure of Physician Assistants," in R. Carter and H. Perry, eds., *Alternatives in Health Care Delivery: Emerging Roles for Physician Assistants,* 78, 79 (1984)]. In an effort to support physicians who became involved in litigation involving the delegation of tasks to their medically trained assistants, two states enacted general delegatory statutes before any consensus on the issue was reached within the PA profession or among state legislatures. In 1963 and 1964, Colorado and Kansas became the first two states to enact delegatory exemptions in their medical practice acts, which essentially permitted nonphysician personnel to carry out delegated medical tasks under physician supervision. Under these delegatory amendments, physicians (rather than state regulatory authorities) had total responsibility for deciding the qualifications and supervision of assistants and for defining the assistants' scope of practice.

Nonetheless, the uncertainty about delegation of medical functions remained among most physicians, especially in the absence of statutes providing explicit legal sanction for such activity, and in light of the occasional court decision indicating potential liability in this area [*see, e.g., Barber v. Reinking,* 411 P.2d 861 (Wash. Ct. App. 1966) (negligence inferred from mere fact that a physician delegated a task to a person not licensed to perform it)]. Founders of the first PA education program at Duke University quickly recognized the need for resolving this issue if they were to successfully maintain the continued growth of the PA profession. Accordingly, PA educators at Duke sought a ruling from the office of the North Carolina Attorney General (AG) as to whether the projected physician-supervised activities of the PA would contravene state licensure laws. In 1966 the AG's office ruled that the state medical practice statutes should not be construed "to prohibit or limit performance by any person of such duties as specified mechanical acts in the personal care of a patient when such care or activities are performed" under direction of a licensed physician [*see* R.D. Carter and J.F. Gifford, Jr., "The Emergence of the Physician Assistant Profession, in H. Perry and B. Breitner, eds., *Physician Assistants—Their Contribution to Health Care* 19, 26 (1982), *citing* "Physician Assistant's Program, 1969–70," *Bulletin of Duke University* (1969)].

Although this ruling provided sufficient authority to justify continuing the Duke PA program, it was understood by PA educators and the first practicing PAs that the advisory opinion was not a formal legal recognition of physician delegation of medical tasks to PAs. Shortly after that opinion was rendered, however, Oklahoma and Arizona enacted delegatory exemptions to their state medical practice statutes, explicitly recognizing the physician's authority to delegate tasks. The Oklahoma statute, for example, provided that services rendered by a PA, registered nurse, or licensed practical nurse were not prohibited if such services were rendered under the direct supervision and control of a licensed physician [OKLA. STAT. tit. 59, § 492 (1969)].

The decisions of medical professional associations, federal policy makers, and the founders of the PA profession provided the impetus for other states to enact delegatory exceptions to their medical practice acts, rather than pursuing the alternative course of enacting separate PA licensing statutes. First, PAs arrived on the health care scene during the late 1960s, a time when the American Medical

Association (AMA) and the American Hospital Association (AHA) were questioning the licensure practices for all health professionals. Within these organizations, physician-members, hospitals, and other health care professionals increasingly expressed concern that existing licensure laws posed significant barriers to educational advancement, effective delegation of tasks, and innovative use of health care personnel, particularly nonphysician providers [*see* C.E. Fasser, P. Andrus, and Q. Smith, "Certification, Registration and Licensure of Physician Assistants," in R. Carter and H. Perry, eds., *Alternatives in Health Care Delivery: Emerging Roles for Physician Assistants* 78, 81–82 (1984)].

Second, in 1971, the U.S. Department of Health, Education and Welfare issued a report that expressed the agency's concern about health manpower shortages and recommended a nationwide moratorium on the licensure of additional health occupations. [U.S. Department of Health, Education and Welfare, *Report on Licensure and Related Personnel* (June 1971)]. Subsequently, the National Advisory Commission on Health Manpower agreed with this viewpoint in its own report, which also emphasized the need for state legislation authorizing the physician delegation of medical tasks to PAs [*see* C.E. Fasser, P. Andrus, and Q. Smith, "Certification, Registration and Licensure of Physician Assistants," in R. Carter and H. Perry, eds., *Alternatives in Health Care Delivery: Emerging Roles for Physician Assistants* 78, 82 (1984)].

Third, in the midst of these policy-making events, the founders of the PA profession held a series of conferences at Duke University between 1968 and 1972, which ultimately resulted in a general consensus among attendees on the issue of establishing a system that would recognize PAs under the licenses of their employing physicians [*see* R. Carter and J. Gifford, Jr., "The Emergence of the Physician Assistant Profession," in H. Perry and B. Breitner, eds., *Physician Assistants—Their Contribution to Health Care* 19, 31–33 (1982)]. According to Dr. E. Harvey Estes, a leading PA educator and one of the founders of the Duke PA program, early discussions about PA credentialing raised doubts as to whether the enactment of independent licensure laws for PAs was the optimal route for ensuring the quality of PA practice. Instead, PA educators and leaders of the time envisioned that legal recognition of PAs under the license of their employing physician would allow more freedom and flexibility than a licensure law, and thus would ensure the "dynamic balance between a doctor and an employed PA." [E.H. Estes, "The PA Experiment After 25 Years: What Have We Learned," *Journal of American Academy of Physician Assistants* 716 (Oct. 1992); *see also* E. Schneller, *The Physician's Assistant: Innovation in the Medical Division of Labor* 21 (1978) (arguing that the founders of the PA profession preferred the delegatory model over enactment of PA practice statutes that might result in a narrow delineation of the PA's role and ultimately be a "deathblow to full [PA] participation in the medical problem-solving process")].

Development of State PA Practice Acts

Although delegatory amendments predominated among the initial statutory enactments affecting physicians' use of PAs, early regulation of PAs based on the delegatory model was subsequently replaced by legislative enactment based on the regulatory model. By the end of 1972, legislation pertaining to PAs had been enacted in 24 states: 7 states had general delegatory statutes, and 17 states had regulatory statutes. Today, almost all states have delegatory amendments in their medical practice statutes as well as PA practice statutes that authorize state licensing boards and/or regulatory agencies to govern PA practice. The number of states choosing not to enact PA practice statutes has dwindled to three (Alaska, South Carolina, and North Dakota), and even in these states, the state PA regulatory board (usually the board of medicine) has promulgated regulations regarding the employment of PAs and permissible practice activities.

The conversion to PA practice statutes has been linked to several historical factors. As the scope of PA practice broadened, concern grew as to whether delegatory laws provided sufficient accountability for services provided by PAs. Under the earliest delegatory statutes, the physician decided who would be a "physician assistant," regardless of the person's educational background. Accordingly, legislators responded to public sentiment by enacting PA practice statutes that imposed stricter requirements on supervising physicians and their PAs, including minimum education standards and other qualification criteria.

Changes in health care delivery and greater numbers of PAs, as well as the need for administrative efficiency, also persuaded many states to enact specific PA practice statutes. From an administrative perspective, conversion to a regulatory-based system enabled the state government to "keep abreast of the number of PAs working within the state and of their qualifications," and place administrative authority within a regulatory body where "rules and regulations [can] be amended easily without involving the possible protracted and political difficulties inherent in legislation." [R.D. Carter and J.F. Gifford, Jr., "The Emergence of the Physician Assistant Profession," in H. Perry and B. Breitner, eds., *Physician Assistants—Their Contribution to Health Care* 19, 36 (1982); see also Chapter 11: Participation in Government Affairs, for a discussion of the difference between legislative enactment and adoption of regulations].

The process of developing such laws was facilitated by model PA legislation drafted after a series of conferences held at Duke University in 1969. [*See* R.D. Carter and J.F. Gifford, Jr., "The Emergence of the Physician Assistant Profession," in H. Perry and B. Breitner, eds., *Physician Assistants—Their Contribution to Health Care* 19, 35 (1982)]. The model legislation retained elements of delegation, but also created new mechanisms for shifting regulatory responsibility from the physician to a state regulatory agency. The two-stage process contemplated by the model consisted of

1. state recognition of PAs through the state medical regulatory body, which would regulate broad aspects of the PA profession such as qualification and examination requirements for certification, applications by supervising physicians to utilize PAs, and disciplinary actions against PAs
2. continued delineation of the individual PA's scope of practice in accordance with the medical tasks delegated by the supervising physician, who would remain liable for PA-provided patient care.

During the 1970s, when many of the PA practice acts were being written and subsequently enacted by state legislatures, an important objective of the PA profession was to eliminate confusion and promote uniformity by developing standard criteria to ensure states of PA competence. The American Academy of Physician Assistants (AAPA) and state PA associations waged a long but successful campaign to convince legislative and regulatory bodies to adopt the two basic qualifications that have been incorporated into most state PA practice laws: (1) graduation from an accredited PA education program and (2) passing the National Commission on Certification for Physician Assistants (NCCPA) examination. In addition, the AAPA and other advocates for improved PA practice opportunities have persuaded many states to regulate PAs under a system in which licensure of the PA is based on the PA's credentials (e.g., meeting the educational and examination requirements of the law), but is not inextricably tied to issues of physician supervision or the PA's employment status. [For a more detailed discussion, see AAPA Model PA Licensing Law.]

LICENSURE UNDER STATE PA PRACTICE LAWS

Although state regulation of PAs was initially a patchwork of various regulatory schemes with divergent requirements for entering PA practice, today PA practice statutes have fairly uniform education and other qualification requirements, and the profession is essentially a licensed health care occupation. The following sections discuss what is meant by "licensure," and why an understanding of regulatory terminology is particularly significant for PAs.

Licensure Defined: How It Differs from Private Credentialing

An individual license, as defined in *Black's Law Dictionary,* is "a permit granted by an appropriate governmental body . . . to a person . . . to pursue some occupation . . . subject to regulation under the [state's] police power" [Black's Law Dictionary 920 (6th ed. 1990)]. In the health care context, licensure is a method of credentialing that attempts to ensure that only qualified people are engaged in health care practice. The primary purpose of licensure laws governing health care professionals is to protect the public health by helping the public to identify qualified providers and by prohibiting unqualified persons from providing services that require expertise. There are many public and private credentialing methods: the public method is individual licensure; the private methods include accreditation of educational programs, certification of individuals, and credentialing by institutions.

National certification of PAs differs from state licensure in that it is sponsored by the NCCPA, a private credentialing organization that certifies, by exam, that PAs meet certain criteria and are considered prepared to practice in the discipline. [See Chapter 2: Education and Certification.] NCCPA certification has become so widely accepted that it is difficult to practice as a PA without successfully passing the NCCPA certifying exam. States can require private certification as a condition of state licensure [*see, e.g., Gilliam v. National Comm'n on Certification of Physicians Assistants,* 722 F. Supp. 1512 (E.D. Pa. 1989), *aff'd,* 898 F.2d 140 (3d Cir.), *cert. denied,* 495 U.S. 920 (1990)], and such is the requirement in most PA practice statutes.

In addition, all hospitals are involved in credentialing health care practitioners. Hospitals have a responsibility for ensuring the competency of physician and non-physician health care providers practicing at the hospital, which they fulfill by evaluating credentials and delineating clinical privileges. For most hospitals, credentialing is handled through the hiring process, hospital and department rules concerning practice patterns, the supervisory system, utilization review, performance evaluation, and verification of relicensure. Qualifications, including verification of licensure and other credentials, are checked before a health care practitioner is hired. The process assists in determining professional competence and detecting other problems that could interfere with proper patient care. [For a detailed discussion of the credentialing process as applied to PAs, see Chapter 8: Credentialing and Peer Review.]

Licensure versus Certification: A Matter of Terminology

In addition to understanding the difference between public and private methods of credentialing, PAs should be aware of the differing terms used to refer to state licensure of PAs. There are three basic terms used by states to describe the regulatory system in place for ensuring that PAs have met certain standards for practicing in the profession: licensure, certification, and registration. Although these terms at one time referred to distinct regulatory schemes, the increasing uniformity of PA regulation has all but eliminated the subtle differences between these state credentialing processes in the context of the PA profession.

As a matter of historical reference, however, the definitions of these three terms are set out here because in knowing the distinctions, PAs may better understand the evolution from differing regulatory processes governing PA practice to the fairly uniform state licensure process that exists today.

1. *Registration* is the creation of an official list of individuals in a particular profession, a process that does not ensure either the public or employers that these individuals are competent or qualified. In general, registration of individuals in an occupation imposes few limitations on an individual's right to practice. Because registration allows essentially unrestricted entry into an occupation, it can be classified as the least restrictive of the three regulatory schemes.
2. *Certification* is a regulatory process directed at limiting the use of a specific occupational title by requiring that the individual seeking to use such title submit to a specific process (e.g., passing a national certifying exam) administered by a nongovernmental agency. Theoretically, this form of regulation does not restrict any individual from entering the occupation, although it makes it very difficult to practice without state certification because both employers and the general public rely on these national and state certification credentials in identifying practitioners that have met state standards.
3. *Licensure* is a regulatory scheme that restricts any individual from practicing in the licensed occupation without permission granted by the state. As such, it is the most restrictive term associated with standards for entering an occupation. In granting a license, the state has the authority to collect fees, establish standards of practice, require certain minimum qualifications and competency levels of applicants, and impose on applicants other requirements necessary to protect the general public welfare.

[*See* D. Bissonette, "The Derivation of Authority for Medical Order Writing by PAs," *Journal of American Academy of Physician Assistants* 358, 360 (June 1991).]

All three terms are still used to refer to PA state credentials, although one term markedly less than the other two (e.g., PAs are currently "registered" in 9 states, "certified" in 20 states, and "licensed" in 21 states). Of critical importance for PAs, however, is that the terms no longer indicate a substantive difference in the regulatory process; now that state requirements for PA practice are fairly consistent across all states, the regulatory system governing PAs, regardless of the terminology used, essentially involves a licensure process.

Because PAs are expressly prohibited from practicing without permission of the appropriate medical licensing authority in all states, PAs who are permitted by law to practice under a regulatory scheme called registration, certification, or licensure are all effectively "licensed" health care practitioners [*see* D. Bissonette, "The Derivation of Authority for Medical Order Writing by PAs," *Journal of American Academy of Physician Assistants* 358, 360 (June 1991)]. Moreover, given that nearly all states restrict PAs from their full range of practice activities until they obtain NCCPA certification, the NCCPA exam effectively serves as a national licensing exam even though sitting for the exam actually comprises one part of a voluntary, private sector certification process. PAs should recognize, however, that there is a significant distinction between NCCPA certification and state licensure, and that each system must be dealt with separately in order to obtain "licensed" status with full PA practice privileges. [NCCPA certification is discussed in Chapter 2: Education and Certification.]

Of the 21 states that currently use "licensure" to indicate that PAs have met state practice standards [*see, e.g.*, Alaska Stat. §§ 08.64.010 *et seq.*, Cal. Bus. & Prof. Code §§ 3500 *et seq.*, 225 Ill. Comp. Stat. 95/1 *et seq.*], many formerly used certification or registration terminology and converted to licensing language to eliminate confusion and resolve problems arising from references to "licensed" practitioners in different state statutes or regulations. [See AAPA Model PA Licensing Law, discussed next.] Moreover, a number of state PA chapters, including chapters in Georgia, Hawaii, South Dakota, Oregon, and Wisconsin, have been expressing interest in, or have experience with, introducing licensure bills in legislative sessions.

AAPA Model PA Licensing Law

Most state laws, including PA practice statutes, vary in structure and content; the creation of a model law is directed at eliminating some of these differences by encouraging states to adopt statutes based on provisions in the model law. The AAPA produced its first model PA practice act in 1982. In 1992, the AAPA incorporated the changes that occurred in the interim decade in its revised model PA licensing law [see Appendix 3-A]. Although the model law contains recommended regulatory language for the entire range of issues covered in PA practice statutes, including qualifications, scope of practice, and physician supervision, this section discusses only provisions pertaining to licensure as a regulatory system. [For a discussion of other model law provisions, see AAPA Model Law: Scope of Practice.]

In the preface to its model law, the AAPA comments that licensing of PAs, rather than state certification or registration, is the most desirable regulatory language. Many states, the AAPA explains, have enacted other laws related to health care (e.g., reimbursement, nursing, etc.), which contain references to "licensed practitioners." Consequently, practicing PAs sometimes encounter problems derived from terminology, including:

- services provided by a PA are denied for reimbursement because an insurance carrier argues that services are not covered unless provided by a "licensed" practitioner
- a nurse refuses to administer treatment under a medical order transmitted by a PA because nursing regulations provide that nurses should act upon only orders issued or relayed by a "licensed" practitioner

Accordingly, states that incorporate "license" in their PA practice statutes or establish a PA licensing authority substantially reduce PA practice obstacles stemming from nonrecognition of PA-provided health care services.

Along with recommending PA licensure, the model law also encourages states to implement a regulatory system in which PAs receive a license independent of a PA's employment status. Under such a system, the PA's credentials are presented to the appropriate regulatory agency, which issues a renewable license based on meeting state requirements. Although PA clinical practice always remains dependent on the existence of a physician supervisor, this approach officially recognizes the PA as a practitioner who has met the state's minimum qualification standards, regardless of whether or not the PA is continuously employed.

In its commentary on the model law, the AAPA notes that such a licensing system should replace the process that developed under many states' original PA laws in which PAs were approved to work for their supervising physicians under the physicians' licenses and, therefore, were required to resubmit to the particular state's medical licensing board all transcripts, test scores, and references every time they changed employers or supervisors. Not only did this system generate paperwork that was unduly burdensome for licensing boards, but, in effect, PAs could not work during periods of job transition because they had no professional or legal identity.

SCOPE OF PRACTICE UNDER STATE PA PRACTICE LAWS

Perhaps the most important regulatory aspects of PA practice statutes and regulations are the limitations they impose on a PA's scope of practice, which is a legal term with which all PAs should be familiar. Every PA should understand scope of practice as a legal concept, as well as know the specific scope-of-practice limitations provided for in the PA practice statutes and regulations of the PA's state of practice or by agreement between the PA and the supervising physician. The following sections outline some of the scope-of-practice provisions common to many state PA practice laws; not addressed here, however, are scope-of-practice provisions delineating PA prescribing privileges. [See Chapter 4: Prescribing and Dispensing.]

Scope of Practice Defined

Scope of practice as a legal term is derived from a concept known as *scope of employment,* which is a test used by courts to determine whether it is the employer or the employee who is liable for harm caused to another by the employee's actions. If the employee's conduct is found to be within the scope of employment, the employer will be held liable for the employee's acts. [For a more detailed discussion, see Chapter 5: Liability, at Imputed Liability, Scope of Employment.] In the context of health care professionals, this concept is known as scope of practice; for PAs, as well as other health care professionals, it not only determines who is liable for the PA's actions, but also defines the range of medical tasks that a PA may legally perform.

State laws defining PA scope of practice are implemented through three different mechanisms: state statutes, administrative regulations promulgated by the PA regulatory board (often the state board of medicine), and delegation of tasks as determined by the supervising physician. In many states, the PA practice laws incorporate a combination of these mechanisms [*see* S. Woomer, "The Physician Assistant's Scope of Practice," *Journal of American Academy of Physician Assistants* 645 (Nov./Dec. 1990)]. Another important element of scope of practice delineated in all PA practice laws is the nature and extent of physician supervision required when the PA performs delegated medical tasks; some statutes and regulations are much more specific than others.

Also, other less formal documents are evidence of the individual PA's scope of practice in many states; for example, the job description developed by the PA or physician-PA team (required by the state licensing board in numerous states), or attorney general opinions on the issue of whether PAs are authorized to transmit orders to other health care personnel. Physician assistants must work within state PA laws and interpretive rulings, as well as job descriptions or guidelines specifically designed for their practice. All of these mechanisms defining scope of practice for PAs are described in greater detail later. Practicing outside of these established boundaries may have serious consequences for PAs, including the finding of personal liability in a malpractice action and licensure suspension or revocation in a disciplinary action. [See Disciplinary Actions and Chapter 5: Liability.]

Statutes and Regulations

Although the language of the PA practice statutes in a few states provides a fairly specific definition of the PA's role, the more common approach is to allow the PA regulatory board to determine, by administrative rule or by regulation, the scope of practice for PAs. Both types of provisions are discussed here through examples from various states' PA practice laws.

An example of statutory language explicitly defining the PA's role is found in Arizona's PA practice statute. Within the body of that statute is a listing of the activities that the scope of practice comprises for PAs, including (but not limited to): performing history and physical examinations; ordering and performing diagnostic and therapeutic procedures; education, counseling, and making referrals to meet patient needs; assisting in surgery and performing specified surgical tasks;

and prescribing medications [ARIZ. REV. STAT. ANN. § 32-2531; *see also* MD. CODE ANN., HEALTH OCC. § 15-301; MO. REV. STAT. § 334.735; N.J. STAT. ANN. § 45:9-27.16(a); and S.D. CODIFIED LAWS § 36-4A-22]. In addition to listing delegable tasks, the New Jersey PA practice statute also specifies procedures, such as suturing traumatic or infected wounds, that the PA may perform only when directed, ordered, or prescribed by the supervising physician or specified in accordance with established protocols [N.J. STAT. ANN. § 45:9-27.16(b)]. Statutes with specific scope-of-practice provisions may be supplemented by administering regulations that also list tasks that are delegable to PAs [*see, e.g.,* N.J. ADMIN. CODE tit. 13, § 13:35-2B.4], or may require the submission of a job description for board approval as a means to further delineate the tasks that the individual PA may perform [*see, e.g.,* MD. CODE ANN., HEALTH OCC. § 15-302].

Numerous PA practice statutes, however, contain broad scope-of-practice provisions, and restrictions on the tasks a PA may perform are provided for in administering regulations. The Alabama PA practice statute, for example, liberally allows PAs to provide medical services under the supervision of a licensed physician approved by the state board of medicine and in accordance with rules adopted by the board [ALA. CODE § 34-24], but administering regulations specify both the tasks that PAs are generally allowed to perform (e.g., patient histories, office lab work, veno- and arterial puncture, applying casts, counseling patients), and the tasks that PAs may not perform (e.g., lumbar puncture, injection of joint, specified invasive procedures) [ALA. ADMIN. CODE r. 540-X-7-.12 & .14; *see also* ARK. CODE ANN. § 72-2004 (authorizing board regulations), and Ark. Med. Bd. Reg. Governing Physician's Trained Assistants, Reg. 4 (Addendum) (listing the delegable tasks and procedures); CAL. BUS. & PROF. CODE § 3502 (authorizing board regulations), and CAL. CODE REGS. tit. 16, §§ 1399.541-.545 (listing tasks PAs may and may not perform); OHIO REV. CODE ANN. § 4730.02 (broad permission to provide services to patients of supervising physicians), and OHIO ADMIN. CODE §§ 4731-4.01-.04 (listing tasks PAs may and may not perform)].

In some states, the administering regulations governing PA practice contain a lengthy list of suggested PA medical or surgical tasks that may be performed under direct (on-site) or indirect (easily available through some form of telecommunication) supervision of a physician [*see, e.g.,* FLA. ADMIN. CODE ANN. r. 59R-30.012 (providing that certain procedures are not to be performed under indirect supervision, such as routine inserting of chest tubes, inserting central venous catheters, and administering anesthesia); WASH. ADMIN. CODE § 246-918-130 (PAs may perform only those services outlined in established guidelines and must practice under direct physician supervision for new procedures not listed)]. Other states' regulations impose such limitations through requiring a detailed job description or written physician-PA agreement [*see, e.g.*, 49 PA. CODE §§ 18.142 & .151-.152 (requiring written agreement outlining services that PAs may and may not perform); see also Job Descriptions].

Delegation by Supervising Physician

Another common approach to defining the PA's scope of practice is by delegation of the supervising physician, which essentially removes the necessity for express statutory or regulatory language pertaining to the tasks the PA is permitted to perform. In Kansas, for example, the PA practice statute simply provides that a PA "may perform, only under direction and supervision, acts which constitute the practice of medicine and surgery to the extent and in the manner authorized by a responsible physician and consistent with board rules" [KAN. STAT. ANN. § 65-2896]. The administering regulations are similarly broad, providing that the PA may perform medical or surgical services when directly ordered, authorized, and coordinated by a responsible or designated physician through direct supervision, telecommunication, written protocols, or in an emergency situation [KAN. ADMIN. REGS. 100-60-8]. In essence, the statute and regulations delegate authority to supervising physicians to determine a scope of practice for their PAs; generally, the physician's delegation of authority to a PA is based on the competency and skill of the PA and cannot reach beyond the physician's scope of practice [*see, e.g.*, CONN. GEN. STAT. § 20-12d(a); MASS. GEN. LAWS ANN. ch. 112, § 9E and MASS. REGS. CODE tit. 243, § 2.08; N.Y. EDUC. LAW § 6542 and N.Y. COMP. CODES R. & REGS. tit. 10, § 94.2; WIS. ADMIN. CODE § Med. 8.07].

AAPA Model Law: Scope of Practice

According to the AAPA, state PA laws should broadly permit PAs to provide any medical services that are delegated to them by the supervising physician when such services are within their skills, form a usual component of the physician's scope of practice, and are provided with direct or indirect supervision of a physician. [See AAPA, *Guidelines for State Regulation of Physician Assistants,* at Appendix 3-B.] The AAPA's model law allows physicians to delegate to a PA any task or responsibility within their scope of practice that the PA is competent to perform [AAPA Model State PA Practice Legislation appears at Appendix 3-A]. Moreover, the AAPA advocates for state PA practice laws that avoid micromanaging the physician-PA team, for example, by limiting the PA's scope of practice through a statutory laundry list of tasks that physicians may delegate to PAs. Accordingly, the model law is based on the concept of allowing physicians the leeway to determine what tasks to delegate to their PAs and the extent to which other limitations should be placed on the PA's scope of practice. The particulars of supervision over the PA are also left to the physician-PA team under the model law, with the exception of language clearly stating that the physician need not be physically on the premises so long as the PA and physician can contact each other whenever necessary through some alternative means of communication.

Physician Supervision

Physician assistant practice statutes and regulations vary widely with respect to required physician supervision. Generally, PA practice laws do not define physician supervision as requiring direct and immediate (or physically present) supervision. The New York PA practice statute, for example, defines supervision as continuous but not necessarily "requiring the physical presence of the supervising physician at the time and place where such services are performed" [N.Y. Educ. Law § 6542(3)]. It is not uncommon, however, for such laws to require that, under certain circumstances or for some procedures, PAs perform delegated tasks only when the physician is present at the practice location.

Proximity Requirements

Physician supervision of PAs can take many forms, as reflected by the wide array of supervision arrangements (some of which allow more PA autonomy than others) authorized under the PA practice laws of these states:

- *District of Columbia* [D.C. Mun. Regs. tit. 17, § 4914 (requiring the supervising physician to be within a 15-mile radius of the city, available in person or by communication device, to countersign all medical orders and progress notes within 48 hours, and to provide immediate consultation for health care tasks not listed in PA's job description); *see also* Ill. Admin. Code tit. 68, § 1350.80 (supervising physician not physically present at PA's practice location must be within reasonable travel distance from facility)]
- *California* [Cal. Code Regs., tit. 16, § 1399.545 (requiring that the supervising physician be available in person or by electronic communication at all times PA is caring for patients, and have on file board-approved written guidelines, including protocols for certain tasks)]
- *Ohio* [Ohio Rev. Code Ann. § 4730.12 (physician must be continuously available for direct communication, either by being physically present or through some means of telecommunication, and under normal circumstances must be within 60 minutes' travel time of PA's practice location); *see also* Del. Code Ann. tit. 24, § 1770A(a)(2) (physician must be readily accessible by some form of electronic communication and able to be physically present within 30 minutes if necessary)]

- *Virginia* [VA. ADMIN. CODE tit. 18, §§ 85-50-50 and 85-50-110 (level of required physician supervision for PAs is determined on an individual basis by medical board; chart review by the physician is required within 24 hours)]

Frequency of Patient Care Review

In addition to setting out requirements as to when and where the supervising physician must be available for consultation with the PA, some PA practice statutes and/or regulations contain provisions regarding how often the supervising physician must meet with the PA to discuss patient management or other problems encountered during day-to-day practice [*see, e.g.,* ALASKA ADMIN. CODE tit. 12, § 40.430 (supervising physician must establish method for periodic evaluation of medical care and clinical management, including at least two days per quarter of direct personal contact at work site of PA or physician and at least monthly telephone or radio review of patient care and records); *see also* IND. ADMIN. CODE tit. 844, r. 2.1-1-1; OKLA. STAT. tit. 59, § 519.6]. Other state PA practice regulations are less specific, indicating only general criteria for adequate supervision [*see, e.g.,* ILL. ADMIN. CODE tit. 68, § 1350.80 (supervising physician responsible for directing and reviewing the work, records, and practice of the PA on a timely basis to ensure that appropriate treatment is being rendered); *see also* KAN. ADMIN. REGS. 100-60-10; 49 PA. CODE § 18.122].

Remote Locations

Many state PA laws authorize supervising physicians to use PAs in locations geographically separate from the physician's primary office [*see, e.g.,* ARIZ. REV. STAT. ANN. § 32-2537; D.C. MUN. REG. tit. 17, § 4911; IOWA ADMIN. CODE r. 645-325.7(4)], although at least one state expressly prohibits such an arrangement [*see* DEL. CODE ANN. tit. 24, § 1770A(a)(2)]. Typically, the legislatures in these states have enacted remote-site authorization provisions as a means to address the problem of medically underserved populations, often in rural settings. In such remote locations, the PA frequently is the primary provider of health care, with a physician on-site infrequently but always available by telephone, and a hospital awaiting emergencies that cannot be handled in the office. This kind of supervision may also be found in clinics run by nonprofit social agencies in the inner city where physicians may be in short supply [*see, e.g.,* GA. COMP. R. & REGS. r. 360-5-.08; KAN. ADMIN. REGS. 100-60-14 (allowing remote-site practice of PAs, but defining such sites as located in medically underserved areas)].

Provisions within PA practice statutes and/or regulations that authorize remote-site practicc of PAs usually impose additional requirements on the supervising physician, or on both the physician and the PA. In Pennsylvania, for example, where the operation of satellite clinics by PAs is allowed, PA practice regulations provide that the supervising physician must:

1. Obtain, and apply separately for, board approval of each satellite location.
2. Demonstrate that the PA is being utilized in an area of medical need.
3. Demonstrate that there is adequate provision for direct physician-PA communication.
4. Personally see each patient every third visit and at least once a year.
5. Visit the satellite clinic at least weekly and personally review records of each patient seen by the PA.

[49 Pa. Code § 18.155; *see also* Alaska Admin. Code tit. 12, § 40.410; Minn. Stat. § 147A.10; Okla. Admin. Code tit. 435, § 15-9-4(e); Wash. Admin. Code § 246-918-120]. Some state PA practice regulations are less specific about supervisory requirements for remote-practice locations and instead require the physician and PA to submit for board approval a plan for working together under a remote-site arrangement [*see, e.g.,* Mont. Admin. R. 8.28.1506].

Number of PAs To Supervise

Nearly all state PA practice statutes also place limitations on the number of PAs a supervising physician can supervise at one time; most allow one or two PAs per supervising physician. Some statutes also specify that the same or different limitations apply for hospitals, clinics, and other facilities employing PAs [*see, e.g.,* Del. Code Ann. tit. 24, § 1770A(e) (no more than two PAs per physician with independent practice and per each physician practicing in the same facility); D.C. Mun. Regs. tit. 17, § 4914 (supervising physician limited to two PA-supervisees or four PA-supervisees if physician is employed by health care facility that provides inpatient care and PAs treat only inpatients)]. In the event of the supervising physician's unavailability or absence for an extended period, most PA practice statutes and regulations allow for the designation of alternative supervising physicians [*see, e.g.,* D.C. Mun. Regs. tit. 17, § 4914; La. Admin. Code tit. 46, §§ 4507–09; Minn. Stat. § 147A.01(5)].

Students and Temporarily Certified PAs

Additional supervision requirements are usually required for supervising student PAs or graduate PA employees who have yet to take the required national certifying exam. [For a comprehensive discussion of the NCCPA certification process, see Chapter 2: Education and Certification.] Along with restricting the tasks that may be delegated to student PAs or newly graduated PAs, many state PA statutes impose stricter supervision requirements, such as prohibiting these PAs from performing any task without direct on-site physician supervision [*see, e.g.,* Alaska Admin. Code tit. 12, § 40.440], or otherwise limiting delegated tasks to those specified in a training plan developed by the supervising physician [*see e.g.,* Code Me. R. § 02-373-002 (10)(C)].

Physician Liability

While the most important statutory and/or regulatory provisions pertaining to physician supervision outline specific supervisory requirements and responsibilities, another significant provision in this area addresses physician liability. Because of the dependent nature of the PA profession, all state PA statutes place liability for PA negligence in providing medical services on the supervising physician; such liability, however, is shared by the PA. [For a discussion of acts or omissions for which PAs may be held liable, see Chapter 5: Liability.]

With slight variations in language, the provisions in state PA practice laws regarding physician supervision generally provide that the supervising physician ultimately retains full professional and legal responsibility for the performance of the PA and the care and treatment of the patient. In Alaska, for example, the PA practice statute states that, "the physician accepts complete personal or employer liability to a patient of the PA for whom malpractice is adjudged." [ALASKA ADMIN. CODE tit. 12, § 40.980; *see also* CAL. CODE REGS. tit. 16, § 1399.545 (supervising physician is responsible for all medical services provided by a PA)].

Related provisions in some states' PA practice laws also address the issue of liability for PA negligence when the PA is employed by a group practice or health care facility and supervised by one or more staff- or member-physicians. In Illinois, for example, PA practice regulations make clear that where the supervising physician is a member of a professional corporation or partnership, sole responsibility for direction and supervision of the PA remains with the supervising physician, who cannot transfer such responsibility to the corporate entity [ILL. ADMIN. CODE tit. 68, § 1350.110; *see also* IND. ADMIN. CODE tit. 844, r. 2.10]. In Louisiana, however, the PA practice statute provides that, where the PA is employed by a group practice or professional medical corporation, both the supervising physician and the group practice or professional medical corporation are legally responsible for the PA's patient care activities in all practice settings [LA. REV. STAT. ANN. § 37:1360.32; *see also* MASS. GEN. L. ch. 112, § 9E (where PA is employed by health care facility, legal responsibility for PA's acts and omissions shall be that of the employing facility)].

Job Descriptions

To clarify the scope of an individual PA's practice, many PA practice statutes and/or regulations require the PA, the supervising physician, or the physician-PA team to submit to the PA regulatory board for approval a job description, also known as a utilization plan, practice description, or written agreement [*see, e.g.,* MINN. STAT. § 147A.09; OHIO REV. CODE ANN. §§ 4730.15–.17; 49 PA. CODE §

18.142]. Job descriptions are typically turned over to the board as part of the PA's application for state licensure, or with an application of the supervising physician or physician-PA team regarding the proposed practice arrangement. [For a discussion of the process of state licensure, see Applications for Licensure and License Maintenance.]

In general, job descriptions explain the relationship of the PA to patients, supervising physician(s), and other health care personnel within the PA's practice location. A job description may include the specific tasks the supervising physician intends to delegate to the PA, the types of patients the PA will see, a schedule of hours or locations of the PA's practice, the nature of physician supervision, the PA's authority to transmit or execute medical orders, and the responsibilities and availability requirements of the PA for on-call shifts. In some states, requirements for a job/practice description or utilization plan are complemented by additional protocol requirements for certain tasks or situations such as prescribing medications or performing tasks in an emergency. [See Protocols.]

In some states, the PA practice laws require a detailed PA job description, but no specific criteria are provided as to the information that should be included in the description. In Illinois, for example, the job description provision of the PA practice statute states, in general terms, that tasks and procedures delegated to the PA by the supervising physician shall be implemented and reviewed under guidelines established by the physician or the physician-PA team [225 ILL. COMP. STAT. 95/4(3) and (7)]. Administering regulations require only that the physician-PA team establish guidelines that are individual to the PA in the practice setting [ILL. ADMIN. CODE tit. 68, § 1350.90(b)]. A number of other PA practice statutes and/or administering regulations also contain job description provisions of a relatively general nature [*see, e.g.,* ALASKA ADMIN. CODE tit. 12, § 40.980; GA. CODE ANN. § 43-34-105, and GA. COMP. R. & REGS. r. 360-5-.04; MONT. CODE ANN. § 37-20-301, and MONT. ADMIN. R. 8.28.1506; UTAH CODE ANN. §§ 58-70-102(12) and 302(1)(h), and UTAH ADMIN. CODE R156-70-308].

Both types of job description or utilization plan (specific and nonspecific) usually must be kept on file at the supervising physician's office or any of the PA's other practice locations in order to provide immediate access to the description to any person seeking to confirm the PA's scope of practice [*see, e.g.,* 49 PA. CODE § 18.142(c); ILL. ADMIN. CODE tit. 68, § 1350.90(b); UTAH ADMIN. CODE R156-70-308(3)].

Protocols

Some physician-PA teams use protocols as a means of ensuring that all appropriate procedures are undertaken in treating a patient's medical problem. Protocols, under a narrow definition of that term, are written statements that typically begin with the patient's presenting complaint and proceed with the steps that should be taken to resolve the medical problem, including the questions that should be asked, the tests that should be run, and the medications that should be prescribed. The definition of "protocols," however, can vary widely; the meaning of that term in a PA practice regulation requiring PAs to follow written protocols may be very different from the definition of protocols as referred to in the PA-specific policies of a particular health care facility.

In general, there is some confusion in this area because "job description," "practice description," and "protocols" are often used interchangeably. As a result, the reference to protocols in one state's regulation may have essentially the same meaning as a job description requirement in another state's regulation, even though these terms have quite different definitions. As discussed earlier, job descriptions are written outlines or reports describing the relationship of the PA to patients and other personnel within the practice, including delegated tasks, hours of work, and specific supervision requirements. The accurate definition of protocol, on the other hand, is a detailed template for treatment of a very specific medical problem. [For additional information in this area, contact the AAPA regarding its *Physician Assistant and Protocols Issue Brief* (1996).] Other terms that also are sometimes interchanged with "protocols" include "standing orders" and "written orders."

Accordingly, in the few states that require the use of protocols as part of the physician-PA working arrangement [*see, e.g.,* CONN. GEN. STAT. § 20-12d; DEL. CODE ANN. tit. 24, § 1770A(e); N.J. ADMIN. CODE tit. 13, § 13:35-6.15; TENN. CODE ANN. § 63-19-106(a)(2)], it is important for practicing PAs to ascertain the meaning of such statutory or regulatory requirements. Moreover, PAs in these states should know the scope of the protocols requirement because it will directly impact upon their daily practice activities. For example, some states' PA practice laws refer to protocols in the context of job descriptions, leaving it to the individual supervising physician to determine the nature of protocols and the extent of their use by PAs; other PA practice statutes, however, may specify under what circumstances protocols must be followed by the PA (e.g., in daily practice or for certain specified tasks) or require board approval of protocols developed by the supervising physician.

Although statutory and regulatory requirements for the use of protocols in performing delegated medical tasks are relatively rare, one area of PA practice—prescribing—should be highlighted as an exception. Protocol language within state PA practice laws more often than not applies to prescriptive privileges; protocol requirements, for example, that apply only to PA prescribing can be found in the PA practice laws of a number of states [*see, e.g.,* DEL. CODE ANN. tit. 24, § 1770A(a)(2); KAN. ADMIN. REGS. 100-60-13; N.H. CODE ADMIN. R. ANN. Med.

602.08; for additional citations to state PA practice laws with prescribing-specific protocol requirements, see Chapter 4: Prescribing and Dispensing, at Prescribing Regulations: Formulary versus Delegatory Approach].

Whether or not a state's PA practice laws refer to protocols, it is likely that practicing PAs will know about protocols and how they are used in clinical practice prior to entering practice. PA educators and health care facilities serving as clinical training sites frequently use protocols in teaching PA students basic clinical procedures, including basic physical examination procedures and procedures for further examination of specific medical conditions. The faculty of the Medical Extension Program (MEDEX) Northwest Physician Assistant Program at the University of Washington, for example, has created a set of protocols for the most commonly performed physical exams starting with the basic screening exam and proceeding with a series of organ-specific exams to be performed in accordance with the specific clinical condition. [*See* H. Stoll, "Physical Examination Protocols and Sample Write-Ups for Physician Assistants," in R. Ballweg, S. Stolberg, and E. Sullivan, eds., *Physician Assistant: A Guide to Clinical Practice* 151 (1994) (reprinting protocols and sample exam write-ups).] Of importance for the newly practicing PA, however, is understanding that protocols developed by the supervising physician in accordance with a statutory requirement may be significantly different from protocols used for academic instruction and in clinical training.

Physician assistants may also be interested in the AAPA's view of protocol requirements. If a supervising physician is required by statute or regulation to use protocols, then supervisee-PAs likewise should follow such requirements. Although acknowledging that protocols are useful for dealing with very specific clinical problems, such as anaphylaxis or advanced cardiac life support, the AAPA recommends against rigidly defining PA practice by the use of detailed treatment protocols. Extensive use of clinical protocols essentially limits PA practice to outlined steps, contends the AAPA, and thereby prevents PAs from using their knowledge to practice medicine with physician supervision [see AAPA, *Guidelines for State Regulation of Physician Assistants*, at Appendix 3-B].

PA Orders

Whether PAs may transmit medical orders to other health care personnel (e.g., nurses), though a matter of controversy among allied health and medical professions in the 1970s and 1980s, is no longer a significant scope-of-practice issue for the PA because it is generally recognized that "order writing" is within the PA's scope of practice. Nonetheless, PAs should be aware of the existing legal authority recognizing PA order writing, including court decisions, state attorney general opinions, and, in some states, statutory and/or regulatory provisions within PA practice laws.

"Transmitting orders" includes any order written by a PA conveying the original intentions of the supervising physician. The supervising physician may communicate these orders through the PA by such mechanisms as written protocols, standing orders, or any form of verbal communication. Although PA authority to transmit medical orders to other health care personnel has been expressly provided for in only a few states' PA practice laws, such authority has been confirmed in numerous state attorney general opinions, as well as in a few court and administrative agency decisions.

Perhaps the most significant court decision addressing the issue of PA transmittal of physician orders as a legally delegated act is *Washington State Nurses Ass'n v. Board of Med. Examiners,* 605 P.2d 1269 (Wash. 1980), in which the state supreme court held that nurses must execute prescriptions and other medical orders issued by a PA because such orders are those of the physician for whom the PA acts as an agent. The state nurses' association challenged a regulation promulgated by the medical board that authorized PAs to issue prescriptions for medication and write medical orders for patient care. The nurses argued that the regulation exceeded board authority, and that they were exposed to potential liability because the regulation required them to execute directions of nonphysicians in violation of nurse practice statutes. Reversing the trial court's decision in favor of the nurses, the state supreme court upheld the regulation as valid, reasoning that it was in accordance with the legislative intent of the PA practice statute: that PAs are agents of their supervising physicians, and therefore PA orders effectively emanate from the physician.

The same rationale appears in state attorney general opinions and regulatory rulings on PA orders. By the early 1990s, attorneys general in 23 states had issued such opinions, the majority interpreting the state PA law to authorize PA transmittal of medical orders, and concluding that other health care personnel must comply with PA orders when the PA is clearly acting under the direction, direct or indirect, of the supervising physician. In Delaware, for example, the Office of the Attorney General concluded that "orders of a physician that are relayed or communicated by a [PA] to a nurse are, in fact, orders of the doctor, not the [PA], and should be honored by nurses" [Letter from Peter S. Feliceangeli, Deputy Att'y Gen., to Delaware Board of Nursing (Nov. 13, 1992); *see also* 71 Cal. Op. Att'y Gen. 296 (Nov. 3, 1988); 1977–78 Iowa Op. Att'y Gen. No. 78-12-41 (Dec. 30, 1978); 1986 Utah Op. Att'y Gen. No. 85-18 (July 9, 1986)]. Regulatory agencies in New York, Oregon, and Wisconsin also have issued specific rulings that affirm the authority of PAs to write orders [for a summary of all state attorney general opinions and agency decisions in this area, *see* AAPA, *Legal Opinions on Physician Assistant Orders* (Aug. 1991)].

In the few states where PA practice laws contain specific language regarding PA orders, usually the relevant provision is no more than a general statement authorizing PA transmittal of medical orders. In Iowa, for example, the regulation on PA order writing simply states that "health care providers shall consider the instructions of the physician assistant to be instructions of the supervising physician if such orders concern duties delegated to the physician assistant by the supervising physician." [IOWA ADMIN. CODE r. 645-325.7(5); *see also* MD. CODE ANN., HEALTH OCC. § 15-301; MINN. STAT. § 147A.09; *but see* OHIO REV. CODE ANN. § 4730.21(D) and 49 PA. CODE § 18.153 (listing specific procedures that PAs must follow when writing medical orders)].

REGULATORY BOARDS AND THEIR POWERS

In a majority of states, the regulatory agency responsible for licensing PAs and regulating PA practice is the state board of medical examiners, which is the same entity that licenses physicians. In a small number of states, however, PAs are regulated by a separate PA licensing board [*see, e.g.*, IOWA CODE § 148C.3; MICH. COMP. LAWS § 333.17025; UTAH CODE ANN. §§ 58-1-202,& -203 and 58-70-201], and in Illinois and New York, the licensure of PAs is administered by departments within state government agencies that license all health care practitioners [*see, e.g.*, 225 ILL. COMP. STAT. 95/9 (Department of Professional Regulation); N.Y. PUB. HEALTH LAW § 3701 (Department of Health)].

All licensing statutes and/or regulations address issues such as composition, terms of appointment, and other powers of the PA regulatory board. In most states, such provisions are found in medical practice statutes because the state medical board regulates PAs. In the majority of these states, a PA committee advises the medical board on issues related to PA practice, and in some states, this committee essentially functions as the regulatory authority over PAs, but must obtain board approval for any rule making action. PAs are members of every PA advisory committee, and thus PAs are able to directly contribute to the regulatory process and assist in shaping the laws that impact on PA practice. [For a more detailed discussion of the composition of PA advisory committees and their role in the regulatory process, see Chapter 11: Participation in Government Affairs; see also Appendix B for a state-by-state list of regulatory boards and, if applicable, PA advisory committees.]

The PA regulatory boards' powers usually include

- rule making
- verifying qualifications, examination, and licensing
- regulating and defining PA practice (see Scope of Practice under State PA Practice Laws)
- approving PA educational programs (in all states except New York and California, however, this approved process is limited to accepting Committee on Allied Health Education and Accreditation/Commission on Accreditation of Allied Health Education Programs accreditation)

- investigating and disciplining PAs through revocation, suspension, reprimand, or denial of license

The following sections outline the primary functions of the PA regulatory board: administering the licensure process, rule making, and disciplining PAs.

Application for Licensure and License Maintenance

The application process for state PA licensure varies significantly from state to state, but usually involves the PA and supervising physician filling out forms provided by the regulatory board. Many state PA statutes require, as part of the PA's application process, that the supervising physician, or the physician-PA team submit a detailed job description indicating how the PA will be used within the physician's practice application, thereby assuring the state that dependent practice regulations are met. [For a discussion of job description provisions in state PA laws, see Job Descriptions.] Some states base their application process on provisions within the AAPA's model law, which provide for a system in which state approval of physicians wishing to supervise a PA is not overly rigorous, but rather involves no more than notification to the state regulatory board by the licensed physician and licensed PA of their intention to work together as a physician-PA team.

Other application requirements may include proof of qualifications and letters of reference from the PA applicant, submission of a separate application for board approval of employment for each supervising physician (where the PA is supervised by more than one physician), a personal interview of the PA applicant and supervising physician by the regulatory board, and, if applicable, a detailed plan regarding PA practice at locations geographically separate from the supervising physician. [For a discussion of remote-site supervision requirements, see Physician Supervision, at Remote Locations.]

Once a license has been granted, most boards require that it be renewed on a regular cycle (e.g., ranging from a one- to three-year basis), and all states impose initial and renewal fees. Many states also require the PA to provide evidence of either maintaining NCCPA certification or completing a minimum number of continuing medical education (CME) credits. [NCCPA certification and recertification processes are discussed in Chapter 2: Education and Certification.]

From state to state, there is significant variation in all of these requirements, and thus PA applicants seeking practice privileges and practicing PAs drawing closer to a renewal date should contact the state regulatory board regarding application, license renewal, continuing education, and any other concerns related to that licensure process. [For a state-by-state list of these regulatory boards' addresses and phone numbers, see Appendix B.]

Rule Making

Licensing boards generally have broad authority to promulgate rules under their enabling statutes, but sometimes controversial rules are found to exceed their authority. Of significance to this issue are fundamental principles of administrative law that govern the exercise of authority by an administrative agency such as a PA regulatory board. Under those principles, the PA regulatory board has limited jurisdiction and authority because the board has only those powers that are expressly conferred by statute (e.g., medical or PA practice acts) or that may be reasonably implied to carry out such express authority.

The following cases involve challenges against licensing board regulations based on exceeding board authority:

- A New Jersey appellate court upheld a rule requiring licensed radiologists who provide diagnostic services for other physicians to also provide those services for licensed chiropractors. Although this service was inconsistent with the practice of many radiologists, the court ruled that it was reasonable, within the board's authority, and promulgated using proper procedures [*Brodie v. State Bd. of Med. Examiners,* 427 A.2d 104 (N.J. Super. Ct. App. Div.), *cert. denied,* 434 A.2d 1068 (N.J. 1981)].
- A Florida appellate court ruled that a Board of Optometry rule authorizing optometrists to use certain drugs was beyond the authority of the board [*Board of Optometry v. Florida Med. Ass'n,* 463 So. 2d 1213 (Fla. Dist. Ct. App.), *review denied,* 475 So. 2d 693 (Fla. 1985)].
- The Maryland Attorney General's office ruled that the licensing board for PAs, the Board of Physician Quality Assurance, has the authority to adopt a regulation specifying the circumstances under which the job descriptions of PAs may include prescribing, but lacks the authority to adopt a regulation authorizing PAs to dispense prescription medications. The Attorney General reasoned that because PA practice statutes allow physicians to delegate prescribing to a PA under an approved job description but do not allow them to delegate dispensing to the PA, the Board is only authorized to promulgate rules regarding PA prescribing [1995 Md. Op. Att'y Gen. No. 95-004 (Feb. 1, 1995)].

There are few court cases dealing with this issue in the context of PAs. Often such challenges are settled by the state attorney general's office, which may issue an opinion in response to a query from an agency or public official as to whether the PA regulatory board exceeded its authority in promulgating a particular rule.

One recent attorney general opinion exemplifies the confusion that may arise with respect to board rule making authority in states where PA practice is regulated by a separate PA board. The Iowa Attorney General's office ruled that it is beyond the authority of the Board of Physician Assistant Examiners to promulgate rules regarding the eligibility of supervising physicians [1995 Iowa Op. Att'y Gen. No. 95-8-3(L) (Aug. 15, 1995)]. The AG reasoned that the PA board only has limited powers that may affect the "conduct" of supervising physicians, while the Board of Medical Examiners has exclusive power to discipline physicians and determine the eligibility of those physicians seeking to supervise PAs. Although clarification of each board's scope of authority is the central purpose of this opinion, it also serves to highlight the importance of cooperation between the PA and medical licensing boards in regulating physician-PA teams.

Disciplinary Actions

Licensing boards have broad authority to discipline licensed professionals when they violate professional standards specified in licensing laws. State legislatures set out general statements as reasons for disciplining the licensed practitioner, and also usually empower their relevant regulatory board to define these grounds further through the rule-making or regulation power. The discipline may be license revocation, suspension, a fine, or a probationary period during which conditions must be met. The most extreme sanction is denial or revocation of a license, and this action is usually reserved for the most severe violations. A wide variety of disciplinary actions is available to PA regulatory boards. Most boards have the authority to impose various conditions, including prohibiting types of practice, requiring substance abuse rehabilitation efforts [see Grounds for Discipline], submitting to random urine screening tests for drugs, consulting about or receiving direct supervision for specified procedures, or completing education programs.

Grounds for Discipline

Most licensing boards for health care occupations promulgate regulations providing detailed grounds for discipline. Although varying from state to state, the PA regulatory board is usually authorized to revoke, suspend, or otherwise restrict PA licensure based on these grounds:

- *impersonating a physician*—PAs holding themselves out or permitting another to represent them as a licensed physician are subject to discipline. Most states' PA practice laws contain additional safeguard provisions that require PAs to explain their role to patients and wear a nameplate indicating PA status [*see, e.g.,* ARIZ. REV. STAT. ANN. § 32-2537; 225 ILL. COMP. STAT. 95/6 & ILL ADMIN. CODE tit. 68, § 1350.60; MICH. COMP. LAWS § 333.17072(4); WASH. ADMIN. CODE § 246-918-130].

- *providing services without required supervision or otherwise attempting tasks beyond the scope of a PA's role*—[see Scope of Practice under State PA Practice Laws].
- *habitual use of intoxicants or other drugs*—In many states, PAs who admit that they have a substance abuse problem do not face immediate disciplinary action; usually they may continue to practice while undergoing a mandatory rehabilitation program, but if they do not meet the conditions of or successfully complete the program, they are subject to disciplinary action [*see, e.g.*, CAL. BUS. & PROF. Code § 3534.1 through -.10; N.C. ADMIN. CODE tit. 21, r. 32 Q.0101 through -.0207; W. VA. CODE § 30-3-9; see also Chapter 9: Employment Laws, at Employee Substance Abuse].
- *conviction of felony or other criminal offense*
- *fraud and deceit*—PAs may lose their license or be disciplined if fraud was committed in the licensing procedure, in employment, or in practice. Most boards, for example, would take some form of disciplinary action against a PA who used fraudulent credentials in obtaining a license.
- *violation of medical or PA practice laws*
- *unfitness or incompetence*—PAs determined to be mentally incompetent or otherwise incompetent or unfit to practice may have their license revoked or suspended; usually a board cannot discipline on this basis unless the particular condition inhibits the PA's ability to provide reasonable and safe care.
- *discipline in another jurisdiction* Some state PA practice statutes list license revocation in another jurisdiction as a ground for discipline.

Due Process and Disciplinary Procedures

Due process requires that PAs and other licensed professionals must have two types of notice. They must have individualized notice of the specific questioned acts and omissions that form the basis for discipline [*see, e.g., Devous v. Wyoming State Bd. of Med. Examiners,* 845 P.2d 408 (Wyo. 1993) (violation of due process not to notify physician of facts and nature of charges against him)]. In addition, the statute and regulations must provide generalized advance notice that conduct of that type will lead to discipline. Courts usually rule, for example, that prohibition of "unprofessional conduct" gives adequate notice that a wide range of inappropriate behavior is prohibited; references to unprofessional conduct in PA practice laws, however, usually avoid any potential for vagueness by enumerating the activities that fall under that term [*see, e.g.,* UTAH CODE ANN. § 58-1-501 and 58-70-102(11)(a) through (d)].

Before imposing disciplinary sanctions, licensing boards must provide due process to licensed professionals, including notice of the wrongful conduct (usually at least 30 days' notice) and an opportunity to present information at a disciplinary hearing [*see* R. Koenders, *Annotation: Rights as to notice and hearing in a proceeding to revoke or suspend license to practice medicine,* 10 A.L.R. 5th 1; *but see Fleury v. Clayton,* 847 F.2d 1229 (7th Cir. 1988) (right to notice, hearing applies only when sanction is censure)]. The procedures followed before and during a hearing are defined in the state's administrative procedures act or other state code provisions. Physician assistants and their attorneys may hold informal conferences with state boards and their counsel before going to a formal hearing.

Many state licensing boards must follow additional hearing requirements for their disciplinary actions to be valid. Some states, for example, require the presence of all or a majority of board members at hearings involving suspension or revocation of licenses [*see, e.g.,* N.H. REV. STAT. ANN. § 330-A:15, and *In re Grimm,* 635 A.2d 456 (N.H. 1993) (violation of due process for some members of hearing panel, acting in fact-finding capacity, to fail to attend all testimony in hearings regarding revocation of psychologist's certificate); CONN. GEN. STAT § 20-8a, and *Pet v. Department of Health Serv.,* 638 A.2d 6 (Conn. 1994) (remand where no board member attended all hearings regarding suspension of psychiatrist's license)]. In other states, however, the licensing board is not allowed to attend evidentiary hearings [*see, e.g., Virginia Bd. of Med. v. Fetta,* 421 S.E.2d 410 (Va. 1992) (proceedings against chiropractor dismissed because board violated law when 4 of 16 members sat with hearing officer at evidentiary hearing)].

APPENDIX 3-A

AAPA Model State PA Practice Legislation

DEFINITIONS

"Physician assistant" means a person who has graduated from a physician assistant or surgeon assistant program accredited by the American Medical Association's Committee on Allied Health Education and Accreditation or by its successor agency, and/or a person who has passed the certifying examination administered by the National Commission on Certification of Physician Assistants.

"Board" means the Medical Licensing Board.

"Supervising physician" means an MD or DO licensed by the board who supervises physician assistants.

"Supervision" means overseeing the activities of, and accepting responsibility for, the medical services rendered by a physician assistant. The constant physical presence of the supervising physician is not required so long as the supervising physician and physician assistant are or can be easily in contact with one another by radio, telephone, or other telecommunication device.

QUALIFICATIONS FOR LICENSURE

Except as otherwise provided in this chapter, an individual shall be licensed by the board before the individual may practice as a physician assistant.

The board may grant a license as a physician assistant to an applicant who:

1) submits an application on forms approved by the board;
2) pays the appropriate fee as determined by the board;

Source: Reprinted with permission from *Model State Legislation for Physician Assistants,* © 1994, American Academy of Physician Assistants.

3) has successfully completed an educational program for physician assistants or surgeon assistants accredited by the Committee on Allied Health Education and Accreditation or by its successor agency, and/or has passed the Physician Assistant National Certifying Examination administered by the National Commission on Certification of Physician Assistants;
4) certifies that he or she is mentally and physically able to engage safely in practice as a physician assistant;
5) has no licensure, certification, or registration as a physician assistant under current discipline, revocation, suspension or probation for cause resulting from the applicant's practice as a physician assistant, unless the board considers such condition and agrees to licensure;
6) is of good moral character;
7) submits to the board any other information the board deems necessary to evaluate the applicant's qualifications; and
8) has been approved by the board.

TEMPORARY LICENSE

(a) The board may grant a temporary license to an applicant who meets the requirements for licensure except that the applicant has not yet taken the national certifying examination or the applicant has taken the national certifying examination and is awaiting the results.

A temporary license is valid:

1) for one year from the date of issuance;
2) until the results of an applicant's examination are available; or
3) until the board makes a final decision on the applicant's request for licensure whichever comes first. The board may extend a temporary license, upon a majority vote of the board members, for a period not to exceed one year. Under no circumstances may the board grant more than one extension of a temporary license.

(b) A temporary license may be granted to an applicant who meets all the qualifications for licensure but is awaiting the next scheduled meeting of the board.

INACTIVE LICENSE

Any physician assistant who notifies the board in writing on forms prescribed by the board may elect to place his or her license on an inactive status. A physician assistant with an inactive license shall be excused from payment of renewal fees and shall not practice as a physician assistant. Any licensee who engages in practice while his or her license is lapsed or on inactive status shall be considered to be practicing without a license, which shall be grounds for discipline under section ___ of this Act. A physician assistant requesting restoration from inactive status shall be required to pay the current renewal fee and shall be required to meet the criteria for renewal as specified in section ___ of this Act.

RENEWAL

Each person who holds a license as a physician assistant in this state will, upon notification from the board, renew said license by:

1) submitting the appropriate fee as determined by the board;
2) completing the appropriate forms; and
3) meeting any other requirements set forth by the board.

EXEMPTION FROM LICENSURE

Nothing herein shall be construed to require licensure under this Act of:

1) a physician assistant student enrolled in a physician assistant or surgeon assistant educational program accredited by the Committee on Allied Health Education and Accreditation or by its successor agency;
2) a physician assistant employed in the service of the federal government while performing duties incident to that employment; or
3) technicians, other assistants or employees of physicians who perform delegated tasks in the office of a physician but who are not rendering services as a physician assistant or identifying themselves as a physician assistant.

SCOPE OF PRACTICE—DELEGATORY AUTHORITY—AGENT OF SUPERVISING PHYSICIAN

Physician assistants practice medicine with physician supervision. Physician assistants may perform those duties and responsibilities, including the prescribing and dispensing of drugs and medical devices, that are delegated by their supervising physician(s).

Physician assistants shall be considered the agents of their supervising physicians in the performance of all practice-related activities, including but not limited to, the ordering of diagnostic, therapeutic and other medical services.

PRESCRIPTIVE AUTHORITY

A physician assistant may prescribe, dispense and administer drugs and medical devices to the extent delegated by the supervising physician.

Prescribing and dispensing of drugs may include Schedule II through V substances as described in [the state controlled drug act] and all legend drugs.

All dispensing activities of physician assistants shall:

1) comply with appropriate federal and state regulations; and
2) occur when pharmacy services are not reasonably available, or when it is in the best interests of the patient, or when it is an emergency.

Physician assistants may request, receive, and sign for professional samples and may distribute professional samples to patients.

SUPERVISION

Supervision shall be continuous but shall not be construed as necessarily requiring the physical presence of the supervising physician at the time and place that the services are rendered.

It is the obligation of each team of physician(s) and physician assistant(s) to insure that the physician assistant's scope of practice is identified; that delegation of medical tasks is appropriate to the physician assistant's level of competence; that the relationship of, and access to, the supervising physician is defined; and that a process for evaluation of the physician assistant's performance is established.

SUPERVISING PHYSICIAN

A physician wishing to supervise a physician assistant must:

1) be licensed in this state;
2) notify the board of his intent to supervise a physician assistant;
3) submit a statement to the board that he will exercise supervision over the physician assistant in accordance with any rules adopted by the board and that he will retain professional and legal responsibility for the care rendered by the physician assistant.

NOTIFICATION OF INTENT TO PRACTICE

A physician assistant licensed in this state, prior to initiating practice, will submit, on forms approved by the board, notification of such intent. Such notification shall include:

1) the name, business address, and telephone number of the supervising physician(s); and
2) the name, business address, and telephone number of the physician assistant.

A physician assistant will notify the board of any changes or additions in supervising physicians within ___ days.

SATELLITE SETTINGS

Nothing contained herein shall be construed to prohibit the rendering of services by a physician assistant in a setting geographically remote from the supervising physician.

EXCLUSIONS OF LIMITATIONS ON EMPLOYMENT

Nothing herein shall be construed to limit the employment arrangement of a physician assistant licensed under this Act.

ASSUMPTION OF PROFESSIONAL LIABILITY

If a physician assistant is employed by a physician or group of physicians, the physician assistant shall be supervised by and be the legal responsibility of the employing physician(s). The legal responsibility for the physician assistant's patient care activities shall remain that of the employing physician(s), including when the physician assistant provides care and treatment for patients in health care facilities.

If a physician assistant is employed by a health care facility or other entity, the legal responsibility for the physician assistant's actions or omissions shall be that of the employing facility or entity. Physician assistants employed by such facilities shall be supervised by licensed physicians.

VIOLATIONS

The board may, following the exercise of due process, discipline any physician assistant who:

1) fraudulently or deceptively obtains or attempts to obtain a license;
2) fraudulently or deceptively uses a license;
3) violates any provision of this chapter or any regulations adopted by the board pertaining to this chapter;
4) is convicted of a felony;
5) is a habitual user of intoxicants or drugs to such an extent that he or she is unable to safely perform as a physician assistant;
6) has been adjudicated as mentally incompetent or has a mental condition that renders him or her unable to safely perform as a physician assistant;

7) has committed an act of moral turpitude; or
8) represents himself or herself as a physician.

DISCIPLINARY AUTHORITY

The board, upon finding that a physician assistant has committed any offense described in section __, may:

1) refuse to grant a license;
2) administer a public or private reprimand;
3) revoke, suspend, limit, or otherwise restrict a license;
4) require a physician assistant to submit to the care or counseling or treatment of a physician or physicians designated by the board;
5) suspend enforcement of its finding thereof and place the physician assistant on probation with the right to vacate the probationary order for noncompliance; or
6) restore or reissue, at its discretion, a license and impose any disciplinary or corrective measure which it may have imposed.

TITLE AND PRACTICE PROTECTION

Any person not licensed under this Act is guilty of a [felony or misdemeanor] and is subject to penalties applicable to the unlicensed practice of medicine if he or she:

1) holds himself or herself out as a physician assistant;
2) uses any combination or abbreviation of the term "physician assistant" to indicate or imply that he or she is a physician assistant; or
3) acts as a physician assistant without being licensed by the board.

An unlicensed physician assistant shall not be permitted to use the title of "physician assistant" or to practice as a physician assistant unless he or she fulfills the requirements of this [act].

IDENTIFICATION REQUIREMENTS

Physician assistants licensed under this Act shall keep their license available for inspection at their primary place of business and shall, when engaged in their professional activities, wear a name tag identifying themselves as a "physician assistant."

RULE MAKING AUTHORITY

The board shall promulgate, in accordance with the provisions of the [state] Administrative Procedures Act, all rules that are reasonable and necessary for the performance of the various duties imposed upon the board by the provisions of this Act, including but not limited to:

1) setting licensure fees;
2) establishing renewal dates.

OPTIONAL REPLACEMENT PARTS FOR MODEL LEGISLATION

SUPERVISING PHYSICIAN-PRACTICE AGREEMENT

Any physician licensed in this state may apply to the board for permission to supervise a physician assistant. The application shall be jointly submitted by the physician and the physician assistant(s) and may be accompanied by a fee as determined by the board.

The joint application shall describe the manner and extent to which the physician assistant will practice and be supervised, including identification of additional licensed physicians who will supervise the physician assistant; the education, training and experience of the primary supervisor and the physician assistant; and other such information as the board may require.

The board may approve, modify or reject such applications.

Whenever it is determined that a physician or physician assistant is practicing in a manner inconsistent with the approval granted, the board may demand modification of the practice, withdraw approval of the practice agreement or take other disciplinary action as defined in section ___ of this Act.

PHYSICIAN ASSISTANT SCOPE OF PRACTICE

The practice of a physician assistant shall include medical services within the education, training and experience of the physician assistant that are delegated by the supervising physician.

Medical services rendered by physician assistants may include, but are not limited to:

1) obtaining patient histories and performing physical examinations;
2) ordering and/or performing diagnostic and therapeutic procedures;
3) formulating a diagnosis;
4) developing and implementing a treatment plan;

5) monitoring the effectiveness of therapeutic interventions;
6) assisting at surgery;
7) offering counseling and education to meet patient needs; and
8) making appropriate referrals.

The activities listed above may be performed in any setting authorized by the supervising physician, including but not limited to: clinics; hospitals; ambulatory surgical centers; patient homes; nursing homes; and other institutional settings.

LOCUM TENENS PERMIT

The board may grant a locum tenens permit to any applicant who is licensed in the state. The permit may be granted by an authorized representative of the board. Such applications for locum tenens permits will be reviewed at the next scheduled board meeting. The maximum duration of a locum tenens permit is one year. The permit may be renewed annually on a date set by the board.

Definition: "Locum tenens means the temporary provision of services by a substitute provider."

REGULATORY OPTIONS

I. Regulation by the Medical Board

The state board of medical examiners shall administer the provisions of this Act under such procedures as it considers advisable and may adopt rules that are reasonable and necessary to implement the provisions of this Act.

II. Regulation by a PA Board

To administer this Act there is hereby established a Board of Physician Assistant Examiners. The board shall consist of five members appointed by the governor, each of whom shall be residents of this state, four of whom shall be physician assistants who meet the criteria for licensure as established by this Act and one of whom shall be a licensed physician experienced in supervising physician assistants.

Initial appointments shall be made as follows:

1) two members shall be appointed for terms of four years;
2) one member shall be appointed for a term of three years;
3) one member shall be appointed for a term of two years; and
4) one member shall be appointed for a term of one year.

Each regular appointment thereafter shall be for a term of four years. Any vacant term shall be filled by the governor for the balance of the unexpired term. No member shall serve more than two consecutive four-year terms and each member shall serve on the board until his or her successor is appointed.

While engaged in the business of the board, each member will receive a per diem of $__ and shall also receive compensation for actual expenses paid in accordance with [other state regulations].

The board shall elect a chairperson and a secretary from among its members at the first meeting of each fiscal year. The board shall meet on a regular basis. A board meeting may be called upon reasonable notice at the discretion of the chairperson and shall be called at any time upon reasonable notice by a petition of three board members to the chairperson.

Powers and duties of the board shall include:

1) promulgation of all rules reasonable and necessary to implement the provisions of this Act;
2) review and approval or rejection of applications for licensure;
3) review and approval or rejection of applications for renewal;
4) issuance of all licenses;
5) denial, suspension, revocation or other discipline of a licensee;
6) determination of the amount and collection of all fees.

III. Regulation by a Medical Board with a PA Advisory Committee

There is hereby created a physician assistant committee which shall review and make recommendations to the board regarding all matters relating to physician assistants that come before the board. Such matters shall include, but not be limited to:

1) practice agreements;
2) disciplinary proceedings;
3) renewal requirements; and
4) any other issues pertaining to the regulation and practice of physician assistants in this state.

Committee Membership

The committee shall consist of three physician assistants, one physician experienced in supervising physician assistants, and one member of the board. All committee members must be residents of this state and hold a license in good standing in their respective disciplines.

The chairperson of the committee shall be elected by a majority vote of the committee members.

Committee members shall receive reimbursement for time and travel expenditures [consistent with usual state practices].

Appointments

The physician assistant and supervising physician members of the committee shall be appointed by the governor. The board of medical examiners shall designate one member to serve on the board. All appointments shall be made within 60 days of the effective date of this Act. All appointments shall be for four year terms, at staggered intervals. Members shall serve no more than two consecutive terms. Reappointments of the physician assistant and supervising physician members of the committee shall be made by the governor.

Meetings

The committee shall meet on a regular basis. A committee meeting may be called upon reasonable notice at the discretion of the chairperson and shall be called at any time upon reasonable notice by petition of three committee members to their chairperson.

IV. Adding a PA to the Medical Board

To assist in the administration of this Act, the governor shall appoint a licensed physician assistant to the board of medical examiners for a term of ___ years, [etc, etc. in accordance with existing law.] The physician assistant member will have full voting privileges.

APPENDIX 3-B

AAPA Guidelines for State Regulation of Physician Assistants

Increased recognition of physician assistants as health care providers has led to development of state laws and regulations to govern their practice. Recognition of physician assistants in state law and delegation of authority to regulate their practice to a state regulatory body serves two main purposes: (1) to protect the public from incompetent performance by unqualified non-physicians, and (2) to promote appropriate expanded delegation within the scope of PA practice by assuring consumers, physicians, and others that PAs are competent. Since the inception of the profession, dramatic changes have occurred in the way states have dealt with PA practice. In concert with these developments has been the creation of a body of knowledge on legislative and regulatory control of PA practice. It is now possible to state which specific concepts in physician assistant statutes and regulations enable appropriate use of physician assistants as health care providers while protecting the public health and safety.

What follows are general guidelines on state governmental control of PA practice. The AAPA recognizes that the uniqueness of each state's political and health care climate will require modification of some provisions. However, standardization of PA regulation will enhance appropriate utilization of PA services nationwide. This document does not contain specific language for direct incorporation into statutes or regulations, nor is it inclusive of all concepts generally contained in state practice acts or regulations. Rather, its intent is to clarify key elements of regulation and to assist states as they pursue improvements in state governmental

---

Source: Reprinted with permission from "Guidelines for State Regulation of Physician Assistants," *1995–1996 Policy Manual,* Position Paper No. 7 (guidelines adopted 1988, amended 1993),

control of physician assistants. For more comprehensive language and discussion, please consult the AAPA's model state legislation for physician assistants.

Definition of Physician Assistant

Many persons assist physicians. The legal definition of physician assistant should include those who have received PA or SA training in approved programs, and those informally trained PAs whose competence is certified by examination. At present only one program accrediting group and one certifying examination should be recognized in state government language. Therefore, the definition of physician assistant should be a person who is a graduate of a physician assistant or surgeon assistant program which is accredited by the American Medical Association's Committee on Allied Health Education and Accreditation, or its successor agency, and/or has passed the physician assistant national certifying examination given by the National Commission on Certification of Physician Assistants. Verification of the PA's credentials by the regulatory body should then create a registry of credentialed physician assistants. This function should be independent of approval or registration of employment.

Supervision

The definition of supervision should convey the idea that direction of the medical practice of the physician assistant is provided and assured by supervising physicians, but that this does not necessarily require the physical presence of a supervising physician at the place where services are rendered. It is imperative, however, that the PA and a supervising physician are or can be in contact with each other by telecommunication.

Supervising physician should be defined as an allopathic or osteopathic physician (MD or DO) licensed to practice in the state, who registers with or is otherwise known to the regulatory agency, and who accepts responsibility for the supervision of services provided by physician assistants. Provisions should be made for alternate supervision in the supervising physician's absence, and for the supervision of groups of physician assistants by groups of supervising physicians. Language that specifies mandatory ratios of PAs to supervising physicians should be avoided.

Supervision in hospitals or other institutional settings should reflect the changing nature of health care delivery and utilization of physician assistants as hospital staff. This may require change or elimination of certain language in state laws and/or regulations. The guiding principles must be to (a) protect patient health and safety, and (b) preserve the physician assistant's access to consultation and supervision. Consequently, it is recommended that the ratio of physician assistants to supervising physicians be determined by the supervising physicians according to the nature of the services being provided by the physician assistants, and according to the tenets of good patient care, adequate supervision and legal responsibility. There should be no limit on the number of supervising physicians each physician assistant may have.

If the state requires registration or notification of the names of supervising physicians, then all physicians using a hospital in which physician assistants are employed as staff and who wish to utilize PAs in the care of their patients should comply with this requirement. Physician assistants should not see the patients of physicians who are not in compliance or who do not wish physician assistants to see their patients. Accountability for physician supervision of physician assistants may be determined prospectively, by scheduling, or retrospectively, by review of charts.

Employment and supervision should be regarded as separate entities. A physician's ability to supervise a physician assistant is independent of the specifics of PA employment.

Scope of Practice

State law should permit utilization of PA services in a wide variety of practice settings. In general, physician assistants should be permitted to provide any medical services which are delegated to them by the supervising physician when such services are within their skills, form a component of the physician's scope of practice, and are provided with supervision of a physician. A list of specific tasks proves to be overly restrictive and should be avoided.

Education of physician assistants, like that of physicians, promotes the development of practical skills in clinical problem-solving and decision making. For this reason, the use of written clinical protocols should not be required as part of state laws or regulations delineating physician assistant scope of practice. Protocols are useful for dealing with very specific clinical entities (e.g., anaphylaxis). However, protocols by their nature are rigid and frequently outdated. Extensive clinical protocols neither enhance the clinical judgment exercised by physician assistants nor improve the diagnosis and treatment of disease.

Prescribing and Dispensing

The ability to prescribe medications should be one of the medical services that physicians may delegate to physician assistants. Supervised prescribing, as regulated by the state and by the physician supervisor, can improve patient access to comprehensive care, and provide for increased efficiency and cost effectiveness. Categories of medications to be prescribed should be consistent with the supervising physician's practice and should not exclude controlled substances. Prescriptive authority should not be circumscribed by protocols, which are too rigid to enhance the dynamic practice of medicine.

Physician assistant education includes extensive training in pharmacology and clinical pharmacotherapeutics. Additional training, education or testing should not be required as a prerequisite to physician assistant prescriptive authority.

Limited dispensing is also appropriate for delegation to physician assistants. The purpose of limited dispensing is not to replace pharmacy services, but rather to increase patient ability to receive needed medication when access to pharmacy services is limited. Pharmaceutical samples should be available to physician assistants just as they are to physicians for the managements of clinical problems.

Regulatory Agencies

Each state must define the regulatory agency responsible for implementation of the law governing physician assistants. A variety of state agencies can be charged with this task. These include the State Board of Medical Examiners, the Department of Health, or independent boards that are selected or created to regulate PA practice. The regulatory agency has a significant impact on the practice and utilization of physician assistants, and some general guidelines, along with each state's administrative realities, should be considered when defining which agency will be responsible for PA regulation. This agency should include a group of members who are knowledgeable about physician assistant education, certification and practice. Consideration should be given to including members who are representative of a broad spectrum of health care settings—primary care, specialty care, institutional and rural based practices.

An increasing number of states are creating separate PA licensing boards. Such boards should be composed primarily of physician assistants and supervising physicians. If regulation is adminstered by a multidisciplinary healing arts or medical board, it is strongly recommended that physician assistants and physicians who supervise PAs be constituent members of the board. It is also recommended in these situations that physician assistant advisory committees be established and actively utilized to assure PA participation in the regulatory process.

Discipline

The American Academy of Physician Assistants strongly endorses the authority of designated state regulatory agencies, in accordance with due process, to discipline physician assistants who have committed acts in violation of state law. Disciplinary actions may include, but are not limited to, suspension or revocation of a license or approval to practice. In general, the basic offenses are similar for all professions and the language used to specify violations and disciplinary measures to be used for physician assistants should be similar to that used for physicians. The Academy also endorses the sharing of information among state regulatory agencies regarding the disposition of adjudicated actions against physician assistants.

CHAPTER 4

Prescribing and Dispensing

INTRODUCTION

During the past decade, the number of states granting PAs prescriptive privileges has significantly increased, and today the vast majority of PAs practice in states where physicians may delegate prescriptive authority. It is the responsibility of PA prescribers to know and comply with state and federal requirements applicable to their prescribing and dispensing privileges. This chapter outlines the pertinent provisions in both federal drug laws and state PA practice statutes.

The chapter first describes the evolution of PA prescriptive authority to highlight the factors underlying widespread recognition among the states of the value of PA prescribing. A brief description of the competing interests that have influenced state legislative developments in the PA prescribing area is also provided. Because drug categories and corresponding prescribing restrictions delineated under federal law are referred to in state PA prescribing statutes, the next section of the chapter outlines relevant federal drug laws, followed by sections providing an overview of prescribing and dispensing privileges typically authorized under state PA practice statutes or administering regulations.

EVOLUTION OF PRESCRIPTIVE AUTHORITY

During the early years of the PA profession, the concept of PA prescribing had not emerged as a significant issue, in part because PA program founders were generally focused on more pressing concerns such as clarifying the PA's role and gaining legal recognition of the supervising physicians' authority to delegate medical tasks to their PAs. [For a more detailed discussion, see Chapter 3:

Licensure and Scope of Practice, at Historical Background.] Only a few of the early PA educators, including Dr. Henry K. Silver, the originator of the Child Health Associate Program at the University of Colorado, advocated for prescriptive privileges as a necessary aspect of physician delegation to PAs [*see* N. Gara, "Regulation of Physician Assistant Prescribing," *Journal of American Academy of Physician Assistants* 71 (Jan./Feb. 1990)].

Accordingly, Colorado became the first state to allow some form of PA prescribing, limiting that authority to only PA graduates of the University of Colorado's child health program, and restricting prescribing privileges to a formulary of 18 drug categories, including vitamins, decongestants, expectorants, and antiemetics but excluding narcotics, antibiotics, injectable medications, and any other drugs not relevant to pediatric health care [*see* COLO. REV. STAT. § 12-31-103 (1969)]. In 1973, North Carolina enacted more comprehensive legislation, authorizing supervising physicians to delegate prescribing authority to all certified PAs practicing in the state. Like the Colorado statute, however, this legislation allowed PAs to prescribe only from a limited formulary developed by the state board of medical examiners [*see* N.C. GEN. STAT. § 90 (1973)]. Several other states followed suit, and by the early 1980s, PA prescriptive authority had been granted in 12 additional states (Alaska, Arizona, California (pilot project), Maine, Michigan, Nebraska, New Mexico, New York, Oregon, Pennsylvania, South Dakota, and Washington).

The first legal challenge to the validity of statutorily authorized PA prescribing privileges was brought by the state nursing association before the Washington state courts. Ultimately, Washington state's highest court upheld this authority, basing its decision on the legal principle of "agency," that is, that the PA is an "agent" of the physician and that orders for medication from the PA are essentially orders from the physician [*Washington State Nurses Ass'n v. Board of Med. Examiners,* 605 P.2d 1269 (Wash. 1980); for a more detailed discussion, see Chapter 3: Licensure and Scope of Practice, at PA Orders]. The decision was the first court opinion confirming that physicians could legally delegate prescribing tasks to PAs and that other health care personnel have an obligation to comply with such prescribing authority.

Physician assistant prescribing authority has expanded at a gradual but consistent pace since the 1980s, with respect to both the number of states allowing supervising physicians to delegate prescribing to PAs and the scope of PA prescribing and dispensing privileges granted under state PA practice laws. Although California dropped off the list of prescribing states upon termination of its pilot project, the total number of states with PA prescribing provisions increased to 24 by 1989. As of the end of 1996, 40 states, the District of Columbia, and Guam have laws or regulations granting PAs some form of prescriptive privileges with physician supervision, nearly all of which allow supervising physicians to delegate prescriptive authority to their PAs as specified by statute or in accordance with specific directions from the physician. [See AAPA state-by-state chart of PA prescribing privileges, at Appendix 4-A].

Of these states, three do not explicitly allow prescribing authority, but rather authorize PAs to "transmit" written and oral prescriptions and orders for drugs as delegated by their supervising physicians [CAL. BUS. & PROF. CODE § 3502.1; KAN. STAT. ANN. § 65-2896e; OKLA. STAT. ANN. tit. 59, § 519.6(D); see also Prescribing and Dispensing under State PA Practice Laws]. Statistics indicate that more than 90 percent of all PAs practice in states where supervising physicians may delegate prescriptive authority to their PAs, and in many states that authority encompasses the prescribing of controlled substances, as delegated by the supervising physician and in compliance with statutory or regulatory restrictions. Other states are in the process of changing laws and regulations and will likely grant PA prescribing privileges in the near future [*see, e.g.,* Haw. Admin. Rules § 16-85-49(8) (proposed regulatory provisions implementing PA prescriptive privileges)].

In the past few years, the federal government has also expanded its recognition of PA prescribing authority, and today federally employed PAs have been granted prescriptive privileges at most agencies. In 1995, for example, the U.S. Department of Veterans Affairs (VA)—the largest federal employer of PAs (approximately 1,100 PAs in 171 VA medical centers)—published a directive allowing PAs at VA health facilities to prescribe and issue orders for noncontrolled substances [*see, e.g.,* Department of Veterans Affairs, "General Guidelines for Establishing Medication Prescribing Authority for Clinical Nurse Specialists, Nurse Practitioners, Clinical Pharmacy Specialists, and Physician Assistants," VHA Directive No. 10-95-019 (Mar. 3, 1995)]. The agency also issued prescribing guidelines for PAs and other nonphysician providers, explaining that a PA's authority to prescribe controlled substances while employed at a VA health facility will mirror the scope of practice in the state where the PA has credentials [*see, e.g.,* Department of Veterans Affairs, "Guidelines for Utilization of Physician Assistants," VHA Directive No. 10-95-020 (Mar. 1, 1995)]. Other federal agencies allowing PA prescribing privileges include the U.S. Public Health Service, the Bureau of Corrections, and U.S. military agencies.

PA PRESCRIBING PATTERNS AND QUALIFICATIONS

The growing number of states that have enacted legislation granting PAs prescribing privileges can be attributed to a variety of factors, including an increasing confidence in PA-provided medical services and the necessities of patient treatment in medically underserved areas. State legislators who have voted in favor of such legislation may well have been influenced by statistical research related to PA prescribing. Data from various surveys and studies have revealed:

- PA prescribing patterns are very similar to those of physicians in terms of appropriateness and safety.
- From the beginning of the PA profession, there have been very few disciplinary actions against PAs for misuse or abuse of prescriptive privileges.
- There is no evidence that PA prescribing has significantly increased liability or malpractice claims.
- In states where physicians are allowed to delegate prescribing to PAs, there is a higher percentage of PAs practicing in rural areas, indicating that PA prescribing can effectively increase the capabilities of PAs to improve access to care, especially in medically underserved areas. In Texas, for example, after the 1991 enactment of legislation providing for PA prescribing privileges, the number of rural health clinics increased from 26 to 99 within 1 year, amounting to a tripling of PAs (from 5 to 15 percent) practicing in rural areas of Texas.

[*See* P.E. Jones and J. Cawley, "Physician Assistants and Health System Reform," *JAMA* 271, 1266, 1271; *see also* J. Willis, "Prescriptive Practice Patterns of Physician Assistants," *Journal of American Academy of Physician Assistants* 39 (Jan. 1990).]

Moreover, a key justification for allowing physicians to delegate prescriptive authority to PAs is that PA students receive pharmacotherapeutic education that is proportionately equivalent to that received by medical students. All PA programs have a formal pharmacology course with instruction averaging 70.4 hours; typically, the course length is two full academic semesters, and course professors are from the pharmacology department of the medical school sponsoring the PA program [*see* D. Oliver, J. Baker, and W. Donahue, *Eleventh Annual Report on Physician Assistant Educational Programs in the United States, 1994–1995* (APAP 1995)]. The PA student's pharmacotherapeutic education is also reinforced during the clinical phase of the PA education program, in which PAs are often intermingled with medical students on the same clinical rotation at the precepting physician's office or health care facility.

In addition, the PA graduate must demonstrate knowledge of pharmacotherapeutics to pass the Physician Assistant National Certification Exam (PANCE) (the National Commission Certification for Physician Assistants' (NCCPA) national certification exam). Passing this exam is a prerequisite to obtaining full practice privileges in many states [for a more detailed discussion of PA certification requirements, see Chapter 2: Education and Certification]. Both the PANCE and the PA recertification exam, developed by NCCPA in conjunction with the National Board of Medical Examiners, contain a statistically valid number of questions (approximately 25 percent) to assess the PA examinee's pharmacotherapeutic knowledge base [*see, e.g.,* W. Wilson, et al., "Shaping a Model Clinical

Therapeutics Curriculum," *Journal of American Academy of Physician Assistants* 51, 52 (May 1995); AAPA, *Physician Assistant Prescribing and Dispensing* (Apr. 1996)].

THE POLITICS OF PRESCRIBING

Given that most states have enacted PA prescribing statutes over the past decade, clearly the legislative trend has been state recognition of PA competency to prescribe and the value of PA prescribing in terms of expanding access to health care. In many states, however, the politics behind the evolution of PA prescribing do not reflect easygoing compromise or acceptance of PA prescriptive privileges. Because delegated PA prescribing authority implicates a range of diverse and competing interests, enacting legislation or adopting regulations in this area has been a long and difficult process in some states.

Unlike many of the basic medical tasks that have been delegated to PAs by supervising physicians, delegated prescribing authority has given rise to opposition from several groups, including physicians, pharmacists, registered nurses, and other nonphysician prescribers (i.e., advanced practice nurses and clinical pharmacists). For varying reasons, each of these groups has attempted to influence the state legislative or regulatory process with respect to PA prescribing issues.

In some states, the legislative battle for PA prescribing has involved opposition from physicians and pharmacists and the state professional societies representing them. One argument posed by some state medical and pharmacy societies is that PAs lack sufficient educational preparation to permit them to prescribe, as evidenced by the fact that physicians usually possess more than eight years of educational preparation and pharmacists specialize in the dispensing of prescriptions, while PAs obtain certification for practice after graduating from a two-year educational program and passing the national certifying exam. Moreover, some physicians have expressed concerns about PA prescribing legislation based on parochial interests such as the physicians' view that nonphysician prescribers result in decreased need for physician supervision, thereby threatening the dominance of physicians. An evaluation of the facts behind PA prescribing, however, counters these arguments (e.g., that PAs receive a comprehensive pharmacotherapeutic education relatively comparable to that received by medical students, and that PA prescribing under all state laws is only authorized if the supervising physician delegates this activity to the PA).

Registered nurses (RNs), pharmacists, and their respective professional associations also have been opponents to state legislation granting PA prescribing privileges. In many states, arguments posed by these professions have centered on whether PA prescribing could expose them to greater susceptibility to legal liability or professional discipline. For example, RNs must comply with state nurse practice statutes, which commonly provide that nurses are to carry out orders only from "licensed" physicians. As a result, nurses in several states have argued that they may be exposed to legal liability or other discipline for violating express language within nursing statutes by accepting orders, including medication orders, from PAs. For the most part, this issue has been resolved by court decisions, attorney general opinions, and explicit statutory language regarding PA orders, which state that the PA is the agent of the supervising physician and therefore the PA's orders can be construed as emanating from the physician. [For a more detailed discussion, see Chapter 3: Licensure and Scope of Practice, at PA Orders .]

Similarly, in some states pharmacists have opposed PA prescribing legislation because it adds another class of prescriber, which could potentially increase risks of legal liability. In support of this argument, pharmacists point to an increase in court decisions holding the pharmacist liable for failing to question a prescriber's dosage instructions or other erroneous prescribing specifications [*see, e.g., Riff v. Morgan Pharmacy,* 508 A.2d 1247 (Pa. Super. Ct. 1986) (holding pharmacist liable for failing to warn patient or inform her physician of inadequacies in prescription's instructions); *Gassen v. East Jefferson Gen. Hosp.,* 628 So. 2d 256 (La. Ct. App. 1993) (holding pharmacist liable for failing to contact the prescribing physician when the physician made clear mistakes in prescription)].

In some states, the legislative battle for PA prescribing has involved pressure on legislators from other nonphysician prescribers such as clinical pharmacists and advanced nurse practitioners. These professions have their own agendas for maintaining or expanding prescribing privileges, and the granting of PA prescribing authority may be viewed as a threat to such objectives. Clinical pharmacists, for example, who specialize in providing patient care through monitoring prescriptions but are authorized to prescribe medications in only a small number of states, sometimes contend that they possess the necessary expertise for helping patients choose the optimal therapeutic treatment, not physicians and other nonphysician health care providers [*see* C.R. Talley, "Pharmacist Prescribing," 52 *American Journal of Health Systems Pharmacy* 1635 (1995)]. Similarly, nurse practitioners, who are authorized in more than 35 states to write prescriptions (usually under protocols) in some states have voiced opposition to PA prescribing legislation in an attempt to block other nonphysician health care providers from gaining prescriptive privileges, although in other states they have joined with PAs in pressing legislators to grant or extend prescriptive privileges for both professions.

Although learning the lines of the PA prescribing debate should be of interest to all PAs, it is particularly important political background for PAs involved in legislative or regulatory processes. Whether striving for the enactment of PA prescribing legislation, or for the expansion of existing prescribing authority, it is essential to understand not only the factors that have influenced legislators and regulators to grant PAs prescribing privileges, but also the obstacles that may hamper progress toward PA prescribing legislation. [For a discussion of PA participation in legislative process, See Chapter 11: Participation in Government Affairs.]

FEDERAL DRUG LAWS

Physician assistants who have prescribing privileges must keep abreast of pharmacotherapeutic developments and demonstrate ongoing competence as qualified prescribers. They also must be very familiar with the state and federal drug laws impacting on PA prescriptive authority. To enable a better understanding of state statutory and regulatory provisions governing PA prescribing and dispensing privileges, PAs should know the basic requirements of two major federal drug laws affecting any person authorized to prescribe medications: the Food, Drug, and Cosmetic Act (FDCA), and the Controlled Substances Act (CSA).

The Food, Drug, and Cosmetic Act

The FDCA [21 U.S.C. §§ 301 through 394], administered by the Food and Drug Administration (FDA), establishes standards for the safety and effectiveness of all drugs and devices in interstate commerce in the United States. Under the FDCA, no new drug may be marketed or transported in interstate commerce until it has been approved by the FDA [21 U.S.C. § 355(a)]. The FDCA, aimed at protecting consumers from unsafe drugs, is a comprehensive drug law, addressing topics as diverse as drug manufacturing practices, labeling requirements, prescription requirements, and pharmacist drug-compounding.

The FDCA classifies drugs either as "over the counter" (OTC) or prescription, based on drug safety, the conditions for which they are indicated, and, in some cases, the strength or dosage form. An OTC drug, also known as a nonprescription drug, is a drug that is generally recognized by experts to be safe and effective for use by patients without supervision, making a prescription unnecessary [21 C.F.R. § 330.10]. A prescription drug is a drug that can only be dispensed pursuant to a valid prescription because the drug is either habit forming or adequate directions for safe use by patients cannot be written [21 U.S.C. § 353(b)]. Prescription drugs are also known as legend drugs derived from the FDCA's requirement that such drugs bear on their commercial labels the "legend" statement: "Caution: Federal law prohibits dispensing without a prescription" [21 C.F.R. § 201.100].

Off-Label Use

In administering the Act, the FDA not only approves all drugs, but also determines what conditions or indications an approved drug may be advertised, labeled, or otherwise marketed for. This determination does not, however, limit the manner in which a physician (or other prescriber) may use an approved drug; accepted medical practice often allows for "off-label use," which is the use of drugs that is not expressly listed on package labeling outlining the FDA-approved uses [*see* J. Yerxa, "Pharmacology: Using Medications," in R. Ballweg, S. Stolberg, and E. Sullivan, eds., *Physician Assistant: A Guide to Clinical Practice* 271, 273 (1994)]. In a 1972 FDA interpretive ruling, the agency clearly pronounced that off-label uses are legal under the FDCA, because the Act is not intended to interfere with the practice of medicine. The ruling states that "[o]nce a new drug is in a local pharmacy after interstate shipment, the physician may, as part of the practice of medicine, lawfully prescribe a different dosage for his patient, or may otherwise vary the conditions of use from those approved in the package insert, without informing or obtaining approval of the [FDA]" [37 Fed. Reg. 16,503 (1972)]. In general, the agency has initiated any enforcement action as a result of promotion of unapproved uses against the drug manufacturer, rather than against the prescriber or pharmacist dispensing for unapproved uses.

Distribution of Drug Samples

Another area regulated by the FDCA is the distribution of drug samples. Although this is an activity primarily engaged in by drug manufacturers that are promoting a drug's use, FDCA restrictions on distributing drug samples also apply to all authorized prescribers. [See Prescribing and Dispensing under State PA Practice Laws.] These restrictions were enacted in 1988 as part of the Prescription Drug Marketing Act (PDMA) [codified at 21 U.S.C. § 353], which amended the FDCA by adding storage, handling, and accounting requirements for drug samples; a ban on the reimportation of prescription drugs; prohibitions against certain wholesale drug distribution practices; and severe criminal and financial penalties for violation of these provisions. In large part, the legislative intent behind the PDMA is to address the problem of prescription drug diversion from the normal stream of distribution culminating in the illegal resale of the diverted drugs and drug samples, and typically involving misbranding and adulteration (e.g., sale of drugs that have been stored improperly or repackaged into improperly labeled containers).

The PDMA places strict limitations on the giving out of drug samples, defined as units of a prescription drug that are intended not for sale, but to promote the sale of the drug [21 U.S.C. § 353(c)]. Under the PDMA amendments, only licensed practitioners, health care professionals with prescribing authority (e.g., PAs), and hospital or health maintenance organization (HMO) pharmacies may request, sign for, and distribute drug samples to patients under procedures prescribed in the statute [21 U.S.C. § 353(d)(1)]. Under those procedures, drug manufacturers may only provide drug samples to prescribers at the written request of the licensed prescriber, and the recipient must sign a receipt that will be returned to the manufacturer. The manufacturer must maintain records of drug sample distributions for three years and report any thefts or significant losses [21 U.S.C. § 353].

The American Academy of Physician Assistants (AAPA) has noted that the process envisioned by Congress in enacting the PDMA's drug sample provisions consists of two steps: (1) the authorized prescriber would fill out a drug-sample request form, and (2) a responsible individual would sign a receipt form on delivery of the drug samples, whether by mail, common carrier, or by a company representative. If samples were distributed under such process, PAs in any state could be the designated recipients because even individuals without prescriptive authority are technically authorized to receive samples. In practice, however, pharmaceutical companies have combined the request and receipt into one form, and therefore only PAs with prescriptive privileges may request (and sign for) drug samples [*see* AAPA, *Physician Assistant Prescribing and Dispensing* (Apr. 1996); for a discussion of state laws governing PA distribution of drug samples, see Prescribing and Dispensing under State PA Practice Laws, at Dispensing Drug Samples].

State FDCAs

Drug distribution is also regulated by state governments. For example, states have independent food, drug, and cosmetic acts that may have stricter or additional requirements and prohibitions than their federal counterpart. When state and federal laws regulate the same activity, and the state law is more restrictive, then state law requirements govern because compliance with the higher state standard also satisfies federal law. PAs should thus be cognizant of any relevant provisions within a state FDCA, as well as state PA statutes or regulations pertaining to distribution of drug products. [See Prescribing and Dispensing under State PA Practice Laws.]

The Controlled Substances Act

The CSA [21 U.S.C. §§ 801 through 970] regulates the handling of drugs that fall within certain categories, known as schedules. These schedules, targeted at deterring drug abuse, rank drugs according to their potential to lead to physical and psychological dependency, as well as their accepted medical use. The federal Drug Enforcement Administration (DEA) administers the CSA and its implementing regulations, which cover areas such as registration of controlled substance prescribers, dispensers, and manufacturers; mandatory records and reports; prescription restrictions; and disposal of controlled substances.

Under the CSA, a drug is determined to be a controlled substance by designation of the attorney general of the United States. In making those determinations, the attorney general relies on the recommendations of the secretary of the U.S. Department of Health and Human Services, who evaluates a drug according to the following criteria:

- the actual or relative potential for abuse
- the scientific evidence of its pharmacological effect, if known
- the state of current scientific knowledge about the drug or substance
- its history and current pattern of abuse
- the extent of risk to public health
- the liability for psychological or physiological dependence
- the chemical similarity to another controlled substance

[21 U.S.C. § 811(c)].

Since the CSA is integral to the practice of prescribing controlled substances, the PA with prescribing privileges should understand what the law requires, as well as the potential consequences of failing to comply with the law.

Drug Schedules

The federal CSA divides controlled substances into five "schedule" categories [21 U.S.C. § 812(a)]. The schedule into which a drug is placed determines which regulations must be followed when preparing, storing, and distributing the drug. The attorney general identifies the appropriate schedule based on the recommendation of the secretary of the U.S. Department of Health and Human Services [21 U.S.C. § 811(b)], and makes a determination on weighing the drug's potential for abuse against the drug's potential medical benefits. Drugs are generally classified into these five schedules as follows:

1. *Schedule I:* Drugs and other substances that have a high potential for abuse, have no currently accepted medical treatment use in the United States, and lack accepted safety for use under medical supervision [21 U.S.C. § 812(b)(1)]. The attorney general may temporarily categorize drugs under this schedule where it is necessary to avoid imminent hazard to the public, and the drug has not yet been scheduled for approval by the FDA [21 U.S.C. § 811(h)]. Some examples of Schedule I substances are heroin, marijuana, LSD, peyote, mescaline, nicocodeine, and nicomorphine.

2. *Schedule II:* Drugs and other substances that have a high potential for abuse, but have a currently accepted medical treatment use in the United States or a currently accepted medical use with severe restrictions. Schedule II substances are those that, when abused, may lead to severe psychological or physical dependence [21 U.S.C. § 812(b)(2)]. Examples of Schedule II substances are certain narcotic, stimulant, and depressant drugs, including opium, morphine, codeine, methadone (Dolophine), meperidine (Demerol), cocaine, oxycodone (Percodan), amphetamines (Benzedrine, Dexedrine), pentobarbital, and secobarbital.
3. *Schedule III:* Drugs and other substances that have less of a potential for abuse than the controlled substances in Schedules I and II, and have a currently accepted medical use in the United States. When abused, Schedule III substances may lead to moderate or low physical dependence or high psychological dependence [21 U.S.C. § 812(b)(3)]. Examples of such drugs are compounds containing limited quantities of certain narcotic drugs, and non-narcotic drugs such as derivatives of barbituric acid (except those that are listed in another schedule), glutethimide (Doriden), benzphetamine, chlorphentermine, mazindol, and paregoric. In 1990, anabolic steroids were also classified as Schedule III substances.
4. *Schedule IV:* Drugs and other substances that have a low potential for abuse relative to Schedule III subtances, have a currently accepted medical treatment use in the United States, and when abused may lead to limited physical dependence or psychological dependence relative to Schedule III subtances [21 U.S.C. § 812(b)(4)]. Examples of such drugs include barbital, phenobarbital, methylphenobarbital, chloral betaine (Beta-Chlor), diazepam (Valium), and lorazepam (Ativan).
5. *Schedule V:* Drugs and other substances that have a low potential for abuse relative to Schedule IV substances, have a currently accepted medical treatment use in the United States, and when abused may lead to limited physical dependence or psychological dependence relative to Schedule IV substances [21 U.S.C. § 812(b)(5)]. Examples are drugs containing limited quantities of certain narcotic drugs generally for antitussive and antidiarrheal purposes (i.e., cough syrups containing codeine, and diphenoxylate/atropine preparations for diarrhea).

DEA Registration Requirements

To legally prescribe and handle drugs contained in Schedules II through V, individuals must have a valid DEA registration number. PAs with prescribing authority under state law are increasingly applying for their own registration numbers under federal regulations specifically allowing “midlevel practitioners,” including PAs, nurse midwives, nurse practitioners, and optometrists, to register as “dispensers” of controlled substances [21 C.F.R. § 1304.03(e)].

PA prescribers should be aware that *dispensing* under the CSA has a much broader meaning than under state PA practice statutes, which typically define that term as delivering or supplying a patient with a quantity of prescription drug or device in accordance with statutory requirements [*see, e.g.,* 49 PA. CODE § 18.122; VA. CODE ANN. § 54.1-3401]. Dispensing under the federal definition encompasses prescribing, administering, packaging, labeling, and compounding necessary to prepare the controlled substance for delivery [21 U.S.C. § 802(10)]. Thus, PAs who prescribe controlled substances under physician supervision, pharmacists who prepare controlled substances, and nurses who administer controlled substances must do so under a valid DEA registration number.

There is an exemption from the registration requirement under the CSA for practitioners dispensing (under the broader, federal definition) controlled substances within the usual course of business of an employer registered to dispense controlled substances [21 U.S.C. § 822(c)(1)]. Federal regulations further specify that agents and employees of a registered individual practitioner (other than a midlevel practitioner), hospital, or institution dispensing or prescribing controlled substances in the course of their official duties or business are exempt from registration [21 C.F.R. § 1304.24(b)]. Under this exemption, some PAs with delegated prescriptive authority prescribe controlled substances under the DEA registration number of their supervising physicians, who are authorized and registered prescribers. In some states, PA prescribers of controlled substances are not allowed to use their own DEA numbers, and thus they use the DEA registration number of their supervising physician(s) [*see, e.g.,* ALASKA ADMIN. CODE tit. 12, § 40.450(d); NEB. REV. STAT. § 71-1,107.30, N.H. CODE ADMIN. R. Med. 608.09]. The DEA also makes its own determination, based on its analysis of state laws and regulations, whether PAs should be considered exempt from registration requirements. [AAPA, *Physician Assistant Prescribing and Dispensing* (Apr. 1996)].

The current trend, however, is toward the separate registration of PAs with the DEA. Several state PA laws now require that PA prescribers of controlled substances register with the DEA [*see, e.g.,* ARIZ. REV. STAT. ANN. § 32–2532(A); MINN. STAT. § 147A.18(b); MONT. CODE ANN. § 37-20-404; OR. ADMIN. R. 847-50-041(2); UTAH CODE ANN. § 58-70-501(4)]. Even in states where separate DEA registration by PAs is not mandated by statute, PAs are increasingly registering for their own DEA numbers; according to a recent AAPA estimate, PAs have separate DEA registration numbers in at least 17 states [*see* AAPA, *Physician Assistant Prescribing and Dispensing* (Apr. 1996)].

In applying for DEA registration, a PA must submit a completed Form DEA-224 to the DEA's Registration Unit in Washington, D.C. [the form appears at Appendix 4-B]. The form can be obtained from the Registration Unit or any DEA regional office listed on the form's last page. When an application for registration has been approved, the DEA issues a certificate of registration that contains the name and address of the registrant, the activity authorized, the amount of the registration fee paid, the expiration date of the registration, and the registration number. Registration numbers issued to PAs begin with the letter M (for midlevel practitioner), followed by a letter corresponding to the first letter of the registered name, and a computer-generated sequence of seven numbers. The DEA registration number must be renewed every three years; typically a re-registration application is mailed to the registered prescriber 60 days prior to the expiration date, and if not received, the PA should make a written request for such form, including a reference to the DEA number, within 45 days prior to the expiration date.

A registering PA prescriber should know that the DEA may deny an application for registration and revoke or suspend such registration if the registrant materially falsifies information in the registration application, is or has been convicted of a drug-related felony, is or has been subject to state license or registration revocation, or commits or has committed such acts as to make registration inconsistent with the public interest [21 U.S.C. § 824]. Registration may only be revoked after the registrant has received due process [21 U.S.C. § 824].

In applying for a DEA registration number, some PAs may also be concerned about requirements under the CSA relating to separate registration for each practice location and maintenance of DEA registration certificates at multiple practice settings. For example, the CSA provides that the practitioner who administers and dispenses (e.g., providing a supply to the patient) controlled substances at more than one practice location must obtain a separate registration for each practice location [21 U.S.C. § 822(e)]. Regulations further provide that separate registration for each practice location is not necessary if the practitioner is prescribing from more than one office, but administers, dispenses, and maintains a supply of controlled substances at only one office [21 C.F.R. § 1301.23(b)(3)].

State CSAs

State legislatures or boards of pharmacy may also designate a drug as a controlled substance, triggering state controlled substance laws. A PA prescriber practicing in one of the many states with a state controlled substance act should know the requirements and prohibitions of that law, which may be stricter than federal controlled substance laws. A DEA-registered PA must comply with the federal agency's rules regarding prescribing and dispensing of controlled substances, but also any relevant restrictions in the state controlled substance laws and PA practice laws, which may regulate matters such as prescription format, refills, and recordkeeping.

PRESCRIBING AND DISPENSING UNDER STATE PA PRACTICE LAWS

It is the responsibilty of every PA to know and comply with the prescribing and dispensing requirements of the PA practice laws and other drug-product regulations of the state in which the PA practices. In general, state laws and regulations governing PA prescriptive authority vary significantly from state to state, and also are subject to frequent amendment. Because of the many different forms of state regulation governing PA prescribing and the ongoing process in many states to expand the PA's scope of prescribing privileges by legislative amendment, it is difficult to present a comprehensive and up-to-date review of state PA prescribing laws. Instead, a number of examples of the relevant language contained in state PA laws are outlined here and in the next section to provide a general overview of state statutory and regulatory approaches to PA prescribing and dispensing.

Prescribing Regulations: Formulary versus Delegatory Approach

PA prescribing provisions within PA state practice statutes generally fall under one of two approaches: delegatory or formulary. A majority of states granting PAs prescriptive privileges have enacted PA prescribing statutes categorizable as "delegatory," in that they allow the state PA regulatory board or the physician-PA team to develop their own prescribing guidelines and patterns. The state medical boards in several states, however, have developed regulations based on the "formulary" approach, which intends to guide PA prescribing practices by allowing PAs to prescribe only those medications listed on a formulary or a list of drug categories. Appearing either directly in the statutory prescribing provisions or in regulations promulgated thereunder, the formulary usually has been approved by the PA regulatory board for use by the supervising physician in delegating prescriptive authority to the PA. Statutory prescribing provisions in Massachusetts and North Carolina are good examples of the delegatory approach to regulation of PA prescribing. The Massachusetts PA practice act specifies certain limitations with respect to PA prescribing of controlled substances, but otherwise leaves to the state commissioner of health the responsibility of promulgating regulations for the registration of PAs with delegated prescriptive authority pursuant to detailed guidelines mutually developed, agreed on, and annually reviewed by the supervising physician and PA [Mass. Gen. L. ch. 94C].

Pursuant to statutory prescribing provisions, the state medical board in North Carolina has promulgated regulations providing that PAs may prescribe, order, and administer drugs and devices if they are licensed, have received from the supervising physician written instructions for prescribing, and there is a written policy for periodic review by the physician. To prescribe controlled substances, the PA must sign a statement with the supervising physician attesting to the fact that both practitioners have read and understand the federal DEA's manual pertaining to midlevel practitioner prescribing. [*See* N.C. Gen. Stat. § 90-18(13) and N.C. Admin. Code tit. 21, r. 32O.0009; *see also* Alaska Stat. § 08.64.100 and Alaska Admin. Code tit. 12, §§ 40.450 & .975; Ariz. Rev. Stat. Ann. § 32-2532 and Ariz. Admin. Code R4-17-401 to -402; Del. Code Ann. tit. 24, § 1770A (b)(2) and Bd. Med. Practice Reg. 25; D.C. Code Ann. § 2.3301.2 and D.C. Mun. Regs. tit. 17, § 4912; Iowa Admin. Code r. 645-325.7(1) and .8; Or. Rev. Stat. § 677.515 and Or. Admin. R. 847-50-041; Tenn. Code Ann. § 63-19-107 and Tenn. Comp. R. & Regs. tit. 63, ch. 0080-3-.21; Wash. Rev. Code Ann. § 18.71A.03 and Wash. Admin. Code § 246-918.030.]

Some states have PA prescribing statutes based on the delegatory approach, but use safeguard measures. Minnesota's PA practice act, for example, broadly allows physicians to delegate prescriptive authority to their PAs, as long as the delegation is appropriate to the PA's practice and within the scope of the PA's training [Minn. Stat. § 147A.18(b)]. That authority, however, is conditioned upon the supervising physician and the PA developing a physician-PA agreement that specifies the PA's scope of practice and manner of supervision including: (1) an internal protocol developed by the physician-PA team listing all categories of drugs, medical devices, or controlled substances from which the PA may prescribe, dispense, or administer, and (2) a delegation form listing, by drug category, each of the legend drugs and controlled substances for which prescribing authority has been delegated [Minn. Stat. § 147A.20].

The Minnesota statute also specifies other standard safeguard requirements, such as the elements that must be included on each prescription written by the PA, but the scope of the PA's delegated prescriptive authority is essentially determined by the physician-PA team, not by explicit statutory language [Minn. Stat. § 147A.18(3); *see also* Conn. Gen. Stat. § 20-12d(3) (protocols established by supervising physician); Colo. Rev. Stat. § 12-36-106(5) and Colo. Bd. Med. Examiners Reg. Physician Assistants § 4 (PAs allowed to issue prescriptions for any noncontrolled substances and Schedule II–V controlled substances pursuant to supervising physician's written protocols); Kan. Stat. Ann. § 65-2896e and Kan. Admin. Regs. 100-60-13 (PAs authorized to transmit physician's prescription orders pursuant to written protocols); Utah Code Ann. § 58-70-501(4) and Utah Admin. Code R156-37-301 (PAs authorized to prescribe certain controlled substances as specified in utilization plan); Wis. Stat. § 448.40 and Wis. Admin. Code § Med 8.08(2) (PAs authorized to prescribe as outlined in written protocols)].

Prescribing regulations pursuant to Florida's PA practice act are based on the formulary approach. Under these regulations, supervising physicians are allowed to delegate to their certified PAs the authority to prescribe any medication used in the practice if it is listed on a formulary that is updated annually. A five-member committee appointed by the Department of Professional Regulation develops the formulary, which currently lists over 500 medications, but is restricted by regulation from including certain categories of drugs, including controlled substances, general anesthetics, and parenteral preparations except insulin and epinephrine [FLA. ADMIN. CODE ANN. r. 59R-30.008; *but see* 22 Fla. Admin. Reg. 7728 (Dec. 20, 1996) (notice of intention to amend regulation to add medications to the approved formulary)]. Supervising physicians and their PAs must keep on file a written agreement outlining which of the drugs in the formulary the PA may prescribe, and the agreement must be kept on file for at least five years and made available on request of the medical board or other appropriate state official [FLA. ADMIN. CODE ANN. r. 59R-30.0007(3)].

Finding the detailed listing of drug categories and medications under a formulary-based regulatory scheme to be burdensome or unnecessary, some states that originally used formularies converted to the delegatory approach. Maine, for example, had an extensive listing of drug categories in its PA prescribing regulations from 1985 until 1994 when the medical licensing board revised the regulations and discarded the formulary (the current regulations contain no formulary) [*see* Maine Board of Registration in Medicine, Admin. R. 10:373, ch. 2, Appendix (1985) and CODE ME. R. § 02-373-002(7); *see also* COLO. REV. STAT. § 12-31-103 (1969) and Colo. Bd. Med. Examiners Reg. Physician Assistants § 4]. Nonetheless, there are several remaining states that continue to use formulary-based PA prescribing regulations, including:

- *Alabama* [Bd. Med. Examiners, Guidelines Governing the Prescription Practices of Assistants to Physicians authorize PAs to prescribe legend drugs pursuant to guidelines listing a formulary of 30 drug categories for which the supervising physician may or may not delegate prescriptive authority to the PA]
- *California* [CAL. BUS. & PROF. CODE § 3502.1(a)(2) allows PAs to transmit prescriptions of supervising physician in accordance with physician's written practice-specific formulary and protocols]
- *New Mexico* [Bd. Med. Examiners R. & Reg. (Physician Assistants), Rule 7(1) authorizes PAs to prescribe legend drugs and controlled substances designated in a board-approved formulary listing over 70 types of drugs]
- *Pennsylvania* [49 PA. CODE § 18.158 authorizes PAs to prescribe and dispense, in accordance with restrictions specified in the regulations, drugs from a board-approved formulary listing categories of drugs for which PA has unlimited prescribing authority and categories subject to exclusions and limitations]

[For a full listing of formulary-based PA prescribing regulations, see AAPA state-by-state chart on PA prescribing privileges, at Appendix 4-A.]

Common Prescribing Provisions

Regardless of the regulatory scheme upon which PA prescribing laws are based, there are a number of prescribing provisions commonly found in most states' regulations of delegated PA prescriptive authority. This section briefly outlines some of the prescribing requirements contained in state PA prescribing statutes or regulations.

Physician Review

Requirements for physician review of PA prescribing and dispensing practices are delineated in the prescribing provisions of several state PA practice laws. The frequency and nature of physician review varies from state to state. For example, states usually allow the physician-PA team to determine the frequency of medication review [*see, e.g.*, Mass. Regs. Code tit. 105, § 700.003; N.C. Admin. Code tit. 21, r. 32O.0009(2)]; but a few states require the supervising physician to review the PA's prescribing practices on a weekly, monthly, or biannual basis, sometimes dependent on the category of drugs being prescribed (e.g., controlled v. noncontrolled) [*see, e.g.*, Ala. Bd. Med. Examiners, Guidelines Governing the Prescription Practices of Assistants to Physicians (weekly review); Ga. Comp. R. & Regs. r. 360-5-.12 (1)(c) (three-month review for controlled substances, six-month review for legend drugs)]. A few states also require the supervising physician's retrospective review and medical record countersignature of the PA's prescribing, dispensing, and administering of drugs and devices on a weekly or daily basis, or within a period of 48 to 96 hours [*see, e.g.*, Cal. Bus & Prof. Code § 3502.1(d) (for transmitted prescription orders, medical record countersignature within seven days); Minn. Stat. § 147A.18(b) (daily); Fla. Admin. Code Ann. r. 59R-30.007(c) (48 hours); Colo. Bd. Med. Examiners Reg. for Physician Assistants § 4 (within three days); 49 Pa. Code § 18.158(e) (within three days)]. A couple of states require review or countersignature within a specified time period on the medical record of patients for whom the PA has prescribed certain controlled substances [*see, e.g.*, Conn. Gen. Stat. § 20-12d (countersignature within 24 hours for Schedule II or III drugs); Mass. Regs. Code tit. 105, § 700.003 (review within 96 hours for Schedule II drugs)].

Items on Prescription

In general, PAs are authorized to sign prescriptions with their names, and prescription blanks are required to bear the name of the PA and the supervising physician. The additional items typically required on prescription blanks used by PAs include:

- PA's license certification number
- addresses and phone numbers of the supervising physician and the PA

- PA's signature followed by designation to identify the signer as a certified PA (e.g., PA-C)
- date of issue
- name and address of the patient
- name and quantity of the drug prescribed, including number of refills permitted
- directions for use

Most state PA practice statutes simply list these items without further explanation [*see, e.g,* MINN. STAT. § 147A.18(3)(c)], but there are a few exceptions. The Georgia PA practice statute, for example, has specific criteria for the PA's signature, requiring the PA to sign a prescription with the language "this prescription authorized through (the prescribing supervising physician) by (the PA's name), physician assistant" [GA. COMP. R. & REGS. r. 360-5-.12 (2)(b); see also N. M. Bd. Med. Examiners R. & Reg. (Physician Assistants), Rule 7(C) (PAs may prescribe only on special prescription pads imprinted for one PA only, which must have a signature line with designation "physician assistant" spelled out; pads must be destroyed when PA leaves practice or there is a change in supervising physician)].

Physicians generally cannot legally presign prescription blanks, which in several jurisdictions is grounds for discipline [*see e.g.,* Code of Wyoming Rules 024-052-004, § 3 (y)(iii)] and in one state is a criminal offense [*see, e.g.,* S.C. CODE ANN. § 44-53-395)]. Presigning of prescription blanks is explicitly addressed in at least one PA practice statute, which prohibits a supervising physician from this practice, including the practice of allowing a PA to use a device (e.g., a rubber stamp) for affixing the physician's signature on a prescription blank [49 PA. CODE § 18.158(d)(2)].

Controlled Substances

In the majority of the PA prescribing states, the scope of PA prescriptive privileges extends beyond the minimum level of signing prescriptions for legend drugs without a physician cosignature. Some state statutes specify which kinds of medications a PA may prescribe—controlled or noncontrolled, and the specific classes of drugs within these broader categories [*see, e.g.*, D.C. MUN. REGS. tit. 17, § 4912 (PAs may prescribe only noncontrolled substances); MICH. COMP. LAWS § 333.17076(3) (PA may prescribe only legend drugs until regulations are promulgated to indicate otherwise)]. Typically, restrictions on the classes of drugs are found in formulary-based PA prescribing regulations, but can also appear in statutes without a formulary [*see, e.g.,* FLA. ADMIN. CODE ANN. r. 59R-30.008 (restrictions within formulary); MINN. STAT. § 147A.09 (no formulary but statutory exclusion of anesthetics other than local); MONT. CODE ANN. § 37-20-404 (restrictions and no formulary); IOWA ADMIN. CODE r. 645-325.7(1)(s)(2) (restrictions and no formulary)].

In at least 29 states, PAs have been granted the privilege of prescribing controlled substances, although several states place limitations on that privilege. Rhode Island and South Carolina, for example, restrict the controlled substances PAs may prescribe to those in Schedule V [S.C. CODE ANN. REGS. 81-100(G)(3); R.I. GEN. LAWS § 5-54-8]. Although under proposed revision, Utah's PA practice statute currently allows PAs to prescribe controlled substances only in Schedules IV and V [UTAH CODE ANN. § 58-70-501]. Ten other states limit PA prescribing or transmittal of prescription order of controlled substances to those in Schedules III through V, while 15 other states permit PAs to prescribe drugs in Schedules II through V. [See AAPA state-by-state chart on PA prescribing privileges, at Appendix 4-A.] It is not uncommon for states that allow PAs the broadest authority to prescribe controlled substances to place restrictions on the supply of drugs with higher abuse potential (i.e., drugs in Schedule II or III) [*see, e.g.,* ARIZ. REV. STAT. § 32-2532(C) (prescriptions for Schedule II–III drugs limited to 72-hour supply; and for Schedule IV–V drugs, 34 days); MONT. CODE ANN. § 37-20-404(3)(b) (Schedule II drugs limited to 34-day supply); N.C. ADMIN. CODE tit. 21, r. 32O.0009 (Schedule II–III drugs limited to 7-day supply); NEB. REV. STAT. § 71-1,107.30 (Schedule II drugs limited to 72-hour supply); 49 PA. CODE § 18.158(c)(4) (Schedule III–V drugs limited to 30-day supply except for chronic condition cases where limit is 90 days)].

Also, PAs in Kansas, Oklahoma, and Tennessee are allowed to call in, but not write, prescriptions for controlled substances [KAN. ADMIN. REGS. 100-60-13; OKLA. ADMIN. CODE r. 435:15-11-1; TENN. COMP. R. & REGS. tit. 63, ch. 0880-3-.21]. Moreover, all PA practice statutes require that prescriptions for controlled substances have the DEA registration number(s) of the supervising physician, or PA, or both. [See DEA Registration Requirements.]

Dispensing Provisions

Under state law, there is a significant difference between prescribing drugs and dispensing them. Unlike the broad definition of dispensing in the federal CSA, which includes prescribing within the meaning of that term, state law separates prescribing from dispensing. Under state law, "dispensing" generally refers to the delivery or distribution of a supply of medication to a patient in accordance with a prescription. [See earlier discussion, at DEA Registration Requirements]. Currently, 25 states, the District of Columbia, and Guam allow physicians to delegate dispensing privileges to PAs. [See AAPA state-by-state chart on PA dispensing privileges, at Appendix 4-C]. In three of these states, however, dispensing privileges are restricted to circumstances when a pharmacist is not readily available or under emergency circumstances [IOWA ADMIN. CODE r. 645-325.7(1)(t); Idaho Bd. Med. Reg., IDAPA 22.01.03.043; NEB. REV. STAT. § 71-1,107.30 (as interpreted by

Bureau of Examining Boards; *see* AAPA, *Physician Assistant Prescribing and Dispensing* 13 (Sept. 1995) (citing informal/unpublished letters from the Bureau, dated July 23, 1991 and July 23, 1992))].

States that grant PAs dispensing privileges generally require PAs to comply with certain labeling requirements, specified either within state PA practice law or by reference to other state prescription labeling regulations. Most dispensing provisions in state PA laws, for example, delineate the items that must appear on the label (i.e., name of the supervising physician, name and address of the PA, name of patient, date dispensed and date of expiration, serial number of prescription, name/strength/quantity of drug, directions for use, and required cautionary warnings about use).

To varying degrees, the dispensing provisions of state PA practice laws specify additional limitations pertaining to the packaging of drug products, the category or quantity of drugs that the PA may dispense to a patient, and the receipt of drugs for subsequent distribution to patients. Examples of such dispensing provisions include:

- requirements that drugs dispensed or administerd by PAs be prepackaged in unit-of-use packages by supervising physicians or by pharmacists acting on a physician's written order [*see, e.g.,* ARIZ. REV. STAT. ANN. § 32-2532(G)(1); D.C. MUN. REGS. tit. 17, § 4912]
- limitations on the types of drugs dispensed or the amount that can be supplied (often in terms of hours or days) to the patient [*see, e.g.,* ARIZ. REV. STAT. ANN. § 32-2532(F) (except in an emergency, Schedule II–III drugs for 72-hour use with board approval; other controlled substances for 34-day use); MASS. GEN. LAWS ch. 12, § 9E and MASS. REGS. CODE tit. 105, § 700.003 (single doses of controlled substances or amount needed for immediate treatment); NEV. ADMIN. CODE ch. 639, § 639.280 (10-day supply for all drugs, except birth control pills; Schedule II drugs in emergency only in amount needed for immediate treatment); N.M. Bd. Med. Examiners R. & Reg. (Physician Assistants), Rule 8(D) (medications dispensed limited to those on board-approved formulary)]
- requirement that the PA not obtain drugs or devices from sources other than supervising physicians, pharmacists, or pharmaceutical representatives [*see, e.g.,* ARIZ. REV. STAT. § 32-2532(H); Colo. Bd. Med. Examiners Reg. Physician Assistants § 4(III); D.C. MUN. REGS. tit. 17, § 4912]

Geographic or Type-of-Facility Limitations

Depending on the state PA practice law, dispensing may be restricted to certain geographical locations or kinds of health care facilities. In some states, only PAs in rural areas or other locations without pharmacy services are authorized to dispense medications from a supply maintained in the offices of the supervising physician or clinic [*see* Wyo. Bd. Med. R. & Reg. Physicians & Physician Assistants § 17; *see also* Iowa Admin. Code r. 645-325.7(1)(t); Idaho Bd. Med. Reg., IDAPA 22.01.03.043]. Rather than geographical limitations on PA dispensing, the PA practice statutes in Connecticut, Georgia, and Oklahoma limit dispensing privileges by type of health care facility. In Oklahoma, for example, PAs are prohibited from dispensing drugs in any practice setting except one that is part of the state health department, mental health department, or other special setting designated by the medical board [Okla. Admin. Code tit. 435, § 15-5-10(f)]. PA practice statutes in Georgia provide that PAs can only dispense if they are employees or agents of public or nonprofit health facilities (except hospitals and HMOs), or if dispensing at a hospital-owned or -operated outpatient clinic where services are provided primarily to medically disadvantaged patients [Ga. Code Ann. § 43-34-26.1(b)(3); *see also* Conn. Gen. Stat. § 20-12d(a)]. This provision further requires that PAs who dispense at such facilities must provide drugs at no cost or at a cost based on the patient's ability to pay [Ga. Code Ann. § 43-34-26.1(b)(3); *see also* Kan. Admin. Regs. § 100-60-13(g)].

Dispensing Drug Samples

Federal law allows all PAs with prescriptive privileges to request, sign for, and distribute drug samples to patients in accordance with specified procedures. Federal law thus recognizes the distinction between giving patients drug samples that have been supplied by a pharmaceutical company and dispensing drugs under a prescription [21 U.S.C. § 353(d)(1); see also Food, Drug, and Cosmetic Act, at Distribution of Drug Samples]. Under state law, however, roughly half of the 40 states granting PAs prescriptive privileges have similarly recognized this distinction by explicitly providing for PA sampling authority in their PA practice laws [*see, e.g.*, Conn. Gen. Stat. § 20-14e; Iowa Admin. Code r. 645-325.7(1)(s)(6); N.C. Admin. Code tit. 21, r. 32O.0009(7); *see also* AAPA, *Summary of State Laws Regarding Physician Assistant Authorization to Request, Receive, Sign for and Distribute Sample Drugs and Devices* (Jan. 1997)]. As a result, PA prescribers in states with specific statutory and regulatory language describing how drug samples should be distributed must comply with these requirements, while PA prescribers in states without such language are authorized to request, sign for, and receive samples pursuant to federal law. [For a discussion about complying with state law when federal law regulates the same activity, see Food, Drug, and Cosmetic Act, at State FDCAs.]

As applied to PAs practicing in California, Kansas, and Oklahoma, where PA practice statutes authorize PAs to "transmit" orally or in writing the prescription orders of their supervising physicians, PAs do not technically have prescribing authority and therefore may not request or receive drug samples pursuant to federal drug law [CAL. BUS. & PROF. CODE § 3502.1; KAN. STAT. ANN. § 65-2896e; OKLA. STAT. ANN. tit. 59, § 519.6(D); *but see* OKLA. ADMIN. CODE tit. 435, § 15-13-1(g) (authorizing PAs to distribute professional samples to patients)].

In all states that grant PAs prescriptive privileges, whether or not state PA sampling is explicitly provided for in statutes or regulations, the authority of PAs to request, sign for, and distribute sample medications to patients may match, but not exceed, their prescribing or dispensing privileges; for example, if a PA is not authorized to prescribe controlled substances under the state PA practice law, then the PA also cannot request or distribute samples of controlled substances. Some PA practice statutes impose additional restrictions such as limiting the type of drug that PAs may distribute to patients as drug samples [*see, e.g.,* Del. Bd. Med. Practice R. & Reg. (Physician Assistants) § C(j) (legend and over-the-counter drugs); N.M. Bd. Med. Examiners R. & Reg. (Physician Assistants) Rule 8 (non-controlled substances in accordance with board-approved formulary); R.I. GEN. LAWS § 5-54-8 (as limited by statute, and controlled substances limited to Schedule V)]. Agency officials in only two states, Georgia and Virginia, have expressly indicated that, because PA sampling is not specifically provided for in their PA practice laws, PAs may not request or sign for drug samples [*see* AAPA, *Summary of State Laws Regarding Physician Assistant Authorization to Request, Receive, Sign for and Distribute Sample Drugs and Devices* (Jan. 1997) (citing informal/unpublished attorney general opinions)].

The AAPA has drafted model sampling language that makes a clear distinction between drug dispensing and distribution of drug samples, and also explicitly identifies each step in the process of requesting, signing, and distributing samples to patients. The model provisions, which may be obtained from the AAPA upon request, may be very useful for state PA associations whose interests include revision of a particular state's PA law to clarify PA sampling authority.

Appendix 4-A

Physician Assistant Prescribing Privileges

	State	#PAs	Restrictions	Controlled Substances
1	Alabama	197	Board formulary	
2	Alaska	226		Sch. III-V
3	Arizona	504		Sch. II-III limited to 72-hour supply Sch. IV-V, 34-day supply
4	California	3000	Prescription transmittal authority based on physician order or protocol/ formulary	Sch. III-V
5	Colorado	639		Sch. II-V
6	Connecticut	602		Sch. II-V
7	Delaware	74		Sch. II-V
8	Florida	1475	Board formulary	
9	Georgia	1027	Board formulary	Sch. III-V
10	Hawaii* (proposed)	98		III-V (proposed)
11	Idaho	123	Board formulary	
12	Iowa	385		Sch. III-V; Sch. II (except stimulants and depressants)
13	Kansas	329		Sch. III-V orally, Sch. II orally in emergency

*Regulations to implement prescribing authority not yet in effect

Source: Reprinted with permission from *Physician Assistant Prescribing and Dispensing*, © 1996, American Academy of Physician Assistants.

continues

	State	#PAs	Restrictions	Controlled Substances
14	Maine	310		Sch. III-V
15	Massachusetts	691		Sch. II-V
16	Michigan	1132		
17	Minnesota	349	Board formulary	Sch. II-V
18	Missouri*	248		
19	Montana	129		Sch. II-V (Sch. II limited to 34-day supply)
20	Nebraska	341		Sch. II-V (Sch. II limited to 72-hour supply)
21	Nevada	150		Sch. II-V
22	New Hampshire	160		Individually determined
23	New Mexico	342	Board formulary	Sch. II-V
24	New York	3163		
25	North Carolina	1457		Sch. II-V (Sch. II-III limited to 7-day supply)
26	North Dakota	174		Sch. III-V
27	Oklahoma	425	Board formulary	
28	Oregon	263		Sch. III-V
29	Pennsylvania	1600	Board formulary	Sch. III-V. Limited to 30-day supply unless for chronic condition
30	Rhode Island	96		Sch. V
31	South Carolina	239	Board formulary	Sch. V
32	South Dakota	186		Sch. II-V (Sch. II limited to 48-hour supply)
33	Tennessee	370		
34	Texas	1752		
35	Utah	211		Sch. IV-V (7-day supply)
36	Vermont	103	Board formulary	Individually determined
37	Virginia	531	Board formulary	
38	Washington	875		Sch. II-V
39	West Virginia	268	Board formulary	Sch. III-V (Sch. III limited to 72-hour supply)
40	Wisconsin	588		Sch. II-V
41	Wyoming	73		Sch. III-V
	District of Columbia	75		
	Guam	12		Sch. III-V

APPENDIX 4-B

Application for DEA Registration

APPLICATION FOR REGISTRATION
UNDER CONTROLLED SUBSTANCES ACT OF 1970

INSTRUCTIONS FOR COMPLETING FORM DEA-224 — *NOTE, this form is for new applicant only and not for renewal of registration.*

This application is for a 3 year registration period; application fee is **$ 60.00.** Checks drawn on foreign banks will not be accepted. Application fees are not refundable.

ADDRESS BLOCK - Information must be **TYPED or PRINTED**. Only 5 lines of address are allowed. The manner in which this information is placed on the application is the way your Certificate of Registration will read. Please use the street address of proposed business location **(DO NOT USE P.O. BOX).**

Practitioner: Line 1 - Last Name, First Name, Middle Initial, Medical Degree
Lines 2, 3, 4 and 5 - Street Address, City, State and ZIP Code

Retail Pharmacy - Hospital/Clinic - Teaching Institution:

Line 1 - Name of Business or Institution
Lines 2, 3, 4 and 5 - Street Address, City State and ZIP Code

Item 1. Business Activity - Check only one.

Retail Pharmacy: Name of pharmacy must appear in address block.

Hospital/Clinic: Applicants applying for Hospital/Clinic registration should check with local State licensing authority to be sure they meet State requirements for that activity

Practitioner: Please furnish medical degree in the space provided, next to practitioner business activity, e.g., DDS, DO, DVM, MD, etc.

Teaching Institution: Registration as a Teaching Institution authorizes purchase and possession of controlled substances for instructional purposes only. Practitioners, teaching institutions or individuals within teaching institutions desiring to conduct esearch with any Schedule I substance, must obtain a "Researcher" registration by submitting Form DEA-225 with applicable fee.

Item 2. Schedules - Check schedules of controlled substance you intend to handle (See Reverse side of this sheet).

continues

Source: Reprinted from the U.S. Department of Justice/Drug Enforcement Administration, Washington, D.C.

Item 3. Order Forms - Check only if you intend to purchase or transfer Schedule II substances. The order form books will be issued to you upon issuance of your DEA registration number.

Item 4. State License and Signature — Federal Registration (DEA) is based upon the applicant being in compliance with applicable State and local laws. Applicants should contact the local State licensing authority prior to completing this application form. If your state requires a separate controlled substance license, please provide the number. If State licensing authority is not required, check N/A. If you have applied for State license and it has not been issued, check "Pending". Questions 4(a), (b) and (c) must be answered. If questions (b) or (c) are answered "Yes", include a statement setting forth the circumstances using the space provided on the Reverse of the application form.

Item 5. Exempt Official - Check only if your DEA registration will be affiliated with Federal, State or local government. The address on the application must be that of the affiliated Federal, State or local government. The application fee will not be required. The signature and title of your supervisor must appear on the application. You cannot exempt yourself from payment of the application fee.

MAIL ORIGINAL & 2ND COPY WITH **$ 60.00** FEE TO:

Drug Enforcement Administration
Central Station
P.O. Box 28083
Washington, D.C. 20038 - 8083

NOTE: Once your DEA registration is issued a renewal application is automatically issued to you 45 days prior to your expiration date.

Title 21, United States Code, Section 827(g) requires all registrants to report any changes of professional or business address to the DEA. Notification of address changes must be made in writing to the DEA office which has jurisdiction for your registered location. (SEE REVERSE SIDE OF COPY 3 OF THE APPLICATION FORM FOR A LIST OF DEA OFFICES AND ADDRESSES).

● RETAIN 3RD COPY FOR YOUR RECORDS ●

Public reporting burden for this collection of information is estimated to average 12 minutes per response, including the time for reviewing instructions, searching existing data sources, gathering and maintaining the data needed, and completing and reviewing the collection of information. Send comments regarding this burden estimate or any other aspect of this collection of information, including suggestions for reducing this burden, to the Drug Enforcement Administration, Records Management Section, Washington, D.C. 20537; and to the Office of Management and Budget, Paperwork Reduction Project No. 1117-0014, Washington, D.C. 20503.

DEA - **224** (6/90)

SCHEDULES OF CONTROLLED SUBSTANCES

The narcotic, depressant, stimulant and hallucinogenic drugs that are covered by the Controlled Substances Act are listed in one of five Schedules. Examples of substances in each are listed below by generic or common name and in some instances by a common trade name in parenthesis.

SCHEDULE I

Schedule I substances have no accepted medical use in the United States and have a high abuse potential. Examples include fenethylline, heroin, LAAM, LSD, marihuana, MDMA, mescaline, methaqualone and peyote.

SCHEDULE II

Schedule II drugs have a high abuse potential with severe psychic or physical dependence liability and in general, are substances that have therapeutic utility. Schedule II narcotics include morphine, codeine, fentanyl (Innovar and Sublimaze), hydromorphone (Dilaudid), levorphanol (Levo-Dromoran), meperidine (Demerol), methadone (Dolophine), oxycodone (Percodan), oxymorphone (Numorphan), opium, anileridine (Leritine) and the veterinary products etorphine hydrochloride (M 99) and diprenorphine (M50-50). Schedule II non-narcotics include amphetamine (Dexedrine), methamphetamine (Desoxyn), methylphenidate (Ritalin), phenmetrazine (Preludin), amobarbital (Amytal), pentobarbital (Nembutal), secobarbital (Seconal), phencyclidine, dronabinol in sesame oil in gelatin capsules (Marinol) and nabilone (Cesamet).

SCHEDULE III

Schedule III drugs have an abuse potential less than those in Schedules I and II. Schedule III narcotics include nalorphine (Nalline) and mixtures of limited specified quantities of codeine, dihydrocodeine, hydrocodone, morphine or opium with non-controlled active ingredients. Non-narcotics include mixtures of amobarbital, pentobarbital or secobarbital with other non-controlled medicinal ingredients; barbiturates not listed in another schedule such as aprobarbital, butabarbital, butalbital, talbutal and thiopental; glutethimide (Doriden), methyprylon (Noludar), benzphetamine (Didrex), phendimetrazine (Plegine), and the tiletamine/zolazepam veterinary combination product (Telazol).

SCHEDULE IV

Schedule IV drugs have an abuse potential less than those listed in Schedule III. Dosage forms of the narcotic dextropropoxyphene are in Schedule IV as are all forms of pentazocine (Talwin), marketed benzodiazepines including alprazolam (Xanax), chlordiazepoxide (Librium), clonazepam (Klonopin), clorazepate (Tranxene), diazepam (Valium), flurazepam (Dalmane), halazepam (Paxipam), lorazepam (Ativan), midazolam (Versed), oxazepam (Serax), prazepam (Centrax), quazepam (Dormalin), temazepam (Restoril) and triazolam (Halcion); long acting barbiturates barbital, mephobarbital and phenobarbital; the ultra-short barbiturate methohexital (Brevital); other depressants including chloral hydrate, ethchlorvynol (Placidyl), ethinamate (Valmid), meprobamate (Miltown), and paraldehyde; and the appetite suppressants diethylpropion (Tenuate), fenfluramine (Pondimin), mazindol (Sanorex) and phentermine (Ionamin); and pemoline (Cylert).

SCHEDULE V

The drugs in this schedule have an abuse potential less than those listed in Schedule IV. Buprenorphine (Buprenex) is a Schedule V narcotic as are antidiarrheal and cough suppressant preparations which contain limited specified quantities of codeine, dihydrocodeine, diphenoxylate (Lomotil), ethylmorphine or opium.

A complete listing of drugs controlled under the CSA may be found in Title 21, Code of Federal Regulations, Part 1300 to END, Sections 1308.11 through 1308.15. This publication may be purchased from the Superintendent of Documents, U.S. Government Printing Office, Washington, D.C. 20402.

continues

*U.S. GOVERMENT PRINTING OFFICE: 1993-350-921

Form **DEA** (Jun 1990) – **224**   OMB No. 1117-0014

APPLICATION FOR REGISTRATION
UNDER
CONTROLLED SUBSTANCES ACT OF 1970

Please PRINT or TYPE all entries.

No registration may be issued unless a completed application form has been received (21 CFR 1301.21).

NAME		
PROPOSED BUSINESS ADDRESS		
CITY	STATE	ZIP CODE

RETAIN Copy 3. Mail Orig. and 1 copy with FEE to:

UNITED STATES DEPARTMENT OF JUSTICE
DRUG ENFORCEMENT ADMINISTRATION
CENTRAL STATION
P. O. Box 28083
WASHINGTON, D.C. 20038 - 8083
For INFORMATION, Call: (202) 307 - 7255

See "Privacy Act" Information on reverse

THIS BLOCK FOR DEA USE ONLY

REGISTRATION CLASSIFICATION: Submit Check or Money Order Payable to the **DRUG ENFORCEMENT ADMINISTRATION** in the Amount of **$ 60.00** (3 year registration period)

● **FEE MUST ACCOMPANY APPLICATION**

1. BUSINESS ACTIVITY: *(Check ☑ ONE only)*

A ☐ RETAIL PHARMACY   B ☐ HOSPITAL/CLINIC   C ☐ PRACTITIONER *(Specify Medical Degree, e.g., DDS, DO, DVM, MD, etc.)*   D ☐ TEACHING INSTITUTION *(Instructional purposes only)*

2. SCHEDULES: *(Check ☑ all applicable schedules in which you intend to handle controlled substances. See Schedules on Reverse of Instruction Sheet.)*

SCHEDULE II ☐ NARCOTIC   SCHEDULE II ☐ NONNARCOTIC   SCHEDULE III ☐ NARCOTIC   SCHEDULE III ☐ NONNARCOTIC   SCHEDULE IV ☐   SCHEDULE V ☐

3. ☐ CHECK HERE IF YOU REQUIRE ORDER FORMS.

4. **ALL APPLICANTS MUST ANSWER THE FOLLOWING:**

(a) Are you currently authorized to prescribe, distribute, dispense, conduct research, or otherwise handle the controlled substances in the schedules for which you are applying, under the laws of the **State** or jurisdiction in which you are operating or propose to operate ?

☐ YES - **State** License No. ____________

☐ Not Applicable ☐ Pending

☐ YES - **State** Controlled Substance No. ____________

☐ Not Applicable ☐ Pending

● *ATTACH CHECK HERE* ●

(b) Has the applicant ever been convicted of a crime in connection with controlled substances under State or Federal law, or ever surrendered or had a Federal controlled substance registration revoked, suspended, restricted or denied, or ever had a State professional license or controlled substance registration revoked, suspended, denied, restricted or placed on probation ? ☐ YES ☐ NO

(c) If the applicant is a corporation (other than a corporation whose stock is owned and traded by the public), association, partnership, or pharmacy, has any officer, partner, stockholder or proprietor been convicted of a crime in connection with controlled substances under State or Federal law, or ever surrendered or had a Federal controlled substance registration revoked, suspended, restricted or denied, or ever had a State professional license or controlled substance registration revoked, suspended, denied, restricted or placed on probation ? ☐ YES ☐ NO ☐ NOT APPLICABLE

IF THE ANSWER TO QUESTIONS 4(b) or (c) is YES, include a statement using the space provided on the REVERSE of this part.

Print or Type Name Here - Sign Below

Applicant's Business Phone No.

SIGN HERE ▶

Signature of applicant or authorized individual

Date

Title (If the applicant is a corporation, institution, or other entity, enter the TITLE of the person signing on behalf of the applicant (e.g., President, Dean, Procurement Officer, etc....))

5. CERTIFICATION FOR FEE EXEMPTION

☐ CHECK THIS BLOCK IF INDIVIDUAL NAMED HEREON IS A FEDERAL, STATE, OR LOCAL OFFICIAL.

The Undersigned hereby certifies that the applicant herein is an officer or employee of a Federal, State or local agency who, in the course of such employment, is authorized to obtain, dispense, or prescribe controlled substances or is authorized to conduct research, instructional activity or chemical analysis with controlled substances, and is exempt from the payment of this application fee.

Signature of Certifying Official

Date

Print or Type Name

Print or Type Title

Name of Institution or Agency

WARNING: SECTION 843(a)(4) OF TITLE 21, UNITED STATES CODE, STATES THAT ANY PERSON WHO KNOWINGLY OR INTENTIONALLY FURNISHES FALSE OR FRAUDULENT INFORMATION IN THIS APPLICATION IS SUBJECT TO IMPRISONMENT FOR NOT MORE THAN FOUR YEARS, A FINE OF NOT MORE THAN $30,000.00 OR BOTH.

Mail the Original and 1 copy with FEE to the above address. Retain 3rd copy for your records.

continues

● **Explanation for answering "Yes", to question(s) 4(b) through (c).**

Applicants who have answered "yes" to questions 4(b) or (c) are required to submit a statement explaining such response(s). The space provided below should be used for this purpose and must be separately signed. If this response involves the revocation, suspension or restriction of a Federal controlled substance registration, provide your previous registration number and the circumstances of its revocation, suspension or restriction. If this response involves the revocation, suspension or restriction of a State professional license or controlled substance registration, provide the license and/or registration number, the names of the issuing state and agency and the circumstances.

____

PRINT or TYPE Name Here - Sign Below

▶ ______________________________ ▶ ______________________

Signature *Date*

PRIVACY ACT INFORMATION

AUTHORITY: Section 302 and 303 of the Controlled Substances Act of 1970 (PL 91-513)

PURPOSE: To obtain information required to register applicants pursuant to the Controlled Substances Act of 1970

ROUTINE USES: The Controlled Substances Act Registration Records produces special reports as required for statistical analytical purposes. Disclosures of information from this system are made to the following categories of users for the purposes stated:

A. Other Federal law enforcement and regulatory agencies for law enforcement and regulatory purposes

B. State and local law enforcement and regulatory agencies for law enforcement and regulatory purposes

C. Persons registered under the Controlled Substances Act (Public Law 91-513) for the purpose of verifying the registration of customers and practitioners

EFFECT: Failure to complete form will preclude processing of the application

DEA OFFICES

ATLANTA DIVISION OFFICE
Richard B. Russell Fed. Building
75 Spring St., S.W. Rm. 740
Atlanta, GA 30303

Georgia
North Carolina
South Carolina
Tennessee

BOSTON DIVISION OFFICE
50 Staniford St., Suite 200
Boston, MA 02114

Connecticut
Maine
Massachusetts
New Hampshire
Rhode Island
Vermont

CHICAGO DIVISION OFFICE
Dirksen Federal Bldg., Suite 500
219 South Dearborn St.
Chicago, IL 60604

Illinois
Indiana
Minnesota
North Dakota
Wisconsin

DALLAS DIVISION OFFICE
1880 Regal Row
Dallas, TX 75235

Oklahoma
Texas

DENVER DIVISION OFFICE
U.S. Customs House Rm. 316
P.O. Box 1860
Denver, CO 80201

Colorado
New Mexico
Utah
Wyoming

DETROIT DIVISION OFFICE
Federal Bldg., Rm. 357
231 West Lafayette
Detroit, MI 48226

Kentucky
Michigan
Ohio

HOUSTON DIVISION OFFICE
333 West Loop North, Suite 300
Houston, TX 77024

Texas

LOS ANGELES DIVISION OFFICE
350 South Figueroa St. Suite 800
Los Angeles, CA 90071

California
Hawaii
Nevada
Trust Territory

MIAMI DIVISION OFFICE
8400 N.W. 53rd Street
Miami, FL 33166

Florida
Puerto Rico
Virgin Islands

NEWARK DIVISION OFFICE
Federal Office Building
970 Broad St., Rm. 806
Newark, NJ 07102

New Jersey

NEW ORLEANS DIVISION OFFICE
1661 Canal St., Suite 2200
New Orleans, LA 70112

Alabama
Arkansas
Louisiana
Mississippi

NEW YORK DIVISION OFFICE
555 West 57th St., Suite 1900
New York, NY 10019

New York

PHILADELPHIA DIVISION OFFICE
William J. Green Federal Building
600 Arch St., Rm. 10224
Philadelphia, PA 19106

Delaware
Pennsylvania

PHOENIX DIVISION OFFICE
3010 N. 2nd Ave., Suite 301
Phoenix, AZ 85012

Arizona

SAN DIEGO DIVISION OFFICE
402 W. 35th Street
National City, CA 92050

California

SAN FRANCISCO DIVISION OFFICE
450 Golden Gate Ave.
Box 36050
San Francisco, CA 94102

California

SEATTLE DIVISION OFFICE
220 West Mercer St., Suite 300
Seattle, WA 98119

Alaska
Idaho
Montana
Oregon
Washington

ST LOUIS DIVISION OFFICE
United Missouri Bank Building
7911 Forsyth Suite 500
St Louis, MO 63105

Iowa
Kansas
Missouri
Nebraska
South Dakota

WASHINGTON, D.C. DIVISION OFFICE
400 6th St., S.W. Rm. 2558
Washington, D.C. 20024

District of Columbia
Maryland
Virginia
West Virginia

Title 21, United States Code, Section 827(g) requires all registrants to report any changes of professional or business address to the DEA. Notification of address changes must be made in writing to the DEA office which has jurisdiction for your registered location. Direct requests for the following actions to the address listed for your State. 1. Request a modification to your DEA Registration (Address or Schedule Changes), 2. Request Order Form Books, 3. Status of Pending Application.

APPENDIX 4-C

Physician Assistant Dispensing Privileges

	State	#PAs	Restrictions
1	Arizona	504	Sch. II-III in emergency, for 72-hour use; other controlled drugs, 34-day supply
2	California	3000	
3	Colorado	639	
4	Connecticut	602	In public and nonprofit clinics
5	Georgia	1027	In public and nonprofit clinics
6	Hawaii*	98	Regulations pending
7	Idaho	123	Drugs in formulary; when pharmacist unavailable
8	Iowa	385	When pharmacist services unavailable; when in patient's best interest
9	Maine	310	
10	Massachusetts	691	Single dose of controlled substance or amount needed for immediate treatment
11	Minnesota	349	
12	Montana	129	
13	Nebraska	341	
14	Nevada	150	10-day supply
15	New Mexico	342	
16	North Carolina	1457	Under pharmacist supervision
17	North Dakota	174	Sch. IV and V
18	Oklahoma	425	In state health or mental health facilities
19	Oregon	263	

*Regulations to implement prescribing authority not yet in effect

Source: Reprinted with permission from *Physician Assistant Prescribing and Dispensing,* © 1996, American Academy of Physician Assistants.

continues

	State	#PAs	Restrictions
20	Pennsylvania	1600	
21	Tennessee	370	
22	Utah	211	At branch pharmacies in rural health clinics
23	Virginia	531	
24	Washington	875	
25	Wyoming	73	In rural clinics
	District of Columbia	75	
	Guam	12	No Sch. I or II

Chapter 5

Liability

INTRODUCTION

The increasing scope of PA practice brings increased risk. As PAs shoulder greater patient care responsibility and act with more independence, medical malpractice suits are of increasing concern to PAs. In addition, although patient education concerning the role of the PA improves the quality of care, it also contributes to the visibility of PAs and, perhaps, the likelihood of litigation against PAs.

A lawsuit, even if successfully defended, carries a high financial and emotional price. To avoid becoming part of the trend of increased litigation, PAs should be familiar with the basic legal theories on which patients may base claims, as well as the types of conduct that may lead to liability. In addition, PAs should understand when their own acts can lead to liability for employers, physicians, and other health care providers. The types of damages that a patient may recover, as well as how to reduce damages, are also discussed here.

Areas of potential liability to patients may also pose important ethical questions that a PA must consider before deciding on a course of action. A few of these areas are highlighted in this chapter. The final portion of this chapter contains an explanation of the events leading up to a medical malpractice trial, known as the "prelitigation phase." Physician assistants should be familiar with this phase of a legal proceeding, as many cases are resolved prior to trial, and a PA's pretrial conduct can contribute to a successful resolution.

NEGLIGENCE

Negligence is a legal theory, or *cause of action,* under which an individual may file a civil lawsuit and recover monetary damages. The essence of a negligence claim is that the individual suing (the *plaintiff* or *claimant*) was injured because the individual being sued (the *defendant*) did not exercise reasonable care. If the plaintiff succeeds and the defendant is found liable, the defendant must pay monetary damages to compensate the plaintiff for the injury.

Negligence is a type of *tort,* a category of causes of action in which one person injures another. *Intentional torts,* such as assault and battery, are distinguished from the tort of negligence by the defendant's willful or knowing injury of the plaintiff. *Malpractice* refers to negligence committed by a professional, such as a physician, lawyer, or PA, in the course of professional activity.

To win a negligence case and recover damages from a PA, a patient must prove each of these three elements:

1. The PA owed the patient a duty of care.
2. The PA breached that duty.
3. The patient was harmed as a result of the PA's action or failure to act.

A patient must prove all three elements by a *preponderance of the evidence.* This level of proof requires the patient to show evidence demonstrating each element under a "more likely than not" test. In other words, the jury or judge must find more than a 50 percent likelihood that the PA owed the patient a duty, breached that duty, and caused the patient's damages.

Duty

A PA's duty to a patient arises out of the provider-patient relationship. The provider-patient relationship generally arises when a provider has agreed to treat a patient and is simply established in most malpractice cases. In the managed care era, however, the question of whether or when a provider-patient relationship was initiated has taken on increased importance, particularly in cases where the provider's contact with the patient was minimal. In these cases, the court will assess whether the physician and PA owed the patient a duty of care as a preliminary matter.

Some courts have ruled that a physician conducting a physical examination for the limited purpose of determining whether an individual is fit for employment does not owe a duty to reveal any findings to the patient, because the physician's relationship is to the employer, not the patient [*see, e.g., Rand v. Miller,* 408 S.E.2d 655 (W. Va. 1991)]. Other courts have ruled, however, that once an examination is undertaken, the physician, or the employer, or both have a duty to reveal dangerous conditions discovered during the course of the examination [*see, e.g., Green v. Walker,* 910 F.2d 291 (5th Cir. 1990) (physician); *Dornak v. Lafayette Gen. Hosp.,* 399 So. 2d 168 (La. 1981) (hospital-employer)].

The existence of a provider-patient relationship, and therefore a duty, is more likely called into question when an "on-call" provider is consulted over the telephone. The highest court in Texas has ruled that a patient who came to a hospital emergency department (ED), for example, could not sue the on-call physician who was consulted by telephone by an on-duty ED physician. The court ruled that the on-call physician owed no duty to the patient because no physician-patient relationship existed, as no consensual relationship with the patient had been established. Specifically, the court reasoned that the on-call physician never agreed to examine or treat the patient and only listened to a description of his symptoms to evaluate whether he should take the case [*St. John v. Pope,* 901 S.W.2d 420 (Tex. 1995)].

Standard of Care and Breach of Duty

The scope of a defendant's duty to a plaintiff is called the standard of care. A defendant who does not comply with the standard of care has breached the duty owed to the plaintiff. If that breach causes harm to the plaintiff, the defendant may be found negligent.

The standard of care for a PA is the level of care that would be provided by a reasonable or prudent PA with similar experience and training under similar circumstances [*Paris v. Kreitz,* 331 S.E.2d 234 (N.C. Ct. App. 1985)]. Under this standard, a PA who specializes in a type of care, oncology for example, is held to a higher standard of care than a primary care PA as the specialist PA may be expected to have superior knowledge and experience in that particular practice area.

Although the standard of care for a PA may be defined as what a reasonable, prudent PA would have done under similar circumstances, courts may discern the standard by determining how a physician would have acted. If the PA, for example, was performing one of the same tasks that the PA's supervising physician performs, the court may reason that the PA was "standing in the shoes" of the supervising physician and consider what the physician would have done under the circumstances.

In each medical malpractice case, the standard of care must be established with respect to the facts of that particular case. In other words, what does the standard of care require a PA to do when faced with a patient under the circumstances that actually occurred in this case? In many cases, the standard of care does not dictate one particular course of action or treatment, but encompasses a range of possible decisions that would have been deemed reasonable under the PA's circumstances.

The evidence that may be admitted to establish the standard of care varies, depending on the jurisdiction. Some courts, for example, will look to the standard of care accepted within the PA's local community, but others will require evidence on a national standard of care. Citing South Dakota law, for example, a federal appeals court ruled that a local standard applied in a medical malpractice case against a PA employed by a hospital, but the court noted that a national standard would apply to a medical specialist such as a board-certified physician [*Goodman v. United States,* 2 F.3d 291 (8th Cir. 1993)].

To determine whether a PA complied with the standard of care in a particular case, the court or jury generally may consider:

- testimony of other PAs and health professionals, known as expert witnesses, concerning what a reasonable and prudent PA would do in the defendant's circumstances (the most common means of establishing the standard)
- whether the PA violated any laws or regulations
- whether the PA followed any clinical practice guidelines or protocols
- whether the PA violated any hospital or other internal policies

Conduct That May Lead to Liability

Although very few reported court decisions expressly discuss PA liability, as the PA profession expands, litigation will probably follow. Physician assistants should be familiar with the types of claims that have succeeded against other health care providers and avoid conduct similar to that which has led to liability. Actions against physicians and nurses fall into a few distinct categories.

Failure To Properly Diagnose

Failure to properly diagnose is the most common action causing negligence allegations. Physician assistants must be on guard for how an improper diagnosis will impact the PA and the supervising physician. A PA may be responsible for the initial screening of a patient, including assessing the patient's complaints, taking a medical history, and conducting a medical examination. The PA may misdiagnose the patient with a minor problem, prescribe treatment, and discharge the patient without review by a physician. To determine whether the PA breached the standard of care, the court is likely to examine whether a prudent PA would have made the correct diagnosis, as well as whether a prudent PA would have referred the patient to a physician.

Failure To Refer

As alluded to in the previous example, PAs should be alert to potential liability resulting from the failure to refer a patient to a supervising physician or other health care provider. To a judge or jury, managed care and other insurance contracts that include financial incentives for health care providers not to refer patients for additional or specialized care may create the perception that the PA who failed to refer was not acting in the best interest of the patient and was negligent.

Exceeding the Scope of Practice

Generally, exceeding the scope of PA practice does not constitute negligence per se (discussed later at Negligence Per Se), however, it probably serves as strong evidence that a PA was negligent, should a patient be injured as a result. That is, a judge or jury would likely examine PA scope-of-practice laws, regulations, and contracts and rule that a PA acting reasonably would not have exceeded those limitations. [For a discussion of scope-of-practice laws, see Chapter 3: Licensure and Scope of Practice.]

Negligent Monitoring

In the inpatient care setting, there is a duty to properly monitor a patient's condition. Although hospitals and other facilities are not obligated to monitor each patient 24 hours a day, a hospital is required to check a patient continually if warranted. Negligent monitoring is a common charge against nurses and their employing hospitals. Physician assistants can also be negligent if a surgeon is not notified of a patient's deteriorating condition. This is particularly important when "on-call." A PA's failure to properly monitor, record, and report changes in a patient's condition can serve as the basis for a malpractice action.

Failure To Question a Physician's Abnormal Orders

Conformity to physician's orders that results in harm to a patient may be the basis for liability, if the PA should have known the physician acted improperly. This is especially true when the PA observed the patient continuing to deteriorate as a result of the physician's prescribed treatment, yet did not act in the patient's interest. Courts have recognized that nurses have an independent duty to patients and have held nurses liable for failing to question physicians' orders. Although there have been no reported cases against PAs for failing to question a physician's orders, the derivative nature of the PA's authority to treat patients probably does not make this legal theory inapplicable to PAs.

Failure To Follow Up

Failure to contact a patient to follow up on a missed appointment, suggested referral, or abnormal lab result can all serve as the basis for allegations of negligence. Physician assistants should be sure their practices have administrative procedures to prevent gaps in patient care—even gaps caused by the patient's own failure to follow through with recommended care. [For further discussion of patient treatment follow-up, see Chapter 6: Quality Review and Risk Management, at Clinical Practice: Reducing Malpractice Risks].

Causation

A patient seeking damages from a PA must prove that the PA's breach of duty caused the patient to suffer an injury. In legal terms, the patient must prove that the PA's error was the proximate cause of the injury. Proximate cause has been described as a forseeable, natural, or direct cause of injury.

In malpractice cases based on a missed or improper diagnosis, causation is sometimes difficult for a patient to prove because the patient must show that an earlier diagnosis would have changed the course of the disease or condition. In a Pennsylvania case, for example, a PA employed by a medical group examined a patient complaining of breast pain. The PA noted that the patient had fibrocystic breasts and ordered a baseline mammogram, which revealed no abnormalities. One year later, a gynecologist in the medical group saw the patient for a different complaint and found a suspicious breast mass, later diagnosed as Stage II cancer. The patient, who underwent a modified radical mastectomy and chemotherapy, sued the medical group, claiming that the PA was negligent by failing to refer her to a physician when she complained of breast pain. The court ruled in favor of the medical group, because the patient did not prove that mastectomy and chemotherapy could have been avoided if the PA had referred her to a physician. Because there was no evidence of a lump or abnormality in the mammogram, the court held, there was no evidence that a physician would have discovered anything more than the PA did. Because it was unknown when the cancer would have been detectable by a physician, the court concluded that the patient did not establish that the failure to refer to a physician could have prevented the cancer from spreading [*Montgomery v. South Philadelphia Med. Group,* 656 A.2d 1385 (Pa. Super. Ct. 1995)].

Contributory and Comparative Negligence

Contributory negligence is a defense to a negligence suit in which a defendant argues that he or she should not be liable for the plaintiff's injuries because the plaintiff also acted negligently. Contributory negligence is a harsh rule, preventing a plaintiff from recovering damages even when the defendant is 99 percent at fault and the plaintiff is one percent at fault. As a result, this defense has fallen into disfavor and is banned in all but a handful of jurisdictions.

Comparative negligence is a more modern defense to negligence claims. In response to the all or nothing approach of the contributory negligence defense, most states have adopted the comparative negligence doctrine in which fault is allocated between the plaintiff and the defendant(s) and damages are apportioned accordingly. For example, a noncompliant patient may be found 40 percent responsible for his or her own injuries despite negligent treatment by a PA. The PA may be ordered to pay only 60 percent of the damages.

Negligence Per Se

Negligence per se is the legal argument that a defendant who violates a statute is automatically negligent because the statute constitutes the standard of care. A plaintiff arguing negligence per se must prove that the defendant violated a statute and that the legislature intended the statute to protect individuals in the plaintiff's situation from the type of harm suffered by the plaintiff. If a defendant is negligent per se, the plaintiff need not offer additional evidence on the standard of care, because the statute conclusively establishes the standard. The plaintiff must still prove, however, that the negligence caused the plaintiff's injury.

For PAs, exceeding the scope of PA practice established by statute could lead to a claim of negligence per se. For example, if a state statute prohibits PAs from writing Schedule II prescriptions, and a PA prescribes a Schedule II drug that harms a patient, the patient could sue on a negligence per se theory. The patient could argue that the legislature enacted the prescribing prohibition to prevent patients from being harmed by improper prescriptions, based on the legislature's judgment that PAs lack adequate medical training to safely prescribe Schedule II medications. Because the PA violated a statute, causing the type of harm the legislature intended to prevent, to a person within the class the legislature intended to protect, the court would likely find that the PA violated the standard of care as a matter of law.

INFORMED CONSENT

Because PAs are often responsible for much of the communication with patients, it is critical for PAs to be familiar with the legal requirements for informed consent. State legislatures and courts require health care providers to obtain informed consent before every complex medical procedure, including surgical procedures, some diagnostic tests, drug therapy, and other treatments. Informed consent is not required for simple procedures, such as routine blood tests, if the procedure does not entail significant risks. Instead, the patient's simple permission is sufficient.

The informed consent process requires the provider to explain the risks, benefits, and alternatives connected with a procedure. Simply requiring the patient to sign a form does not satisfy informed consent requirements, as the form serves merely as evidence of the informed consent process. The patient must understand and voluntarily consent to the procedure.

There are two lines of legal reasoning on which a patient can base a lawsuit after undergoing a procedure in the absence of informed consent: the informed consent theory and the battery theory.

Informed Consent Theory

Under the *informed consent* theory, the patient argues either that no consent was given, or that the patient's consent was not informed. In both cases, patients must prove that they would not have undergone the treatment had they been given a choice based on adequate information, and that the particular medical procedure resulted in injury.

To determine whether consent is "informed," courts will generally examine the consent process from the patient's point of view, deciding what information a reasonable patient would have wanted to know before deciding whether to consent. Many state laws have adopted the patient-based standard, rather than adopt the provider's perception of what the patient should know. In Pennsylvania, for example, a physician must inform a patient of the nature of the proposed treatment, its risks, and the alternatives that a reasonable patient would consider material to the decision whether to undergo treatment [40 PA. CONS. STAT. § 1301.103].

Over the years since "informed consent" came into use, courts have been developing, on a case-by-case basis, a list of items that the health care provider must disclose. This list, and the detail required, varies from state to state. In general terms, however, the list includes:

- patient's diagnosis
- nature and purpose of the proposed procedure
- risks and consequences of the procedure
- potential benefits and probability that the procedure will be successful
- feasible alternatives to the procedure
- prognosis if the procedure is not undertaken

Most informed consent cases have arisen from the provider's failure to reveal sufficient information about the risks and consequences of the proposed treatment. A provider is not required to disclose every possible risk. Risks that are very remote and improbable can generally be omitted from disclosure because they are not material to the patient's decision. While courts have not set a specific probability figure to trigger the requirement of disclosure, this threshold is directly related to the severity of the risk in question. For example, one court has held that a provider must disclose even a one percent risk of paralysis [*Canterbury v. Spence,* 464 F.2d 772 (D.C. Cir. 1972)]. By contrast, the risk of a hematoma from drawing a blood sample would not trigger informed consent requirements in any state. Physician assistants should be familiar with the consent procedures followed in their hospital or community, and the detail of information commonly provided by other health care providers in their state. [For further discussion of informed consent, see Chapter 6: Quality Review and Risk Management, at Clinical Practice: Reducing Malpractice Risks.]

Battery

An intentional touching of another person without authorization constitutes *battery.* Unlike the informed consent theory, battery does not require the patient to prove that she suffered any injury—only that the touching was not consented to. Although the absence of an injury may not preclude liability, it will reduce damages to a nominal amount.

As under the informed consent theory, a health care provider can be liable for battery even if a patient has consented to a treatment, if the provider exceeds the scope of the patient's consent. An appeals court in Illinois ruled, for example, that a patient who specifically requested that no male view or touch her unclothed body during childbirth may sue a male nurse who attended the procedure for battery [*Cohen v. Smith,* 648 N.E.2d 329 (Ill. App. Ct. 1995)].

Special Consent Statutes

In addition to statutes delineating the general requirements for informed consent, states have enacted laws governing informed consent in specific situations. Consent laws for minors may specifically address the age at which a minor may consent to treatment for drug or alcohol addiction, psychiatric counseling, sterilization or abortion, emergency treatment, and basic health care. Some state legislatures have addressed the problem of obtaining informed consent from incompetent patients by outlining whose consent may be substituted for the patient's, and under what circumstances. Statutes may also address the consent process for specific medical procedures such as breast cancer treatment, human immunodeficiency virus (HIV) testing, sterilization, or electroconvulsive treatments. Physician assistants should familiarize themselves with any state consent legislation relevant to their practice area. As discussed earlier, violation of a statute may not only lead to the penalties specified in the statute, but can also serve as evidence of negligence, or even serve as the basis of a negligence per se claim.

IMPUTED LIABILITY

Imputed liability is imposed when a nonnegligent party is held liable for the acts of a second, negligent party, on the basis of the relationship between the two parties. Employers, for example, may be held liable for the acts of negligent employees if the employer has supervision and control over the employee and the employer is responsible for that person's actions. For PAs the employment relationship is not the only relationship that can be the basis for imputed liability. Agency principles and the relationship between the PA and supervising physician can also result in imputed liability.

Vicarious Liability

One type of imputed liability is the legal doctrine known as *vicarious liability* or *respondeat superior,* which holds employers responsible for negligent acts of employees even if the employer is without fault. When there is a bona fide employer-employee relationship between a PA and a hospital, for example, the hospital may be held vicariously liable for the PA's negligent acts occurring within the scope of employment. The rationale for this rule is that an employer has the right to control the conduct of an employee and, therefore, should be liable for the employee's negligent conduct.

To recover damages from an employer on the basis of vicarious liability, a plaintiff must prove these elements:

- the negligent actor was the defendant's employee
- the employee who committed the negligent act was acting within the scope of employment
- the employee was negligent
- the employee's negligence caused the plaintiff's injury

Identifying Employees

Although identifying employees may seem straightforward, it is not always easy to do. Providers who are independent contractors working for more than one health care entity, providers exercising hospital privileges, and providers who participate in managed care plans should examine their business relationships to identify who may be required to share liability or defense costs in the event of a malpractice suit. [For a discussion of identifying employees versus independent contractors in a different context, see Chapter 9: Employment Laws.]

The key to identifying an employer who may be liable for an employee's negligence is the degree of control that the defendant exerts over the negligent actor. The courts will not simply rely on the language in any contract between the defendant and the negligent individual, even if the language specifies that the individual is an independent contractor, not an employee. Rather the courts will look at the totality of the circumstances to determine the defendant's level of control, examining factors such as whether the defendant paid a salary, provided fringe benefits, determined the work schedule, and directed day-to-day conduct. [For additional discussion of independent contractors versus employees, see Chapter 9: Employment Laws.]

For example, health care professionals who enter into participation agreements with managed care organizations (MCOs) may be characterized as employees by courts, leading to vicarious liability for the MCO. A New Jersey court, citing *respondeat superior* principles, held a health maintenance organization (HMO) liable for a participating physician's actions. The physician was a specialist and a member of a group that had contracted with the HMO. The court looked at several factors in drawing its conclusion, including the following:

- The contract specified that the physicians' group would abide by HMO policies and procedures, and that each physician would work a certain number of hours at the HMO each week.
- The HMO controlled the number of patients seen and maintained all patient charts and records, including the specialists' records.

- The physicians agreed that they would not let their private practice interfere with their contractual obligations to the HMO.
- The HMO had control over the laboratory facilities and outside consulting services available to the specialists who were required to use in-house medical services available at the HMO unless a procedure was not available, and could not order outside tests unless the primary care physician approved the tests.
- HMO clerks and staff physicians scheduled outside testing, handled the paperwork, and arranged billings.
- The HMO arranged all patient appointments.

[*Dunn v. Praiss,* 606 A.2d 862 (N.J. Super. Ct. 1992)].

Scope of Employment

Scope of employment is the test that courts apply to determine whether an employee was on the job at the time of the negligent act, such that the employer should be held vicariously liable for the employee's acts. Typically, courts have held that an employee was within the scope of employment if the employee was acting in furtherance of the employer's business interests. For example, a PA who escorts a patient to an examination area is acting within the scope of employment, even if the PA acts negligently. Courts presented with an employee who committed an intentional injury such as assault or battery will often find that the employee did not act within the scope of employment. For example, a Georgia appeals court refused to hold a hospital liable after a nurse intentionally gave an unauthorized lethal injection to a patient. The nurse claimed she injected the patient to end his suffering. The court concluded that she was pursuing her own interests and the hospital could not be liable for the injection [*Lucas v. Hosp. Auth. of Dougherty County,* 388 S.E.2d 871 (Ga. Ct. App. 1989)]. Physician assistants sued for acts committed outside the scope of employment should not expect to be reimbursed for defense costs by their professional insurance carriers, nor should they expect their employers to participate in a joint defense. [Notification of professional liability insurers is discussed later at The Filing of a Lawsuit, Service of Summons; see also Chapter 3: Licensure and Scope of Practice, at Disciplinary Actions, Due Process and Disciplinary Procedures for a related discussion on exceeding the scope of employment as a ground for PA discipline.]

Apparent Agency

Another type of imputed liability is *apparent agency,* also known as *ostensible agency*—a legal theory that can be used to hold health care organizations (such as hospitals, physicians' offices, and HMOs) liable for the acts of a negligent PA, even if the PA is not an employee. Understanding agency liability is an important part of evaluating business relationships. A PA who appreciates the significance of contract clauses and other conduct that may establish an agency relationship is a more attractive candidate to a managed care plan, group practice, hospital, or other health care entity.

Unlike the vicarious liability theory, which focuses on the actual relationship between the negligent actor and the employer, the apparent agency theory focuses on how the relationship appeared to the injured party. A patient suing a health care organization under the apparent agency theory must show that (1) the patient reasonably viewed the organization, rather than the individual health care provider, as the source of care, and (2) the organization engaged in conduct that led the patient reasonably to believe that the source of care was the organization or that the individual provider was an employee of the organization. The organization need not actually disclose to patients that they are being treated by employees for this doctrine to apply. Rather, the representation of agency may arise from marketing and other affirmative acts or from omissions that in some way lead patients to conclude that they are receiving treatment from an organization employee.

This doctrine is well illustrated in the ED, where physicians who are not hospital employees typically provide emergency care to the public. The highest court in Illinois has ruled, for example, that a hospital may be liable for the negligent acts of an ED physician, even if the physician is not the hospital's employee. A patient sought treatment at a hospital ED for chest and left arm pain. An ED physician performed several tests, then discharged the patient, who died later that day due to a myocardial infarction. The patient's wife sued the hospital on the basis of the independent contractor physician's negligence under the apparent agency theory. She argued that the hospital was liable because the physician appeared to be a hospital employee, as the hospital consent form stated that care would be provided by "physicians and employees of the hospital." The court agreed, emphasizing that hospitals promote themselves as full-care facilities in advertisements, the public relies on the reputation of particular hospitals, and patients are unlikely to know that ED physicians are not hospital employees. Further, the court concluded that a patient may recover damages if the hospital held itself out as a provider of emergency care without informing the patient that the ED physicians are independent contractors and the patient relied on the hospital to provide complete emergency care, rather than relying on a specific physician [*Gilbert v. Sycamore Mun. Hosp.*, 622 N.E.2d 788 (Ill. 1993)].

In the managed care context, some courts have extended the apparent agency doctrine to hold MCOs liable not only for independent contractor health care providers, but also for nonparticipating providers to whom plan physicians have referred patients. A Michigan court held an independent practice association model HMO liable on agency grounds for the negligence of a specialist who was not a member physician. An HMO primary care physician had referred a patient to the specialist in violation of the HMO's policies. The court cited public policy in its ruling, noting that HMOs collect fees based on the representation that they provide complete health care services, making it unfair to allow HMOs to escape liability by referring members outside the plan [*Decker v. Saini,* No. 88-361768 NH (Mich. Cir. Ct. Sept. 17, 1991)].

Physician Liability

The legal relationship between physician and PA is well established by tradition, case law, statutes, and regulations. As a result of the dependent nature of the PA profession, liability for PA negligence is likely to be imputed to the physician, even if the physician does not employ the PA.

State laws and regulations addressing the supervisory responsibilities of physicians with regard to PAs are the most likely basis of imputed liability. [See Chapter 3: Licensure and Scope of Practice, at Scope of Practice under State PA Practice Laws, for a more detailed discussion of these laws.] Some state laws specifically state that a physician is liable for the negligence of the PA whom the physician supervises. In Ohio, for example, the law states: "A physician assistant's supervising physician assumes legal liability for the services provided by the physician assistant." [Ohio Rev. Code Ann. § 4730.22]. In Vermont, "the supervising physician delegating activities to a physician's assistant shall be legally liable for such activities of the physician's assistant, and the physician's assistant shall in this relationship be the physician's agent." [Vt. Stat. Ann. tit 26, § 1739]. All state PA statutes contain similar provisions that provide a clear basis for supervising physician liability.

DIRECT LIABILITY FOR SUPERVISORS

In addition to liability for the negligence of PAs on the basis of an employment or agency relationship, physicians, physician groups, hospitals, and other PA employers may be directly liable for failing to properly supervise PAs. This type of claim is referred to as negligent supervision. Even if a court or jury finds that a PA is not liable, it may impose liability on a physician for negligent supervision. In this type of case, violation of laws and regulations on PA supervision can serve as evidence in a suit brought by a patient that the supervisor acted negligently. [Chapter 3: Licensure and Scope of Practice, at Scope of Practice under State PA Practice Laws, discusses the statutory and regulatory requirements for PA supervision, and how state medical boards enforce those regulations.]

Even where a state statute or regulation regarding physician supervision of PA practice does not apply, courts may find liability against the PA's employer based on the employer's policies regarding the use of PAs. A federal court in Pennsylvania took this approach and found negligence in a naval medical center's policy of allowing patients to be seen by PAs in the ED and released without having a licensed physician review the patient's chart. A patient came to the ED and was examined by a PA who diagnosed her with the flu, prescribed flu medication, and sent her home. In accordance with ED policy, the patient was not seen by a physician, nor was her chart reviewed by a physician. The patient was later diagnosed with a subarachnoid hemorrhage and died after surgery. The patient's family sued the federal government, arguing that the naval medical center's policy of allowing PAs to evaluate, diagnose, treat, and discharge patients without physician oversight was negligent. The court agreed. Not only did an expert witness testify that even interns who had graduated from medical school were customarily required to have patients' charts reviewed before or soon after discharge, the court explained, but "reason alone" dictated that "a person with only two years of general medical training cannot hope to have the same ability to recognize medical disorders as that possessed by a licensed physician having four years of medical training." Thus, the court concluded that the ED policy in this case violated the standard of care [*Polischeck v. United States,* 535 F. Supp. 1261 (E.D. Pa. 1982)].

DAMAGES

There are two types of damages: *compensatory* and *punitive.* A patient injured by PA negligence may recover compensatory damages, that is, damages that will financially compensate the patient for the injury. Compensatory damages theoretically restore the patient to the position the patient was in prior to the injury. Compensatory damages typically include past and future medical expenses, past and future lost wages, compensation for pain and suffering, and possibly compensation for loss of consortium (loss of society, comfort, and support of one's spouse).

Alleviating Damages

As a practical matter, it is important for PAs to reduce a patient's potential damages as soon as, and as much as, possible once a bad outcome has occurred. If a patient obtains an improved clinical outcome, the potential monetary award, as well as the potential for filing a lawsuit, is greatly reduced. Physician assistants and other health care providers can also facilitate a good malpractice defense by exercising good clinical judgment after possible negligence, as it will allow defense attorneys to portray the providers in a positive light.

More specifically, PAs should not be embarrassed about an unexpected outcome or after making a mistake in patient care. Rather, the PA should be very direct with the supervising physician and ask the physician to become involved in the patient's care as soon as possible. Depending on the circumstances, the PA should consider asking the supervising physician or a specialist to examine the patient and take an active role in the patient's care, rather than merely acting as a consultant. The PA who struggles alone for too long may not only violate the standard of care, but may also open the door to claims that the PA exceeded the scope of practice and that the supervising physician negligently supervised the PA.

It is important to do everything possible to obtain a good clinical outcome for a patient who may sue (or has filed suit) for malpractice. A PA should consult the supervising physician and employer to determine what treatment avenues are available for a dissatisfied patient, advocating the best course of care. In doing so, the PA and supervising physician should consider the highest level of care possible. If an expert surgeon, for example, has developed a treatment technique that can effectively correct the patient's problem, the PA and supervising physician should seriously consider making a referral to that surgeon, rather than continuing with a more conservative course of care that is less likely to succeed.

Caps on Damages

One legislative response to the perceived malpractice crisis has been the enactment of state statutes that impose ceilings on the amount recoverable in an action by a patient against a health care provider. In some statutes, the cap on recovery applies to the total amount of damages that a plaintiff may seek in a malpractice action, while in others, the statutory limit only restricts the amount of noneconomic damages. Noneconomic damages are damages awarded for pain and suffering and loss of consortium, as opposed to economic damages awarded for lost wages and medical expenses. Current caps range from approximately $150,000 to $1 million.

Apportioning Damages

Often, PA liability to a patient is shared with other health care providers, raising the issue of what portion of the damages each provider will pay. In some states, the jury or court will make this determination as part of the medical malpractice verdict. Each provider found liable will only pay a portion of the damages, depending on the level of the provider's responsibility for the patient's injuries. For example, in a case in which a physician and hospital failed to properly supervise a negligent PA, the PA might be liable for 40 percent of the damages, the physician for 40 percent, and the hospital for 20 percent. In other jurisdictions, liability is not apportioned. Rather, each health care provider has *joint and several* liability for the patient's injuries. The patient can sue any or all of the providers, and they are each legally responsible for all of the damages, either as a group, or individually. The patient will collect a full settlement, then the health care providers determine who pays each portion of the damages after the malpractice trial.

Punitive Damages

In some cases, patients may also recover punitive damages. Punitive damages are damages awarded to deter wrongful conduct, rather than to compensate the plaintiff. As a result, they are more commonly awarded against corporations than individuals. Individual health care providers, however, have been ordered to pay punitives in certain circumstances. Punitive damages can be assessed in millions of dollars, because they are meant to punish the defendant and are not proportionate to any actual injury. A court or jury may only order a defendant to pay punitive damages if the defendant's conduct was not merely negligent, but can be characterized as reckless, wanton, or intentional. The standard of wrongfulness necessary to justify a punitive award varies from state to state.

A suit against two physicians demonstrates how courts might loosely interpret the willful and wanton standard in order to award punitives to remedy dramatic suffering. A twenty-three-year-old patient with a puncture wound and infected finger was treated by two physicians on three occasions over the course of several days. Although she was eventually diagnosed with sepsis and treated by a third physician, she died a disfiguring death. A jury awarded the patient's family $1.5 million in punitive damages against the first two physicians. The physicians appealed the punitive damages, arguing that there was no evidence of willful, wanton, or reckless disregard of the patient's rights. The court disagreed and upheld the verdict. The court pointed to the failure to diagnose and treat the patient within the standard of care on three separate occasions, failure to order timely diagnostic tests in light of the patient's continuing complaints, failure to appreciate the seriousness of the patient's deteriorating condition and abnormal blood work, failure to "aggressively monitor" the patient's deteriorating condition, and failure to promptly seek the immediate aid of a specialist once the seriousness of the patient's condition became apparent [*McCourt v. Abernathy,* 457 S.E.2d 603 (S.C. 1995)]. Conduct that may support only compensatory damages in some courts may be deemed willful misconduct supporting punitive damages in other courts.

BALANCING LEGAL AND ETHICAL ISSUES

Certain practice settings and factual circumstances have been the focus of debate concerning the legal and ethical duties of PAs. Physician assistants embarking on a new practice area should consider their ethical obligations, as well as the relationship between ethical duties and liability risks. Ethical duties may impose obligations where liability is not a concern, may be subsumed in legal requirements, or may directly conflict with legal principles. The following legal topics serve as examples of these sometimes problematic interactions. Although these issues may not present an increased risk of liability, PAs should understand the legal implications of their choices in these areas.

Death and Dying Issues

Fearing civil or criminal liability, health care providers have sometimes been reluctant to honor the wishes of terminally ill or persistent vegetative state patients or their families. Although liability is possible, it seems no more likely that health care providers will be held liable for withholding or withdrawing treatment than for the many other decisions and actions they make every day. The best indication of the limited exposure to civil liability is the apparent absence of lawsuits brought against physicians for withholding or withdrawing medical treatment from terminally ill patients with the concurrence of the patient or the family. Nor does participation in assisted suicide seem to present a civil liability risk. Rather, criminal prosecution, discussed later, is a concern for health care providers in some states that have laws against the practice of assisted suicide.

Ethical considerations, on the other hand, play an important role in a health care provider's decision whether to withhold lifesaving or life-sustaining treatment, or to assist a terminally ill patient wishing to commit suicide. Physician assistants should consult the PA code of ethics, as well as articles and discussions addressing these complex issues before deciding on a course of action. [Patient education and advance directives are discussed in Chapter 6: Quality Review and Risk Management, at Clinical Practice: Reducing Malpractice Risks.]

Do Not Resuscitate and No Code Orders

A medical order given by a physician that indicates that in the event of a cardiac or respiratory arrest, no resuscitative measure should be used to revive the patient is known as a "do not resuscitate" (DNR) or no code order. Because the patient has the right to refuse treatment, including life-sustaining measures, it is the patient's choice whether to have the physician write such an order. Just as a patient has the right to refuse all medical treatment or to refuse certain specific treatments such as blood transfusions, the patient may also refuse all or some life-prolonging measures. If refused treatment is given, liability for battery or negligence is possible.

Do not resuscitate orders must be in writing and be signed and dated by the physician. An appropriate consent form or refusal of treatment form should also be signed by the patient, the patient's family, or the patient's surrogate or proxy.

Although DNR orders are common practice in hospitals, some states do not allow their use outside the hospital setting. Physician assistants should consult with counsel or check state laws to determine the effect to be given to the DNR order in their practice setting.

For prehospital and ED care, consent for cardiopulmonary resuscitation is implied unless a valid, written, advance directive states otherwise. The American Medical Association (AMA) Council on Ethical and Judicial Affairs has stated: "Efforts should be made to resuscitate patients who suffer cardiac or respiratory arrest except when circumstances indicate that administration of cardiopulmonary resuscitation (CPR) would be futile or not in accord with the desires or best interests of the patient." [American Medical Association, *Current Medical Opinions* A-96 (June, 1994)]. With respect to emergency care, the presumption at law is that the patient would choose to be resuscitated were the patient able to express such an opinion.

If the patient is incompetent, any health care provider should proceed with caution before placing a DNR order in the medical record or in failing to respond in the event of cardiopulmonary arrest, unless a written advance directive such as a living will clearly indicates the patient's choice. In one leading case, a court ruled against a physician who concluded that a patient was incompetent and issued a no-code order in response to a relative's request. Although a nurse gave evidence that the patient was able to communicate coherently up to a few minutes before his death, the physician relied on the patient's sister, who requested the DNR order. No efforts were made to resuscitate the patient when he stopped breathing. The court held that the patient should have been consulted before the physician gave the DNR order. In addition, the court noted that a year prior to the incident, the patient had suffered from the same type of illness and recovered. Thus, there was a good possibility that the patient would have survived if there had been concerted resuscitation efforts [*Payne v. Marion Gen. Hosp.,* 549 N.E.2d 1043 (Ind. Ct. App. 1990)]. However, it is worth noting that a physician is not required to obtain court approval before entering a DNR order [*see In re Dinnerstein,* 380 N.E.2d 134 (Mass. Ct. App. 1978)].

Physician assistants should never independently determine when not to respond to a patient in need of resuscitation. Rather, this issue must be discussed ahead of time with the attending physician and the patient's family, when possible. If a DNR order is written, it must be signed by the physician and be clearly indicated in the patient's record. The physician's signature will reflect that the PA did not independently decide not to respond to the medical needs of the patient. [Do not resuscitate orders are also discussed in Chapter 6: Quality Review and Risk Management, at Clinical Practice: Reducing Malpractice Risks.]

Assisted Suicide

The medical community has taken a strong position with respect to assisted suicide. Again, PAs should begin consideration of this subject by examining their code of ethics. In addition to the (seemingly low) risk of civil liability for participating in assisted suicide, PAs should consider the criminal ramifications. Currently, many states have statutes that specifically criminalize participation in assisted suicide. These statutes have been challenged by terminally ill patients and their health care providers, who have argued that such patients have a constitutionally protected right to end their lives with the assistance of another person who can protect their dignity and prevent further suffering that may result from an unsuccessful attempt at suicide.

This argument has met with mixed results. The Michigan Supreme Court, for example, rejected that argument and upheld a statute criminalizing assisted suicide, finding that a patient's right to an assisted suicide is not analogous to the recognized right to refuse unwanted medical treatment. The Court emphasized the distinction between suicide and the refusal of life-sustaining medical treatment, and concluded that the due process clause of the federal Constitution does not include a fundamental right to commit suicide, with or without an assistant, and regardless of whether the assistant is a physician [*Michigan v. Kevorkian,* 527 N.W.2d 714 (Mich. 1994), *cert. denied sub nom. Hobbins v. Kelley,* 115 S. Ct. 1795 (1995)]. Other courts have ruled, however, that state legislation criminalizing assisted suicide violates the federal Constitution. The Ninth Circuit has ruled, for example, that a Washington state law making it a crime to aid another person to attempt suicide is unconstitutional because it violates the due process rights of terminally ill competent adults [*Compassion in Dying v. Washington,* 49 F.3d 586 (9th Cir. 1995)].

The U.S. Supreme Court recently heard arguments concerning whether there is a fundamental right to assisted suicide that makes such statutes unconstitutional [*Washington v. Glucksburg,* No. 96-110, *Vacco v. Quill,* No. 95-1858]. Because the Court's decision has not yet been announced, PAs should investigate whether a law criminalizing assisted suicide exists in the states where they practice and whether the statutes continue to be valid.

Treating Patients with HIV or AIDS

According to the AAPA, professional ethics require PAs to provide medical care to patients with HIV or acquired immune deficiency syndrome (AIDS). [AAPA, "Human Immunodeficiency Virus (HIV) Infection," *1995–1996 Policy Manual,* Position Paper No. 9 (1995) (adopted 1989, amended 1990, 1992)].

From a legal perspective, refusing to treat patients with HIV or AIDS also creates a risk, not of medical malpractice, but of liability under federal and state antidiscrimination statutes. The Americans with Disabilities Act (ADA) prohibits discrimination against individuals with disabilities, including HIV and AIDS, by public accommodations, including hospitals and physicians' offices [42 U.S.C. §§ 12181 through 12189]. The Rehabilitation Act is a similar federal antidiscrimination statute, but only regulates entities that accept federal funds [42 U.S.C. § 794]. Courts have held that health care providers that accept Medicare and Medicaid payments are governed by the Rehabilitation Act [*see, e.g., Wagner v. Fair Acres Geriatric Ctr.,* 49 F.3d 1002 (3d Cir. 1995); these laws are discussed in the employment context in Chapter 9: Employment Laws].

An ADA case illustrates the duty of nondiscrimination. A federal court in Ohio ruled that the on-call admitting physician at a hospital violated the ADA when he refused to admit an HIV-positive man who had a skin condition from an allergic drug reaction [*Howe v. Hull,* 873 F. Supp. 72 (N.D. Ohio 1994)]. The patient had a severe allergic reaction to a new prescription medication. He sought treatment in the ED at the nearest hospital, where the attending physician determined that the reaction was not related to AIDS or HIV infection, but that the patient should be admitted to the hospital for further treatment. The hospital's on-call admitting physician expressed primary concern over whether the patient had progressed from HIV-positive to full-blown AIDS status, however, and ultimately denied admission. The patient sued the hospital and the admitting physician, alleging violations of the ADA and the Rehabilitation Act. A jury awarded the patient damages under the Rehabilitation Act, while the ADA claims were submitted to the district judge.

The court ruled that both the hospital and the admitting physician were liable for discrimination under the ADA. In this case, the admitting physician could be personally liable, the court found, because he had the authority and discretion to admit the patient to the hospital, and his decision was not the implementation of an institutional policy at the hospital. The court ruled that the decision not to admit the patient was discriminatory, because the patient's HIV status was the motivating factor in the admitting physician's refusal to admit the patient. Because the ADA does not permit damage awards for violations of its public accommodations provisions, the court permanently ordered the hospital not to further violate the ADA.

In contrast, several courts have held that health care providers did not discriminate against HIV-positive or AIDS patients by exercising precautions to prevent the spread of infection [*see, e.g., North Shore Univ. Hosp. v. Rosa,* 86 N.Y.2d 413 (Ct. App. 1995); *Doe v. Comm'n on Human Rights,* 624 A.2d 440 (D.C. 1993); for a discussion of infection control and standard precautions in the health care setting, see Chapter 6: Quality Review and Risk Management, at Clinical Practice: Reducing Malpractice Risks].

Physician assistants treating patients with HIV or AIDS should also take care not to violate confidentiality rules. [See Chapter 6: Quality Review and Risk Management, at Clinical Practice: Reducing Malpractice Risks, and Chapter 7: Medical Records, at Access to Medical Record Information, for further discussion.] Also, PAs should be aware of federal health and safety regulations pertaining to preventing transmission of blood-borne pathogens. [See Chapter 9: Employment Laws, at Occupational Safety and Health Act.]

Managed Care Participation

The linchpin of managed care is the cost-effective delivery of health care services. Toward this goal, MCOs impose contractual requirements on health care providers who provide health care services to MCO members. Some of these contractual clauses have created a conflict for PAs—whether to comply with the clause in order to continue participating in the plan and receiving payment for services, or reject the clause in the interest of patient care and avoid ethical and legal difficulties.

For example, when an MCO denies coverage for recommended medical treatment, health care providers must examine their ethical obligations and decide whether to provide the treatment at the risk of not being paid. A patient who cannot afford treatment without coverage may later sue the MCO, utilization reviewer, and health care providers for negligently refusing to provide necessary health care. Court decisions in this area have focused on the liability of the MCO (the defendant with the deepest pocket), rejecting the argument that MCOs cannot be liable because patients are free to obtain the desired treatment in the absence of coverage. Courts have found that the denial of coverage does equate to the denial of care [*see, e.g., Wickline v. California,* 239 Cal. Rptr. 810 (Ct. App. 1986)]. Health care providers, including PAs, may be included as parties in these suits, and should assist patients by providing medical information needed to appeal negative coverage decisions to their highest level. Further, a health care provider who discharges or refuses to treat a patient clearly in need of immediate care could be liable for negligence, especially if a provider-patient relationship existed.

"Gag clauses" prohibiting a participating health care provider from informing patients about treatment options not covered by the health plan also conflict with ethical codes and traditional liability principles. The doctrine of informed consent requires health care providers to educate patients about treatment alternatives in the process of obtaining patient consent to a treatment or procedure. Providers who do not comply with gag clauses face deselection from managed care plans, while those who do comply may be liable for failure to obtain informed consent or for malpractice. Recognizing this dilemma, many state legislatures have made these clauses unenforceable. In California, for example, contracts between physicians (or other licensed health care providers) and health care service plans may not contain provisions that

> "interfere with the ability of [the health care provider] to communicate with a patient regarding his or her health care, including, but not limited to, communications regarding treatment options, alternative plans, or other coverage arrangements." [Cal. A.B. No. 3013 (New Laws 1996), to be codified at CAL. BUS. & PROF. CODE § 2056.1].

The law goes on to state that any contract provisions inconsistent with the statute are "void and unenforceable." At the federal level, the Health Care Financing Administration (HCFA) has taken the position that contractual provisions violate the law if they limit a physician's ability to counsel a Medicare beneficiary concerning medically necessary treatment options. [HCFA, Office of Managed Care, *Operational Policy Letter* No. 44, (Nov. 25, 1996)].

WHAT TO EXPECT WHEN A LAWSUIT IS FILED*

A medical malpractice lawsuit is initiated when the plaintiff serves a summons (an order from the court) on the defendant and files a complaint (a document that sets forth the plaintiff's allegations) with the appropriate court. In almost every case, however, a great deal of prelitigation activity precedes the actual filing of a lawsuit. The prelitigation phase can be crucial in determining the ultimate outcome of a lawsuit. For this reason, the PA must behave judiciously and must exercise extreme caution regarding responses to any request for information or any other such prelitigation activity.

Prelitigation Activity

Commonly, the practitioner is put on notice that a patient is dissatisfied with care rendered when the patient fails to appear for a scheduled appointment, when the PA receives an oral or written complaint from the patient, or when the patient orders a copy of the patient's medical record. The PA may also receive inquiries from a subsequent treating physician or from the patient's attorney.

If the PA strongly suspects that a lawsuit is forthcoming, the PA should notify the supervising physician. The PA (or the PA's employer) should also notify any involved insurance carriers (i.e., the employer's insurance carrier, the PA's

---

**Source:* Adapted with permission from S. Huntington, "Untangling the Legal System," in *Managing Risk Through Quality PA Practice: A Guide For Health Care Providers,* pp. 163–172 © 1994. American Academy of Physician Assistants.

insurance carrier, and the carrier for the supervising physician). The PA and the supervising physician can then review the patient's medical record and make a preliminary determination on whether the care administered may have been improper.

It is imperative that the PA exercise extreme caution in discussing the patient's care or allegations. Generally, the PA should refrain from discussing information with anyone other than the defense attorney(s) and the supervising physician. In some cases, the PA should not even discuss the case with the supervising physician if the physician wishes to blame the PA for a bad outcome. Discussions with coworkers are tempting, but should be avoided because coworkers can be called to testify about prior conversations. Most importantly, both the PA and the supervising physician should resist the temptation to speak with the patient or the patient's attorney in an attempt to discourage the filing of the lawsuit or try to explain what may have happened in the care of the patient. A PA facing the threat of a lawsuit, for example, may try to explain the reasons for the patient's treatment or may offer to pay for the alleged damage in an effort to prevent the lawsuit from being filed. These conversations, however, can sometimes be used at trial. Statements may be taken out of context and inconsistencies can be used to impeach the credibility of the PA.

The PA should never alter the patient's medical record in any way. If the PA makes such changes and is discovered, it may completely destroy the PA's credibility before the judge or jury. Moreover, in some states improper record alteration is a criminal offense. If a written request for records is received, the PA should ensure that the request has been signed by the patient or legal guardian, if the patient is incompetent or is a minor. Only in extremely rare instances, and only after consulting an attorney, should the PA forward a copy of the patient's medical records.

Medical records should be carefully secured, because lost records markedly lessen the credibility of the PA and make preparation of defense more difficult. When complying with a record request, the custodian of the records should number them and copy them without making any additions, deletions, or alterations. If X-rays are requested, these, too, should be duplicated or, if this is not feasible, the person who requests the record should be required to go to court to obtain original records.

The Filing of a Lawsuit

Once a PA receives notice that a lawsuit has been filed, the PA should consider a variety of practical issues, from who to inform to what information to collect for attorneys defending the suit.

Service of Summons

The service of a summons means that a lawsuit has been filed and brings that defendant within the jurisdiction of the court. The summons advises the defendant which court has jurisdiction over the lawsuit, the basis for bringing the lawsuit in that court, the identities of the parties to the lawsuit, and the name of the plaintiff's attorneys. The date on which the summons was served on the defendant (date of service) is important because it may provide the basis for a statute of limitation defense if the summons is served too late. The date of service also determines the deadline by which the defendant PA must respond. Failure to respond in time may result in a judgment against the defendant.

Upon receiving the summons, the PA should notify the supervising physician and all involved insurance carriers. The supervising physician and PA employer may or may not also have been served. In addition, the PA must forward the summons to the proper insurance carrier after making a copy. The insurance carrier will assign an attorney to represent the PA. [A detailed discussion of professional liability insurance is beyond the scope of this chapter; physician assistants seeking to obtain liability insurance separate from that of their employer should contact the AAPA for more information; *see also* G. McCammon, "Evaluating Insurance for Professional Liability Risks," in *Managing Risk Through Quality PA Practice: A Guide for Health Care Providers* 3–13 (AAPA 1994).]

If the PA does not carry individual insurance but is covered under the employer's or supervising physician's policy, the PA must immediately provide the summons to the employer so the employer can forward it to the insurance carrier. If a PA is covered by the employer's or supervising physician's insurance, the insurance carrier may appoint one lawyer to represent all defendants. That may result in one attorney representing the PA, several supervising physicians, and a health care entity, such as a hospital or HMO. Depending on the situation, the PA may wish to retain personal counsel. Retaining private counsel can be costly and generally is not reimbursed by the insurance company. However, the PA may be able to convince the carrier of the need for separate representation, particularly if the PA suspects that his or her personal interest may be different than that of the supervising physician or employer and, therefore, may not be fully represented by a single attorney. In some cases, the insurance company may be obligated to retain and pay for separate counsel for the PA. Where the PA has a separate policy from the supervising physician, the PA will be assigned a personal attorney by the insurance carrier.

There are two situations in which a PA should seriously consider retaining personal counsel:

1. if the supervising physician infers that the PA's actions regarding the patient treatment were outside the scope of the responsibilities delegated by the supervising physician
2. if the supervising physician carries minimal or no insurance coverage, and the plaintiff's injuries are so large that the judgment may greatly exceed the amount of coverage provided by the physician's policy

If a summons is served without the *complaint,* the attorney will simply send notice of the PA's appearance to the court and the plaintiff's counsel. The plaintiff's attorney must then send the complaint to the PA's attorney within a specified time period before the summons expires.

The Complaint

The complaint must set forth the PA's duty to the plaintiff, how the PA allegedly breached that duty, how the alleged breach caused the injuries to the plaintiff, and the damages the plaintiff allegedly sustained. The complaint is referred to as a pleading. Specific procedural rules define the requirements for the complaint. Many states require that the complaint not only include a statement of the facts upon which the plaintiff relies in stating the cause of action, but also state the plaintiff's allegations with enough specificity to reasonably inform the defendant of the nature of the claims to be defended against. Regardless of the form of the complaint, the defendant is required to file a responsive pleading called an answer.

Meeting with the Defense Attorney

As soon as feasible, and ideally as soon as possible after receiving the complaint, the PA and the PA's attorney must meet to discuss the case. The PA should provide the attorney with a copy of the pertinent medical records so that the attorney can become familiar with the patient's medical care in light of the PA's alleged violation of the standard of care. The PA should offer assistance in identifying the issues and explaining what happened in the case, especially with regard to clinical issues.

The attorney may be unfamiliar with the PA profession, yet the role of the PA is a pivotal issue in the case. Thus, the attorney may require additional education regarding PAs. Information in a written form is particularly helpful, such as copies of state laws and regulations in the PA's jurisdiction and surrounding states, written policies or position statements from state or national PA associations, medical staff rules and regulations, if applicable, and, most importantly, any written protocols. It is important for the PA's attorney not only to have a copy of applicable state laws regarding PAs, but also to understand how the law is interpreted. In addition, the PA will need to describe the nature of the PA's practice, the responsibilities that have been delegated by the supervising physician, and any protocols, job descriptions, or routines that are practiced in the office, either formal or informal. The PA should also describe the manner in which the supervising physician oversees the PA's activities and any agreements that have been reached with the supervising physician concerning delegation. [For a general discussion of PA scope of practice, see Chapter 3: Licensure and Scope of Practice, at Scope of Practice under State PA Practice Laws.] This educational process may require several encounters. Further, it is important for the PA to be patient and to understand that some confrontational questioning by the attorney is common in order for the attorney to develop a full understanding of the situation.

In general, the PA is an agent of the supervising physician. The PA's practice is composed of those duties delegated by the supervising physician within the allowable scope of practice established under state law. Therefore, in a malpractice suit involving a PA, the first issue generally is whether the care rendered by the PA to the plaintiff was within the scope of the PA's employment. The next issue is whether the care rendered by the PA was consistent with the applicable standard of care or somehow violated any protocols, supervising physician instructions, or applicable laws.

The PA and the PA's attorney should meet with the supervising physician and the physician's attorney. It is likely that the supervising physician also has been sued under the doctrine of vicarious liability. The supervising physician may also be sued for his or her own acts under the theory of negligent supervision. The PA's employer (other than the supervising physician, such as a health care institution) will probably also be named as a defendant. The theories against the employer are usually similar to those brought against the supervising physician.

A *unified defense* among codefendants (i.e., using the same attorney or cooperating jointly in a defense) has tactical advantages such as allowing for more efficient *discovery* (the fact-finding phase of a lawsuit). However, a unified defense may not be possible due to potential cross-claims among the codefendants, or even testimony in which one defendant criticizes another. A cross-claim is a separate cause of action filed by one codefendant against another, usually based upon the existence of a contractual agreement such as an indemnity clause. This may occur, for example, if a PA is providing services in an emergency room through an independent contractor agreement that contains an *indemnity clause* (i.e., the parties are each responsible for the consequences arising out of their respective actions).

If the PA is uninsured, the plaintiff may elect to proceed against the supervising physician or the employer alone under the theory of vicarious liability without specifically naming the PA as a defendant. Suits against a PA that do not also name a supervising physician, however, are extremely rare. The physician or employer is often named as a codefendant under the theory, otherwise known as the "deep pocket" strategy, that the physician or employer has more assets and better insurance coverage than the PA. If a PA is uninsured, the PA is not a deep pocket, while if insured, the PA may be. The plaintiff's attorney usually tries to collect as much money as possible to compensate the patient for damages. A PA's insurance policy alone may not satisfy the judgment for damages. The PA should consider these issues when deciding whether to obtain personal insurance and what limits to choose. [*See, e.g.*, G. McCammon, "Evaluating Insurance for Professional Liability Risks," in *Managing Risk Through Quality PA Practice: A Guide for Health Care Providers* 3–13 (AAPA 1994); M. Hickey and L. DeFacio, "Your Malpractice Insurance Policy: What You Need to Know," in *Professional Liability Handbook: A Basic Guide for Physician Assistants* 9–19 (AAPA 1990)].

Preanswer Motions

Pretrial activities come before the court through *motions*. A motion is a request filed with the court on behalf of a party that seeks a final determination on an issue by the court. The defendant may file a motion to dismiss, asking the court to dispose of the plaintiff's case based on grounds such as inadequacy of the plaintiff's service of process, the court's lack of subject matter jurisdiction, or expiration of the applicable statute of limitations. For instance, the practitioner may not have received a copy of the summons and complaint within the time frame prescribed by law, or the practitioner may be from out of state and allege that the court does not have jurisdiction. If the judge grants such a motion, the case may be forever barred from being brought in any court, or the judge may dismiss it without prejudice, which allows the plaintiff to correct any errors and refile the case at a later date.

The defendant may also file a motion for a *change of venue* (location of the court). Because the plaintiff brings the lawsuit, the plaintiff's attorney normally chooses the venue and may choose a location where the court tends to grant plaintiffs large damage awards, rather than another location that exhibits more deference toward medical practitioner defendants. By motion, the defendant's attorney may convince the court that the cause of action arose in another county, or that both parties reside in another county, or that the suggested county is otherwise more convenient for the parties because of the location of the witnesses and other factors. The court then can order a change of venue to the county where the defendant resides or where the venue would otherwise be proper.

The Answer

If the defendant's attorney finds no grounds to move for dismissal at the complaint stage of the proceedings, or if the court denies the defendant's motion to dismiss, the attorney must file an *answer* to the complaint. As with pretrial motions, a PA should offer to review the *answer* in detail to make sure that the answer is accurate in every way. The answer must separately address each individual allegation in the complaint. Allegations that are not denied in the answer are deemed to be "admitted," which means that the defendant agrees that they are true and may not disagree later. In many cases, the allegations will be answered by a statement that the defendant lacks knowledge or information sufficient to form a belief as to the truth of the allegation. The answer is not the vehicle to explain away the allegations. At this stage it is unlikely either party is aware of all the facts with which to either pursue or defend the matter.

Discovery

Germane facts are learned by both parties through a pretrial process called *discovery.* Discovery normally includes written requests for written answers from the other party called *interrogatories,* requests for relevant documents (e.g., medical records), *depositions* (questions that are asked and answered under oath), *admissions* or *stipulations* (uncontested positions or statements), *examinations,* and *identification of witnesses,* including expert witnesses. Discovery is governed by the procedural rules of the court that address filing requirements, deadlines, and other substantive issues. A party has the right to object to a discovery request, but must state a good-faith reason for the objection. The judge will make a final ruling on all matters relating to discovery.

Interrogatories

Usually, the defendant's attorney will send the plaintiff's attorney a set of interrogatories along with the answer to the complaint. Interrogatories are merely a series of written questions that must be fully and truthfully answered by the party who receives them. The interrogatories must be signed by the party answering them and answered under oath. Acknowledgment by a Notary Public is usually required. Only parties to the lawsuit may serve interrogatories on each other, and interrogatories cannot be served on lay or expert witnesses.

Interrogatories sent to the plaintiff will inquire, among other things, into the plaintiff's past medical history, the identity of other treating health care providers seen by the plaintiff, both before and after the alleged medical malpractice of the defendant, the description of the plaintiff's alleged injuries, disabilities, and disfigurement, the alleged financial losses incurred, and the identity of any expert witnesses. The PA's attorney will also receive interrogatories from the plaintiff that must be answered. The PA should carefully review all answers to interrogatories, even if they seem routine, because any error, even minor or typographical, can be used later to challenge the PA's credibility.

Obtaining Medical Records

Just as the plaintiff obtains as much information from the defendant as possible, the defendant's attorney may also obtain relevant information from the plaintiff. The plaintiff's answers to interrogatories will provide substantive information and will usually list all of the physicians, hospitals, and other health care providers from which the plaintiff has received treatment, both before and after the treatment in question. The defendant's attorney will then *subpoena* (get an official demand from the court) the medical records from each of the health care providers listed.

The acquisition of all of the plaintiff's medical records is crucial because the records may contain information that tends to disprove that the plaintiff's injuries were caused by the PA's treatment. Once a plaintiff has filed a lawsuit alleging personal injuries, the defense is entitled to obtain all of the medical records that it deems pertinent. The defense obtains these records by asking the plaintiff to sign authorizations to release medical records. Most hospitals or other health care providers will not forward the medical records until they have received this release from the plaintiff. The PA's attorney will also subpoena other pertinent records, including employment records, that may either substantiate or refute the plaintiff's claims for lost wages.

The Deposition

Attorneys for each party in a lawsuit are allowed to *depose* (take sworn statements) from the other parties, their employees, fact witnesses, and expert witnesses. Thus, at some point during the pretrial period, the plaintiff's attorney will want to take a deposition from all defendants. Although most practitioners consider the deposition an emotionally grueling ordeal, thorough predeposition preparation will ensure that the process progresses more smoothly. The PA should expect to meet with the personal attorney at least once for a lengthy preparation before the deposition. Although the exact questions are not known before the actual deposition, the defense attorney will advise the PA what questions will probably be asked. Adequate preparation entails a comprehensive review of the medical records and a thorough familiarity with the underlying medical condition for which the PA rendered care to the plaintiff. Moreover, it is often necessary to revisit the scope of practice of a PA and applicable state laws.

Normally any party being deposed (called a deponent) is accompanied by an attorney. While the deponent's attorney may not answer the question or tell the witness how to answer, the attorney will object to any improper questions and generally be on guard for any problems that arise during the deposition. The defense attorney can be very helpful to a PA during a deposition, and the PA should be willing to take counsel from the attorney.

The plaintiff's attorney will probably ask the PA about the standard of care in the clinical scenario in which the plaintiff was treated. If the PA is qualified to answer the question (i.e., has the necessary knowledge), the PA must answer the question. However, if a PA does not understand a question or does not know the answer, the PA should not guess. The PA should be sure to wait after each question before answering in case the defense attorney objects.

During a deposition, the PA may also be asked hypothetical questions. In order for the hypothetical question to be proper, the plaintiff's attorney must phrase the question so as to incorporate the salient facts of the plaintiff's case. Therefore, the attorney may ask whether a plaintiff's injuries could have been caused by the particular course of action taken by the PA. Furthermore, if the PA is qualified through training or experience, the plaintiff's attorney may also ask if the plaintiff's disabilities are likely to be permanent, or whether a particular course of additional therapy will be required to treat the disability. It is crucial for the PA to answer "I do not know" if the PA does not have the requisite knowledge or training to answer specific questions.

A composed, straightforward demeanor is imperative. All answers should be concise. Speculation or personal opinion should be avoided. A deponent who does not know an answer or does not recall certain facts should not hesitate to admit it. The deposition is not a memory test. Medical records should be reviewed during a deposition prior to responding to some questions. If the deponent does not understand a question, or it is improperly phrased or medically incorrect, the PA should tell the attorney that the question cannot be answered in its current form. The attorney will then request that the examiner rephrase the question. Most importantly, a PA should refrain from volunteering information that can provide new grounds for attack. If a question cannot be answered by a mere yes or no, however, a brief qualification may be provided with a preface in order to prevent misinterpretation. If opposing counsel's questions are speculative, harassing, repetitive, irrelevant, or otherwise improper, the deponent's attorney will object to them. After placing the objections on the record, the attorney will then instruct the deponents as to whether to answer the questions. The PA should follow his or her attorney's instructions.

The plaintiff's attorney may depose any health care professional who saw the plaintiff after treatment by the PA, and will also take the depositions of expert witnesses who have been retained to testify on behalf of the PA. The PA's attorney will take the plaintiff's deposition. The PA should attend these depositions if possible. The PA can help the attorney before and during such depositions with issues and questions to ask. In addition, the plaintiff may be less likely to distort or falsify testimony if the PA is present. The defendant's attorney will also take depositions of critical witnesses, including the plaintiff's family members, eyewitnesses, other treating physicians, and the plaintiff's expert medical witnesses. Whenever the PA can be present for depositions, it will be very helpful.

Expert Witnesses

Because the field of medicine is outside the general understanding of the average person, the plaintiff is unqualified to testify as to the applicable standard of care regarding the treatment by a PA and how that standard was allegedly breached or how the breach caused the plaintiff's injuries. Therefore, the plaintiff is generally required to present medical-expert testimony to establish these elements of the malpractice case. The PA must also present expert witnesses. It is not enough merely for the defendant to state under oath that there was no breach in the standard of care. Many jurisdictions have held that standards of practice for a PA can be established either by another PA or by a physician, either because it is the physician who ultimately delegates responsibility to the PA or because the standard of care provided by the PA is the same as the physician standard of care for services provided by the PA.

Expert witnesses should be devoid of any potential bias. Thus, the use of personal friends or coworkers should be avoided. The plaintiff's attorney will frequently retain an expert from a prestigious medical center, which may be outside of the state, or hire a witness through a medical expert organization. The general rule is that if a national standard exists (i.e., a specialty field in which there is a national board), any practitioner certified in that specialty is qualified to testify as an expert to establish the standard of care. However, if the plaintiff's expert is from outside the area in which the defendant practices, the expert may be unfamiliar with the clinical setting or the state laws and regulations about PAs. In addition, many hired medical-expert witnesses may not be familiar with the actual practice of PAs or the appropriate scope of practice. The PA should make every attempt to attend the depositions of the opponent's expert witnesses to identify these issues and to assist in cross-examination of the opposing expert witnesses.

Physical and Mental Examinations

Under both federal and state court rules, a party may be ordered to submit to an independent physical or mental examination when the physical or emotional condition of the party is in controversy. Obviously, this applies in medical malpractice cases. The defendant's attorney may schedule the plaintiff for such an examination to determine whether the plaintiff is suffering from the particular injury or disability claimed. In general, the party who schedules the independent medical examination can choose the type of practitioner to perform the examination. Often, the attorneys for the plaintiff and defense stipulate where they would like the examination to be performed based upon geographical location and specialty. A plaintiff may also be ordered to submit to certain testing such as X-rays, genetic testing, or psychological testing, if those conditions are at issue in the case.

Trial Alternatives

Not every medical malpractice suit results in a trial. Many states either require or encourage parties to resolve the dispute prior to trial by first submitting the claim to a review panel or an arbitrator. In addition, a large percentage of suits are settled by the parties prior to trial to avoid the cost and uncertainty of litigation. Because these methods of resolving disputes are commonplace, PAs should be familiar with these processes.

Pretrial Screening Panels

In response to the tremendous growth in the number of medical malpractice claims, many states have enacted laws that establish either mandatory or voluntary procedures that employ screening panels, either as a preliminary proceeding or as an alternative to litigation of malpractice claims in court. The composition, function, and procedural effect of these panels varies from state to state.

Many states that have enacted pretrial systems have adopted the use of a screening panel, also known as a medical review panel. The screening panel is designed to provide both parties in a malpractice dispute with an impartial, nonbinding assessment of the validity of the plaintiff's claim. The use of these panels is generally mandatory in the states that have enacted them. When a malpractice claim is filed, the dispute is immediately referred to a panel often composed of physicians and attorneys for review of the facts and an evaluation of the merits of the claim. In some states, the panel's findings are introducible as evidence in a subsequent trial. A screening panel's finding is nonbinding and the court is free to accept or reject, in full or in part, the findings of the panel. Use of screening panels encourages the settlement of claims.

Arbitration

Some states have adopted the use of arbitration for resolution of malpractice claims. Arbitration is a process outside of litigation that uses a disinterested third party (or panel of persons) to evaluate the merits of a claim and make a determination to resolve the dispute. There are two types of arbitration proceedings: binding and nonbinding.

A nonbinding arbitration panel is functionally indistinguishable from a screening panel. Its findings serve only as indications of the validity of the plaintiff's claim and as evidence for the court to consider if the parties fail to settle the matter privately.

Binding arbitration, however, is a substitute for the trial system and its decision is binding on the parties and precludes litigation. Binding arbitration of a claim can arise from either a contractual agreement between the parties (called private arbitration) or a state statute providing for mandatory arbitration. A private arbitration agreement is a contract executed by a patient before or during medical care in which the patient agrees to submit any malpractice dispute to arbitration. These agreements have been generally determined to be valid, provided the patient has freely consented to the agreement. State statutes creating mandatory arbitration for malpractice claims, however, have been challenged on constitutional grounds.

Settlement

Settlement offers may arise in various circumstances, such as:

- a request by the defense attorney to the plaintiff's attorney to make a demand for settlement prior to the completion of discovery
- a settlement offer by the defense to the plaintiff's attorney
- an order by the court for the attorneys representing the parties to appear in the judge's chambers for a settlement conference
- an offer by the plaintiff to settle the case to ensure receipt of some compensation for the injuries sustained rather than taking a chance on going to trial and not receiving a favorable verdict

If the case is settled, the parties are barred from ever bringing the lawsuit again. However, if the parties agree to a settlement, the plaintiff must go before the judge and testify under oath that he or she is fully aware that the amount of settlement to be received is a final and full payment, and that the plaintiff understands that he or she is now precluded from ever refiling the case against any of the defendants. In some states, the plaintiff's attorney must also have the court approve the attorney's fees. After the plaintiff goes on record, the attorneys ask the court to approve the settlement. The plaintiff's attorney must execute a release and hold harmless agreement, which is normally drafted by the defense attorney and reviewed by the plaintiff's attorney. Since this actually defines the settlement terms, the release and hold harmless agreement is crucial and should be carefully drafted. The release may include a confidentiality provision forbidding the parties from discussing the allegations in the case or the settlement amount. After the execution of this agreement, the defense attorney then provides plaintiff's counsel with a check in the amount of the agreed settlement.

The PA and defense attorney should take into account seven important considerations in making the decision to settle a case:

1. the strengths and weaknesses of the PA's case and that of the plaintiff's case
2. the amount of the insurance policy and the possibility that the verdict may exceed that amount
3. the appearance and demeanor of the parties
4. the appearance or absence of unified defense among codefendants
5. the estimated length of the trial
6. the availability of key witnesses
7. the amount of money needed to resolve the case

CHAPTER 6

Quality Review and Risk Management

INTRODUCTION

In today's health care environment, PAs must be familiar with the concepts of quality improvement (QI) and risk management (RM), and the methods for implementing them through effective QI/RM programs. During the past decade, these programs have been integrated into the organizational structure of all health care organizations, and all health care practitioners, including PAs, are increasingly expected to apply QI and RM in their daily practice routines. This chapter provides historical background on quality review, as well as a comprehensive review of QI/RM principles and methods. The chapter also provides PAs with a basic understanding of QI and RM concepts and the mechanics of QI/RM programs, including monitoring and evaluation of the quality of patient care, identification of problem areas, implementation of corrective actions, and risk reduction techniques. The chapter concludes with a general overview of some measures PAs may use for reducing risk and enhancing the quality of patient care in their day-to-day practice activities.

HISTORICAL BACKGROUND

The health care industry has long recognized the importance of monitoring health care services with the goal of improving patient care, but the starting point for discussions on the historical development of health care quality review is often dated at 1951, the year that the Joint Commission on Accreditation of Healthcare Organizations (Joint Commission) was established. With the initial objective of developing standards and a monitoring system by which the quality of hospital-based patient care could be objectively measured, the Joint Commission published its *Accreditation Manual for Hospitals,* which has been updated annually since its first publication. Today, hospitals must obtain accredited status to qualify for government funded programs and payment reimbursements. As a result, the standards and quality review concepts outlined in the manual are now widely implemented in hospital QI/RM programs.

To enable a better understanding of QI concepts and the extent to which they currently impact the delivery of health care services, some of the significant changes in both the substance and applicability of the Joint Commission's standards are outlined here.

Conventional Quality Assurance

For most of the 1970s, the Joint Commission standards used quality assurance (QA) terminology and QA programs primarily involved retrospective random medical audits or chart review. The underlying assumption of the early QA process was that quality was determined largely by the actions of individual physicians and other nonphysician health care providers (at the time, predominantly nurses), and that identifying good and bad practitioners would highlight who needs to be better controlled or eliminated from health care delivery systems. Accordingly, hospitals concentrated their efforts on conducting a prescribed number of formal audits that were carried out by physicians or nurse reviewers who compared performance of clinical activities recorded in the medical record to established criteria.

Practitioners identified for such review were subject to peer review and possible reprimand such as restriction of practice privileges or, in the most egregious cases, prohibiting the practitioner from practicing at the hospital. Random surveillance of health care practitioners under the conventional QA approach served to create an incentive for such practitioners to conform to a minimum acceptable standard. While such an approach did identify practitioners rendering care below standard, it did little to foster measurable improvement over time.

As a result, the Joint Commission developed a new QA standard in 1979 that was intended to eliminate the random nature of audits by promoting the development of an organized program directed at coordinating information generated from multiple quality review activities within a health care facility. By 1979, the Joint Commission's quality assurance standards had extended beyond hospitals and were being applied to many types of ambulatory care facilities. The new process became known as the "problem-focused" approach because its goal was to achieve resolution of identified problems.

Continuous Quality Assurance

Although moving toward quality improvement, the problem-focused approach was still an essentially reactive process, which not only failed to identify all potential problems but also maintained quality assurance mechanisms that dealt with problems as they arose rather than looking forward to resolve potential patient care problems on an ongoing basis. In response to these deficiencies, the Joint Commission introduced a new approach in its 1984 *Accreditation Manual for Hospitals,* calling for "monitoring and evaluation" (M&E) of the quality of patient care. M&E emphasized ongoing identification of existing and future problems and encouraged working toward resolutions before the occurrence of any adverse event.

The M&E process was not the only new aspect of QA programs, however; also different from previous QA efforts was the emphasis on monitoring and evaluation of all clinical components of an institution, rather than just provider performance. For the first time, the Joint Commission's QA process focused on the concept that quality of patient care is rarely linked exclusively to physician-clinician performance, but more often to the entire system that supports health care delivery.

The M&E process quickly became the foundation of QA programs at hospitals and other health care facilities, including health maintenance organizations (HMOs) for which the Joint Commission began to develop survey and review systems in 1985. Four years later, the Joint Commission published its *Ambulatory Health Care Standards Manual,* which provided QA standards (including M&E process design) for assessing all types of ambulatory health care. With a large staff of QA professionals, the Joint Commission has been able to continually revise their series of manuals and standards for accreditation.

From the mid to late 1980s, the M&E process was further developed and refined, increasingly reflecting QI concepts. [For a more detailed discussion of the Joint Commission recommendations for implementing an effective M&E process, see Joint Commission Standards.] While the role of the physician's knowledge and judgment continues to remain central to the quality of patient care, the M&E process highlights the fact that there are many points in the continuum of service delivery that are beyond the control of the clinician. The process of managing a bleeding patient, for example, involves numerous clinicians, laboratories, technicians, and information systems and defects in health care delivery can occur at any step of this process—the decision to triage, the drawing and transporting of blood samples, or the decision to operate. The evolving QA/QI approach thus took the focus off the competence of the individual and put it on the design and execution of the entire health care delivery process. [For a more detailed discussion, see Quality Improvement Management Theory.]

Transition to Modern Quality Improvement

During the 1990s, the conversion to QI principles has occurred at a fairly rapid pace within the health care industry, and today continuous quality improvement (CQI) and total quality management (TQM) have become predominant terms in the language of health care quality review. These two terms, and several others, are frequently interchanged, making the vocabulary used to describe new quality review concepts confusing; for example, there appears to be only a subtle distinction between TQM, which refers to the management principle used to guide an organization in a continuous quality improvement effort, and CQI, which can be defined as quality improvement processes that are guided by management theory and systematic information. For the basic overview of quality review provided in this chapter, QI is meant to encompass the numerous labels ascribed to quality improvement philosophy and process.

The concept of QI is derived from a philosophy of management first introduced into American business industry in 1980, following years of successful results in Japanese organizations operating under QI principles since post–World War II. Although formulated by an American statistician, Dr. W. E. Deming, QI management theory was applied in Japanese businesses and industries prior to catching the attention of the business world in the United States. Dr. Deming's original QI concepts outlined step-by-step procedures for improving quality and decreasing costs, and QI management theory has since developed into numerous variations applicable to divergent industries, including the health care industry.

Generally, QI initiatives in the health care realm are built on a strong QA foundation, which remains the most significant component of an effective QI effort. Additional mechanisms for ongoing quality improvement, however, are what separate today's QI process from yesterday's QA approach. The concept of QI, as applied in the health care organization, focuses on all key organizational functions, including governance, management, and support functions as well as direct patient care. Accordingly, implementation of QI efforts involves education at all levels, from top executives to employees paid by the hour, such that the entire organization is following the flow of health care services provided from beginning to end, continuously working together to improve quality at every stage of patient care.

QI process relies on statistical evaluation of appropriately collected data to produce information by which management decisions can be made; a central component of QI is the use of objective data to address any process that has a direct or indirect effect on patients. [For a more detailed discussion of data collection and evaluation, see sections on Outcomes Measurement and Comparative Performance Measurement.] The use of such data under QI principles focuses on opportunities to improve processes rather than individual performance.

The conversion to QI principles throughout the health care industry is partially related to the Joint Commission's transition to QI concepts in the 1990s. In 1992, the Joint Commission introduced a new chapter in its accreditation manuals for hospitals and ambulatory health care entitled "quality assessment and improvement," which marked the beginning of the Joint Commission's transition to advising health care organizations to implement QI concepts. In the managed care realm, the infiltration of QI principles is more accurately linked to the QI focus of the National Committee on Quality Assurance (NCQA), the predominant accrediting body for managed care organizations (MCOs), including HMOs.

QUALITY IMPROVEMENT MANAGEMENT THEORY

The central purpose of QI management theory is to create organizations with a clear vision of what constitutes quality for their "customers" and how individuals working for the organizations can contribute to continually improving the quality in their daily work. A multidisciplinary approach with a highly developed philosophy of management and organizational change, QI relies on scientific and managerial techniques to evaluate and improve quality of services. For health care providers, QI principles of particular significance are derived from six basic concepts:

1. *Process improvement and system analyses.* Process improvement refers to a scientific approach to studying and improving the way small tasks are performed, for example, in the health care context, the process of triaging a patient in the emergency room or booking appointments for acute patient visits. QI theory emphasizes that work is composed of small, interrelated processes, and that the quality of these processes and their outcomes determines the overall quality and efficiency of organizations. The general strategy of process improvement is to study and improve the design of individual processes, including their resultant outcomes.
2. *Knowing and meeting customer expectations.* QI assumes that an organization cannot achieve high quality service or production unless everyone working in the organization knows who the customers are and understands their needs and expectations. In QI theory, "customer" refers to any person who depends on a supplier for a product or service; thus, for PAs, customers include not only patients and their families, but also supervising physicians, other staff physicians, nurses, and ancillary hospital departments. Because each of these customers has particular needs and expectations and specific criteria for quality, knowledge of the full spectrum of needs and expectations in explicit terms is a crucial element of designing QI processes that can satisfy everyone's definition of quality.
3. *Building quality into the process of providing services.* To prevent the costs of poor quality, QI emphasizes that analyzing how a service is provided for the purpose of designing an improved process of service delivery is more important than investing financially and organizationally in inspection systems (such as measuring outcomes and reporting adverse

patient care incidents). In the health care context, low quality of care leading to a poor clinical outcome often does not involve practitioner incompetence; rather, such outcomes frequently result because the design of certain work processes failed both the providers and the patients. Reporting incidents such as misdiagnosis of a breast lump, for example, simply identifies the frequency of bad outcomes. For health care providers with QI training, the more critical questions are where and why processes failed in the particular episode of care (e.g., physician's initial exam, scheduling tests, technician's performing the test), and how scientific skills and QI principles can be utilized to improve process design.

4. *Emphasis on process design rather than individual blame.* Quality improvement places the responsibility on leaders and managers to analyze and develop processes that allow workers to take pride in their performance and encourage them to do the best job possible. Quality improvement principles seek to improve process design within which workers do their jobs, rather than place blame on workers, and as a result of an environment free from doubt and defensiveness, workers are far more likely to participate in and contribute to QI initiatives within their organization.
5. *The importance of teamwork.* In the model QI organization, QI objectives become a part of every worker's daily efforts, workers regularly participate in the planning and development of QI initiatives, and the organization rewards each worker for his or her QI efforts. The primary role of management in organizations utilizing QI principles is to involve workers in a particular process in striving for improved process design and function. To accomplish this objective, QI management theory relies on the formation of cross-functional project teams assigned to study and improve specific work processes. [See Implementing Quality Improvement Programs.]
6. *Scientific approach to evaluating processes.* A key QI principle is that quality services are the outgrowth of methodical efforts by everyone in an organization applying a scientific approach to solving problems. Within such approach, quality improvement is considered a process itself; the measurement of quality through gathering of data and formulation of statistics reflecting performance becomes part of a systematic, ongoing process directed at continuous quality improvement. [See Monitoring and Evaluation Process and Objective Measurement of Quality.]

JOINT COMMISSION STANDARDS

In its various accreditation manuals, the Joint Commission provides that accredited health care organizations (i.e., hospitals, ambulatory health care facilities, and other health care networks) work toward the goal of improving organizational performance on a continuous and ongoing basis. Improvement is defined as activities undertaken by leaders and support staff for the purpose of continuously measuring, assessing, and improving performance of clinical and other processes, and ultimately improving patient health outcomes [*see, e.g.,* Joint Commission, *1997 Hospital Accreditation Standards, Overview: Standard for Improving Organization Performance,* § 2, Standard PI, p. 129 (1997)]. While there are many approaches to improving organization performance, the Joint Commission's standards indicate that all QI programs should contain these elements:

- *Plan.* The hospital has a planned, systematic, organizationwide approach to designing, measuring, assessing, and improving its performance [PI.1].
- *Design.* New processes implemented at the hospital must be designed well [PI.2].
- *Measure.* The hospital must have in place a systematic process to collect data needed to design and assess new processes [PI.3].
- *Assess.* The hospital must also have a systematic process for assessing collected data to determine whether design specifications for new processes were met [PI.4].
- *Improve.* The hospital must systematically improve its performance [PI.5].

In addition to the standard specifically addressing improvement of organizational performance, the Joint Commission's standards cover a wide range of other functions including patient rights and organization ethics, continuum of care, patient and family education, leadership, management of human resources, and management of information. Within those standards, the Joint Commission addresses these areas of performance and quality improvement: member rights and responsibilities; utilization management; credentialing of practitioners; medical records; preventive health services; ethical standards; withdrawal of care and end-of-life treatment policy; satisfaction of consumers, providers, and purchasers; safety of the care delivery environment, including infection control; emergency preparedness planning; and compliance with laws and regulations. Physician assistants practicing in hospitals, ambulatory care facilities, or health care networks that are accredited under the Joint Commission's standards should be familiar with QI requirements and recommendations applicable to their particular practice setting.

NCQA STANDARDS

Established in 1990 under the auspices of the Group Health Association of America (GHAA) and the American Managed Care and Review Association (AMCRA), NCQA has evolved into the primary accrediting organization for MCOs. NCQA's review of MCOs, typically conducted by a team of physicians and administrative personnel with experience in MCO quality management, focuses on clinical and administrative mechanisms for quality assurance and improvement, and on the communication process for problem identification, analysis, and follow-up. NCQA also relies on the Health Employer Data and Information Set (HEDIS) system as a core set of performance measures. [For a more detailed discussion, see Health Plan Employer Data and Information Set.]

NCQA standards are used to evaluate a MCO in the areas of quality management and improvement, utilization management, credentialing, members' rights and responsibilities, preventive health services, and medical records, and to rate the organization on a compliance scale ranging from full compliance to noncompliance. As of August 1996, NCQA had reviewed 330 MCOs: 40 percent received full accreditation, 37 percent received one-year accreditation, 11 percent received provisional accreditation, and 11 percent failed to receive accreditation (with 1 percent of plans under current review and thus having no status) [*see* S. Dacso and C. Dacso, *Managed Care Answer Book* 8–12, 8–13 (2d ed. 1996)].

Physician assistants practicing in MCOs accredited by NCQA should be familiar with NCQA's standards. With respect to quality improvement, NCQA requires that the MCO have a well-organized, comprehensive quality assurance program accountable to its highest organizational levels. NCQA measures quality improvement through review of QI program structure, accountability and coordination with management, content of the QI program, and delegation. Some inquiries NCQA attempts to answer in the course of its review are:

- Does the plan fully examine the quality of care given to its members?
- How well does the plan coordinate all parts of its delivery system?
- What steps does it take to make sure members have access to care in a reasonable amount of time?
- What improvements in care and service can the plan demonstrate?

[*See* S. Dacso and C. Dacso, *Managed Care Answer Book* 8–13, 8–14 (2d ed. 1996).]

During the evaluation process, NCQA focuses on the tracking of issues uncovered by the MCO's QI process, including whether that process follows problems through to their resolution, and will likely review the MCO's QA/QI program description and related policies and procedures; QA/QI studies, projects, and monitoring activities; QA/QI committees; and governing body reports and meeting minutes.

COMPONENTS OF QUALITY IMPROVEMENT PROGRAMS

Largely because of the impetus of the Joint Commission and NCQA, QI principles have been integrated into the organizational structure of an increasing number of hospitals, health care networks, and other health care settings. With this in mind, the following sections focus on the practical and operational aspects of QI programs with which PAs should be familiar if they are to play an effective role in a systematic approach to improving patient care, including specific QI processes, sources of QI information such as outcomes and performance profiling data, and actual implementation of QI programs in the workplace.

Monitoring and Evaluation Process

Despite dramatic changes in the approaches used to ensure quality of patient care, one function that has remained a central part of QA/QI programs through their evolutionary transitions is the M&E process. To assist health care providers in understanding what that process involves, the Joint Commission published recommendations for implementing an effective M&E process, which is essential to an effective QI program [*see* Joint Commission, *Using QI Approaches to Monitor, Evaluate, and Improve Quality* (1991)]. Because these recommendations may be the underlying rationale for a health care organization's particular policies and procedures, and because such policies will likely impact upon clinical practice and performance criteria, PAs should be aware of the Joint Commission's guidelines for developing an M&E process.

As a first step, the Joint Commission recommends that the health care organization's leaders *assign responsibility* amongst themselves for developing and implementing M&E and QI processes, including how implementation priorities will be established and how other staff members will be trained in QI efforts. Organization leaders include members of the governing body, directors of medical staff, clinical departments, nursing, and senior administrative positions.

The organization then, as a second step, needs to *delineate its scope of care and service* or, in other words, identify its key functions, which are those functions that have the greatest impact on quality care and service to the patient. Such functions may include medication use, nursing, blood use, performing minor surgery, or conducting laboratory tests. The organization should involve all of its health care providers in this process to ensure that the full range of activities and services provided to patients is identified within the organization's scope of care.

The third step, according to the Joint Commission's recommendations, requires the organization, typically through functional experts within its various departments and services, to *identify important aspects of care* based on the functions comprising the organization's scope of care. The important aspects of care are those activities that each department determines should receive priority for monitoring, which can include any of the organization's key functions, and/or department-specific procedures, treatments, or other activities related to patient care. The Joint Commission recommends that priority be given to activities that are:

- *high volume*—frequent and repetitive patient care tasks (e.g., suturing of minor lacerations, treatment of upper respiratory infections, or diagnosis of sexually transmitted diseases)
- *high risk for patients*—patient care tasks that possess inherent risks to either patients or staff (e.g., use of medications with a significant risk of anaphylaxis, treatment of sprains and fractures by applying casts, or psychological counseling of suicidal patients)
- *commonly prone to arising in health care delivery problems*—patient care tasks that have traditionally caused problems or resulted in lawsuits for staff and the health care organization (e.g., follow-up of abnormal test results, consulting with patient via telephone, communication problems arising from language barriers, errors in dispensing prescription medications)

Once these priorities have been identified, the organization's leadership should agree with the aspects of care identified for monitoring.

The fourth step involves *identifying indicators of quality,* which typically precedes establishing methods for outcomes measurement within an organization. [For a more detailed discussion of outcome indicators, see Outcomes Measurement.] As defined by the Joint Commission, indicators are measures of objective events occuring during the course of providing care or service to a patient or in support of patient care. After indicators have been identified, they are used to define the activities, procedures, or outcomes that are to be monitored. For each indicator that is identified, objective criteria are developed that describe what the organization considers to be an acceptable level of care for that indicator; for example, blood pressure control as an indicator would be assessed by an objective measure such as maintenance between 100/60 mmHg and 140/90 mmHg, rather than subjective language such as "blood pressure within an appropriate range." Objective criteria allows support staff to assist in data collection for identified indicators.

After indicators and objective criteria are developed, the fifth step calls for *establishing thresholds for evaluation,* also known as TFEs. Particular indicators are pinpointed for further evaluation by using TFEs, which demonstrate levels of noncompliance with established criteria and thereby indicate problem areas or opportunities for improvement of patient care. TFE values are set very low (meaning any occurrence will be reviewed) for significant adverse outcomes such as the patient's death following a cardiac arrest. At the other end of the scale, organizations may set comparatively high TFE values (meaning review only for occurrences clearly not meeting accepted standards) for areas such as a low quality of service rating on patient satisfaction surveys. Other factors may impact upon the determination of a TFE value for a particular indicator, for example, an adverse trend such as an increase in infections following wound care over a period of consecutive months.

The sixth step of the M&E process, *collection and organization of data,* enables the organization to make use of TFEs. Before setting up any elaborate systems for collecting massive amounts of data, however, health care organizations should utilize any existing data tracked by the organization. Where data are lacking, the organization should institute simple methods for data collection, which allow for support staff involvement in the process, as well as readily accessible information. Within a department, an individual or group should be assigned to gather information from specific sources and to organize the data for evaluation; such sources may include patient records and charts, department logs, incident reports and occurrence screens, patient complaints, utilization review documents, laboratory and autopsy reports, infection control reports, and QI committee reports and meeting minutes. The Joint Commission cautions, however, that meaningful evaluation of the data can only be accomplished if the type and number of sources provide for a representative sampling of the health care organization's patient population. [To assist organizations in this area, the Joint Commission outlines various sampling methods in its recommendations and other publications, *see, e.g.,* Joint Commission, *Using QI Approaches to Monitor, Evaluate, and Improve Quality* (1991)].

The next stage of the M&E process calls for *comparing,* at predetermined intervals, the *collected data with the TFE for each indicator.* If such comparison indicates that the TFEs' established criteria were complied with, then no further evaluation is necessary. In cases where the TFE is reached or exceeded, however, an in-depth review and subsequent evaluation is needed to determine whether substandard care exists for the relevant indicators. A health care organization may establish a team of representatives working within the sections involved to undertake further evaluation and determine the problem areas.

In-depth review teams may also be authorized to take corrective actions they consider appropriate, although some health care organizations restrict the teams' role to making recommendations for actions to organization leaders. In either case, *developing and implementing a plan of corrective action* is the eighth step of the M&E process. Plans of action should include, if possible, a way to eliminate the problem. If not possible, an action plan should at least recommend measures for resolving deficiencies, providing necessary staff education, and otherwise improving quality of patient care. Moreover, corrective actions should include risk management elements, including emphasis on ways to prevent occurrences of identified problems in the future and on measures that can be instituted in daily practice for the purpose of reducing the risks of malpractice lawsuits. [For a more detailed discussion, see Risk Management and Clinical Practice: Reducing Malpractice Risks.]

The next stage of the M&E process involves *assessing the effectiveness of corrective actions.* Monitoring and evaluation of the results of the corrective action should be undertaken on a periodic basis. The duration of repeat monitoring is usually determined when the action is first implemented, and if results indicate that further action is needed, additional measures may be implemented. The Joint Commission recommends maintaining a log of identified problems that indicates when each problem was discovered, the parties considered responsible, the planned corrective action, the frequency of review after implementing the action, and a date of completion (detailing results of the action). A log can then be reviewed at meetings of QA/QI committees, which may review each problem for the purpose of assessing the need for further measures or recognizing other QI opportunities.

The tenth and final step, which is vital to the integration of QI into daily practice of health care providers, requires *communicating the conclusions, recommendations, and effectiveness of corrective actions* to affected individuals, including practitioners involved, QA/QI team members, and organization leaders. Information regarding the successful results of an M&E process needs to be disseminated to encourage and reward those individuals and groups undertaking QI efforts. Additionally, information regarding clinical competence needs to be provided to individuals authorized to assign clinical privileges in accordance with each practitioner's proficiency level. [For a more detailed discussion of clinical privilege delineation and potential legal implications, see Chapter 8: Credentialing and Peer Review.]

Physician assistants can play an important part in the M&E process. Due to a high degree of contact with patients and their families, PAs are in a unique position to observe patient care and identify problem areas and opportunities for improvement. Moreover, PAs are particularly well-suited for involvement on QI teams and committees because of their clinical knowledge and their collegial relationship with supervising physicians and other members of the medical staff. [For a more detailed discussion on getting involved in QI activities, see Implementing Quality Improvement Programs.]

Review of Specific Functions

The M&E process must be integrated with other QI functions, including review processes that should be routinely conducted by medical staff, and organization-wide review activities requiring medical staff participation. The Joint Commission's *Hospital Accreditation Standards* requires medical staff to perform certain quality improvement functions considered to be critical to appropriate oversight of quality of care, and addresses the scope of several of these functions including:

- *review of surgical and other invasive procedures*—ongoing review by the department or service performing such procedures

- *drug usage evaluation*—systematic review of the appropriate use of drugs conducted by medical staff in cooperation with the pharmacy department, nursing services, and administrative staff
- *medical records review*—review of medical records, usually at least quarterly, by multidisciplinary group, including individuals from medical staff, nursing, medical records department, management, and administrative services
- *blood utilization review*—ongoing review of utilization of blood components, including in-depth evaluation of any incident involving adverse reaction to blood products
- *pharmacy and therapeutics*—ongoing evaluation of policies and procedures for selecting, distributing, and administering drugs and diagnostic testing materials performed by medical staff in cooperation with pharmacy, nursing, and management departments
- *risk management activities*—identifying risks of clinical practice and developing programs and procedures to reduce such risks

[For a more detailed discussion of risk managment activities, see Risk Management and Clinical Practice: Reducing Malpractice Risks.]

Medical staff participation in organizationwide review functions also requires the integration of the M&E process. Such activities are usually conducted through facilitywide programs developed and implemented by multidisciplinary committees including members of medical staff, nursing, organization management, and other department-specific personnel. Organizationwide functions include areas such as infection control, hospital safety and emergency preparedness, utilization management, credentialing and peer review, and risk management.

Objective Measurement of Quality

In addition to understanding the essential steps in the M&E process, PAs should also learn the vocabulary and concepts related to measuring outcomes and performance because methods utilized for objective measurement of quality are central to all QI programs. Many of today's health care organizations have begun to use performance profile information, primarily based on outcomes measurement, in compliance with state licensing or accreditation surveying by the Joint Commission (for hospitals) or NCQA (for MCOs). Usually the gathering of such information as part of an M&E process includes review of credentialing and delineation of clinical privileges, which may directly impact on a PA's scope of practice. Outcomes reporting and performance measurement techniques, including the information systems used to organize the collected data into a meaningful format, are discussed in the sections that follow.

Outcomes Measurement

Outcomes measurement refers to a technique for measuring the quality of care through the use of clinical outcomes. Outcomes are measurable changes in the health status of persons, groups, or communities that can be attributed to a specific clinical intervention. Outcomes data include provider-specific performance information, patient reported improvement in functional status, patient satisfaction surveys, and other indicators that are clinically valid and objective measurements of performance. Some of the systems associated with outcomes measurements are described here.

Outcome Indicators. Outcome indicators show whether a health care goal has been achieved. Whether prenatal evaluation and clinical intervention resulted in the outcome of improved birth-weight of live-born infants, for example, is one type of outcome indicator. The Joint Commission recommends the use of outcome indicators and, in the process of accrediting health care organizations, has beta-tested several indicators, including cardiovascular, oncology, trauma, medication use, and infection control indicators. The M&E process within QI programs includes the development and implementation of an outcome indicators monitoring system for the identification of trends or patterns in performance.

To evaluate the significance of an outcome indicator, the measurement must be adjusted for expected frequency of the outcome, which is called risk-adjusted outcome rating. If the outcome indicator demonstrates mortality after coronary heart surgery, for example, the mortality rate can be expected to be substantially different for 55-year-old female nonsmokers as compared to 75-year-old male smokers. It is crucial to the accurate representation of the health care organization's quality of care to adjust outcome indicators for the patient population.

Occurrence Screening. Occurrence screening refers to the use of objective criteria, including outcome indicators, to identify events or elements in patient care that deviate from normal procedure or expected outcome. Although often used in risk management functions (i.e., identifying potential claims), occurrence screening data can be charted and used for QI functions such as identifying problem areas and developing plans for corrective action. [For a more detailed description of occurrence screening, see Sources of Risk Management Information, at Incident Reports.]

Patient Satisfaction Surveys. Outcomes measurement encompasses evaluation of both clinical outcomes for measuring quality of health care and other indicators, such as patient satisfaction surveys, for measuring quality of service. Quality of service usually relates to how the health care system performs in meeting the patient's nonclinical needs and expectations, which may include appointment waiting times, telephone response times, claims handling, courtesy, and overall responsiveness. A patient satisfaction survey can take many forms, from simple conversations between physician and patient as to whether needs were met, to more comprehensive questionnaires asking the patient about access, availability, continuity of care, financial aspects of care, interpersonal aspects of care, and general satisfaction. As discussed earlier, data collection for any outcome indicator, including patient satisfaction surveys, will yield statistically significant results only if the survey relies on proper sampling techniques; to obtain objective data, the structure of questions contained in the survey is also important. [See Monitoring and Evaluation Process.]

Comparative Performance Measurement

Performance data comparisons, based on outcomes measurement, are showing a rapid growth in popularity among both health care organizations and purchasers of health care. Otherwise known as performance profiling, this form of measurement relies on outcome measures to develop performance profiles of individual providers or organizations. In today's health care environment, purchasers of health care plans are increasingly seeking out such data to compare the value of health plans; health care organizations, on the other hand, are utilizing such data in seeking out contracts for services or setting capitation rates [discussed in greater detail at Report Cards]. Regardless of how performance comparison data are utilized, some form of comparative evaluation of provider performance is rapidly becoming a standard practice in the health care industry [*see* W. Burke, "Tools for Evaluating Performance Quality," *Journal of American Academy of Physician Assistants* 21, 23 (Sept. 1996)].

Health care organizations also use performance profiling of individual providers to encourage quality improvement. If performance profiles are presented to individual providers in a way that does not make them fear reprisal or other negative consequences, the health care organization will likely encourage open discussion about unrecognized deficiencies and areas for improvement in a provider's skills. Such discussion may lead affected providers to share information with other interested physicians and clinicians, ultimately resulting in increased education among providers as to the best practices for achieving desired clinical outcomes.

The following sections describe some of the information systems and other tools currently utilized to produce and consolidate health care outcomes data for performance profiling purposes.

Morbidity and Mortality Statistics

An early system of performance data comparison was pioneered by the Health Care Financing Administration (HCFA) when it began publishing crude mortality data for hospitals. Although these statistics certainly reflected accurate counts of deaths as a function of discharges, their use for quality assessment has been widely criticized. Hospitals ranked in accordance with the statistics argued that the data were skewed, inaccurate, and not severity-adjusted. One notable deficiency in the rankings was their reliance on statistics that did not take into account the differences among patient populations served by the hospitals studied [*see, e.g.,* J. Green, "Problems in the Use of Outcome Statistics to Compare Health Care Providers," 58 *Brook L. Rev.* 55 (1992)]. The statistics upon which the ranking was based ignored crucial distinctions, for example, the fact that large urban medical centers, as compared to suburban hospitals, handle a much higher volume of trauma patients and victims of violence, all of whom will have a higher mortality rate. In the past decade, mortality statistics for the purpose of comparing hospital performance have been replaced by more objective and accurate means of measuring quality and performance.

Health Plan Employer Data and Information Set

The HEDIS is a set of standardized performance measures designed to ensure that purchasers and consumers have the information they need to reliably compare the performance of managed health care plans. It is sponsored, supported, and maintained by NCQA and involves 21 HMOs that serve 9.6 million enrollees. The first version of HEDIS was produced in September 1991. Since then, the system has been updated in three subsequent versions; the current HEDIS version 3.0 became operational in 1997.

The HEDIS measures are based on the size of the population served by a participating health plan and clinical outcomes such as breast, cervical, prostate, and colon cancer screening rates; pediatric immunization rates; frequency of emergency department visits (and subsequent admissions) for acute asthma; incidence of first-trimester prenatal visits; and standardized patient satisfaction survey results. In addition to providing third-party payers, employers, and consumers with a standard set of measurements to evaluate the efficacy of a health plan in comparison to other health plans, HEDIS enables a health care provider, through evaluation of HEDIS measures, to identify opportunities for improving the quality of care it provides for its patient population.

A central objective of HEDIS version 3.0 is aggregation of data that improves upon former techniques of performance measurement. Significant features of the new version include:

- *outcomes orientation.* Health plans will be expected to measure how well their patients are able to function in their daily lives, emphasizing the importance of patient care that improves functional health; as with the earlier versions of HEDIS, version 3.0 will include a mix of outcome measures (which examine whether a desired health objective was achieved) and process measures (which examine the steps involved in delivering a particular health care service to a patient).

- *full spectrum of health care.* The data set covers a full range of health care issues from prevention and early detection to acute and chronic care for populations of children, adolescents, adults, and seniors and for conditions of high prevalence such as acquired immune deficiency syndrome (AIDS), breast cancer, smoking addiction, heart disease, and diabetes.
- *uniform measurement standard.* The same measurement standard will be applied to care, whether provided to private consumers or to Medicare or Medicaid beneficiaries and will cover a range of issues, including clinical results, access, satisfaction with patient care, and cost of care; applying the same standard to private and public sector measurements may enable comparison of care across populations as well as across health plans.
- *ongoing improvement.* The value of ongoing improvement is acknowledged by including a set of measures still under development, which serve as "testing" mechanisms for evaluation of performance measures that may be used in future HEDIS versions.

[*See* S. Dacso and C. Dacso, *Managed Care Answer Book* 8–38, 8–39 (2d ed. 1996).]

To fully comprehend health plan performance measures included in HEDIS, PAs who are unfamiliar with this information system may want to review its components. A free draft copy of HEDIS version 3.0 can be obtained by accessing NCQA's online information at http://www.ncqa.org.

Report Cards

A relatively new concept in comparative performance measurement is the notion that a "report card" can be issued for a health care plan or for providers for the purpose of facilitating consumer choice among plans and providers. In the early 1990s, several pioneering health plans—United HealthCare, Group Health Cooperative of Puget Sound, Kaiser Permanente, U.S. Healthcare Corporation, and Ethix Corporation—set out to publish report cards on their activities. Since then, with the rise of commercial health plans and consequent increased competition, many other plans have started to utilize report cards as a means to attract purchasers [*see* S. Dacso and C. Dacso, *Managed Care Answer Book* 8–39 (2d ed. 1996)]. Report card initiatives have also been developed by state agencies [*see, e.g.,* FLA. STAT. ANN. § 408.05(3)(i)]. Although state agency data have typically addressed only hospital performance on specific procedures, a growing number of states have begun to enact health reform legislation that provides for publicly available report cards on health plans.

Individual consumers have also demonstrated an increased interest in comparative data useful to them (e.g., selecting a provider in accordance with performance factors most important to the consumer). Moreover, consumer information surveys have shown that the more information that consumers obtain in the form of report cards, the more sophisticated they become in their ability to use the data [*see, e.g.,* A.G. Gosfield, "Measuring Performance and Quality: The State of the Art and Legal Concerns," in *Health Law Handbook* 31, 46 (1995)]. In such an environment, PAs should be sufficiently familiar with the concept of the report card system in order to engage in conversations with patients who inquire about report card ratings and the methods used to arrive at such ratings.

In formulating a report card system, health care plans use outcome measures to create a performance profile for an individual provider or institutional health care provider. A report card usually addresses these key aspects of health care delivery:

- *Access.* Are health services obtained easily and provided in a timely manner?
- *Appropriateness.* Was the care provided necessary and, where necessary, was that care actually provided?
- *Efficiency.* Was care provided with optimal efficiency and without unnecessary delays?
- *Outcome.* Was the expected outcome achieved successfully and without complications?
- *Patient satisfaction.* Are members satisfied with the health care they are receiving and have the provided services had the desired effect on improving patients' functional health?

[*See* S. Dacso and C. Dacso, *Managed Care Answer Book* 8–3, 8–4 (2d ed. 1996).]

To effectively grade the health care plan's performance in these areas, a report card includes quantitative measurement of quality of care and utilization of services. Data for quality-of-care assessments may be collected from patient satisfaction surveys, chart audits to determine adherence to clinical practice guidelines, access studies demonstrating provider availability, and statistics indicating the level of provider participation in continuing education programs. The outcomes measures typically used in report card systems to evaluate utilization of services include rates of inpatient hospitalization, use of emergency services, frequency of referrals to a specialist, pharmacy costs and adherence to formulary, and use of ancillary providers for laboratory or radiology services.

Aside from using a report card system as a marketing and information dissemination tool, some health care plans use report cards in deciding whether to initially contract (or renew a contract) with an individual provider or medical group. Moreover, some health care networks have based their determinations regarding capitation rates and bonuses for member-providers on report cards. Several years ago, for example, U.S. Healthcare Corporation instituted a quality compensation system that rewards high quality providers by tying the basic capitation rate for each provider to a multiplier "quality factor" that is the sum of scores totaled from measurements in three areas: quality review, comprehensive care, and utilization of services.

Despite consistently high demand, particularly among corporate purchasers, for the type of comparative data that can be ascertained from health plan report cards, there are still considerable doubts about the accuracy of data collected and its validity for comparison purposes. In developing report card systems, health care plans have disagreed, and continue to disagree, about the accuracy of data collection. Difficult questions have persisted as to the selection of indicators and whether they measure anything relevant to quality. Also, reliable, common risk adjustment of data has continued to cause problems with respect to accuracy [for an explanation of risk-adjusted outcomes measurement, see Outcomes Measurement, at Outcome Indicators]. Whether data collected is in fact comparable has proved to be another problematic issue in using report cards for performance comparisons; in comparing, for example, data from plan-specific report cards, reliable methods still need to be developed for ensuring that the population selected and the calculation for indicated events is similar. [*See* A.G. Gosfield, "Measuring Performance and Quality: The State of the Art and Legal Concerns," in *Health Law Handbook* 31, 45 (1995)].

Computer Software for Data Collection

Several commercial software packages are available to health care providers seeking ways to extrapolate clinical information from claims data for the purpose of performance measurement. These programs collect data in several areas, including office encounters; preadmission certification rates; hospital, laboratory, and imaging utilization rates; prescriptive practice patterns; and patient satisfaction and functional assessment survey responses. Most provider-profiling software programs collect International Classification of Diseases, ninth edition (ICD-9) and Current Procedural Terminology, fourth edition (CPT-4) codes from raw claims data. The ICD-9 represents the diagnostic coding system used by providers, hospitals, and medical facilities. The ICD-9 deals with diagnoses, while the CPT coding system concentrates on actual procedures performed. CPT-4 refers to the current coding system used by physicians and clinicians such as PAs to describe medical procedures performed [see Chapter 10: Third-Party Reimbursement, at Billing and Coding Issues, for a discussion of coding for medical services provided by PAs].

Practicing PAs can assist in ensuring the quality of the data processed by becoming familiar with methodologies employed for categorizing disease-specific diagnostic (ICD-9) and treatment (CPT-4) codes. Moreover, PAs can also benefit from a basic understanding of the statistical processes that are used to assimilate these data sources into performance profiles. Contacting the American

Academy of Physician Assistants (AAPA) is a good first step for gathering information in this area [*see, e.g.*, AAPA, *CPT Documentation Guidelines* (available through AAPA's Fast Fax line)].

Because a full explanation of these processes is beyond the scope of this chapter, only a basic description of the software programs for consolidation of data is provided here. Although ICD-9 and CPT-4 encompass thousands of codes, data collection methods usually involve funneling the codes into a few hundred disease-specific categories or conditions such as asthma, diabetes, or congestive heart failure. Computer software programs enable quantification of each disease-specific category by severity of illness, with ratings of low, medium, or high. This is done through program mechanisms that assess an accumulation of codes for a given condition over time (which allows for reconstruction of an episode of illness). These software programs also typically provide for further categorization of data; for example, each disease category can be stratified by demographic factors, including age, sex, and adverse health-related habits such as smoking or drug abuse, and an episode of care can be assessed as brief, intermediate, or prolonged based on codes for a patient and patient-encounter information (e.g., frequency and volume of office visits). [For a more detailed discussion of computer-based evaluation of provider performance, *see* W. Burke, "Tools for Evaluating Performance Quality," *Journal of American Academy of Physician Assistants* 21 (Sept. 1996).]

Implementing Quality Improvement Programs

The ultimate success of a QI program requires commitment by the health care organization's leadership, including the governing body, administration, medical staff, clinicians, and nurses. From the leadership, involvement in QI efforts must be expanded to include the entire organization. A first step in implementing an effective QI program, therefore, is the establishment of a QI steering committee comprised of some senior leaders within the organization. The committee is responsible for providing direction, designing and implementing a QI program, overseeing the progress of that program, assessing the results to identify strengths and weaknesses of the organization, determining QI strategies, creating and tracking management indicators, and providing the appropriate and necessary resources for a successful QI program.

QI Teams

QI teams are multidisciplinary groups of individuals that meet regularly to identify opportunities for improvement, generate ideas as to how to make improvements, select and implement a preferred improvement, and monitor and evaluate the progress of improvement measures. In some health care organizations, an executive committee of the medical staff is appointed to act on behalf of the entire medical staff, which has significant QI responsibilities including ensuring quality patient care, and conducting effective M&E of care and clinical performance of individuals with clinical privileges. [For a related discussion on delineation of clinical privileges for PAs, see Chapter 8: Credentialing and Peer Review, at Clinical Privileges.]

Clinical departments and services may appoint QI teams whose members are assigned to the M&E process and are responsible for communicating the results of implemented corrective actions to other QI committees within the organization. QI teams typically have a chairperson whose responsibilities include continuously assessing and improving services provided within a department, and surveillance of the professional performance of individuals assigned to making clinical privileges recommendations.

Physician assistants interested in active involvement in QI efforts should seek out opportunities for becoming a member of a QI team; in fact, for PAs, initial participation in QI initiatives usually stems from participation on a QI team, which assigns its members M&E responsibilities such as conducting special studies or audits, or developing new M&E indicators. Because PAs possess clinical knowledge and frequently interact with physicians, patients, and other clinical staff, QI team coordinators are usually very receptive to involving PAs in QI activities.

Regardless of whether or not a PA chooses to become a member of a QI team, all PAs should recognize the importance of participating in QI efforts through continuing education in QI and through clinical and medical staff training in QI. An effective QI program requires continuous self-assessment and ongoing education in the principles of QI at every level of the organization.

RISK MANAGEMENT

Following a comprehensive review of quality improvement, perhaps the best way to introduce risk management concepts is to explain their relation to quality improvement. The purposes of RM and QI often are viewed as complementary. The patient safety aspect of RM—preventing events most likely to lead to patient injury—is the area of greatest interaction between QI and RM. Poor quality of care that creates a risk of injury to patients poses financial risks both to health care practitioners and to health care facilities; identification and resolution of problems in patient care—the cornerstones of QI—ultimately prevent events that may result in patient injury and consequently reduce the potential risk of liability to the health care provider. In addition to the common aim of ensuring patient safety, QI and RM use similar methodologies. Both depend on the establishment of screening criteria, collection and analysis of data pertaining to those criteria, and correction of identified problems through improvements in individual practices and the overall health care delivery system.

Nevertheless, QI and RM differ in at least one significant respect related to the perspective each brings to the analysis of data. QI generally approaches the identification and analysis of patient care problems and issues from the perspective of goals for what should occur in the health care organization, whereas RM tends to approach these tasks from the perspective of what should not occur in that organization. Accordingly, QI monitors patient care on an ongoing basis and aims to improve quality of care and prevent adverse outcomes, while RM focuses on risk identification, protecting the organization's financial and personnel assets, and investigating specific incidents that may result in liability for the organization.

In its accreditation manuals, the Joint Commission requires that health care organizations demonstrate integration of QI and RM functions by showing an appropriate sharing of information between established QI and RM committees and a coordinated approach to resolving identified problems [*see* Joint Commission, *1997 Hospital Accreditation Standards,* Standard PI.3.3.2 (1997)]. For example, information obtained through the M&E process conducted in relation to policies and procedures on hospital safety must be shared by QI and RM committees, although each committee ultimately reviews such information and conducts further investigation from differing perspectives.

Process of Risk Management

Risk management can be described as a four-step process used to identify, confront, and prevent risks and to accomplish the goals of an RM program.

1. *Risk identification*—the process of identifying activities that potentially expose the organization to the risk of liability or financial loss. RM committees and risk managers rely on many data sources to identify risks, including incident reports and occurrence screening systems, verbal communication, safety and QI committee reports, and patient complaints [for a more detailed discussion, see Sources of Risk Management Information]. Risk identification is most commonly accomplished retrospectively (based on information on past events or incidents), but is often combined with other approaches, including prospective risk identification (based on an analysis of likely potential exposures), and concurrent risk identification (based on monitoring of situations and events as they occur).
2. *Risk evaluation*—the process of using analytical skills to determine the potential for risk and the financial impact the risk could have on the practitioner or organization. Risk managers attempt to predict the expected loss frequency (how often will an identified risk generate a loss) and loss sever-

ity (how much will the generated loss cost), so that the organization may be prepared to address the consequences of loss events and can prioritize necessary RM efforts. Risk evaluation usually entails analysis of incident reports and claims generated by the health care organization, as well as analysis of relevant statistical studies and surveys from industry associations, government agencies, and independent organizations [see Sources of Risk Management Information, at Surveys and Statistical Studies].

3. *Risk handling*—the process of taking steps to respond to the risks that have been identified. Risk managers must analyze available methods for reducing exposure and potential losses and implement an appropriate course of action. The primary approach utilized for risk handling is risk control (preventing losses from occurring in the first place and reducing the effect of losses that do occur), which can be further classified into several categories, including *risk elimination* (totally avoiding a particular exposure by limiting or completely eliminating an activity, procedure, or particular service as, for example, when a medical group stops offering obstetrical services to avoid exposure to malpractice) and *risk reduction* (reducing or preventing loss through
   a. *loss prevention mechanisms directed at reducing recurrence of adverse events* (e.g., patient, staff, and visitor education programs; updating and revising policies and procedures; and strict credentialing requirements)
   b. *loss control mechanisms directed at minimization of the severity of loss* (e.g., claims management follow-up, preventive maintenance, safety and detection devices, and staff training programs such as early detection methods for adverse drug reactions)).
   [For an excellent source on methods of risk control, *see* C. Benda and F. Rozovsky, *Managed Care and the Law—Liability and Risk Management* § 15.2, at 15-2 through 15-17 (1996).]
4. *Risk monitoring*—the process of continuously monitoring and evaluating the results of RM initiatives. Risk managers must modify techniques as appropriate and review RM processes on an ongoing basis, updating approaches in accordance with changing circumstances or revealed inefficiencies. [For a more detailed discussion, see Implementing Risk Management Programs.]

The first two steps are the most critical in the RM process, and essentially form the core of risk management activities. Prompt identification and evaluation of risk are key to the success of an RM program because it enables the risk manager to initiate appropriate follow-up procedures in a timely manner and to create an accurate priority list of necessary RM interventions, including the appropriate allocation of resources for implementing an effective plan of action.

Sources of Risk Management Information

To identify risks, an RM committee relies on a wide range of collected data, documents, and records. It is essential that the RM committee or department has access to all sources of information required to perform its functions. Moreover, when a particular risk is identified, whether it is an isolated occurrence or a pattern that indicates a recurring problem, there must be a formal mechanism in place for reporting such event(s) to risk managers. Some common sources used for risk identificaton purposes are:

- incident and accident reports
- data on members who utilize greater than average levels of service
- length-of-stay data
- unexpected patient returns for acute care
- variations from clinical practice guidelines and outcome indicators
- patient complaints and patient satisfaction surveys
- accreditation and federal/state inspection reports
- credentialing, recredentialing, and clinical privileges files
- audit reports of internal committees (e.g., safety or infection control) or insurance surveyors

[*See, e.g.,* C. Borda and F. Rozovsky, *Managed Care and the Law—Liability and Risk Management* § 15.2.1, at 15-6 (1996).]

Risk management staff usually find access to these materials necessary for use in analysis and reporting activities or for purposes of deciding upon proposed RM initiatives. Access to some of these materials, however, may require review to be limited to a few specific members of an RM committee in order to maintain any claim to the material's privileged nature and prevent unauthorized disclosure of medical record information. [For a discussion of the confidentiality of peer review documents and medical record information, see Chapter 7: Medical Records; see also Chapter 8: Credentialing and Peer Review for a discussion of confidential peer review information.] The following sections describe in greater detail some of the most commonly used risk identification data sources.

Incident Reports

Incident reports are forms filled out upon the occurrence of an adverse event at the health care organization; they identify the who, what, where, and why of such events, and, if properly completed, they should elicit as many facts as possible from all witnesses and participants in the event. The use of incident reporting systems for identifying risks is widespread among health care institutions. To implement an effective incident reporting system, the institution (through its risk management committee/department) must provide clear definitions and procedures to guide staff members in their incident reporting activities; for example, "incident" should be clearly defined so that staff have an accurate understanding of what sort of events necessitate filling out an incident report. Some examples of reportable events include medication errors, failure of important equipment (defibrillators) during treatment, fires, falls causing injury, electric shocks, and all deaths occurring at the health care facility. Moreover, procedures must be clear as to when and within what time frame such reports should be completed and returned to risk management staff. Clear reporting forms that are easy to complete and analyze (i.e., questions structured to elicit short, objective answers and use of checklists) also enhance the usefulness of incident reports.

In the past decade, many hospitals and other health care institutions have expanded their incident reporting systems into occurrence screening systems. Occurrence screens are predetermined indicators utilized to signal the need for evaluation of some aspect of patient care. For example, events such as unexpected deaths, returns to the surgical suite, adverse drug reactions, or other high-risk incidents typically are included within an occurrence screen, which serves to notify clinicians and medical staff members that such events always require prompt reporting to RM staff and a subsequent investigation. In addition to identifying individual potential claims, occurrence screening data can be charted to assist in identifying trends and problem areas [for discussion of occurrence screening in the QI context, see Outcomes Measurement, at Occurrence Screening]. Many health care organizations have instituted concurrent occurrence screening of high-risk areas or frequently performed procedures associated with risks to enhance the potential for RM intervention prior to an adverse occurrence.

Data from Quality Improvement Evaluations

QI data are an important source of RM input. Just as identification of potential liability risks raises quality of care issues, all outcomes and performance measurements revealing low quality care or opportunites for improvement are of concern to risk managers. As mentioned earlier, the relationship between RM and QI departments must be collaborative, and health care facilities are required to demonstrate coordination of RM and QI efforts.

Surveys and Statistical Studies

For both risk identification and risk evaluation, risk managers at health care organizations frequently make use of their own inspection surveys and questionnaires, as well as those provided by insurance companies and RM consultants. For example, the Emergency Care Research Institute (ECRI), an independent non-profit organization focusing on the safety and efficacy of health technology, puts out a self-assessment questionnaire intended for use by health care providers in identifying potential risk areas. In addition, assessment tools of the Joint Commission, NCQA, the American Hospital Association, and other medical and allied health professional organizations can assist in the process of risk identification and evaluation. Many risk managers also rely on relevant statistical studies during these two steps, although statistics are often available only for the most common exposures that generate frequent or severe losses. Some examples of such studies include statistics published by:

- federal agencies (e.g., the Occupational Safety and Health Administration (OSHA), the Department of Labor, and the Centers for Disease Control)
- state agencies (e.g., workers' compensation commissions and health departments)
- independent organizations (e.g., Jury Verdict Research, an organization that collects and publishes data on jury verdicts related to medical malpractice and other claims)

Patient Complaints

Patient complaints about a particular provider, general dissatisfaction with care, billing procedures or inaccuracies, or angry letters and phone calls about any aspect of health care service provided at the health care organization are excellent sources of risk identification information. A patient's expressed disappointment over an outcome that is less favorable than expected based on the patient's view of information provided by the physician or clinician is another common signal, from the risk manager's perspective, of a potential breakdown in the patient-provider relationship that may lead to professional liability claims. An important RM objective is to reduce the risk of potential legal actions arising from patient dissatisfaction through careful handling of patient complaints, including staff training in effective communication with patients. [See Clinical Practice: Reducing Malpractice Risks, at PA-Patient Communication.] Risk managers also seek to reduce risks in this area by surveying patients about their patient care experience at the health care facility for the purpose of identifying areas of care, procedures, or provider-patient relations that can be improved. Patient satisfaction surveys are used to learn about potential patient-relations problems before an actual complaint occurs. [See Outcomes Measurement, at Patient Satisfaction Surveys, for a discussion of the use of patient surveys as a source for identifying opportunities for quality improvement.]

Clinical Practice Guidelines

Clinical practice guidelines are standardized specifications for medical care developed by a formal process that incorporates the best scientific evidence of effectiveness with expert opinion. Practice guidelines are intended to specify recommendations for treatment methods regarding medical diagnosis and procedures, and should assist the health care practitioner and the patient in making decisions about appropriate health care for specific circumstances.

Over 1,800 practice guidelines have been developed by national medical specialty societies, including the American Cancer Society, the National Institutes of Health, the American Medical Association, and the federal Agency for Health Care Policy and Research. The use of practice guidelines, also known as practice parameters, clinical pathways, and clinical protocols, by health care facilities has recently shown rapid expansion, and guidelines have been developed for application in most areas of medical practice. [For a listing of clinical practice guidelines and organizations that regularly publish them, *see* J. Forster, "Applying Practice Guidelines Wisely and Effectively," *Journal of American Academy of Physician Assistants* 67 (Sept. 1996).]

Because of their widespread use in the health care industry, PAs should understand the purpose of clinical practice guidelines, and how their development and use involves both QI and RM programs. From the QI perspective, clinical practice guidelines are useful tools for enhancing quality of patient care because they are directed at reducing the amount of practice variation and inappropriate care. Moreover, guidelines have been shown to reduce the use of ineffective medical therapies and thereby minimize unnecessary costs for uncertain medical treatments. These results are supported by QI initiatives that stress the reduction of variability as a way of enhancing quality and reducing costs.

Risk management departments or committees, however, are interested in clinical practice guidelines from the perspective of loss prevention (e.g., Will they reduce the frequency of adverse occurrences?). Risk managers, along with legal counsel, should be consulted during the practice guideline development process to ensure that guidelines are reasonable and will be reasonably applied. Moreover, it is the role of the risk management staff to act as advisors to the medical staff regarding the implementation and proper use of practice guidelines; physicians, in particular, need to be educated on the significance of guidelines' structure and format and their relation to how a court will interpret guidelines as reliable authority on the standard of care.

Related and equally important functions of risk managers are to work with legal counsel to ensure that practice guidelines are used appropriately in litigation and to be aware of any state laws that may allow a physician to use compliance with practice guidelines as a defense in a malpractice suit. Several states, for example, are currently conducting projects that use clinical practice guidelines for medical specialties with high risk liability claims [*see, e.g.*, ME. REV. STAT. ANN. tit. 24, §§ 2971 through 2979]. Under such projects, physicians charged with negligence can achieve dismissal of a malpractice case by demonstrating that they complied with clinical practice guidelines, which sufficiently proves that they met the standard of care without the need for additional expert testimony. Risk managers should also be aware of statistics on the evidentiary use of clinical practice guidelines by malpractice litigants, and of the malpractice cases decided in the relevant jurisdiction wherein facts before the court included evidence of deviation from a clinical practice guideline. [*See, e.g.,* A.L. Hyams, et al., "Practice Guidelines and Malpractice Litigation: A Two-Way Street," *Annals of Internal Medicine* 122(6): 450–455 (1995).]

From both QI and RM perspectives, it is clear that the development and implementation of clinical practice guidelines must be done in a careful and thoughtful manner. [For a detailed discussion of the clinical practice guideline development process, *see* S. Mitchell, et. al., "Legal Issues Associated with the Use and Development of Practice Guidelines," in B. Youngberg, ed., *Managing the Risks of Managed Care,* (1996).] A multidisciplinary approach is needed to ensure that all aspects of guidelines are evaluated and that both the risks and benefits of using guidelines are understood and planned for. PAs can play an important role in this process by serving on panel and consensus groups that create and review clinical practice guidelines prior to their implementation in health care facilities [*see* A. Davis, et al., "Managed Care: Do Corporatized Medicine and PAs Make a Match?" *Journal of American Academy of Physician Assistants* 74, 82–83 (Oct. 1995).]

Implementing Risk Management Programs

When a health care organization's governing body and administrators establish an RM program, they must consider national, state, and local laws pertaining to their particular type of practice. Several states mandate risk management programs as a condition for licensing health care facilities and such statutes often contain specific criteria for developing such programs. [*See, e.g.,* A. Diosegy, "Risk Management" in A. Dellinger, ed., *Healthcare Facilities Law: Critical Issues for Hospitals, HMOs, and Extended Care Facilities* 389, at § 5.1; *see also* FLA. STAT. ANN. § 641.55 (health care facilities, including HMOs); ALASKA STAT. § 18.20.075 (hospitals); N.Y. PUB. HEALTH LAW § 2805-j(1)(a) (hospitals); MD. HEALTH-GEN. CODE ANN. § 19-319(g)]. Establishing an RM program also requires consideration of the Joint Commission standards, OSHA regulations, and other regulatory requirements related to the scope of an RM program's activities and authority [*see, e.g.,* Joint Commission, *1997 Hospital Accreditation Standards,* Standards PI.3 and IM.8 (1997)]. Because there are numerous legal issues involved in establishing and operating an RM program, legal counsel should be at hand during program development, and should remain available for consultation on medico-legal issues that arise in the day-to-day operation of any RM program.

A health care organization's RM committee should be comprised of representatives from the governing body, as well as administration and medical staff. The RM committee ideally should be chaired by a person trained in medical audits and the risk management process; the chairman should be responsible for investigating all incidents that pose significant risk or potential risk to patients, staff, or the organization itself, and for developing and coordinating strategic risk prevention and control measures. Information from all committees (e.g., pharmacy, transfusions, infection control, safety, audit, utilization, medical records, personnel, credentialing, continuing education, product review) regarding potential liability hazards, as well as any other RM-related documents, should be funneled to the chairman or RM committee for review, evaluation, and appropriate action. After identifying potential claims, the chairman and members of the RM committee must have authority to intervene by means of interviewing staff, reviewing all necessary documentation, conducting a thorough investigation, and implementing corrective action plans.

As with QI opportunities for PAs, risk management programs benefit from PAs' input and active participation. As clinicians who have substantial contact with patients and physicians, PAs are in a unique position to identify and report loss control issues and to provide valuable data through careful attention to incident reporting and occurrence screen systems. Moreover, the field of risk management provides new professional opportunities for PAs; if interested and qualified in areas such as insurance, finance, or law, PAs may be particularly well suited for risk management positions.

Practicing PAs, however, can also play a significant role in the analysis, intervention, and monitoring phases of the risk management process, and thus should continually strive to increase their awareness of clinical practice activities that may give rise to liability for the individual clinician and for the health care organization.

CLINICAL PRACTICE: REDUCING MALPRACTICE RISKS

The American Academy of Physician Assistants adopted a policy in 1993 regarding QI and RM initiatives: PAs are strongly encouraged to pursue a pattern of continuous quality improvement in their professional lives, and to incorporate quality and risk management into their clinical practice activities [*see* AAPA, *1995–1996 Policy Manual,* Policy No. 1308-03-03, at 27 (1995)]. The following sections provide a general overview of some of the main areas where PAs can employ risk reduction mechanisms in their clinical practice activities, and thereby prevent potential lawsuits while also enhancing the quality of patient care.

Physician-PA Relationship

As described in Chapter 3 on licensure of PAs, state laws and statutes define the scope of practice for PAs and the supervisory nature of the physician-PA relationship. In addition, some state PA practice statutes require that written job or practice descriptions be on file to further delineate the scope of activities the PA will perform under direct or indirect physician supervision and explain other aspects of the working arrangement (e.g., frequency of chart review). These documents are intended to assist the PA and the physician, as well as other office staff, in understanding the roles and duties of the PA.

Accordingly, a critical element of reducing the liability risks of clinical practice for PAs is knowing applicable state law requirements for PA practice, and practicing in conformity to that law, as well as any physician-PA practice agreement in place. All issues regarding physician supervision and delegation of duties must be addressed and clearly understood by the PA before the PA enters into any employment situation or treats any patients. The best strategy to minimize risks potentially generated by the dependent nature of PA practice is to practice at all times in accordance with both state law requirements and job description criteria established by the supervising physician. [For a more detailed discussion, see Chapter 3: Licensure and Scope of Practice, at Scope of Practice under State PA Practice Laws.]

Office Environment

Physician assistants should be aware of their role in preventing malpractice claims arising from patient dissatisfaction with some aspect of the patient care environment or with the manner in which health care or other services were delivered. This is a part of health care services for which each and every employee of the health care system or physician's office bears some responsibility. Beyond the visit with the clinician or physician, patient dissatisfaction can arise from a wide array of factors, for example, the physical environment of the patient reception area, the length of time a patient has to wait, the way the patient is escorted to the physician's office, the amount of time spent in an examination room prior to the arrival of a clinician or physician, the handling of billing complaints and patient care complaints, and time spent listening, educating, and counseling a patient. [The extent to which every aspect of patient care, including office environment, may give rise to malpractice concerns is reflected in Appendix 6-A: Risk Indicators for the Physician's Office Practice.] For every patient encounter, PAs should keep in mind the ways in which they can reduce patient complaints with respect to the health care environment.

Although PAs may not be directly involved in the first stage of a patient encounter (i.e., responding to calls for appointments, the physical surroundings of the reception area, waiting time, and escorting the patient to an examination), they can, nonetheless, take notice of problem areas and make suggestions for improvement. For example, some points of contact that PAs may want to review when considering ways to improve patient satisfaction during this first interval of the patient visit are:

- *initial phone calls to set up a visit.* A bad impression may be created if a patient is either repeatedly put on hold when calling for an appointment or experiences a "hold" phone call of long duration; receptionists must be informed of the importance of sensitivity and prompt response in taking such calls, which often constitute the first contact between patient and office/health care system.
- *physical environment.* While physical surroundings need not be lavish, they must be clean and organized; the reception area is a significant basis of first impression for some patients who may focus on cleanliness, inconvenience factors, or lack of adequate precautions for protecting patient confidentiality (e.g., telephone conversations or small talk amongst staff can be overheard by patients).
- *waiting time and greeting from reception.* Patients also receive a poor first impression when they are greeted by a receptionist in a manner that does not make them feel cared about; far more important, however, is the length of waiting time in the reception area, which has consistently been highlighted as a predominant patient complaint in patient satisfaction surveys. In offices or facilities where health care providers do not know how long patients are waiting in the reception area, an audit or survey should be conducted on a yearly basis to assess whether waiting time is a problem area, and if it is, scheduling changes should be implemented to improve the situation.

Because of the nature of PA practice, however, the role of PAs in creating an optimal health care environment for patients is obviously centered around the second stage of a patient encounter, which encompasses patient examination, discussion of treatment alternatives, patient education, and treatment follow-up. Physician assistants should make every effort to minimize patient dissatisfaction in performing these functions and should constantly remind themselves of areas that commonly lead to patient complaints, including:

- *quality time spent with the patient.* History-taking and interviews, especially when they are part of initial encounters between the PA and patient, should be patient centered and patient led. It is important to communicate with the patient, and not just talk at the patient. PAs must find ways of communicating that put the patient at ease, thus helping the patient to discuss health concerns and problems; for example, PAs should always introduce themselves, and should welcome the patient, use the patient's name, ensure the patient of privacy and comfort, and engage in some conversation about nonhealth-related topics.

- *ending the patient encounter.* Along with spending quality time with the patient during examination and consultation, PAs should attempt to end the patient encounter with some assurance that the patient has understood the results or treatment and that the patient's concerns have been fully addressed; for example, PAs should strive to end a patient encounter with confidence that the patient's questions have been answered, that the patient understands the next step in the patient's treatment as well as follow-up of laboratory test results, and that the patient has not had a negative patient care experience.
- *informed consent.* This is perhaps one of the most important areas where PAs can reduce the risk of patient dissatisfaction, and it is also a very important concept from a legal standpoint. All PAs should recognize that a patient who does not understand puts the health care provider at great risk if the outcome of treatment is anything less than the patient's expectations. [See PA-Patient Communication, at Informed Consent; for a discussion of the legal doctrine of informed consent, see Chapter 5: Liability, at Informed Consent.]

These are just some of the areas that affect the environment of a health care provider. Physician assistants should evaluate the environment where they practice by objectively reviewing some of these patient points-of-contact, looking at them from the patient's perspective in an effort to identify three or four areas for improvement. Implementing such improvements is usually an easy and inexpensive undertaking, and, ultimately, improved patient care reduces the potential of a medical liability claim and also increases patient satisfaction.

PA-Patient Communication

Effective communication with patients is a fundamental aspect of PA practice, and PAs should recognize the importance of good communications as a means to reducing the risks associated with clinical practice. Physician assistants can play an important part in controlling risk by taking every opportunity to educate patients and their families, and the staff and physicians with whom they work. Patient education is an essential component of both RM and QI efforts, and PAs are particularly well-positioned to educate patients and their families on a continuing basis. [*See, e.g.,* U.S. Preventive Services Task Force, "Disease Prevention: Educating and Counseling Patients," *Journal of American Academy of Physician Assistants* 51 (Mar. 1996)]. From the risk management perspective, thorough education of patients through effective communication is a powerful tool for helping to prevent misunderstandings and patient dissatisfaction, which may lead to malpractice lawsuits [*see* L. DeFacio, "Practical Advice for Preventing Malpractice," in *The Professional Liability Handbook: A Basic Guide for Physician Assistants* 34, 36 (AAPA 1990)].

A particularly important function of good patient education is eliminating patients' unrealistic expectations or misunderstandings about treatments or their results. PAs can play a very significant part in reducing some of the most commonly cited elements of a malpractice allegation, such as the patient's surprise about an unknown complication or anger over an outcome less satisfactory or less desirable than expected, by providing the patient with an accurate and well-communicated explanation of what to expect during the course of treatment (including possible complications) and as an ultimate outcome.

The following sections briefly outline two areas of PA-patient communication subject to specific legal considerations. Both areas are discussed in greater detail in other chapters of the book [see Chapter 5: Liability, at Informed Consent, and Chapter 7: Medical Records, at Liability for Unauthorized Disclosure of Medical Record Information] but are included here because of their importance as measures for reducing malpractice risks.

Informed Consent

All PAs should know that there are legal requirements for informed consent, and that obtaining informed consent is an essential communication process between provider and patient. Although informed consent law varies from state to state, generally, all health care providers must receive permission before performing any operative or invasive procedure on a patient or before prescribing any treatment that involves material risks to the patient. This permission can only be obtained after the patient is aware of the proposed procedure or treatment and alternatives, and the risk associated with each. Every PA should have a routine for consistently and thoroughly engaging in the process of informed consent with the patient and documenting the process in the medical record.

Also falling under this area of communication is the process that PAs should follow in cases of *informed refusal,* involving patients who have obtained information from the health care provider about a proposed procedure or treatment and associated risks, but who refuse to accept treatment or to undergo a particular procedure or therapy. If the patient's refusal has the potential for resulting in injury or deterioration of health, PAs must explain these potential consequences to the patient. If serious medical consequences are at issue, informed refusal should be documented very carefully, including filling out a form detailing the circumstances of refusal and sending a letter to the patient acknowledging the patient's withdrawal from treatment [*see* C. Legler, "What You Must Know About Discontinuing Care," *Journal of American Academy of Physician Assistants* 24 (May 1996)].

Confidentiality

Another significant issue for PAs regarding their communications with patients is the law protecting the confidentiality of information shared between patient and health care providers. All PAs should understand the legal implications of unauthorized, unnecessary, or inappropriate disclosure of information obtained from or communicated to the patient. Although already recognized by most PAs, it is worth reiterating here that, assuming a private setting, breach of patient confidentiality is not at issue when confidential, medically relevant information about a patient is shared with a supervising physician or other physicians and colleagues involved with the patient's care. However, PAs can and should proactively prevent the risk of lawsuits arising from breach of patient confidentiality through careful attention to protection of privacy when conversing or consulting about a patient with physicians and other health care staff. In discussing a patient's medical problem with a physician, for example, PAs must choose an appropriately private setting so that information is not overheard by persons uninvolved in the patient's care (i.e., other patients or family members).

Physician assistants also need to be aware that the same risk of breaching patient confidentiality exists with respect to unauthorized disclosure of information contained in patients' medical records. [See Chapter 7: Medical Records, at Liability for Unauthorized Disclosure of Medical Record Information.] Finally, PAs should know the confidentiality laws and public health reporting requirements (including reporting of human immunodeficiency virus (HIV)-positive test results) of the state in which they practice. These laws specify circumstances when confidentiality of patient information is considered less important than the government's access to information obtained via mandatory reporting requirements. [See Chapter 7: Medical Records, at Access to Medical Record Information.]

Patient Treatment Follow Up

Because PAs are frequently involved with the steps for follow up of patient treatment, this is another area where PAs can play a significant role in reducing potential failure-to-treat malpractice allegations. Strict attention to detail in conjunction with systematic approaches to following up patient care will minimize the risk of missed diagnosis and/or a treatment error. Several measures can be taken by PAs in their daily practice routines to protect against the risk of problems arising from follow-up patient care under various circumstances, including:

- *abnormal lab or X-ray results.* PAs can assist in developing and ensuring the effectiveness of a system for following up all abnormal diagnostic test results (laboratory and X-ray); in some offices and facilities, clinicians have a follow-up system that includes a patient notification mechanism for all diagnostic tests (abnormal and normal). Regardless of what type of follow-up system is implemented, a consistent and uniform method should be adopted throughout the office or facility for review of test results, follow-up, recall, and documentation.
- *compliance with prescribed treatment.* PAs should be careful to recognize that follow-up may be neglected if the patient has not complied with advice to obtain recommended tests. To guard against such occurrences, PAs should take measures to ensure that their practice settings have adequate follow-up and recall systems for handling incomplete test results generated by patient noncompliance.
- *missed appointments.* PAs should be aware of the importance of a system for physician-PA notification and follow-up of patients who have missed scheduled appointments. In the actual follow-up for such patients, PAs should know what information needs to be relayed to the patient, including the risks for failing to keep an appointment or to follow a prescribed treatment or test order.
- *patient referrals or transfer of care.* PAs should understand the liability concerns related to transferring patients to another practitioner for care; this may happen when the patient's problem can be more effectively treated by a specialist or when the provider decides to withdraw from caring for a patient with an ongoing medical condition who refuses to comply with prescribed treatments. Both situations necessitate follow-up steps and other measures to safeguard against malpractice claims; for example, the office or facility should have a system for ensuring that referred patients actually received care from the specialist, as well as a procedure for sending out withdrawal-from-providing-care letters to noncompliant patients [*see* C. Legler, "What You Should Know About Discontinuing Care," *Journal of American Academy of Physician Assistants* 24, 30 (May 1996)].

Documentation

Physician assistants can prevent many malpractice claims simply by making good documentation a central aspect of patient care. This includes knowing when and how to properly document patient care, as well as documenting conversations regarding patient care. PAs should recognize, for example, the importance of documenting not only examination and test results, but also the dates and manner (i.e., any telephone conversations where clinical information is exchanged) in which instructions were given to the patient about the patient's treatment [*see* S. Keavey, "Using the Telephone to Give More and Better Care," *Journal of American Academy of Physician Assistants* 41, 45 (Sept. 1996); for a discussion of legal requirements pertaining to recordkeeping, see Chapter 7: Medical Records, at Recordkeeping Practices].

Advance Directives and Do Not Resuscitate Orders

An advance directive is a legal document designed to communicate to health care providers a patient's wishes with respect to life-sustaining treatments in the case of permanent loss of communication. Advance directives may include living wills, durable powers of attorney, or similar documents portraying the patient's preferences. To provide adequate patient education in the difficult area of end-of-life choices, PAs should be able to address inquiries from patients about advance directives and related laws; indeed, PAs should incorporate the giving of advice about these instruments into their clinical practice, especially when caring for elderly or terminally ill patients [*see, e.g.,* AAPA Professional Practice Council, *End-of-Life Choices* (Mar. 1996); B. Glasz and G. Morrison "Advance Directives: What Your Colleagues Are Thinking and Doing," *Journal of American Academy of Physician Assistants* 51 (Oct. 1995)].

Although beyond the scope of this chapter, the many requirements of the federal Patient Self-Determination Act of 1990 [42 U.S.C. § 1395 cc] should be familiar to the PA. The Patient Self-Determination Act, in brief, requires hospitals, nursing facilities, hospices, home health agencies, and HMOs that participate in Medicare and Medicaid to provide all patients written information about their rights under state law to accept or refuse medical or surgical treatment and to formulate advance directives. PAs also must be familiar with any relevant state law regarding advance directives.

Do not resuscitate (DNR) orders and related legal issues are other areas with which PAs must be familiar. Typically, hospitals have DNR policies affirming the legal right of a patient to direct caregivers. In recent years, states have begun to allow DNR orders outside the hospital, but only a physician may enter a DNR order. The PA should be familiar with the policies and procedures of the hospital or other facility where the PA practices regarding how DNR orders are to be documented and interpreted by health care staff. A typical DNR policy may address the following points (in accordance with any relevant state law requirements):

- statement that orders to resuscitate are standing orders and that cardiopulmonary resuscitation (CPR) should be initiated unless there is a specific written order to the contrary

- statement regarding the patient's wishes
- statement concerning the medical conditions that should be present to justify a DNR order
- statement regarding the role of family members or close friends
- statement regarding placing the DNR order in the patient's medical record
- statement concerning the scope of the DNR order
- statement regarding the obligation of various persons responsible for the care of the patient

[*See generally* K. Darr, "Availability and Use of Advance Directives," Hospital Topics 74: no. 3, at 4 (1996).]

Infection Control

All PAs should be familiar with a guideline issued by the Centers for Disease Control and Prevention (CDC) regarding infection control steps for preventing the transmission of infectious diseases. These steps have gained widespread use in all health care settings as the principal means of preventing parenteral, mucous membrane, and skin exposures of health care providers to HIV and other blood-borne pathogens. The infection control guideline has recently been updated, and the new guideline supersedes previous CDC recommendations for isolation precautions, including the *universal precautions* and *body substance isolation* practices followed in many hospitals.

The new isolation guideline has two "tiers." The first tier consists of *standard precautions* to be followed for the care of all patients in hospitals, regardless of their diagnosis or presumed infection status. The second tier, *transmission-based precautions,* consists of three additional sets of precautions to be used depending on whether the patient poses a risk of transmission that requires airborne, droplet, or contact precautions, or any combination of the precautions. The standard precautions include:

- washing hands after touching body fluids, after removing gloves, between patients, and during procedures on the same patient when necessary to prevent cross-contamination
- wearing clean gloves when touching body fluids, mucous membranes, and nonintact skin; changing gloves between procedures on the same patient after contact with material that may contain a high concentration of microorganisms; removing gloves promptly after use; and washing hands immediately
- wearing eye and mask protection or a face shield, as well as a gown, during patient care activities likely to generate splashes or sprays of body fluids
- handling patient-care equipment soiled with body fluids in a manner that prevents contamination

- taking care to prevent injuries when using sharp instruments
- placing patients who cannot maintain appropriate hygiene in a private room

[Centers for Disease Control and Prevention, "Guideline for Isolation Precautions in Hospitals," reprinted from *Infection Control and Hospital Epidemiology,* 17:53 (1996)]. Although the CDC infection control guideline is specific to hospital settings, PAs in all practice settings are responsible for learning and complying with the infection control requirements of their jobs, as well as any other institutional policies and procedures regarding disease-specific isolation precautions.

APPENDIX 6-A

Risk Indicators for the Physician's Office Practice

Risk Indicator	Yes/No	Score
Credentialing/Competency (Score 3 for each "no" response.)		
1. Is there a current file on each physician?	[ ]/[ ]	________
2. Is there a procedure in place to check the credentials of the physician (group)?	[ ]/[ ]	________
3. Does this procedure include checking information from the National Practitioners Data Bank (NPDB)?	[ ]/[ ]	________
4. Is there a reappointment process in place?	[ ]/[ ]	________
Documentation (Score 3 for each "no" response.)		
1. Does the physician's office record reflect the method of patient referral?	[ ]/[ ]	________
2. Does the record indicate date and time of visit?	[ ]/[ ]	________
3. Does the record reflect discussions with the patient regarding the patient's presenting complaint?	[ ]/[ ]	________
4. Does the physician's office record reflect proposed treatment?	[ ]/[ ]	________
5. Does the record reflect diagnostic tests ordered?	[ ]/[ ]	________
6. Are the results of tests communicated to the patient?	[ ]/[ ]	________
7. Does the record reflect the patient's understanding of the proposed treatment?	[ ]/[ ]	________

Source: Reprinted from V. Masta-Gornic and B. Youngberg, "Developing Tools To Identify and Manage the Risks of Managed Care," in *Managing the Risks of Managed Care*, B. Youngberg, ed., pp. 45–48, © 1996, Aspen Publishers, Inc.

continues

Risk Indicator	Yes/No	Score
8. Does the record reflect unplanned events (complications of treatment)?	[ ]/[ ]	________
Therapeutic Misadventure (Score 3 for each "no" response.)		
1. Is there a specific process for identifying adverse events?	[ ]/[ ]	________
2. Are the physicians knowledgeable regarding communication with the patient/family regarding adverse events?	[ ]/[ ]	________
3. Is there a procedure for evaluating an incident that results in serious injury or death?	[ ]/[ ]	________
Misdiagnosis (Score 3 for each "no" response.)		
1. Is there a system in place for notifying the appropriate personnel if a misdiagnosis is identified?	[ ]/[ ]	________
2. Is there a policy regarding communication to the patient and family with reference to misdiagnosis?	[ ]/[ ]	________
Coordination of Diagnostic Tests (Score 3 for each "no" response.)		
1. Is there a procedure in place for labeling of blood samples?	[ ]/[ ]	________
2. Is there a procedure in place for shipment of blood samples?	[ ]/[ ]	________
3. Is there a procedure in place for reporting laboratory results to patients?	[ ]/[ ]	________
4. Does the physician's office record reflect discussion with patients regarding test results?	[ ]/[ ]	________
5. Is there a procedure in place for reporting test results to a referring physician?	[ ]/[ ]	________
6. Does the physician's office record reflect discussion with the referring physician regarding test results?	[ ]/[ ]	________
7. Is there a procedure in place for "re-call" of patients in the event that an incorrect value or test result was reported to them?	[ ]/[ ]	________
Documented Telephone Advice (Score 3 for each "no" response.)		
1. Is there a procedure in place that addresses documentation of telephone calls?	[ ]/[ ]	________
2. Does the procedure indicate whether the doctor must take the call or if it is appropriate for other staff to give advice?	[ ]/[ ]	________

Risk Indicator	Yes/No	Score
3. Does the procedure require date, time, person calling, patient, problem, name of the office staff member who answers the call, and advice given?	[ ]/[ ]	________
4. Does the procedure address communication regarding this call to the patient's physician (if the physician did not take the call)?	[ ]/[ ]	________
5. Does the procedure address follow-up?	[ ]/[ ]	________
Delay in Treatment/Scheduling (Score 3 for each "no" response.)		
1. Is there a procedure in place to ensure that a patient's complaints are evaluated and an appointment is scheduled in a timely manner?	[ ]/[ ]	________
2. Is there a procedure in place to address follow-up calls to the patient regarding test results?	[ ]/[ ]	________
3. Is there a procedure in place for identifying patients who require a referral?	[ ]/[ ]	________
4. Is there a procedure in place that addresses a process by which the patient's records and a referral letter are transmitted to the consulting physician?	[ ]/[ ]	________
5. Does the physician's office record or reflect discussions held with the patient regarding the referral?	[ ]/[ ]	________
6. Is there a procedure in place for follow-up with the patient who is referred?	[ ]/[ ]	________
7. Does the office record reflect any conversations or correspondence held with the referring physician?	[ ]/[ ]	________
Equipment (Score 2 for each "no" response.)		
1. Is there a policy that controls the purchase of equipment?	[ ]/[ ]	________
2. Is there a procedure in place for preventive maintenance of office equipment?	[ ]/[ ]	________
3. Is there a procedure in place for the replacement or updating of equipment?	[ ]/[ ]	________
4. Is there a policy that mandates the removal of defective equipment?	[ ]/[ ]	________
5. Is there a policy that addresses the disposition of equipment involved in a patient incident?	[ ]/[ ]	________

continues

Risk Indicator	Yes/No	Score
Informed Consent (Score 2 for each "no" response.)		
1. Is there a policy requiring documentation of an "informed consent" discussion with the patient?	[ ]/[ ]	______
2. Is there a form used for general consent to treatment?	[ ]/[ ]	______
3. Is there a consistent methodology for documented informed consent?	[ ]/[ ]	______
Confidentiality (Score 2 for each "no" response.)		
1. Is there a policy in place that discusses the importance of patient confidentiality?	[ ]/[ ]	______
2. Is there a procedure in place for education of the office staff regarding the importance of patient confidentiality?	[ ]/[ ]	______
3. Is there a policy established for the release of medical records?	[ ]/[ ]	______
4. Is there a procedure/policy that establishes a responsible party to speak for a patient who is unable to speak for himself or herself?	[ ]/[ ]	______
5. If a fax machine is used by the office to transmit and receive patient information, is it located away from the sight of patients and/or visitors?	[ ]/[ ]	______
Sufficiency of Insurance Limits (Score 1 for each "no" response.)		
1. Is there an annual review of all physicians' insurance policies substantiating minimum limits of $1 million to $3 million? ($1 million per individual incident with $3 million annual aggregate limit)	[ ]/[ ]	______
2. Is an annual insurance audit performed on the facility to verify appropriate limits?	[ ]/[ ]	______
3. Is there a system in place for notifying the risk manager prior to assuming new risk, to verify the existence of coverage, or to procure additional coverage?	[ ]/[ ]	______
4. Are all nurse practitioners or physician assistants insured at a limit consistent with that for the primary care physicians?	[ ]/[ ]	______
Safety/Security (Score 1 for each "no" response.)		
1. Are all personnel working in the physician's office provided with mandatory yearly reviews regarding fire, electrical, and biohazard safety?	[ ]/[ ]	______

Risk Indicator	Yes/No	Score
2. Are all needles and syringes kept in a location away from patients and visitors?	[ ]/[ ]	________
3. Are all drugs or controlled substances kept in a location away from patients and visitors?	[ ]/[ ]	________
4. Are all staff provided with annual updates for handling of security emergencies?	[ ]/[ ]	________
5. Is there a mechanism in place for reporting all safety and security problems to risk management?	[ ]/[ ]	________
Managed Care Contract Reviews (Score 1 for each "no" response.)		
1. Is there a specific process in place for review of all managed care contracts prior to their signing?	[ ]/[ ]	________
2. Are there a limited number of designated persons within the organization who have authority to sign managed care contracts?	[ ]/[ ]	________
3. Is the maximum potential financial risk assessed prior to the signing of any managed care contract?	[ ]/[ ]	________
4. Are stop-loss products evaluated when the potential financial risk of the managed care contract is deemed to be high?	[ ]/[ ]	________
Appropriate Billing (Score 1 for each "no" response.)		
1. Is there an integrated billing system that allows for a single bill to be sent to the patient for all services provided, including office visit, laboratory tests, X-rays, and physical therapy?	[ ]/[ ]	________
2. Is there a system in place for the reviewing of all bills being disputed by the patient or insurance provider?	[ ]/[ ]	________
3. Is there a system in place for handling payment denials by a managed care plan?	[ ]/[ ]	________
4. Is there a system in place for explaining health plan denials for care to patients and for estimating the cost of that service, if paid for by the patient?	[ ]/[ ]	________
	Total Score	________
	Maximum Score	154

If your score is:

<15	your physician office practice risks are well controlled
16–36	you have opportunity to further mitigate your risks in a physican office practice but are well on the way
>36	you have identified some of the important risks in physician office practice, but there is work to be done

CHAPTER 7

Medical Records

INTRODUCTION

Medical records and the information they contain play a crucial role in the delivery of all health care services. Most importantly, the delivery of appropriate and timely medical care to patients themselves would not be possible without adequate medical record documentation. In addition, risk management and quality assurance programs rely heavily on medical records for information to determine if patient care measures up to specific standards and to identify potential risks. Medical staff peer review is also heavily dependent on information obtained from medical records. Payment and reimbursement of the health care services provided requires accurate and current data about the nature of these services and the identity of the recipient. Finally, any litigation involving the medical treatment or health of an individual will rely on the information contained in the medical record, which frequently will provide the most efficient defense to a malpractice claim.

As health care providers, PAs not only create medical record data, but also rely on the information a record contains. Often the entries by PAs are in records for patients who are cared for by several health care professionals. Because the treatment PAs provide is frequently part of a continuum of medical services, PAs are well-placed to understand the need for accurate and complete medical record information and the importance of proper recordkeeping procedures.

This chapter outlines the legal requirements that apply to the content of a medical record, including contents, authentication, corrections, and destruction. The chapter also illustrates some examples of poor recordkeeping procedures with respect to legibility, the type of information included and excluded from the record, errors, additions, signatures, and countersignatures. Rules governing access to medical record information and liability for the improper disclosure of such information are also examined. The chapter also discusses some of the special legal requirements that apply to specific types of medical information, such as advance directives, consent forms, records from outside providers, and acquired immune deficiency syndrome (AIDS)-related information.

PATIENT RECORD REQUIREMENTS

A variety of statutes and regulations require hospitals to maintain medical records. The public health laws of most states require those who own, manage, or supervise health care facilities to make records of personal and statistical data relating to their patients [*see, e.g.,* N.Y. Pub. Health Law §§ 4165 & 4170]. Although the specific data requirements differ from state to state, each jurisdiction mandates that health care facilities include certain basic information concerning the history and treatment of each patient.

The medical record consists of four types of data concerning an individual: (1) personal, (2) financial, (3) social, and (4) medical. Personal information is usually obtained upon admission and includes name, birth date, sex, marital status, occupation, and other items of identification. Financial data include the name of the patient's employer, the patient's health insurance company, type of insurance and policy number, and other information that enables the facility to bill for its services. Social data include the patient's race, family relationships, community activities, and other information related to the patient's position in society. Also included are any court orders or other directions concerning the patient and other information that may indicate a need for special confidentiality protection.

By far, the most important component of the record is the medical data it contains—a continuously maintained history of the treatment provided to the patient. Depending on the type of health care facility maintaining the record and the nature of the treatment provided, the medical data can include the patient's chief complaint, results of physical examinations, medical history, treatment administered, progress reports, physician's orders, clinical laboratory reports, examinations, X-ray reports, consultation reports, anesthesia records, operation records, signed consent forms, nurses' notes, and specialty reports. Medical data may also include information obtained from outside sources, including diagnostic tests performed at another facility, where reliance on outside reports by in-house health care professionals is reasonable medical practice and consistent with policy.

The medical record may be written, typed, or computer-generated. Regardless of its form, the medical record should be a complete, accurate, and current account of the history, condition, and treatment of the patient. Depending on the format of the record, practices governing the entry of information must strive to achieve these goals. Poor recordkeeping practices can create a multitude of difficulties affecting the quality of care the patient receives, the usefulness of the data for peer review and scientific research, and the potential liability of the health care providers responsible for the patient's treatment.

RECORDKEEPING PRACTICES

The quality of medical records is determined by specific practices relating to the gathering and recording of information in the patient chart itself and, therefore, depends largely on the individuals making the entries. All health care professionals who are called on to make such entries as part of the services they provide to a patient must understand the importance of creating legible, complete, and accurate records.

Importance of a Legible Medical Record

Medical record entries should be made in clear and concise language that can be understood by all professional staff members attending the patient. An ambiguous or illegible record often is worse than no record since it documents a failure of the health care facility and professional staff involved to communicate clearly, and thus may impair the ability of the staff to provide proper treatment.

Legibility is a function of the language used as well as the visual clarity of the information transcribed, whether it be written in cursive, printed, typed, or word-processed. Physician assistants should examine the quality of their handwriting, and have it assessed by a coworker or supervisor. Physician assistants should also be aware that medical records are frequently copied, and that the reproduction process distorts poor handwriting even further. Questions that PAs should answer to determine if they are entering information in a legible fashion include: Are coworkers and colleagues able to decipher the words? Are the spelling and abbreviations accurate? Can colleagues tell what was diagnosed and what diagnostic workup plan was intended? For those with illegible handwriting, a variety of courses and workbooks can offer valuable assistance. Attention to the type of writing instrument used can also make a difference. Finally, transcription is an option for those who have illegible handwriting.

Transcription, however, is not without risks. While dictated records can serve to eliminate legibility problems, they can generate other difficulties with respect to the accuracy of the information transcribed. Physician assistants who adopt this method of entering information in a record should read the transcription and sign or initial the work as they would other entries. The turnaround time for the transcription also contributes to the quality of the record, as the practitioner dictating the report is less able to check the accuracy of the transcription as more time has elapsed. It is important, therefore, to pay close attention to this detail.

Importance of a Complete Medical Record

In addition to being legible, a medical record should contain a complete account of the treatment given to the patient. A record is complete if it contains information sufficient to show clearly what treatment the patient received, why it was given, and if some routine procedure was not given, the reason it was not. The statutes and regulations of several states, Medicare Conditions of Participation, and Joint Commission on Accreditation of Healthcare Organizations (Joint Commission) standards require hospitals to maintain a complete record of the care rendered to a patient during hospitalization [*see, e.g.,* N.J. REV. STAT. § 26: 8-5; 42 C.F.R. § 482.24; and Joint Commission, *Hospital Accreditation Standards,* Standard IM 3.2 (1997)].

The information that a PA should include in a patient's medical record should contain the facts necessary for all professionals involved with the patient to understand the patient's course of treatment. A PA should list the type of contact, specifying whether the information entered in the record was gathered during the course of an office visit, a telephone call, or a hospital visit. Other sources of information, including letters or information received from third parties, should be indicated.

Telephone calls and messages received by other staff members should also be documented if the communication involved evaluating or providing advice for the patient. Symptoms that a patient describes over the phone should be reflected in the chart using the patient's words because clinical descriptions would indicate that a direct examination of the patient took place.

It is also crucial to document a patient's consent or refusal of treatment in the medical record. Obtaining informed consent is more than having a patient sign a form; PAs need to understand that it is the actual process of providing information to the patient that governs whether consent has been given. Although the form is only evidence of consent, this documentary evidence can be crucial in establishing that the patient did give informed consent. In all cases, information on a consent form must be consistent with the information given to the patient. If the information provided is different from that on the consent form, a PA should revise it accordingly before having the patient sign. Even when no form is used, it is essential to record that a complete discussion took place, and that the patient has a complete understanding of the risks and benefits of the recommended treatment. [For a more detailed discussion of liability for failing to obtain a patient's informed consent, see Chapter 5: Liability, at Informed Consent.]

An important subset of consent forms consists of documents that reflect a patient's choices with respect to life-sustaining treatment. The vast majority of states have enacted legislation recognizing the right of competent adults to execute advance directives expressing their wishes as to medical care if they become incapacitated or otherwise unable to make decisions personally. These directions are recorded in documents known as living wills or durable powers of attorney for health care. Patients will frequently execute these documents outside the treatment setting, but copies of the forms must be part of the medical record. The medical record system should prominently display the presence of these forms in a record. [See also Chapter 6: Quality Review and Risk Management, at Clinical Practice: Reducing Malpractice Risks.]

Physician assistants who are providing consultation services or who are evaluating and treating a single condition should indicate the capacity in which they are acting, and document follow-up decisions in the patient's record. For instance, information indicating whether the patient is to be sent back to the referring provider, whether the PA will continue to treat the patient, or whether the PA will take over management of the case should be included in the medical record.

Follow-up and review information must also be carefully charted in a patient's medical record, as this is one of the areas where the risk of malpractice liability is the greatest. Before filing lab, X-ray, or consultation reports in a medical record, the results contained in the report should be reviewed and the document initialed to indicate that such a review has been conducted. Follow-up information about patients relating to missed, canceled, or rescheduled appointments; referral tests; prescribed treatments; and reminders to the patient regarding the treatment plan should all be included in the record. Card file systems or computerized scheduling systems can track and record much of this type of information.

In recording all of this information, a PA should use clear and concise language. The use of abbreviations or other symbols or acronyms should follow the approved list for the facility where the record is maintained. No changes to the meaning of an approved abbreviation should be made. In addition, PAs should be aware that these approved lists frequently do not contain many of the abbreviations commonly found in medical literature. If a PA needs to abbreviate a term that is not on the list or part of standard practice, the PA should spell out the word the first time it is used and include the abbreviation in parentheses.

Authentication and Countersignatures

There are generally no legislative requirements restricting or mandating the identity of professionals who may make entries in a chart. Given the lack of formal requirements in this area, any individual providing care to a patient should be permitted to document that care in the patient's medical record. It is up to the facility to ensure that professionals function within the scope of practice as authorized by state licensing statutes or certification statutes or, in the absence of such statutes, as defined by their professional competence.

The requirement that a PA or other medical practitioner sign the record or a portion thereof exists to ensure authenticity. Authentication is the key element in system reliability and security. The Joint Commission requires that all entries in a medical record be dated and authenticated, and that a method be established to identify the authors of entries [*see* Joint Commission, *Hospital Accreditation Standards,* Standard IM 7.8 (1997)]. Medicare Conditions of Participation also require that entries to a patient's record be authenticated and dated promptly by the person responsible for ordering, providing, or evaluating the service furnished [42 C.F.R. § 482.24(c)(1)].

Traditionally, authentication was made by handwritten signature, but numerous regulatory and accrediting organizations also contemplate authentication by a rubber stamp or computer key. To safeguard against abuses in the utilization of rubber stamps or computer keys, however, many of the standards for authentication contain a requirement that a signature stamp or computer key may be used in lieu of a signature only where the practitioner has placed a signed statement in the administrative files of the health care facility stating that the practitioner is the only person who has possession of the stamp or key and is the only one who will use it [*see, e.g.,* CAL. CODE REGS. tit. 22, § 70751(g)].

A PA's signature on the notes in a medical record indicates that the PA has checked the notes and confirms the facts as they are entered in the record. Entries made by PAs will often require a countersignature by the supervising physician. A supervising physician's countersignature indicates that the physician has reviewed the care provided and the record of that care. State PA practice laws often stipulate how often and to what extent the supervising physician must countersign the medical records of patients treated by supervisee-PAs [*see, e.g.,* CAL CODE REGS. Tit. 16, § 1399-545 (review and countersignature of at least 10 percent of medical records within 30 days for patients treated by PAs); D.C. MUN. REGS. tit. 17, § 4914 (countersignature of all medical orders and progress notes within 48 hours); KAN. ADMIN. REGS. 100-60-10 (countersignature of all patient records at least weekly, and within 48 hours for records of patients seen by PAs in hospitals or medical facilities or for cases wherein PA provided emergency treatment that exceeded the PA's normal scope of practice); N.J. ADMIN. CODE tit. 13, § 13:35-2B (regular review of patient records and countersignature of all medical orders within 24 hours; in outpatient setting, countersignature of patient records must occur within 7 days)].

Health care facilities, health insurance plans, liability insurance carriers, and government benefit programs for disability or social services may also impose similar rules. It is important for PAs to verify these requirements, as well as those specified in state PA practice laws, before performing services and documenting care in medical records for any organization.

Corrections and Alterations

Some medical record entry errors are inevitable. Generally, two kinds of errors occur: (1) minor errors in transcription, spelling, and so forth and (2) more significant errors involving test results, physician orders, inadvertently admitted information, and similar substantive entries. As a general rule, the person who made the incorrect record entry should correct it.

A PA who has made a charting error should cross out the incorrect entry with a single line, enter the correction, initial it, and enter the time and date of the correction. The line through the original entry should be drawn so that it can still be read and leave no doubt as to the original information being corrected. If a correction requires more space than is available near the original entry, the person correcting the record should enter a reference to an addendum to the record and enter the more lengthy correction in the addendum. If the correction is not obvious, is made later, or appears somewhere else in the record, the annotation *error* can be inserted and an explanation for why the correction is made provided. Mistakes in the record should never be erased or obliterated because erasures and obliterations could arouse suspicions in the mind of a jury as to the contents of the original entry.

CONSEQUENCES OF MAINTAINING AN INCOMPLETE MEDICAL RECORD

Maintaining a complete record is important not only to comply with licensing and accreditation requirements, but also to enable the hospital to establish that adequate care was provided. If a health care provider can demonstrate by testimony that the provider regularly keeps complete and accurate records in accordance with established policies and procedures, the absence of certain notations may be used to defend against a malpractice claim. In *Smith v. Rogers Mem. Hosp.* [382 A.2d 1025 (D.C. Ct. App. 1978)], for example, the record did not show that the patient had complained of certain symptoms, and testimony that the hospital's records were generally reliable was important evidence in rebutting the patient's claim that she had complained of the symptoms and had not received proper care.

Conversely, the failure to maintain a complete record may lead to a finding of negligence on the part of a health care provider. In one case, a patient alleged that the nursing staff at a hospital had negligently failed to observe the condition and circulation of his leg during the time it was in a cast and that his leg had to be amputated as a result of that failure. The court examined the patient's medical record and concluded that the absence of nursing notes documenting observations of the leg during seven critical hours, particularly in view of the physician's order to "watch condition of toes," reasonably could have led the jury to infer that no observations were made during that time. In that case, there was testimony that nurses do not always record observations on the chart when patients are checked, that usually they only record abnormal findings, and that this procedure is consistent with the principles of problem-oriented medical records, which many hospitals have adopted. Nonetheless, the court allowed the jury to infer from the absence of documentation that no observations had been made.

The failure to insert proper notations of care on a patient's chart may lead not only to a finding of medical malpractice, but also to difficulties in recovering the financial cost of the care that was provided. This was illustrated in a ruling by an Arizona court on the accuracy of a computerized bill containing charges for services and medication that were not reflected in the patient's chart. Because the evidence revealed the strong possibility that the bill contained charges for medication not given, services not rendered, procedures not performed, and supplies not delivered, the court ruled that the bill was insufficient to sustain the hospital's claim for the cost of the medical care [*Tracor/MBA v. Baptist Med. Ctr.,* 780 S.W.2d 26 (Ark. Ct. App. 1989)].

These cases all illustrate the difficulties that arise when health care providers fail to create proper records: the possibility for a patient to rely on an inference or presumption of negligence concerning the actions omitted from the record and the risk for the provider of being unable to rebut the patient's re-creation of what occurred based on the memory of lay persons present during the time in question.

ACCESS TO MEDICAL RECORDS INFORMATION

Under legislation in most states, a patient's medical record is owned by the provider or facility that creates the record. The medical record is a confidential document and access to it generally should be limited to the patient or an authorized representative, the attending physician, and health care professionals possessing a legitimate interest in the record relating to the patient's care. The facility or provider that owns the record has the obligation to respect the pertinent rules of confidentiality and access with respect to the information the record contains.

The basic rules of confidentiality and access to medical records are established in most states by statute and regulation. A few states simply specify that a medical record is confidential and impose a general obligation on the facility with custody of the record to develop an appropriate policy for record confidentiality without further statutory or regulatory guidance [*see, e.g.,* S.D. ADMIN. R. 44.04:09:04]. Enactments in other states similarly embody the principle of confidentiality and the patient's right of access. In Connecticut, for example, a patient's Bill of Rights statute [CONN. GEN. STAT. § 19a-550(b)(9)] provides that patients are entitled to confidential treatment of personal and medical records. Patients may approve or refuse their release to any individual outside the facility, except in the case of the patient's transfer to another health care institution, or as required by law or a third-party payment contract. Numerous other statutes, including those of Maryland and Michigan, provide that medical records are confidential and may be disclosed only with the patient's consent or as provided in the statutes [MICH. COMP. LAWS § 333.6112 and MD. CODE ANN. HEALTH–GEN. § 4-302(a)(2)].

In most states, the statute encompassing confidentiality rules for patient records contains exceptions for access by persons other than the patient. Typically, health care professionals who are caring for a patient may review the records without consent for purposes related to the care they are providing [*see, e.g.,* FLA. STAT. ch. 395.3025(3)(a)]. Medical records information may also be released to a facility's personnel as required for billing purposes [*see* WIS. STAT. § 146.82(3)]. State legislation also establishes the release of medical record information to the patient's insurance carrier, employer, or health services plan for billing and reimbursement purposes [*see, e.g.,* CAL. CIV. CODE §§ 56.10(c)(2) and (3)]. Finally, many state laws grant access to professional licensing bodies and peer review committees [*see, e.g.,* CAL. CIV. CODE § 56.10(c)(5)].

State and federal legislation also sets forth special rules relating to the release of specific types of information from medical records, usually imposing stricter requirements for confidentiality. Provisions in the Public Health Service Act, for example, address access to the records of drug or alcohol abuse patients [21 U.S.C. §§ 1101 through 1800], providing that patient identity, diagnosis, prognosis, or treatment in any patient record maintained in connection with these programs are confidential. In a number of jurisdictions, the rules on access to the medical records of mental health patients differ from those applicable to medical records generally, frequently granting patients the right to review their records but also imposing limits on the exercise of that right [N.Y. MENTAL HYG. LAW § 33.16 (b)(1)]. The records of minor patients are also subject to specific rules, allowing for the disclosure of information from such records only with the authorization of one of the patient's parents. Parents are also typically allowed to access the record on behalf of the minor child [*see, e.g.,* MINN. STAT. § 144.335(1)(a)].

The records of human immunodeficiency virus (HIV)-infected patients also represent a complex area of medical record management, particularly with respect to special confidentiality and reporting provisions. Most states impose a duty on health care providers to report all cases of "contagious," "infectious," or "sexually transmitted" diseases to the state's department of health. The statutory or regulatory definitions of reportable diseases typically include AIDS, and some jurisdictions also require reporting of AIDS-related complex and HIV diagnoses to the state's department of health. In conjunction with these reporting requirements, most statutes or regulations also contain special confidentiality provisions strictly prohibiting the release of AIDS-related information except under specific circumstances. These exceptions to the strict confidentiality rule often allow the disclosure of information to emergency assistance personnel, spouses, persons with whom the patient has shared needles, blood banks, and funeral directors. These laws are important because they authorize the release of information in a patient's record without the individual's consent and, in some cases, in spite of the person's opposition.

RECORD SECURITY

Record security is critical to protecting patient confidentiality and preventing intentional alteration or falsification of records by hospital staff or others. Storage, retrieval, and use of medical records should involve procedures that ensure the integrity and confidentiality of the information they contain.

In particular, a medical practice or health care facility should adopt security measures that provide for the following:

- Original records should never be removed from the premises unless required by legal process or pursuant to a defined procedure that permits inpatients going to another facility for testing to take their medical records with them. When a patient requires the transfer of his or her records to another provider, the facility should send copies of the originals.
- A competent medical records or risk management staff member should review a record before it is examined by the patient or representative. The reviewer should notify a manager if the record is incomplete or otherwise defective, or if it reveals a problem that could give rise to liability.
- All releases of medical records should be centrally logged, including information relating to what records have been copied and where they were sent.
- Reviews of a record by the patient or the patient's representative should always take place under supervision. The facility should provide accommodations for record inspection in its medical records department or in another location that allows for proper surveillance.
- A practice or health care facility should centralize its response to subpoenas by designating specific members of its staff to respond to this type of request for medical records. Procedures that these staff members should follow in complying with subpoenas include examining the record for completeness, proper patient identification, and legibility; removal of material that may not be within the scope of the subpoena such as correspondence and copies of records from other facilities; enumeration of each page of the medical record and writing the total number of pages on the record jacket; preparation of a

list of the medical record contents to be used as a receipt for the contents if they must be turned over to a court or an attorney; and finally, the use of a photocopy, whenever possible, when responding to legal process.

- Special precautions must be taken when transmitting medical record information via fax or fax modem because of the risk of a misdirected communication. A provider sending confidential information by fax should verify that the recipient is authorized to receive it. Some protection against unauthorized access can be obtained by calling the recipient before sending the transmission, alerting the recipient to stand by for the transmission, and verifying that the fax number to which the transmission will be directed is the correct number. Encrypting faxed information is another method of protecting its confidentiality, but this process generally requires that the receiving fax machine or computer be equipped to decode the encrypted information. Highly sensitive health information should probably never be sent via fax except in encrypted format. In all cases, a cover sheet on the document should include a confidentiality legend emphasizing the nature of the information contained in the transmission and requesting that the recipient contact the sender if the fax is received by someone other than the recipient as indicated on the cover sheet.
- When destroying medical records upon expiration of the mandatory retention period, health care facilities should follow the method of destruction indicated in state legislation, if one is specified. The states that have specified the method of record destruction generally permit destruction by shredding or burning [*see, e.g.*, TENN. CODE ANN. § 68-11-305(c)]. Facilities that destroy their own records must establish procedures to protect the confidentiality of the information and ensure that the records are destroyed completely. The employee responsible for the task should certify that the records have been properly destroyed and the facility should maintain certificates of destruction. If a commercial enterprise is hired to destroy the records, the facility should spell out in writing the requirements for safeguarding against breach of confidentiality, indemnifying the facility for unauthorized disclosure, and providing certificates of destruction.

COMPUTERIZED MEDICAL RECORDS

Security for computerized medical records raises special concerns. Although a computer-based patient record system can improve efficiency and the quality of care rendered by a provider, it may also increase a provider's exposure to liability for improper disclosure of personal health information and for computer sabotage committed by persons gaining unauthorized access to a computerized record system.

Legal confidentiality obligations do not vary with the medium on which patient records are stored. Because of the potential for large-scale breaches of data security in a computerized medical record system, however, a provider must implement special safeguards to protect confidentiality against both internal and external users of the system. The medical record system must provide for both system and data security. Data security exists when data are protected from improper disclosure or unauthorized or unintended alteration. System security implies that a defined system functions in a defined operational environment, serves a defined set of users, contains prescribed data and operational programs, has defined network connections and interactions with other systems, and incorporates safeguards to protect the system against defined threats to the system and its resources and data.

Appropriate computer security can generally be achieved through a combination of technical measures, system management, and administration and procedures. It is generally preferable to incorporate the technical safeguards into the system application or program (i.e., the medical record system) rather than relying on network infrastructure for security. Some of the technical safeguards relevant to computerized medical record systems are:

- *personal identification and user verification*—verifies user's identity, frequently through a secret password or code, or a combination of identifiers
- *access control software and audit trails*—limit the user's access to authorized data and resources and locate suspicious patterns of access
- *computer architecture*—enhances security by monitoring the computer's activities, preventing users from gaining access to unauthorized data and, in some cases, can prevent tampering and sabotage
- *encryption*—encodes data so as to permit interpretation only with the appropriate key

With respect to its inside users, the system should permit only authorized users to have access to medical records. Access may be controlled, and users identified in one or more of the ways discussed previously, including passwords, keycards, access codes, and biometric identification. In addition, a system should allow access through only one workstation at a time for each user identifier. It is wise to program a system to log off automatically when a workstation has not been used for a predefined period of time. A user's access to the system should be limited to that portion of the system or record that relates to the user's position and duties. A system can be programmed to lock out an individual who attempts to retrieve files that the person is not authorized to access or who repeatedly attempts to gain access to the system using an improper access code. Such information includes HIV antibody test results, AIDS patient records, alcohol and drug abuse patient records, and records of celebrities. Provider policy should specifically prohibit revealing or sharing passwords, and this policy should be strictly enforced.

Improper access to computerized medical records must also be prevented with respect to outside users of a medical records system. There are several possible methods to combat attempts of external parties to gain unauthorized access to a patient records system. Such methods include recording and monitoring attempts to gain access to the system, having the computer system call back users requesting remote access, and requiring remote users to have physicians' "keys," such as encoded disks, to gain access.

Computerized patient record systems make possible widescale alteration or destruction of patient data through computer sabotage. Viruses and other forms of sabotage such as worms, bombs, and trojan horses can jeopardize both the integrity and accessibility of information on the system by causing the system to slow or crash. Although both outside and inside users of the system potentially can commit sabotage, the biggest threat to computer security is often internal. Health care facilities also need to be sensitive to the risk of sabotage from software vendors. This type of sabotage involves the insertion of a virus or keylock into system software, enabling the vendor to lock or shut the system down in the event of a payment dispute. Contracts for the purchase, lease, license, or maintenance of a computerized medical records system should obligate the vendor and its agents to refrain from inserting viruses or keylocks into the system.

While no computer security technology or method available to the provider can totally protect against breaches of security, it is important to employ system security technology and techniques. Nevertheless, the need to preserve the confidentiality and ensure the integrity of patient records will have to be balanced against the practical constraints on achieving perfect computer security.

LIABILITY FOR UNAUTHORIZED DISCLOSURE OF MEDICAL RECORD INFORMATION

State statutes may impose both criminal sanctions and civil liability on health care providers that improperly disclose medical records information [*see, e.g.*, TENN. CODE ANN. § 68-11-311]. Many states also impose specific penalties for revealing particular medical records information, such as whether a patient is HIV-positive. In Wisconsin, for example, an individual who negligently discloses a patient's HIV status may be liable for actual damages and costs, as well as $1,000 in exemplary or punitive damages.

Patients may also bring civil liability suits on a variety of legal theories. One theory of recovery in suits alleging the improper disclosure of medical information is invasion of privacy, based on either state common law, state or federal constitutional law, or state statutory law. The use of a patient's photograph, in connection with an advertisement for a provider or medical education, without the patient's consent, can lead to liability under this theory [*see, e.g., Estate of Berthiaume v. Pratt,* 365 A.2d 792 (Me. 1986)]. Courts have also held that an unwarranted intrusion on a patient's privacy occurs when nonmedical personnel are allowed to witness medical procedures or to examine a patient without the latter's consent [*see, e.g., Knight v. Penobscot Bay Med. Ctr.,* 420 A.2d 915 (Me. 1980)]. Finally, one of the most likely practices to give rise to invasion of privacy liability is the release of information concerning patients to news entities. Although a facility should be reluctant to release patient information to the news media, it may determine in some cases that the release of information of legitimate news value is appropriate. In such circumstances, the risk of liability is dependent on the specific nature of the disclosure. Merely releasing the status of the patient's condition may not create liability exposure, but disclosing more detailed information or a photograph without the patient's consent should be avoided.

Yet another legal theory under which a patient may sue a health care provider who improperly discloses medical record information is breach of confidentiality, also known as breach of the patient-physician privilege. Patient-physician privilege is frequently defined in state law and in some jurisdictions has developed through common law.

Courts have routinely held that physicians have a legal duty to maintain their patient's confidentiality and have awarded damages to patients when that duty was breached [*see, e.g., Bower v. Murphy,* 444 S.W.2d 883 (Ark. 1969)]. Courts have also extended the patient-physician privilege when a third party has worked with the patient under close supervision of a physician, on the premise that a patient is entitled to trust someone who acts in that capacity. Courts have ruled that public policy and professional codes of conduct justify extending the privilege under these circumstances [*see, e.g., In the Matter of C.P.,* 563 N.E.2d 1275 (Ind. 1990)]. The American Academy of Physician Assistants' Code of Ethics of the Physician Assistant Profession, under tenet nine, specifically requires PAs to uphold the doctrine of confidentiality regarding privileged patient information unless required to release such information by law, or the release of such information becomes necessary to protect the welfare of the patient or the community [*see* AAPA, *Guidelines for Professional Conduct* 6-8 (March 1992) (pamphlet reprinting AAPA Code of Ethics and providing examples relevant to clinical practice)]. A PA's unauthorized disclosure of medical information, therefore, could lead to liablity for breach of confidentiality.

The improper disclosure of medical information can also lead to a suit for defamation. Defamation is a written or oral communication to someone other than the person defamed of matters that tend to injure a living person's reputation. There are two types of defamation. Libel is the written form of defamation while slander is oral. Medical records may contain information that is inaccurate and that, if published, would affect a person's reputation in the community adversely and cause damages. It should be noted that the possibility of recovery against a health care provider for the release of medical records information is slight. Medical entries are ordinarily true and, as a general rule, truth of the published statement is an absolute defense to a civil suit for libel or slander.

CHAPTER 8

Credentialing and Peer Review

INTRODUCTION

The term *credentialing* has been used very broadly by some commentators to mean any type of certification or approval. National certification and state licensure, for example, discussed in Chapters 2 and 3, can all be characterized as credentials. This chapter discusses credentialing in a narrower context, that of medical staff membership and clinical privileges conferred by a hospital or other health care entity.

The credentialing process developed with a focus on physicians. As a result, court decisions and statutes have addressed the physician credentialing process in great detail, but have not shed as much light on legal issues related to PAs and other nonphysician health practitioners. This chapter discusses general credentialing issues, as well as credentialing issues specific to PAs.

CREDENTIALING

Credentialing is the process of obtaining information, verifying the information, and evaluating applicants who want to obtain or renew medical staff membership, and/or obtain, renew, or revise clinical privileges at health care facilities. Managed care organizations (MCOs), such as health maintenance organizations (HMOs) and preferred provider organizations (PPOs), also credential health care providers who seek to become participating providers in the MCO. Large group practices, independent practice associations (IPAs), and some medical societies may also perform credentialing activities.

Credentialing is generally performed at:

- initial appointment to the staff
- initial determination of clinical privileges
- reappointment to the staff and renewal or revision of clinical privileges

The credentialing process generally applies whether the individual is a contract practitioner such as a member of a medical group that has an exclusive contract for emergency department services, a health practitioner employed by the facility, or an independent contractor. Even individuals seeking temporary privileges must be subject to the credentialing process.

The medical staff have a responsibility to ensure the qualifications and competence of nonphysician practitioners. Nonphysician practitioners such as PAs are subject to evaluation processes delineated in the medical staff bylaws, rules and regulations, or policies. In these documents, nonphysician practitioners may be classified as allied health staff, ancillary staff, auxiliary staff, or specified professional personnel. Mechanisms for ensuring the competency of nonphysician practitioners include staff membership, clinical privileges (also called practice prerogatives or protocols), or detailed job descriptions. Nonphysician practitioners also are subject to evaluation through the quality assurance and utilization review process.

In a hospital, the governing body is ultimately responsible for credentialing decisions. The governing body delegates certain credentialing duties to the hospital administration and medical staff through its medical executive committee, credentials committee, and the clinical department chair. [For a sample hospital policy outlining the credentialing process, see Appendix 8-A.] In addition, other health care providers and other committees contribute valuable information regarding provider performance that is essential in properly evaluating providers. Other entities that credential practitioners include:

- *MCOs,* such as HMOs, in the form of decisions regarding who will be allowed to participate in the particular MCO.
- *physician hospital organizations (PHOs).* PHOs are organizations that form alliances between hospitals and physicians mainly for the purpose of pursuing managed care contracts.
- *medical (or management) services organizations (MSOs).* MSOs are organizations that typically provide various services to physicians, although there are freestanding, hospital-affiliated, physician-affiliated, joint venture (hospital-physician), and MCO models. MSOs may provide all of the services of a PHO, including credentialing.
- *large group practices and IPAs.* When an IPA contracts with a managed care plan, the responsibility for credentialing may be delegated to the IPA.
- *medical associations* such as the American Medical Association. Hospitals and other health care organizations can access credentialing services provided by such associations.

The primary reason for performing credentialing is to ensure that patients receive quality medical care from qualified practitioners. The vast majority of PAs do not have credentialing problems. When there are problems, however, and they are not detected and appropriately addressed by the credentialing entity, the consequences to patients can be devastating. Many state courts and legislatures have recognized that hospitals have a duty to the public to properly credential their medical staff members. Therefore, to minimize legal liability to patients and to ensure compliance with federal and local laws, hospitals must ensure that credentialing procedures are properly carried out. In addition, hospitals must meet certain credentialing standards set by the Joint Commission on Accreditation of Healthcare Organizations (Joint Commission) in order to be accredited by that organization. Joint Commission standards are discussed later in this chapter.

In MCOs, credentialing is performed because of the same concern for quality patient care and limitation of liability. In addition, MCOs focus on the economic aspects of health care delivery to a greater degree than hospitals have in the past. Part of the credentialing process in MCOs may include an evaluation of whether the care is rendered in a cost-effective manner, also known as economic credentialing or utilization management.

PEER REVIEW

Peer review is an essential part of the initial credentialing process and ongoing evaluation of practitioners. In peer review, a committee composed of the practitioner's peers reviews the practitioner's clinical skills and professional conduct. Peer review also involves ongoing quality assurance functions. Entities that conduct peer review include hospitals, MCOs, third-party payers, professional liability insurers, and professional associations.

MEDICAL STAFF MEMBERSHIP

Each hospital's governing board must decide whether, considering applicable federal and state laws, PAs are eligible to be medical staff members. A hospital's governing body may decide to include PAs as medical staff members or in an alternative category, such as the allied health staff or paramedical staff.

To become a member of the medical staff, a practitioner must meet the requirements described in the medical staff bylaws. These requirements typically include valid licensure, relevant training and experience, current competence, good physical and mental health, and evidence of insurance. As a condition of appointment to the staff, the practitioner may be asked to assume certain duties and responsibilities, such as serving on various medical staff committees. Medical staff membership does not automatically include clinical privileges. The practitioner must apply for clinical privileges separately.

There are three ways that hospitals and other health care entities typically approach medical staff membership for PAs.

1. Allow nonphysician practitioners, such as PAs, to become members of the medical staff, along with physicians, dentists, and podiatrists.
2. Create a medical staff subcategory for nonphysician practitioners. This subcategory may be known as the allied staff, paramedical staff, or affiliated staff.
3. Prohibit staff membership for allied health practitioners, relying on the privileging process or detailed job descriptions to regulate the quality of care given by PAs and other nonphysicians.

More than one approach may apply at a single hospital. For example, PAs supervised by physicians on the medical staff may be in a medical staff subcategory, while PAs employed by the hospital operate under a detailed job description.

The advantages of medical staff membership include the voting rights and procedural protections conferred on the medical staff in rules, regulations, and bylaws. Therefore, the bylaws must be examined carefully to determine what requirements and protections have been granted to PAs. The allied or paramedical staff may be represented on medical staff committees, but without full voting rights on policy matters and without full procedural protections granted to medical staff members. Physician assistants who have privileges but no staff membership may have even fewer protections against adverse actions.

To determine whether PAs can be members of the medical staff at a facility, a PA should first examine the medical staff bylaws and rules and regulations. These documents will list the categories of medical staff membership (full membership, allied health staff membership, etc.) and describe the qualifications for admission to the medical staff, as well as the requirements for membership renewal. The bylaws and rules and regulations will also contain the procedures that must be followed when the hospital denies or terminates medical staff membership or clinical privileges.

Applying for Staff Membership

A PA applying for medical staff membership, regardless of the category, bears the burden of proving eligibility. Thus, a PA must fill out the application completely and truthfully, as the failure to provide material information or falsifying information may serve as a basis for denial. For example, if a PA feels dismissal by a former employer was unfair and omits that job from the employment history section of an application, the hospital may automatically reject the application on the basis of the material omission. If the PA includes and explains the previous employment situation, however, the hospital must investigate before making a determination.

State Laws

State laws and regulations describe the requirements for medical staff membership, and may determine whether PAs may be members of the full medical staff (along with physicians) or whether they must be relegated to a subcategory for allied health practitioners. In New York, for example, regulations state that the medical staff "shall be composed of persons practicing medicine, and may also be composed of other licensed and currently registered health care practitioners appointed by the governing body." [N.Y. COMP. CODES R. & REGS. tit. 10, § 405.4]. Thus, hospitals may include PAs on the medical staff. In Pennsylvania, by contrast, regulations state that "the medical staff shall be limited to physicians and dentists." [28 PA. CODE § 107.2]. In California, regulations expressly limit medical staff membership to physicians, dentists, podiatrists, and psychologists [CAL. CODE REGS. tit. 22, § 70701(a)(1)(E)]. In such states, excluded licensed practitioners such as PAs may obtain privileges, but may not be admitted to the medical staff.

Joint Commission Standards

The Joint Commission accredits hospitals and other health care entities after conducting a survey to assess compliance with Joint Commission standards. Accreditation by the Joint Commission is a voluntary process, but benefits that inure to an accredited hospital are considerable. The hospital that is accredited is "deemed" to comply with the Medicare Conditions of Participation. Further, participation in other state and federal programs, as well as third-party payer contracts, may require accreditation. Undeniably, in the public's mind there is an element of prestige associated with accreditation.

The Joint Commission standards of accreditation require a hospital's medical staff to assume responsibility for the quality of professional services provided by individuals with clinical privileges [Joint Commission, *1997 Hospital Accreditation Standards,* at MS.1 (1997)]. The Joint Commission standards regarding clinical privileges are discussed later in this chapter.

Although the standards do not specifically mention PAs, they do limit medical staff membership to "licensed independent practitioners," defined as "licensed individuals permitted by law and by the hospital to provide patient care services independently." [MS.1.1.1]. In response to concerns that these statements would seem to preclude medical staff membership for PAs, the Joint Commission has clarified its position as to medical staff membership for PAs. In a letter to the American Academy of Physician Assistants (AAPA), the Joint Commission explained, "Hospitals may, and do permit PAs to be members of the medical staff if the hospital chooses to grant membership. Some PAs are 'admitted' to membership categories known as 'auxiliary staff' or 'ancillary staff.' Other hospitals permit the PA membership in the same department as his or her supervising physician. In all such cases, membership is a nonissue under the Joint Commission Standards." [Letter from Carole H. Patterson, Deputy Director, Department of Standards, Joint Commission to Ellen Rathfon, Director, Professional Affairs, AAPA, May 22, 1996.]

Amending Bylaws

If PAs are not currently included on the medical staff at a particular facility and state law allows, an individual PA may petition the governing body to amend the bylaws to allow PAs on the staff. To do so, a PA should consult existing bylaws to determine the process for adding new categories of practitioners. The AAPA has outlined the considerations relevant to such an amendment [AAPA, *Guidelines for Amending Hospital Staff Bylaws, Hospital Privileges Summary* (March 1996)].

Definition of Physician Assistant

The medical staff bylaws should include a definition of PA that is consistent with the definition used in state law. The definition should make reference to PA competence to practice and state licensure.

Composition of the Medical Staff

The bylaws should identify the categories of health care practitioners eligible for staff membership. Categories of practitioners should also be identified for any subcategory of medical staff such as allied health staff or ancillary staff.

Requirements for Staff Membership

The bylaws should specify uniform criteria for initial and continued membership on the medical staff. Examples include state licensure, relevant training and experience, current competence, and adequate professional liability insurance.

Clinical Privileges

Clinical privileges are distinct from medical staff membership and are discussed later in this chapter in greater detail. Any change in medical staff bylaws regarding PA staff membership should, however, also address clinical privileges. The bylaws should require that all clinical privileges granted to PAs conform to applicable state laws and regulations, providing, for example, for appropriate physician supervision. Hospitals cannot waive state law limitations on PA practice in their bylaws. The bylaws should also specify the criteria for delineating the PA's clinical privileges.

Corrective Action and Due Process

The medical staff bylaws should describe the criteria and process for disciplining PAs. A PA seeking to amend the bylaws should attempt to obtain the same processes applied to physician members of the medical staff. The PA should also request that the bylaws give the PA the right to request due process or procedural fairness (discussed later in this chapter) when medical staff or governing board action adversely affects the PA's clinical privileges.

Quality Assurance and Continuing Education

The bylaws should include a description of mechanisms for quality assurance with respect to PAs, typically including monitoring and evaluation by a supervising physician. The bylaws may also require PAs to participate in continuing education.

Committees

Physician assistants should seek bylaw amendments allowing PA membership on medical staff committees. It is important, especially when PAs are first granted staff membership, for PAs to serve on committees to educate others regarding the PA's role in the health care institution, even if PAs are nonvoting committee members. Offering to participate on committees (and encouraging supervising physicians to do so) may increase the level of fairness that PAs encounter.

Institutional Employment

The medical staff bylaws should also allow PAs who are not medical staff members to obtain clinical privileges when properly supervised.

CLINICAL PRIVILEGES

Clinical privileges represent specific procedures or groups of procedures and patient care services that the hospital or MCO governing body authorizes a practitioner to perform. With regard to PAs, privileges may be called, among other terms, practice prerogatives or protocols. The Joint Commission defines clinical privileges as authorization "to provide specific patient care services in the hospital within defined limits, based on the following factors, as applicable: license, education, training, experience, competence, health status, and judgment" [Joint Commission, *1997 Hospital Accreditation Standards,* at 328 (1997)].

Individuals, including PAs, may hold clinical privileges without being medical staff members. For each privileged health practitioner, privileges must be *delineated.* That is, the scope of the practitioner's permissible practice must be outlined. For PAs, state laws and regulations on scope of practice establish outside parameters on PA practice. In some states, laws or regulations specifically address the scope of privileges for PAs practicing in institutional settings. [See Chapter 3: Licensure and Scope of Practice, at Scope of Practice under State PA Practice Laws.]

A PA's education, training, and experience also affect the delineation of privileges, as these factors can either expand or contract the specific list of procedures that a hospital will permit the PA to perform. Finally, medical staff bylaws should specifically address the delineation of PA privileges, setting forth the criteria for granting clinical privileges. The bylaws should also address requirements and procedures for renewal of privileges. [Sample hospital forms delineating PA clinical privileges appear at Appendixes 8-B and 8-C.]

Not all PAs who care for hospital patients have clinical privileges. Some institutions that employ PAs oversee the scope of PA involvement in patient care with a detailed job description, rather than through the privileging process.

State Law Limits on Scope

State laws and regulations addressing the scope of practice for PAs may determine the permissible scope of clinical privileges. [For detailed information on scope of practice statutes and regulations, see Chapter 3: Licensure and Scope of Practice, at Scope of Practice under State PA Practice Laws.] Some states specifically address PA duties in the hospital setting, defining the permissible scope of clinical privileges. Health care entity bylaws must incorporate these state-specific rules. For example:

- In Massachusetts, PAs employed by health care facilities may not be the sole medical personnel in charge of emergency or outpatient services, or any other clinical service where a physician is not regularly available [MASS. GEN. L. ch. 112, § 9E].
- In New Mexico, a PA may not deliver babies unless the PA has received specific training in a board-approved obstetrics course and the PA's supervising physician practices obstetrics. Physician assistants may assist a physician in a health care institution, within the institution's bylaws, provided the PA's duties are delineated by the credentials committee and approved by the institution's governing body [N.M. Bd. Med. Examiners R. & Reg. (Physician Assistants), Rule 6].

- In Pennsylvania, a PA may be employed by a medical care facility, such as a hospital, ambulatory clinic, HMO, corporation medical center, or nursing home, but may not be supervised by more than three physicians [49 PA. CODE § 18.161].

Medicare Conditions of Participation

To be reimbursed under both the Medicare and Medicaid programs, hospitals must comply with federal regulations called Conditions of Participation. These regulations set out the standards hospitals must meet in a variety of operational and strategic areas in order to participate in the Medicare program and thereby receive Medicare reimbursement [42 C.F.R. §§ 482.1 *et seq.;* for a related discussion, see Chapter 10: Third-Party Reimbursement, at Medicare].

The Conditions of Participation address PA practice in hospitals, affecting the delineation of PA privileges. First, the Conditions of Participation now direct hospitals to delineate surgical privileges for *all* practitioners who perform surgery. This requirement may implicitly allow PAs to assist at surgery. The regulations originally allowed only physicians to exercise surgical privileges [51 Fed. Reg. 22,010, amending 42 C.F.R. § 482.51].

Second, the regulations recognize that there is a legitimate role for nonphysicians in emergency department care. The regulations, which previously required that every emergency patient be examined by a physician, now allow the medical staff to develop emergency service procedures that will ensure that care is provided by a physician when necessary. The regulations do require, however, that emergency service personnel be qualified in emergency care [51 Fed. Reg. 22,010, amending 42 C.F.R. § 482.55].

Third, the Conditions of Participation require that every patient be under the care of a physician. To implement this requirement, the regulations state that "a physical examination and medical history be done . . . for each patient by a doctor of medicine or osteopathy." The regulations point out, however, that this provision is not intended to restrict a physician's ability to delegate tasks to appropriate personnel such as PAs [51 Fed. Reg. 22,010, amending 42 C.F.R. §§ 482.12 (c) & 482.22(c)(5)].

REPORTING ADVERSE CREDENTIALING ACTIONS

An adverse action against clinical privileges can have consequences for a PA beyond being unable to practice at a particular facility. Federal and state regulations may allow or require a facility that limits or revokes a health care provider's clinical privileges to report the adverse action to a government agency or databank, which may then disseminate the report to other interested entities. Physician assistants should understand the circumstances that may trigger databank reporting and who has access to reported information.

Health Care Quality Improvement Act

The Health Care Quality Improvement Act of 1986 (HCQIA) is a federal law that seeks to improve the quality of health care, in part by establishing the National Practitioner Data Bank (NPDB), which disseminates information on a variety of health care practitioners. The HCQIA, a statute primarily aimed at physicians and dentists, requires health care entities to report certain adverse actions taken against health care practitioners. The NPDB is a database that contains adverse information regarding certain health care practitioners. The intent of the NPDB was to prevent incompetent practitioners from moving from state to state without detection. The HCQIA provisions regarding the NPDB contain both reporting and inquiry requirements.

Reporting

HCQIA requires health care entities to report certain information to the NPDB through their state licensing boards. Health care entities required to report include hospitals or other entities that provide health care services and engage in professional review activities through a formal peer review process for the purpose of furthering quality health care. Health care entities must report any professional review action that adversely affects the clinical privileges of a physician or dentist for a period of longer than 30 days. Hospitals *may* report adverse actions taken against other health care practitioners, such as PAs, but it is not mandatory [42 U.S.C. § 11133; see also Appendix 8-D, for a list of NPDB reporting requirements].

"Professional review action" means an action or recommendation of a professional review body:

- taken in the course of professional review activity by a health care entity to determine whether a physician or dentist may have clinical privileges with or membership in the entity, to determine the scope or conditions of such privileges or membership, or to change or modify such privileges or membership
- based on the professional competence or professional conduct of an individual physician or dentist, which affects or could affect adversely the health or welfare of a patient
- that adversely affects or may adversely affect the practitioner's clinical privileges or membership in a professional society

[42 U.S.C. § 11151(9)].

"Adversely affects" means reducing, restricting, suspending, revoking, or denying clinical privileges or membership in a health care entity.

Reports of adverse actions on clinical privileges must be made within one month of the action becoming final. Health care entities must submit an adverse action report to the state medical or dental board within 15 days of the action being taken. The state boards are responsible for submitting all reports directly to the databank and the appropriate licensing agency, if necessary, within 15 days from the date of its receipt [45 C.F.R. §§ 60.5 & 60.6(b)].

In addition to adverse actions affecting clinical privileges, a health care entity that is also a self-insurer must report medical malpractice payments of any amount on behalf of all licensed health care practitioners (not only physicians) within one month of the payment [42 U.S.C. §§ 11131 & 11134]. Payments that must be reported include those in satisfaction of a legal judgment as well as those made under a settlement or partial settlement agreement. A health care entity that fails to report such payments may be fined up to $10,000 for each failure [42 U.S.C. § 11131].

Hospitals need not report actions that are primarily based on association or lack of association with a professional society or association; fees, advertising, or other competitive acts intended to solicit or retain business; participation in pre-paid group health plans, salaried employment, or any other manner of delivering health services; association with a member or members of a particular class of health care practitioners or professionals (such as PAs); or any other matter that does not relate to the competence or professional conduct of the health care practitioner [42 U.S.C. § 11151].

The HCQIA reporting requirement refers to final actions only. Therefore, if the time to appeal an action has not expired, the action is not yet final. In addition, if an appeal is requested, the action does not become final until appeal measures are exhausted in most cases. A practitioner who is reported receives a copy of the report and an opportunity to submit comments that will subsequently be sent out with the report when the databank is queried.

If a health care entity fails to report an adverse action on clinical privileges, after appropriate hearings, the Department of Health and Human Services will publish the name of the health care entity in the Federal Register and the immunity provisions of HCQIA (discussed later) will not apply to professional review activities that occur during the three-year period beginning 30 days after the date of the publication [42 U.S.C. § 11111(b)].

Other health industry entities must also report to the NPDB. [For a listing of NPDB reporting requirements, see Appendix 8-D.] Medical malpractice insurers must report all medical malpractice payments on behalf of a health care practitioner, including PAs, regardless of the amount [42 U.S.C. § 11131]. State licensing boards must report all adverse actions against physicians' and dentists' licenses [42 U.S.C. § 11132], and may report adverse actions against the licenses of other health care practitioners, including PAs. Professional societies such as the AAPA may report disciplinary actions to the NPDB also, but are not required to do so [42 U.S.C. § 11133].

Information reported to the NPDB is confidential and may not be disclosed, except in connection with peer review and as necessary to carry out the requirements of HCQIA [42 U.S.C. § 11137(b)]. Entities that receive information directly from the NPDB may disclose it to others only for the purpose of professional review activity within the entity. According to federal regulations, those who receive NPDB information indirectly may use the information only for the purpose for which it was provided, presumably professional peer review activity [45 C.F.R. § 60.13]. Further, an attorney who receives information from the NPDB in connection with a malpractice suit may use the information only within the context of that particular suit. HCQIA confidentiality provisions do not protect the original documents from which the reported information was obtained, however, and do not prevent disclosure otherwise authorized by state law. To protect the confidentiality of the information, a civil money penalty of up to $10,000 for each violation may be assessed against any person or entity wrongfully disclosing confidential information [42 U.S.C. § 11137 (b)].

Querying

Physician assistants should distinguish between circumstances under which querying the NPDB by a health care entity is mandatory and circumstances under which querying is merely permitted. [For a listing of NPDB querying requirements, see Appendix 8-D.] Hospitals and HMOs *must* request information from the NPDB when licensed practitioners, including PAs, apply for positions on the medical staff, clinical privileges at the hospital, or participation in an HMO. A NPDB report on the PA also must be requested every two years or at the time of reappointment [42 U.S.C. § 11135]. A hospital *may* request information concerning a physician, dentist, or other health care practitioner who is a member of the medical staff or has clinical privileges at the hospital at any time [45 C.F.R. § 60.11].

Other health care entities, such as group practices, *may* request information if they have established an employment or affiliation relationship with a physician, dentist, or other health care practitioner, or if they may establish such a relationship. Health care entities may also request information if a practitioner has applied for clinical privileges or appointment to the medical staff or in connection with a professional review activity [45 C.F.R. § 60.11].

A hospital that does not request information required by HCQIA is presumed to have knowledge of any information reported to the NPDB concerning a particular physician, dentist, or other practitioner. Because courts in most states have found that hospitals have a corporate duty to properly and thoroughly credential practitioners, failure to do so could result in hospital liability. Therefore, this presumption of knowledge could be damaging to a hospital in a lawsuit by any patient harmed by a practitioner who was the subject of an NPDB report.

An attorney (or individual representing himself or herself) who has filed a medical malpractice action against a hospital may request information from the NPDB regarding a physician, dentist, or other health care practitioner also named in the malpractice claim. This information will be disclosed only after the attorney shows evidence that the hospital failed to comply with NPDB querying requirements. The information may be used solely in connection with the lawsuit against the hospital [45 C.F.R. § 60.11].

State Law Reporting Requirements

In addition to the HCQIA reporting requirements, PAs should consider state laws addressing the circumstances under which adverse credentialing decisions must be reported, as disciplinary actions may have implications beyond a single facility. Some examples follow:

- West Virginia law requires each health care facility to report to the state medical board the name of any PA practicing in the facility whose privileges have been revoked, restricted, reduced, or terminated for any cause (including voluntary resignation). The health care facility must also report any other formal disciplinary action against a PA relating to professional ethics, medical incompetence, medical malpractice, moral turpitude, or drug or alcohol abuse. Health care facilities need not report temporary suspensions for failure to complete medical records or failure to attend staff meetings [W. Va. Code § 30-3-16].
- In Minnesota, any hospital, clinic, prepaid medical plan or other health care institution must report to the state medical board any action taken to revoke, suspend, restrict, or condition a PA's privilege to treat patients, as well as any denial of privileges, or any other disciplinary action. Health care entities must also report the resignation of any PA prior to the conclusion of any disciplinary proceeding, or prior to the commencement of formal charges, but after the PA knew that charges were in preparation [Minn. Stat. § 147A.14].
- Ohio's PA practice statute states that a hospital or health care facility must report to the board any formal disciplinary action against any registered PA, including the PA's name, the action taken, and a summary of the underlying facts. The health care facility must provide copies of patient records (minus identifying information) to the board upon request [Ohio Rev. Code Ann. § 4730.32].

IMMUNITY FOR PEER REVIEW PARTICIPANTS

Physician assistants should think about volunteering to participate on peer review committees to educate other health professionals about the role of the PA and to learn about the peer review process firsthand. However, before joining a committee, or even offering assistance to a committee, a PA should consider whether he or she will be exposed to individual liability should another health care provider file suit as a result of a peer review action. Both federal and state laws provide limited immunity from liability for peer review activities.

Health Care Quality Improvement Act

In addition to the reporting requirements described previously, HCQIA also seeks to improve the quality of health care by granting immunity under federal and state law for certain participants in the peer review process to encourage full and free participation in peer review. The immunity provisions of HCQIA provide peer review committee members, participants, and witnesses limited immunity from damages that may arise as a result of adverse decisions that affect a physician's medical staff privileges. The immunity provisions apply only if certain procedural safeguards, specified in HCQIA, are satisfied. If the procedural and reporting requirements of the act are met, members of a professional review body will not be liable in damages as, for example, in a defamation suit brought by a practitioner. HCQIA immunity does not shield peer review participants from civil rights suits, suits for injunctive relief, or suits filed by the United States or a state attorney general.

Hospitals have the discretion to seek or forgo the protection of HCQIA immunity. If a hospital chooses not to follow the procedural safeguards necessary to obtain immunity, health care practitioners may not sue the hospital under HCQIA for failing to provide the procedures required for immunity. (Practitioners may be entitled, however, to procedural protections under state hospital licensing law or as a result of violations of the hospital bylaws.) Similarly, HCQIA immunity applies only to "professional review actions," defined as actions or recommendations "based on the competence or professional conduct of an individual physician which conduct affects or could adversely affect the health or welfare of a patient or patients. . . ." [42 U.S.C. § 11151]. Therefore, a health care entity may decide to follow the HCQIA procedural requirements only when an adverse action is based on the competence or professional conduct of a practitioner, using a different or more streamlined set of procedures when immunity may not be invoked. (The hospital bylaws or other laws, however, may require that the hospital provide procedural protections.)

Although HCQIA's immunity provisions apply only to peer review of physicians and dentists, the statute's protections extend to all participants in the peer review of physicians and dentists, including PAs. Thus, it is important for a PA who participates in the peer review process as a committee member, an investigator, or merely by providing information on a physician's performance, to understand when HCQIA immunity will apply to protect the PA from liability.

HCQIA immunity protects a health care entity and the participants in the peer review process only if the challenged peer review action was taken in the reasonable belief that the action was in furtherance of quality health care, the action was taken after reasonable effort to obtain the facts of the matter, the entity afforded the affected physician adequate notice and hearing procedures, and there was a reasonable belief that the action was warranted [42 U.S.C. § 11112].

Because HCQIA provides immunity for the peer review of physicians and dentists only, a PA participating in the peer review of another PA or other allied health practitioner is not protected by HCQIA. Thus, careful consideration should be given to the potential for liability under state and federal law before participating in the peer review of a nonphysician provider. Further, a PA should inquire whether the institution's insurance will cover the PA in the event of a suit over peer review participation.

State Law Immunities

Even if a hospital does not follow the HCQIA procedural protections to avail itself of immunity, many states have enacted legislation that provides legal immunity to those engaged in reviewing the hospital practice of medical staff members. These laws vary with respect to the type of review activity protected, which individuals enjoy the protection, and the conditions under which immunity is granted. Physician assistants participating in the peer review process should consult state law to determine whether they are shielded from liability.

In Alabama, for example, members of medical staff committees of licensed hospitals are immune from civil liability. Immunity extends to members of utilization review or similar committees formed to evaluate or review the diagnosis or treatment of patients. To be immune, these actions or decisions must be made in good faith, without malice, based on facts reasonably known or believed, and within the scope of the committee's purpose [ALA. CODE § 34-24-58]. Thus, informal conversations that occur outside the peer review process, for example, in a restaurant, are probably not immune.

In many states, including Indiana, immunity extends beyond the members of the committee to any person who, in good faith, furnishes records, information, or assistance to a peer review committee engaged in the evaluation of the qualifications, competence, or professional conduct of a professional health care provider or the evaluation of patient care [IND. CODE § 34-4-12.6-3]. Oregon similarly protects individuals on medical staff committees, as well as individuals who, in good faith, communicate information to the medical staff committees [OR. REV. STAT. § 41.675].

PROCEDURAL PROTECTIONS FROM ADVERSE DECISIONS

A PA who faces an adverse credentialing decision (such as a limitation on or revocation of privileges) may be entitled to certain procedural protections, such as a hearing and a notice of the basis for the adverse decision. These procedures may be required by law or may be voluntarily adopted by a health care institution. Physician assistants must consult the bylaws at their facility to determine the specific procedures that apply.

Physician assistants considering invoking procedural protections when facing an adverse action should consider the cost. A formal hearing can easily result in tens of thousands of dollars in legal expenses that are not covered by the PA's professional insurance. Also, PAs should note that while they bear the burden of proving their eligibility and competence at the initial medical staff membership and privileging stage, the hospital bears the burden of proving incompetence when revoking membership or privileges.

Due Process

The Fifth Amendment to the United States Constitution prohibits the federal government from depriving any person of property without due process of law. The Fourteenth Amendment is held to apply this principle to the states and their subdivisions. Several states have constitutional provisions similar to the federal due process clause, adding an additional set of due process provisions to be met. Although not all practitioners are entitled to due process protections (as discussed later), due process is a fundamental concept that PAs should understand.

There are two aspects to due process: substantive and procedural. Substantive due process refers to rights that must be protected. For example, if state law mandates that medical staffs include podiatrists, podiatrists may claim the substantive right to be considered for medical staff membership and cannot be automatically denied because of their school of practice. That does not mean that every podiatrist has a right to be granted medical staff membership or privileges, because every medical staff applicant must meet all of the admission criteria and must be individually evaluated and approved. The mainstay of substantive due process is reasonableness. Hospitals must make rules for governing the medical staff that are reasonably calculated to achieve some legitimate hospital purpose. They must not be arbitrary, capricious, or vague. Hospital bylaws and rules dealing with the qualifications for medical staff membership and privileges or limiting professional discretion within the hospital are examples of measures that must be reasonable and clear in order to comport with substantive due process.

Procedural due process refers to the procedures put in place to protect the substantive rights; it can be thought of as fundamental fairness. State statutes and regulations may require that certain due process procedures be afforded to practitioners. In addition, court decisions may govern whether certain procedures are required in a particular jurisdiction. There are several elements that have come to be accepted as necessary to procedural due process. Basically, procedural due process includes notice and an opportunity to be heard. A right to notice of the charges against the practitioner, to be informed of the facts relied on as the basis for an adverse action, as well as what hospital rule or bylaw is being applied, are essential. The practitioner also has a right to be heard, to present evidence and argument in opposition to the adverse action, and to cross-examine witnesses who testify on behalf of the body taking action. The practitioner must be given a reasonable amount of time to prepare for the hearing and reasonable access to records in the possession of the hospital that were used as the basis of the adverse action. A fair hearing includes the right to be heard by an unbiased tribunal. The practitioner is entitled to a written determination of the outcome, which must be forthcoming within a reasonable amount of time. The practitioner should also be given the opportunity to appeal the decision within a reasonable amount of time.

Due process protections need not be extended to practitioners whose privileges have been adversely affected for reasons unrelated to competence, such as failure to complete medical records in a timely manner. Further, practitioners who fail to meet minimum requirements for membership do not have a right to a hearing.

Public hospitals, such as those operated by the state or county, are required to preserve the constitutional rights of practitioners to both substantive and procedural due process. There is a large body of law addressing the question of whether due process requirements apply to private hospitals. In some cases, the answer turns on whether the hospital is viewed as engaging in state action, which would render it subject to due process requirements. In other cases, the important question is whether a "property right" is implicated. While private hospitals may or may not be required to do so, the reality is that they generally do provide a fairly high level of due process. This is especially true of hospitals that seek the benefit of HCQIA's immunity provisions, thus following the procedures set out in that law. As a general rule, HCQIA's procedural provisions are similar to those required by due process principles. This is because HCQIA was intended in part to establish a national standard for practitioner due process rights in peer review actions.

State Laws on Credentialing Procedures

State laws may grant both substantive and procedural rights in connection with the credentialing process. Florida, for example, confers substantive rights on PAs seeking hospital privileges by stating that certified PAs may not be denied clinical privileges except for good cause as long as the PA's supervising physician is a staff member in good standing [FLA. STAT. ch. 458.347]. Most state laws, however, do not explicitly grant such rights to PAs.

States may be quite specific with regard to procedures for credentialing PAs. Massachusetts regulations, for example, dictate that a physician who wishes a PA to assist in the care of hospitalized patients must contact the credentials or other appropriate hospital medical staff committee, as well as the hospital administration. The physician must provide the medical staff committee and administration with a detailed description of the PA's proposed responsibilities, training, and qualifications [MASS. REGS. CODE tit. 105, § 900.154]. In California, a PA seeking privileges in a health care facility must be supervised by an active staff physician approved by the Division of Allied Health Professions of the Board of Medical Quality Assurance. Physician assistants must also be approved by the executive committee of the medical staff [CAL. CODE REGS. tit. 22, § 70706.1].

Joint Commission

The Joint Commission standards require that all health care practitioners with delineated privileges be subject to medical staff and departmental bylaws, rules, regulations, and policies. This requirement includes medical staff members, as well as health care practitioners who have privileges, but who are not members of the medical staff. Privileged practitioners must also be subject to peer review as part of the health care organization's performance improvement activities. [Joint Commission, *1997 Hospital Accreditation Standards,* at MS.1.1.3 (1997).] Although the credentialing process may differ for medical staff members and other individuals with clinical privileges, all privileged practitioners must be granted a fair hearing and appeal in the course of adverse decisions concerning renewal, revocation, or revision of clinical privileges [MS.5.2.1 & MS.5.2].

Credentialing decisions must be based on professional criteria that are uniformly applied to all applicants for medical staff membership and clinical privileges. At the least, the professional criteria must pertain to evidence of current licensure, relevant training or experience, current competence, and ability to perform the privileges requested. The Joint Commission encourages hospitals to also consider information from sources such as federal and state disciplinary databanks. Applicants must provide information such as previously successful or pending challenges to any licensure or registration, voluntary or involuntary termination of membership or privileges at another hospital, and final judgments or settlements in professional liability actions [MS.5.4 through MS.5.5]. It is very important to be candid and absolutely comprehensive in responses to questions on a medical staff application. Lack of candor on an applicant's part is rapidly becoming a ground for denial of membership or clinical privileges.

ANTITRUST IMPLICATIONS OF CREDENTIALING

Broadly speaking, antitrust laws are intended to remedy abuses associated with the acquisition of market power. If one entity acquires and maintains too much market power and there is little or no competition, consumers may consequently suffer economic harm. Market power can be legitimately acquired and maintained by any competitor in the market. Antitrust concerns are raised, however, when a single entity employs unfair methods to acquire or maintain market power or when two or more entities combine to aggregate their market power.

Antitrust concerns may arise in the credentialing or peer review context when health care practitioners participate in an adverse action against a competing health care practitioner under circumstances indicating that reducing competition, rather than protecting the welfare of patients, was the motivation behind the adverse action. Traditionally, physicians have sued to recover under antitrust laws. With the number of PAs obtaining privileges and staff membership increasing, there is potential for PAs to join this trend of litigation. It is very difficult, however, for a health care provider to win an antitrust suit.

Cases have been brought under antitrust laws to challenge exclusions, expulsions, and suspensions from staff, as well as other limitations placed on a practitioner's use of hospital facilities. In addition, alleged exclusions from referral lists have been challenged, as has exclusion from an emergency department on-call roster. Any action that unfairly impinges on a practitioner's unfettered right to practice may be the subject of an antitrust challenge. Physician assistants participating in staff membership, privileging, or peer review decisions should consider the following advice:

- PAs involved in credentialing or peer review should consider whether anti-competitive motives are driving an adverse recommendation.
- The medical staff should focus only on a practitioner's competence and conduct qualifications. Criteria such as competitive strategy and the hospital's needs should be considered by hospital officials, not in the credentialing or peer review process.
- PAs attending committee meetings must avoid making comments, even in jest, about "getting rid of" or "freezing out" another practitioner.

- All credentialing and peer review participants must scrupulously follow medical staff bylaws, especially the fair hearing plan, to avoid charges of unfairness.
- PAs should avoid voting in a credentialing or peer review process concerning another economic competitor. To determine whether a health care provider is an economic competitor, a PA should consider whether the provider could take over the PA's patients or whether the PA would economically benefit from the loss of that practitioner's privileges—a nurse practitioner, for example [S. Borden, "Peer Review: A Guide to Implementation in Your State," in *Professional Liability Handbook: A Basic Guide for Physician Assistants* 64–71 (AAPA 1990)].

If peer review activities are undertaken in compliance with HCQIA, all practitioners involved are immune from antitrust liability. These procedures are usually required by medical staff bylaws or fair hearing plans. Compliance with state law will also help eliminate the risk of liability.

APPENDIX 8-A

Credentialing Process for Allied Health Professionals

1. St. Vincent Hospital has designated the following groups as Allied Health Professionals who will be credentialed as outlined by the process below: **Licensed Independent Clinical Social Workers, Acupuncturists, Certified Nurse Midwives, Physician Assistants, Nurse Practitioners, Certified Psychiatric Nurse Mental Health Clinical Specialists, Certified Registered Nurse Anesthetists.**

2. **AHP receives:**
   a) Cover Letter
   b) AHP Application
   c) Specific Services Form
   d) Medical Staff's Rules & Regulations
   e) For NPs, CNMs, PAs, and RNCSs who have prescriptive writing authority, also send the appropriate Medication Guidelines and Agreement package.
   f) For PAs only—A physician agreement form should be included with the application.

3. Upon receipt of completed AHP application, the verification process begins. For employed AHPs, Human Resources (HR) has agreed to complete the verification process and to transfer the requisite documents to Medical Staff Services (MSS) for review by the appropriate committees.

4. **Verification process**
   a) Write to all places of training to verify attendance and graduation. — Letter
   b) Write or call license board(s) to verify licensure currency. — Form
   c) Write to professional liability insurance carrier requesting verification of coverage and claims experience. — Letter

continues

Courtesy of St. Vincent Hospital, Worcester, Massachusetts.

d) Write or call specialty board(s) to verify year and currency of certification. Letter
e) Electronically query National Practitioner Data Bank (Done in MSS).
   1. HR call MSS x36110 to request query.
f) Write to the two listed references, requesting written responses. Letter
g) Send reference request to any health care facility where the AHP has worked. Form

5. **Documents to be collected: Use Checklist**
   a) AHP application (completed, dated, and signed)
   b) Specific Services Form appropriate to AHP (dated and signed)
   c) Copy of license(s)
   d) Copy of specialty certificate(s)
   e) **For PAs, NPs, CNMs, and RNCSs**—If they have prescriptive writing authority:
      1. Copy of Mass. Controlled Substances Certificate
      2. Copy of Federal DEA certificate
      3. Completed Medication Guidelines and Agreement
   f) Curriculum Vitae/Resume
   g) **For PAs only**
      1. Supervising Physician Agreement
      2. Letters from Board of Registration in Medicine:
         A. Letter to PA re supervising physician
         B. Letter to supervising physician

APPENDIX 8-B

Physician Assistant Privilege Sheet

PHYSICIAN ASSISTANT NAME

INSTRUCTIONS: Supervising physician(s) may request the following privileges to be granted to the above-named physician assistant by checking the applicable box(es) and signing at the end of the form.

REQUESTED	GRANTED	DENIED	
			HISTORY, PHYSICAL, DIAGNOSIS
☐	☐	☐	Evaluate patient presentation and suggest diagnosis.
☐	☐	☐	Perform physical examination.
☐	☐	☐	Record pertinent patient data on medical record.
☐	☐	☐	Review patient records to determine health status.
☐	☐	☐	Take patient history.
☐	☐	☐	Other: ______________________________
			LABORATORY AND SCREENING PROCEDURES
☐	☐	☐	Catheterization and routine urinalysis.
☐	☐	☐	Collection of and examination of stool.
☐	☐	☐	Nasogastric intubation and gastric lavage.
☐	☐	☐	Perform and read skin tests.
☐	☐	☐	Perform audiometry.

continues

Courtesy of The Hospital of the Good Samaritan, Los Angeles, California.

Laboratory and Screening Procedures (continued)

REQUESTED	GRANTED	DENIED	
☐	☐	☐	Perform endoscopic procedures limited to nasoscopy, otoscopy and anoscopy.
☐	☐	☐	Perform pelvic examinations, including biannual examinations and pap smears.
☐	☐	☐	Perform tonometry.
☐	☐	☐	Perform venipunctures both to obtain blood specimens and to start intravenous fluids.
☐	☐	☐	Take cultures.
☐	☐	☐	Take EKG tracings.
☐	☐	☐	Other: ____________________________
			THERAPEUTIC PROCEDURES
☐	☐	☐	Anterior nasal packing for epistaxis
☐	☐	☐	Application traction
☐	☐	☐	Application of physical therapy modalities
☐	☐	☐	Cast removal
☐	☐	☐	Debridement of minor superficial burns
☐	☐	☐	Debridement, suture and care of superficial wounds
☐	☐	☐	Immunizations
☐	☐	☐	Incision and drainage of superficial skin infections
☐	☐	☐	Injections
☐	☐	☐	Removal of foreign bodies from the skin
☐	☐	☐	Removal of impacted cerumen
☐	☐	☐	Removal of sutures
☐	☐	☐	Subcutaneous local anesthesia, excluding any nerve blocks
☐	☐	☐	Start, superimpose and discontinue intravenous fluids.
☐	☐	☐	Strapping, casting and splinting of sprains
☐	☐	☐	Other: ____________________________
			EMERGENCY PROCEDURES
☐	☐	☐	Assist in cardiopulmonary resuscitation.
☐	☐	☐	Control external hemorrhage.
☐	☐	☐	Other: ____________________________

REQUESTED	GRANTED	DENIED	
			PATIENT INSTRUCTION AND COUNSELING (Specify examples)
☐	☐	☐	______________________
			______________________
			ASSIST IN INSTITUTIONAL SETTING
			Act as first assistant in the following surgeries:
☐	☐	☐	______________________
☐	☐	☐	______________________
			Act as second assistant in the following surgeries:
☐	☐	☐	______________________
☐	☐	☐	______________________
☐	☐	☐	Order occupational therapy treatment.
☐	☐	☐	Order physical therapy treatment.
☐	☐	☐	Order respiratory therapy services.
☐	☐	☐	Order routine diagnostic lab tests and procedures.
☐	☐	☐	Order routine diagnostic radiological services.
☐	☐	☐	Order therapeutic diets.
☐	☐	☐	Schedule patient admissions.
☐	☐	☐	Other: ______________________
☐	☐	☐	**FACILITATE REFERRAL TO OTHER FACILITIES, AGENCIES & RESOURCES (Specify examples)**
☐	☐	☐	______________________
☐	☐	☐	______________________
☐	☐	☐	**TRANSMIT ORALLY OR IN WRITING ON PATIENT'S RECORD A PRESCRIPTION FROM SUPERVISING PHYSICIAN (Specify examples)**
☐	☐	☐	______________________
☐	☐	☐	______________________

STATEMENT BY SUPERVISING PHYSICIAN: In recommending that the above privileges be approved, I have evaluated the physician assistant and found him/her to be qualified to perform those tasks. I will conduct routine reviews and

continues

spot-check reviews as required. My written evaluation of the quality of his/her performance and competence will be entered into his/her file in the Medical Staff Office.

Supervising Physician's Signature	*Date*
Supervising Physician's Name Printed	
Chairman, Interdisciplinary Practices Committee	*Date*
Chairman, Department of	*Date*
Chairman, Medical Staff	*Date*
Chairman, Board of Trustees	*Date*

Appendix 8-C

Delineation of Privileges for Emergency Department Physician Assistant

One-Year Appointment
Dates:

Two-Year Appointment
Dates:

NAME ____

PREPARING FOR BOARD CERTIFICATION: Yes ____ No ____

Emergency department physician assistant: Yes ____ No ____

Privileges in the department of emergency medicine will be granted to those physician assistants who have fulfilled the necessary requirements as required by the hospital bylaws for medical assistants and who follow the rules and regulations for the department of emergency medicine.

Requirement: The physician assistant must be certified by the appropriate certifying agency and must be licensed by the State of _______. Each individual shall be advanced cardiac life support (ACLS) certified. Advanced trauma life support (ATLS) certification is encouraged.

The applicant should have successfully completed training in one of the approved programs for physician assistants in the United States.

The exact privileges accorded to each physician assistant of this department shall vary with the qualifications of the applicant. This matter will be decided by the chairman of the department.

NOTE: No emergency medicine physician assistant may routinely treat patients on an inpatient basis.

continues

Courtesy of Brandywine Hospital, Coatesville, Pennsylvania.

In accordance with the emergency department policy and procedure on physician assistants (#1.17), the emergency department physician assistant will always operate under the supervision of an attending emergency department physician. Appropriate consultation with the emergency department attending physician is mandatory in all those cases beyond the scope of practice of the emergency department physician assistant and in all cases in which there is a question as to the proper evaluation and management of the patient.

PRIVILEGES

GENERAL: The emergency department physician assistant will provide history/physical examination and evaluation on those patients who present to the department of emergency medicine judged to be within their area of care in accordance with Policy 1.17 of the emergency department policy and procedure on physician assistants.

NOTE: In life-threatening or limb-threatening cases in which the emergency department attending physician is caring for a patient of equal or more severe injury or illness, the physician assistant may provide care to patients presenting with life- or limb-threatening injuries to thus prevent morbidity and mortality. The attending emergency department physician will become involved with the patient's care as soon as is possible.

The following list of procedures will be listed in three groups: (1) procedures that can be performed without direct physician oversight and direct physician discussion; (2) procedures that require physician consultation prior to the procedure; (3) procedures that require prior physician discussion and direct one-on-one supervision.

	To Be Completed by Applicant		To Be Completed by Medical/Dental Staff	
Procedure or Therapeutic Modality	Privilege Requested	Approx. No. of Times Performed in Past Two Yrs.	Privileges Approved by the Board	Special Conditions
A. Procedures that the physician assistant may complete prior to emergency department attending consultation and oversight:				
Administration of Tylenol	_______	_______	_______	_______
Nonsteroidal anti-inflammatory medication	_______	_______	_______	_______
Tetanus prophylaxis	_______	_______	_______	_______
Antacids	_______	_______	_______	_______
Inhaled adrenergic agents	_______	_______	_______	_______
Oral antibiotics	_______	_______	_______	_______
Donnatal	_______	_______	_______	_______
Nonprescription medication	_______	_______	_______	_______

Procedure or Therapeutic Modality	To Be Completed by Applicant: Privilege Requested	To Be Completed by Applicant: Approx. No. of Times Performed in Past Two Yrs.	To Be Completed by Medical/Dental Staff: Privileges Approved by the Board	To Be Completed by Medical/Dental Staff: Special Conditions
EMERGENCY DEPARTMENT				
WOUND EVALUATION				
Laceration management				
Closure in injuries not involving tendon, bone, nerve or blood vessel, or the face	______	______	______	______
Cervical spine immobilization via Philadelphia collar	______	______	______	______
Simple foreign body removal	______	______	______	______
Local and regional nerve block	______	______	______	______
Slit lamp usage	______	______	______	______
Ocular tonometry	______	______	______	______
Urethral catheter insertion	______	______	______	______
Application and/or inflation of medical antishock garment	______	______	______	______
Nail bed repair	______	______	______	______
Evaluation of extremity injuries with application of appropriate splinting material	______	______	______	______

B. Procedures in which the attending emergency department physician will be consulted (however, the performance of the procedure does not require the direct personal one-to-one supervision by the emergency department attending physician):

Procedure or Therapeutic Modality	Privilege Requested	Approx. No. of Times Performed in Past Two Yrs.	Privileges Approved by the Board	Special Conditions
Repair of facial lacerations	______	______	______	______
Abscess incision and drainage	______	______	______	______
Arthrocentesis of the knee joint	______	______	______	______
Reduction of dislocations of the digit and patella	______	______	______	______
Epistaxis management via cautery or anterior nasal pack	______	______	______	______
Arterial blood gas	______	______	______	______
Intravenous cannulation via percutaneous, external jugular, or scalp vein	______	______	______	______
Indirect mirror laryngoscopy	______	______	______	______
Nail trephination	______	______	______	______

continues

Procedure or Therapeutic Modality	To Be Completed by Applicant: Privilege Requested	To Be Completed by Applicant: Approx. No of Times Performed in Past Two Yrs.	To Be Completed by Medical/Dental Staff: Privileges Approved by the Board	To Be Completed by Medical/Dental Staff: Special Conditions
Preservation of severed extremity (digit, ear, nose, penis)	_______	_______	_______	_______
Anoscopy	_______	_______	_______	_______
Surgical debridement	_______	_______	_______	_______

C. Procedures that may be performed as an assistant to the emergency attending physician:

Procedure or Therapeutic Modality	Privilege Requested	Approx. No of Times Performed in Past Two Yrs.	Privileges Approved by the Board	Special Conditions
Arthrocentesis of elbow, wrist, ankle	_______	_______	_______	_______
Central venous pressure measuring	_______	_______	_______	_______
Reduction of dislocation of the elbow and shoulder	_______	_______	_______	_______
Cricothyroidotomy	_______	_______	_______	_______
Endotracheal intubation	_______	_______	_______	_______
Central venous catheter insertion	_______	_______	_______	_______
Lumbar puncture	_______	_______	_______	_______
Postnasal packing	_______	_______	_______	_______
Peritoneal lavage	_______	_______	_______	_______
Split thickness skin grafting	_______	_______	_______	_______
Thoracostomy tube insertion	_______	_______	_______	_______
Emergency delivery	_______	_______	_______	_______
Culdocentesis	_______	_______	_______	_______
Defibrillation	_______	_______	_______	_______
Cardioversion	_______	_______	_______	_______
Rhythm interpretation	_______	_______	_______	_______
ECG interpretation	_______	_______	_______	_______
Transvenous pacing	_______	_______	_______	_______
Transcutaneous pacing	_______	_______	_______	_______

PLEASE NOTE: Indicate the name of the hospital where procedures were performed:

____

____

I agree to abide by the above Delineation of Privileges.

______________________	______________________
Signature of Department Chairman	Signature of Applicant
______________________	______________________
Date	Date

Appendix 8-D

Reporting and Querying—The National Practitioner Data Bank

Table 1 Reporting to the National Practitioner Data Bank

Entity/Action	*Physicians and Dentists*	*Other Licensed Health Care Practitioners*
Medical Malpractice Insurers Payment resulting from written claim or judgment	Must report	Must report
State Licensing Boards Licensure disciplinary action based on reasons related to professional competence or conduct	Must report	No reporting requirements*
Hospitals and Other Health Care Entities Professional review action, based on reasons related to professional competence or conduct, adversely affecting clinical privileges for a period longer than 30 days Voluntary surrender or restriction of clinical privileges while under, or to avoid investigation	Must report	May report
Professional Societies Professional review action, based on reasons related to professional competence or conduct, adversely affecting membership	Must report	May report

*Must report when the requirements of Section 5 of P.L. 100-93 are implemented.

Source: Reprinted from *National Practitioner Data Bank Guidebook: A Reference for Individuals and Entities Reporting to and Querying the Data Bank,* p. 3, U.S. Department of Health and Human Services, August 1992.

Table 2 Requesting Information from the National Practitioner Data Bank

Entity	*Information Request (Query) Status*
Hospitals Screening applicants for medical staff appointment or granting of clinical privileges every two years for physicians, dentists, or other health care practitioners on the medical staff or granted clinical privileges	Must report
Hospitals At other times as is deemed necessary	May request
State Licensing Boards As is deemed necessary	May request
Other Health Care Entities Screening applicants for medical staff appointment or granting of clinical privileges Supporting professional review activities	May request
Professional Societies Screening applicants for membership or affiliation Supporting professional review activities	May request
Plaintiff's Attorney Plaintiff's attorney or plaintiff representing himself or herself (*pro se*) who has filed a medical malpractice action or claim in a state or federal court or other adjudicative body against a hospital when evidence is submitted revealing that the hospital failed to make a required query of the National Practitioner Data Bank on the practitioner(s) also named in the action or claim	May request
Physicians, Dentists, and Other Health Care Practitioners Regarding their own files	May request
Medical Malpractice Insurers	May not request

Source: Reprinted from *National Practitioner Data Bank Guidebook: A Reference for Individuals and Entities Reporting and Querying the Data Bank,* p. 4, U.S. Department of Health and Human Services, August 1992.

Table 3 Examples of Other Health Care Practitioners

The following list of health care practitioners other than physicians and dentists is provided solely for illustrative purposes. The inclusion or exclusion of any health care occupational group in the list noted below should not be interpreted as a mandate or a waiver of compliance with National Practitioner Data Bank reporting requirements.

Acupuncturists
Audiologists
Chiropractors
Dental assistants
Dental hygienists
Denturists
Dietitians
Emergency medical technicians
Home health aides
Homeopaths
Medical assistants
Medical technologists
Mental health counselors
Midwives, lay
Naturopaths
Nuclear medicine technologists
Nurses aides
Nurse anesthetists
Nurse, licensed practical
Nurse, licensed vocational
Nurse midwives
Nurse practitioners
Nurse, registered
Nutritionists
Occupational therapists
Occupational therapy assistants
Ocularists
Opticians
Optometrists
Orthotics/prosthetics fitters
Pharmacists
Pharmacists, nuclear
Pharmacy assistants
Physical therapy assistants
Physician assistants
Physical therapists
Podiatric assistants
Professional counselors
Psychiatric technicians
Radiation therapy technologists
Radiologic technologists
Rehabilitation therapists
Respiratory therapists
Respiratory therapy technicians
Social workers, clinical
Speech/language pathologists

Source: Reprinted from *National Practitioner Data Bank Guidebook: A Reference for Individuals and Entities Reporting to and Querying the Data Bank,* p. 5, U.S. Department of Health and Human Services, August 1992.

CHAPTER 9

Employment Laws

INTRODUCTION

Both state and federal laws govern the relationship between employers and employees. These laws are applicable to PAs employed by hospitals, health maintenance organizations (HMOs), and other types of health care providers. To determine the effect of employment laws on a particular PA's circumstances, it is necessary to determine whether the PA is an employee or independent contractor.

The most important employment laws relate to either equal employment opportunity or labor standards. Equal employment opportunity laws deal with aspects of discrimination based on race, color, religion, national origin, age, sex, disability, and other protected classifications. Labor standards laws establish minimum standards that employers must maintain with respect to working conditions. The principal laws in this field deal with minimum wages, overtime pay, maximum hours worked, safety, and health.

Ordinarily, when federal law and state law conflict, federal law supersedes or preempts state law. In some instances, however, state and federal law may be simultaneously effective and may afford the PA a choice of jurisdiction in which to exercise employment rights. Because this chapter focuses on federal legislation, PAs concerned with employment rights should also consider state law remedies.

Although there are few cases discussing the application of employment laws to PAs specifically, the employment law principles explained in this chapter are of importance to PAs, as they are to all employees.

DETERMINING EMPLOYEE STATUS

The first step in any employment law analysis is determining whether the individual is an employee. This may be particularly difficult in the health care context, where many workers are classified by employers as independent contractors, rather than as employees. Employee status determines what federal employment taxes apply to a particular worker, whether the individual is protected by minimum wage and overtime provisions, whether civil rights laws apply, and whether the employer can be liable for the employee's actions on the job. Each of these legal issues is dealt with differently depending on whether a PA is an employee or independent contractor.

The determination of whether a PA is an employee or an independent contractor is based on the circumstances of the relationship. A contract specifying that a worker is an independent contractor is relevant to the analysis, but is not dispositive if other facts reveal that an employer-employee relationship exists. Cases and statutes illustrate the circumstances that characterize an employer-employee relationship, generally focusing on the degree of control that the employer exerts over the employee's day-to-day work.

The Internal Revenue Service (IRS) takes a particular interest in employee status, as employers are responsible for a higher share of federal taxes for employees than for independent contractors. The IRS has scrutinized the use of independent contractors in the health care industry recently, relying on a 20-factor test to determine whether an individual is actually an employee. Similar factors have been considered in court decisions assessing employee status for other purposes, such as the application of civil rights laws. The IRS will examine whether the employer:

- can require a worker to comply with instructions about when, where, and how the work is to be performed
- provides training for the worker
- integrates the worker's services into the employer's business operations
- requires the worker to perform the services personally
- hires, supervises, and pays assistants for the worker
- uses the worker's services in a continuing or frequently recurring relationship
- sets the hours of work for the workers' services
- requires the worker to devote substantially full-time hours to the employer's business
- requires the work to be performed on the employer's premises
- establishes the order or sequence of work to be performed by the worker
- requires the worker to submit reports
- makes periodic (hourly, weekly, or monthly, as opposed to lump sum or per job) payments to the worker
- pays or reimburses the worker's expenses
- furnishes the worker with tools and supplies
- retains the right to discharge the worker
- does not have a claim against the worker if the worker quits

Four additional factors measure the independence of the individual worker by examining whether the worker:

1. invests in facilities or equipment used to perform the services
2. can expect a profit or suffer a loss (other than mere nonpayment by the facility for services rendered)
3. performs services for more than one unrelated individual or entity at the same time
4. makes services available to the general public on a regular and consistent basis

[Rev. Rul. 87-41].

In the past several years, IRS rulings on the status of hospital-affiliated physicians have emphasized the hospital's control over the physician's business operations to conclude that many physicians were employees for tax law purposes. For example, the IRS concluded that physicians paid on a per-read basis to interpret electrocardiograms for an outpatient surgery center were employees. The physicians maintained their own practices, did not receive any fringe benefits from the hospital, and purchased their own malpractice insurance. The IRS emphasized, however, that the readings were part of the hospital's operations, the physicians did not assume any financial risks, and the physicians were paid a flat fee for their readings, whether the hospital was reimbursed or not [*see* Tech. Adv. Mem. 95-35-001 (Mar. 14, 1995)].

For PAs, individual state laws may also pose a barrier to independent contractor status, based in part on the dependent nature of PA professional status. Some states specifically prohibit independent contractor status for PAs. In Wisconsin, for example, regulations state that no physician assistant may be self-employed [Wis. Admin. Code § Med. 8.09]. Other states may require PAs to keep the state medical board informed as to the identity of the PA's supervising physician or practice location, notifying the board of any change within 30 days or less [*see, e.g.,* Fla. Admin. Code Ann. r. 59R-30.004; Ind. Admin. Code tit. 844, r. 2.1-1-3]. This notification requirement may hinder independent contractor status for PAs by limiting mobility. [Refer to Chapter 3: Licensure and Scope of Practice, at Physician Supervision, for further discussion of requirements for physician supervision of PAs.]

Federal regulations may also work against an independent contractor relationship. Medicare regulations state that payment for PA services may be made only to the employer of a PA, for example, not to the PA. At one time, the Health Care Financing Administration (HCFA) looked for a W-2 tax form to identify a PA's employer, as opposed to the 1099 form filed by independent contractors. Presently, however, HCFA looks for a "valid employment relationship" which may be found even in the absence of a W-2 employment relationship. PAs considering becoming independent contractors should determine whether local Medicare carriers will look beyond a 1099 form when identifying a PA's employer [*see* AAPA, *Issue Brief: The Physician Assistant as an Independent Contractor* (1996) (prepared by AAPA Professional Practice Council); for a more detailed discussion of reimbursement regulations, see Chapter 10: Third-Party Reimbursement].

OVERVIEW OF FEDERAL ANTIDISCRIMINATION LAWS

The most significant pieces of federal legislation governing discrimination in employment are Title VII of the Civil Rights Act of 1964 (Title VII), the Age Discrimination in Employment Act (ADEA), the Vocational Rehabilitation Act of 1973 (Rehabilitation Act), and the Americans with Disabilities Act (ADA). This body of legislation governs a variety of employment practices, and is primarily aimed at prohibiting various forms of employment discrimination.

Title VII

Title VII is the most comprehensive and far-reaching antidiscrimination statute. It prohibits employers from discriminating against individuals on the basis of race, color, national origin, religion, or sex in decisions regarding the employment relationship, including hiring, promotion, compensation, discipline, and termination decisions [42 U.S.C. §§ 2000e through 2000e-17]. Title VII applies to private employers, as well as to state and local governments, governmental agencies, and political subdivisions. Only religious groups and their educational institutions are exempted.

Since 1964, Congress has amended Title VII in several significant ways, in particular through the enactment of the Pregnancy Discrimination Act (PDA) and the Civil Rights Act of 1991. The PDA prohibits discriminatory treatment of pregnant women for all employment related purposes [42 U.S.C. § 2000e(k)]. The Civil Rights Act of 1991 reverses several Supreme Court rulings narrowing the scope of Title VII and extends the damages available to victims of some forms of intentional discrimination [Pub. L. No. 102-166, amending 42 U.S.C. § 1981].

ADEA

Title VII does not cover discrimination based on age or disability. However, the ADEA was enacted in 1967 to prohibit arbitrary age discrimination in employment [29 U.S.C. §§ 621 through 634]. As it was originally enacted, the ADEA granted protection to employees aged 40 to 65. Subsequent amendments to the statute extended the upper age limit to 70 and then eliminated the upper cap completely. In 1990, Congress enacted the Older Workers Benefit Protection Act, amending the ADEA to extend the prohibition against age discrimination to employee benefit programs [29 U.S.C. §§ 621, 623 & 626].

Disability Discrimination Statutes

The Rehabilitation Act and the ADA generally prohibit employment discrimination against qualified individuals with disabilities. The Rehabilitation Act prohibits this type of discrimination by government agencies and federal contractors, but does not apply to private employers [29 U.S.C. §§ 793 through 794d]. Courts have held that hospitals receiving federal funds, for example, through Medicare, are subject to the Rehabilitation Act. In 1990, the ADA was enacted to extend the ban on disability discrimination to private companies employing 15 or more workers [42 U.S.C. §§ 12100 through 12213].

LEGAL THEORIES OF DISCRIMINATION

The Supreme Court has established two distinct legal theories of discrimination: disparate treatment and disparate impact. The more easily understood of these two notions is disparate treatment, simply defined as unequal treatment. Direct evidence of an employer's intent to discriminate is not necessary to prove a violation of Title VII; illegal discrimination can occur if an employer treats a person in a protected class differently from a similarly situated person in another class, and is unable to justify the difference in treatment on nondiscriminatory grounds. A protected class is a segment of the population that historically has been subjected to discriminatory treatment such as on the basis of race, religion, or gender. For example, an employer's discharge of a female employee for insubordination can constitute disparate treatment discrimination if there is evidence that a similarly situated male employee was not discharged for a comparable insubordinate act.

Unlike disparate treatment, the disparate impact theory of discrimination focuses on the *effects* of an alleged discriminatory practice. The results or consequences of the employer's policies, rather than the employer's motivation or intent, are the primary focus of this type of claim. An employee will generally attempt to prove that a practice has a substantial adverse impact on a protected class, even though it is applied equally to all employees. In a well-known Supreme Court ruling regarding a disparate impact case, the Court held that an employer's requirement that all employees, except those working in the maintenance department, have a high school diploma was discriminatory [*Griggs v. Duke Power Co.*, 401 U.S. 424 (1971)]. At that time, many more White employees had high school diplomas than did Black employees, and as a result, almost all of the positions outside the maintenance department (the lowest in pay) were filled by White employees. The Court decided that although the requirement of a high school diploma was neutral on the surface, it had a discriminatory impact on Black employees and therefore violated Title VII.

RACE DISCRIMINATION

The use of the word *race* in Title VII includes all racial distinctions, making it as illegal to discriminate against a White employee as it is against a Black employee. Title VII also specifically bans discrimination on the basis of color, which has been interpreted either as synonymous with race or as a subclass of a race that is itself subject to disparate treatment, such as African Americans with lighter skin tones or more Caucasian features.

Historically, the most common form of racial discrimination occurs when a White individual is selected for a position instead of an equally qualified non-white person because of race. However, under the disparate impact theory of discrimination, there are a wide range of other more subtle practices that could constitute racial discrimination in an employment relationship. Employment practices that may discriminate against certain minorities include consideration of an individual's poor credit rating or arrest record, discharge of an employee whose wages are garnished or who is an unwed mother, and non–job-related criteria such as the need for a high school diploma.

An employer may defend charges of race discrimination by pointing to a legitimate business necessity for its actions. For example, a hospital that moved from an inner city location to an outlying suburban area was charged with discrimination because the total number of minority employees decreased significantly. However, the hospital could rebut the charge by producing evidence of the poor financial condition of the hospital at the old site, the decline in its usage, and the need for the hospital in the suburbs. Such a defense would constitute a business necessity [*see, e.g., EEOC v. North Hills Passavant Hosp.,* 466 F. Supp. 783 (W.D. Pa. 1979)].

SEX DISCRIMINATION

An employment decision to hire, discharge, or classify an individual on the basis of gender is the most obvious form of sex discrimination, but sex discrimination also can take a variety of other forms. Sexual harassment, decisions based on pregnancy or pregnancy-related disabilities, and unequal pay for equal work are other forms of sex discrimination.

Both case law and administrative guidelines have contributed to defining the types of behavior that can generate liability for sex discrimination. The Equal Employment Opportunity Commission (EEOC) has issued guidelines on sex discrimination. Under the guidelines, an employer will violate Title VII if it classifies or advertises a job as either requiring a "male" or "female." [But see the later discussion regarding gender as a bona fide occupation qualification.] Other types of sex discrimination, according to the EEOC, include separate seniority lists based on gender, rules that limit the employment of married women but not married men, and the automatic exclusion of all women in jobs where physical strength is required [*see* EEOC, *Guidelines on Discrimination Because of Sex,* 29 C.F.R. Part 1604].

Case law has also illustrated what types of conduct amount to gender bias in the context of an employment relationship. The Supreme Court has held, for example, that suggestions that a female lawyer wear more makeup, change her hairstyle, and enroll in charm school were sexual stereotypes that could be the basis for liability for refusing to admit the woman as a partner in a law firm [*Price Waterhouse v. Hopkins,* 490 U.S. 228 (1989)]. The Sixth Circuit has ruled that requiring a newly married employee to change her name on personnel forms to that of her husband violated Title VII [*Allen v. Lovejoy,* 553 F.2d 522 (6th Cir. 1977)]. A Michigan appeals court ruled that a hospital discriminated against female technologists by requiring them to wear white or pastel-colored uniforms, while male technologists were permitted to wear white lab coats over regular street clothes [*Department of Civil Rights v. Sparrow Hosp. Ass'n,* 326 N.W.2d 519 (Mich. Ct. App. 1982)].

Defenses

An employer can successfully defend a sex discrimination suit by proving that gender is a bona fide occupational qualification (BFOQ) for a particular job. A psychiatric hospital, for example, treating emotionally disturbed and sexually abused children and adolescents may require the presence of female and male staff members on all shifts, the Third Circuit has ruled, because sex is a BFOQ. A female child care specialist sued, arguing that the hospital discriminated against her on the basis of sex in violation of Title VII by assigning her to the night shift because of her gender. The federal appeals court ruled in favor of the hospital, finding that although the hospital's policy was facially discriminatory, the policy is justified because gender is a BFOQ for child care specialists at the facility. The essence of the hospital's business is to treat emotionally disturbed and sexually abused adolescents and children, the court reasoned. Expert testimony established that this type of therapy requires staff members of both genders, depending on the gender of the patients and their abusers. Further, privacy concerns justify the staffing policy because patients discuss hygiene and sexuality more freely with staff members of the same sex. Thus, the court concluded, the hospital established a BFOQ justifying the discriminatory employment practice [*Healey v. Southwood Psychiatric Hosp.*, 78 F.3d 128 (3d Cir. 1996)].

Pregnancy and Childbirth

Title VII was amended in 1978 to prohibit discrimination in employment based on pregnancy. The amendments, known as the PDA, contain an expansive prohibition against employment decisions made on the basis of pregnancy, childbirth, or related medical conditions. The amendments expressly ban the use of pregnancy as a factor in employment decisions, and also prohibit practices that have an adverse effect on pregnant women, unless the practice is justified by business necessity.

The PDA requires that policies relating to the commencement and duration of pregnancy leave treat pregnancy as any other disability. Further, such policies may not have a disparate impact on pregnant women unless the policy can be justified by business necessity. A policy that denies leaves of absence of any kind until an employee has completed at least one year of service, for example, will violate Title VII if there is evidence that significantly more female employees are denied leave than male first-year employees [*see, e.g., Floca v. Home Health Care Servs.*, 845 F.2d 108 (5th Cir. 1988)]. Similarly, a leave of absence policy that limits maternity leave to three months while authorizing an indefinite leave of absence for an "illness" would also violate the PDA [*Maddox v. Grandview Care Ctr.*, 780 F.2d 987 (11th Cir. 1986)].

The Family and Medical Leave Act of 1993 (FMLA) also directly addresses the issue of maternity and paternity leave [29 U.S.C. §§ 2601 through 2654]. Under the FMLA, an eligible employee is entitled to up to 12 workweeks of unpaid leave during any 12-month period for a serious medical condition or to care for a newborn child or a newly adopted child.

Sexual Orientation

Courts have generally ruled that Title VII does not protect employees from discrimination on the basis of sexual preference. In one case, for instance, the Fifth Circuit ruled that an employer could refuse to hire an applicant because he was effeminate, ruling that Title VII does not forbid discrimination based on an affectional or sexual preference [*Smith v. Liberty Mut. Ins. Co.*, 569 F.2d 325 (5th Cir. 1978)]. Several courts have also ruled that Title VII does not protect transsexuals; the law simply provides that it is unlawful to discriminate against women because they are women and against men because they are men [*Ulane v. Eastern Airlines,* 742 F.2d 1081 (7th Cir. 1984), *cert. denied,* 471 U.S. 1017 (1985); *Dobre v. National R.R. Passenger Corp.,* 850 F. Supp. 284 (E.D. Pa. 1993)]. However, certain states, such as California, have specifically included sexual orientation as a protected class under state employment discrimination law [CAL. LAB. CODE § 1102.1].

Sexual Harassment

Sexual harassment, which is prohibited under Title VII's ban on sex discrimination, includes unwelcome sexual advances, requests for sexual favors, and other verbal or physical conduct of a sexual nature. Such behavior constitutes sexual harassment when submission to such conduct is a term or condition of employment; submission to such conduct becomes the basis for employment-related decisions; or such conduct unreasonably interferes with an employee's job performance. Both men and women can be the victims of sexual harassment. There are two types of sexual harassment: *quid pro quo* harassment and hostile environment harassment.

Quid Pro Quo Sexual Harassment

Quid pro quo harassment occurs when submission to unwelcome sexual advances, requests for sexual favors, and other verbal or physical conduct of a sexual nature becomes the basis for employment-related decisions. *Quid pro quo* is a Latin term meaning "this for that." In other words, an employee is required to "trade" conduct of a sexual nature in order to keep or obtain employment.

To prove this type of harassment, the victim must show that sexual advances were made, the advances were unwelcome, and the harasser either threatened or pursued retaliation for rejection of advances. The harasser need not explicitly inform the victim, however, that adverse employment consequences will flow from the refusal to submit to the harasser's advances to constitute *quid pro quo* harassment. The victim can prove such harassment by either direct or indirect evidence.

Hostile Environment Sexual Harassment

Hostile environment sexual harassment occurs when the conduct creates a hostile or intimidating work environment to the degree that it interferes with the person's ability to do his or her job. To prove hostile environment harassment, an employee must show that acts of a sexual nature occurred in the workplace; these acts were unwelcome, repeated, and pervasive; and the hostile environment either interfered with the employee's ability to do the job or made the job more difficult or severe.

A federal appeals court case illustrates hostile environment harassment in the health care context. During the course of a medical residency program, several male residents were involved in conversations to the effect that women in general, and one of the female residents in particular, should not be surgeons. In the male residents' rest facility, they displayed *Playboy* centerfolds, sexually explicit drawings of the female resident's body, and a list of sexually-oriented nicknames they had given the female residents. The conditions described were sufficiently severe and pervasive to create an abusive work environment for female residents [*Lipsett v. University of Puerto Rico,* 864 F.2d 881 (1st Cir. 1988)].

The Supreme Court has ruled that for hostile environment sexual harassment to violate Title VII, it must be sufficiently severe or pervasive to alter the conditions of the victim's employment and create an abusive working environment [*Meritor Sav. Bank v. Vinson,* 477 U.S. 57 (1986)]. To prove the severity of the conduct, there must be evidence that the conduct unreasonably interferes with an individual's work performance or creates an intimidating, hostile, or offensive working environment. Whether an environment is hostile must be determined by looking at all of the circumstances, and no single factor is required.

An employee suing for sexual harassment does not have to offer evidence that he or she suffered concrete psychological harm. The psychological well-being of the victim will be relevant, however, to the overall analysis of whether the environment was abusive. According to the Supreme Court, courts must also consider other factors such as the frequency and severity of the discriminatory conduct, whether the conduct is physically threatening or humiliating, and whether it interferes unreasonably with the employee's work performance [*Harris v. Forklift Sys. Inc.,* 510 U.S. 17 (1993)].

Employer Liability for Sexual Harassment

To determine whether an employer, such as an HMO or hospital, is liable for sexually harassing conduct of an employee, courts will first examine whether the harasser is the victim's coworker or supervisor. According to the EEOC, an employer is liable for a coworker's sexual harassment if the employer knows or should have known of the offensive conduct but fails to take "immediate and appropriate corrective action" [29 C.F.R. § 1604.11(d)]. This is true for both *quid pro quo* and hostile environment sexual harassment.

An employer is always responsible for acts of *quid pro quo* harassment committed by an employee's supervisor, although the employer's prompt and remedial action to complaints of harassment can limit liability. The employer's liability is predicated on the fact that in making or threatening to make a decision affecting the victim's employment, the supervisor is exercising authority delegated by the employer.

Employers are not automatically liable for sexual harassment by supervisors in hostile environment cases, however. Rather, courts will apply agency principles to determine employer liability. A person qualifies as an agent if the person is a supervisory or managerial employee to whom employment decisions have been delegated by the employer. An employer will be liable for acts by a supervisor that amount to hostile environment sexual harassment if the acts represent the exercise of authority that others reasonably believe the supervisor to have because of the employer's conduct. The District of Columbia federal circuit court has ruled, for example, that an employer will not be liable for a supervisor's hostile environment sexual harassment if the employer has adopted policies and implemented measures such that the complaining employee should have known that the employer did not tolerate the supervisor's conduct. At the time the harassment took place in that case, the employer had sponsored seminars on sexual harassment, distributed notices to all employees to the effect that harassment would not be tolerated, publicized its civil rights policy statement, and made available names and phone numbers of equal employment opportunity counselors to whom harassment could be reported. Thus, the employer could not be held liable [*Gary v. Long,* 59 F.3d 1391 (D.C. Cir. 1995), *cert. denied,* 116 S. Ct. 569 (1995)].

Same-Sex Harassment

Some courts have allowed same-gender sexual harassment claims under Title VII, but other rulings have rejected same-sex harassment claims. The Fifth Circuit, for example, stated that "harassment by a male supervisor against a male subordinate does not state a claim under Title VII, even though the harassment has sexual overtones" [*Giddens v. Shell Oil Co.,* 12 F.3d 208 (5th Cir. 1993), *cert. denied,* 115 S. Ct. 311 (1994)].

Along the same lines, the Fourth Circuit has decided that Title VII does not create a right to sue based on hostile environment sexual harassment, where both the harassers and the victim are heterosexuals of the same sex. Reasoning that Title VII's requirement that the conduct take place "because of" sex cannot be extended to include all sexually focused conduct, the court found that the federal law does not protect against harassment because of the victim's shyness, prudery, or vulnerability, or because of the harassers' vulgarity, insensitivity, or meanness. The court declined to address the issue of sexual harassment involving homosexual employees, however [*McWilliams v. Fairfax County Bd. of Supervisors,* 72 F.3d 1191 (4th Cir. 1996)].

In some jurisdictions, however, courts may permit same-sex sexual harassment cases to go forward under Title VII, refusing to distinguish traditional sexual harassment cases [*Yeary v. Goodwill Indus.,* No. 96-5145 (6th Cir. Feb. 24, 1997)].

NATIONAL ORIGIN DISCRIMINATION

Title VII prohibits employment discrimination on the basis of national origin. EEOC guidelines indicate that national origin discrimination includes these practices:

- use of tests in English where English language skill is not a BFOQ
- denial of employment or job advancement to, or firing of, people who marry or associate with people of a specific national origin or whose name indicates a specific national origin
- denial of employment opportunities because of an individual's physical, cultural, or linguistic association with a particular national origin
- denial of employment or job advancement to, or firing of, individuals because of association with people, or organizations, schools, or religious institutions identified with any national origin
- denial of employment or job advancement based on height and weight where height and weight have an adverse impact on the selection of minorities, unless height and weight are BFOQs

[29 C.F.R. Part 1606].

RELIGIOUS DISCRIMINATION

Discrimination based on religion has not been litigated as much as discrimination based on race or sex. Nevertheless, there have been a number of religious discrimination cases concerning dress codes and observance of the Sabbath and other religious holidays. Title VII requires that, absent undue hardship, an employer must reasonably accommodate the religious needs of its employees [29 U.S.C. § 2000e(j)]. Whether a particular employment decision regarding these issues constitutes religious discrimination is largely based on the facts of each case, which indicate in particular instances whether an employer can reasonably accommodate an employee's specific religious practice. Accordingly, in some instances, an employer may be required under Title VII to allow an employee to wear a costume, headpiece, or emblem unique to a particular religion.

AGE DISCRIMINATION

Under the ADEA, it is unlawful for an employer:

- to fail or refuse to hire or to discharge any individual or otherwise discriminate against any individual with respect to his or her compensation, terms, or privileges of employment because of the individual's age

- to limit, segregate, or classify employees in any way that would deprive or tend to deprive an individual of employment opportunities or otherwise affect his or her status as an employee because of such individual's age

Courts have generally ruled that an employee who sues under the ADEA must demonstrate age discrimination, without which the adverse employment decision would not have been made [*see, e.g., Taggart v. Time, Inc.*, 924 F.2d 43 (2d Cir. 1991)]. This means that an employee does not need to prove that age was the sole determining factor in the negative employment decision. It is sufficient for the employee to prove that age was a determining factor even if there were other more compelling factors.

An employer may violate the ADEA even if both employees at issue are in the protected age bracket (40 and over). The United States Supreme Court recently ruled that a 56-year-old worker who was replaced by a 40-year-old worker could sue under the ADEA. The court emphasized that a significant difference in age, even among workers protected by the federal statute, can show age discrimination [*O'Connor v. Consolidated Coin Caterers Corp.*, 116 S. Ct. 1307 (1996)].

DISABILITY DISCRIMINATION

Under the Rehabilitation Act, employers that receive federal financial assistance may not, on the basis of an employee's or job applicant's handicap, exclude the individual from participating or enjoying the benefits of the federally assisted program or activity. The definition of who is handicapped is quite broad, and includes any person who:

- has a physical or mental impairment that substantially limits one or more major life activities
- has a record of such an impairment
- is regarded as having such an impairment

The definition does not include any individual who is an alcoholic or drug abuser and whose use of such substances prevents the individual from performing the duties of the job or whose employment would constitute a direct threat to property or the safety of others because of current alcohol or drug abuse.

The ADA prohibits employers from discriminating against qualified individuals because of a disability. A disability under the ADA is a physical or mental impairment that substantially limits one or more major life activities, a history of such impairment, or being regarded as having such an impairment. A "qualified individual" is defined as an individual with a disability who satisfies the requisite skill, experience, and educational requirements of an employment position and who, with or without reasonable accommodation, can perform the essential functions of the position.

Employment decisions covered by the disability discrimination statutes include job application procedures, hiring, advancement, discharge, compensation, job training, and other terms and conditions of employment.

Reasonable Accommodation

Generally defined, reasonable accommodation refers to any change in the work environment or in the customary way of doing things that enables an individual with a disability to perform a particular job's functions. Under the Rehabilitation Act, an employer may not discriminate against a qualified but handicapped individual, defined as an individual who "with reasonable accommodation can perform the essential functions of the job." Regulations adopted under this law require that an employer accommodate the physical or mental impairment of a handicapped applicant or employee unless the accommodation would impose an "undue hardship" on the operation of the employer's business. The regulations provide several examples of reasonable accommodation, such as modification of work schedules, job restructuring, physical modifications, or relocations of particular offices or jobs [45 C.F.R. §§ 84.3 & 84.12].

Similarly, under the ADA, reasonable accommodation may include making existing facilities accessible, job restructuring, part-time or modified work schedules, reassignment to a vacant position, acquisition or modification of equipment or devices, provision of qualified readers or other effective methods of making visually delivered materials available to the visually impaired and/or the provision of a qualified interpreter or other effective methods of making aurally delivered materials available to the hearing impaired. Under ADA regulations, reasonable accommodation can be broken down into three categories:

1. measures required to ensure equal opportunity in the application process
2. measures that enable employees to perform the essential functions of a position
3. measures that enable employees with disabilities to enjoy the same benefits and privileges of employment as are enjoyed by employees without disabilities

[29 C.F.R. § 1630.2(o)].

Health Care Cases

The following disability discrimination claims against health care employers illustrate how courts and administrative agencies have determined whether an individual is entitled to the protections offered by the Rehabilitation Act and the ADA.

- The Rehabilitation Act did not protect a head nurse whose mental illness caused her to consistently report late to work. The ability to arrive at work for the early shift was an essential requirement of the head nurse position, and the hospital could not reasonably accommodate her disability [*Guice-Mills v. Derwinski,* 967 F.2d 794 (2d Cir. 1992)].
- The Rehabilitation Act did not protect a physical therapist with colon cancer that had metastasized to her brain, where no reasonable amount of accommodation could have compensated for the therapist's difficulty with essential job functions such as performing normal documentation and recalling patients' names [*Klein v. Manor Healthcare Corp.,* 19 F.3d 1433 (6th Cir. 1994) (table format)].
- The ADA did not require a medical group to accommodate a disabled physician by hiring an assistant to perform physical aspects of the physician's job or by limiting the physician's duties to supervision and administration. Such accommodations would place an undue hardship on the business by requiring the medical group to hire two persons to do a task ordinarily assigned to one, or by necessitating the medical group's involuntary restructuring [*Reigel v. Kaiser Found. Health Plan,* 859 F. Supp. 963 (E.D.N.C. 1994)].
- A hospital's discharge of a human immunodeficiency virus (HIV)-positive surgical worker did not violate the ADA, because the technician posed a significant risk to the health and safety of patients undergoing surgical procedures and the risk could not be eliminated by reasonable accommodation [*Mauro v. Borgess Med. Ctr.,* 886 F. Supp. 1349 (W.D. Mich. 1995)].
- A hospital was not required by the ADA to reinstate an alcoholic physician to the position of Chief of the Department of Internal Medicine because the physician posed a direct threat to patient safety and was not qualified for the position under the ADA [*Altman v. New York City Health and Hosp. Corp.,* 903 F. Supp. 503 (S.D.N.Y. 1995)].
- A hearing-impaired nurse working at a Veterans Administration outpatient clinic may sue her employer for constructive discharge under the Rehabilitation Act. According to the nurse's suit, the employer rejected the nurse's repeated requests for transfer to a nonpatient care unit and never provided the nurse with medical equipment, including a stethoscope for hearing impaired individuals. In addition, the nurse argued that supervisors and coworkers demeaned the nurse and told her that she was incompetent because of her disability [*Hurley-Bardige v. Brown,* 900 F. Supp. 567 (D. Mass. 1995)].

FEDERAL LAWS GOVERNING WAGES, HOURS, AND BENEFITS

Aside from these equal employment opportunity laws, federal statutes governing wage and hour issues and leaves of absence also impact the working conditions of PAs. The most significant legislation in this area is:

- the Fair Labor Standards Act (FLSA) [29 U.S.C. §§ 201 through 219]
- the Equal Pay Act (EPA) [29 U.S.C. § 206]
- the FMLA [29 U.S.C. §§ 2601 through 2654]

Fair Labor Standards Act

For covered or "nonexempt" employees, the FLSA affects working conditions related to wages, hours, and child labor. Most employees are nonexempt and protected under the act. Exempt employees, on the other hand, include outside salespersons and workers in bona fide executive, administrative, or professional positions. One type of professional employee exempt from FLSA's protections is an employee whose primary duty requires advanced knowledge in a field of science or learning, customarily acquired by a prolonged course in specialized intellectual instruction and study, as distinguished from a general academic education, apprenticeship, and training in the performance of routine mental, manual, or physical processes. A court would therefore likely find a PA to be exempt.

For an employer to take advantage of this exemption and avoid paying overtime to professional employees, the employee must be paid on a salaried, not hourly, basis. To maintain an employee's salaried status, the employer must not "dock" the employee's wages or benefits because of variances in the quantity or quality of work, or the exemption is destroyed. This includes docking for partial day absences and for disciplinary reasons.

A suit filed by a registered nurse illustrates the possible effect of docking pay on an exempt employee's salary. A registered nurse serving in a locked psychiatric acute care unit for hospital patients was entitled to overtime pay because she was not a salaried employee under the FLSA, a federal appeals court held. Instead of being paid for hours worked, the nurse received a set wage, based upon 80 hours of work. The hospital also followed a compensatory-time policy, however, in which hours worked in excess of eight per shift were "banked." If the nurse worked less than eight hours on a shift, she would need to make up the difference by either subtracting from banked compensatory time or accruing negative compensatory time. The hospital also docked compensatory time for violations of its disciplinary code. The Seventh Circuit ruled that the nurse in this case, suing to recover unpaid overtime, was not a salaried employee and therefore not an exempt professional under the FLSA, and was entitled to overtime. By assigning negative compensatory time to the nurse for partial days docked, the hospital had essentially reduced her pay, the court explained. Under the FLSA regulations, the court continued, a salaried employee can only be penalized for infractions of significant safety rules, not for variations in work quality as in this case [*Klein v. Rush-Presbyterian–St. Luke's Med. Ctr.*, 990 F.2d 279 (7th Cir. 1993)].

Under the FLSA, employers must pay nonexempt employees at least the specified minimum wage per hour. Further, employers must compensate any nonexempt employee required to work in excess of 40 hours per week at a rate of at least one and one-half times the worker's regular rate. In the private sector, compensatory time can be awarded in lieu of overtime *only* if the time is granted and used during the same pay period during which the overtime was worked. In other words, compensatory time cannot be banked. Like overtime pay, compensatory time must be awarded at the rate of one and one-half times the number of overtime hours worked.

In the health care industry, time spent on call has triggered suits for unpaid overtime, as illustrated by a case involving PAs. Four PAs employed by a state correctional facility with multiple sites each worked 40 hours per week at one particular site. In addition, the PAs rotated through on-call time, during which they would provide emergency medical services when needed after regular working hours. The state paid the PAs one and one-half times their regular rate for hours when they were physically present at a facility on a call, but did not compensate them for time spent waiting for calls. The PAs sued to recover overtime pay for all hours spent on call, pointing out that because the employer required a 20-minute response time to any of the seven facilities in an eight-mile radius, they could not use on-call time for personal pursuits, such as taking a walk, entertaining guests, doing yard work, attending sporting events, or spending time with their children without a babysitter. The state defended that the PAs had agreed to be paid only for time spent at a facility in response to a call, and that the PAs were free to spend on-call time as they wished [*Casserly v. State,* 844 P.2d 1275 (Colo. Ct. App. 1992)].

The court rejected both defenses and ruled that the state owed the PAs overtime pay for all time spent on call. Employers and employees cannot supersede the FLSA by contracting to reduce compensation required by the federal statute, the court ruled. Nor can such an agreement be used as a defense against employee claims. Turning to whether on-call time constituted working time, the court explained that the test is whether the time is being used predominantly for the employee's or the employer's benefit. In this case, the court concluded, the short response time, the number of facilities, and the geographical radius put severe restrictions on the PAs' activities, such that they were entitled to time and a half for hours spent waiting for calls.

The FLSA prohibits retaliation against an employee who files a complaint or who in any way participates in an FLSA action. Employers who willfully violate the FLSA may be fined, imprisoned, or both. Willful violators also are liable for the amount of unpaid minimum wages, unpaid overtime compensation, and an additional amount as liquidated damages.

Equal Pay Act

Under the EPA, which was enacted as an amendment to the FLSA, salary disparities based on gender are prohibited. The statute prohibits an employer from paying employees of one sex less than employees of the other sex for work requiring equal skill, effort, and responsibility, performed under similar conditions at the same establishment. The EPA protects men as well as women.

The law contains several exceptions that allow unequal payments. Unequal payments may be lawfully made pursuant to a seniority system, a merit system, a system measuring earnings by quantity or quality, or other non–sex-based differences.

Complaints relating to possible EPA violations can be filed with either the EEOC or the Department of Labor's Wage and Hour Division. An employee may also file a lawsuit in federal or state court without first exhausting the administrative remedies. Aggrieved employees may sue for damages in the form of back pay plus attorney's fees and court costs. A two-year statute of limitations exists for nonwillful EPA violations, and three years for willful violations.

Equal Pay Act suits have been filed by female nurses and nurse practitioners, charging that male PAs perform equal work, but receive higher pay. A decision by a federal trial court in Georgia demonstrates the factors that courts may rely on to determine whether a pay disparity is justified. In that case, six female nurse practitioners (NPs) employed at a primary health care facility for university students claimed that a male PA (the first one hired at the facility) was given a significantly higher salary for equal work. The university defended that the PA's higher salary was justified by his education and training, which qualified him to perform tasks beyond those the nurse practitioners performed. The court reviewed in great detail the education and training, regulatory and professional association requirements, types of medical care provided, and job duties of the NPs and the PA. The court concluded that the PA's higher salary was justified, as the nurses had not proven "equal skill, effort, and responsibility." The court noted the following in its ruling:

- The PA training program was based on a medical model, as opposed to a nursing model, and was taught by the same faculty that taught medical students.
- The overlap in the types of care actually provided by PAs and NPs at the facility does not discount their different levels of medical competence, skill, expertise, and responsibility.
- The PA had skills, by virtue of experience, training, education, and ability that the NPs did not have, particularly in the area of trauma.
- Even if trauma cases did not make up a significant percentage of cases seen at the facility, rarely used skills can be used to distinguish employee salaries.

- The NPs' greater experience in gynecological care did not offset the PA's trauma management skills, because the PA could quickly become adept at gynecological care, while the nurses could not acquire trauma treatment skills through experience or short-term training.
- The PAs were included in night call rotation, while the NPs were not.
- The state PA practice act allowed PAs to perform "any function performed by the applying physician which the physician's assistant is qualified to perform." The NPs, by contrast, were limited by regulation to practicing in accordance with written protocols, and were prohibited from treating a condition for which a protocol was not established.

[*Beall v. Curtis,* 603 F. Supp. 1563 (M.D. Ga. 1985), *aff'd without opinion,* 778 F.2d 791 (11th Cir. 1985)].

Family and Medical Leave Act

Under the FMLA, employers must provide eligible employees with up to 12 weeks of leave per year for an employee's own serious illness, the birth or adoption of a child, or to care for a sick spouse, child, or parent. The law applies to all private employers with 50 or more employees within a 75-mile radius of the work site as well as federal civil service, state, and local government employers. To be eligible for leave under FMLA, an employee must have been employed for 12 months at the time the leave is requested and have completed at least 1,250 hours of service with the employer during the previous 12-month period. Employers must guarantee that employees on leave will return to the same or comparable position if they return to work within the maximum allowable leave period. An employer may, however, refuse to restore an employee to a former position if the employee is salaried and among the highest paid 10 percent of the employer's work force, and the refusal is necessary to prevent substantial economic injury to the employer. FMLA also requires employers to maintain health care coverage during the leave on the same basis and under the same conditions as if the employee were not on leave status.

OCCUPATIONAL SAFETY AND HEALTH ACT

The Occupational Safety and Health Act (OSH Act) establishes safety and health standards for workers in establishments that affect commerce, including nongovernmental hospitals and nursing homes [29 U.S.C. §§ 651 through 678]. The OSH Act imposes a general duty on employers to provide a workplace free from recognized safety and health standards. In addition to safety standards, the

OSH Act imposes recordkeeping and reporting requirements, nondiscrimination or "whistleblower" provisions, and notice-posting requirements. Certain exceptions apply to employers with 10 or fewer employees and federal and state governments. The provisions of the OSH Act are particularly relevant to the health care industry, including PAs, due to dangers such as airborne and bloodborne pathogens.

Covered employers must maintain a log and summary of all "recordable" occupational injuries and illnesses, as defined in the OSH Act, as well as supplementary records that must be posted annually and maintained for five years. Employers also must maintain medical and exposure records showing employees' exposure to toxic substances.

The OSH Act forbids any person from discharging or discriminating against any employee who has instituted a violation proceeding, but does not recognize an individual right to sue for employees alleging such discrimination. Instead, all complaints must be filed with the Occupational Safety and Health Administration (OSHA).

Under the OSH Act, an employer's workplace may be subject to inspection at any reasonable time. Anyone connected with a business undergoing inspection may be questioned. If an investigation reveals unacceptable conditions, OSHA will issue a citation describing the violation and the proposed civil or criminal penalties or both. Citations may be contested before the Occupational Safety and Health Review Commission.

OSHA has issued enforcement inspection guidelines to clarify a health care facility's duty toward its employees regarding preventing transmission of airborne disease hazards, such as tuberculosis. For example, OSHA may issue citations for failure to: establish a method for early identification of anyone with active tuberculosis (TB), establish an employee educational program regarding the TB hazard and its symptoms and disease controls, use approved high-efficiency particulate air (HEPA) respirators when employees are in the same room with confirmed or suspected TB sufferers, and provide free medical screening every six months for high-risk employees who might be exposed to TB. [*See* Occupational Safety and Health Administration, *Enforcement Procedures and Scheduling for Occupational Exposure to Tuberculosis,* OSHA Instr. CPL 2-106 (Feb. 9, 1996)].

OSHA has also issued a standard on preventing the transmission of bloodborne diseases in health care settings. The standard provides detailed guidance on health care employers' duties to protect employees from bloodborne pathogens in eight key provisions.

1. Employers must develop written exposure control plans that identify employees at risk of exposure and the methods to be used to protect and train these workers.

2. Employers must implement engineering controls, such as puncture-resistant containers for used needles, self-sheathing needles, protective shields, and biosafety cabinets.
3. Employers must provide, at no cost to employees, personal protective equipment when engineering and work practice controls cannot fully protect an employee from occupational exposure.
4. Employers must take certain measures to clean the worksite and dispose of contaminated waste.
5. Employers must give all employees who have occupational exposure the option to receive a free hepatitis B vaccine.
6. Employers must conduct postexposure evaluations of employees who are exposed on the job.
7. Employers must communicate the hazards of bloodborne pathogens to employees through employee training and education.
8. Employers must maintain medical records for each employee with occupational exposure for the duration of the employee's employment plus 30 years.

[29 C.F.R. §1910.1030; *see also* Occupational Safety and Health Administration, Enforcement Procedures for the Occupational Exposure to Bloodborne Pathogens Standard, 29 C.F.R. § 1910.1030, and OSHA Instr. CPL 2-2.44C (Mar. 6, 1992)].

EMPLOYEE SUBSTANCE ABUSE

Many employers, including health care employers, have instituted employee drug testing programs. Drug testing is limited by important federal and state constitutional protections of an individual's right to privacy. Further, state legislation may define the specific circumstances under which these employers may administer drug tests.

For safety, productivity, and other purposes, an employer may decide to test for substance abuse at various stages of the employment relationship. A Management Advisory adopted by the American Hospital Association in 1992 recommends that health care institutions adopt substance testing policies and implement drug screening for all applicants for employment, regardless of job descriptions. [American Hospital Association, *Management Advisory, Substance Abuse Policies of Health Care Institutions* (Jan. 1992)]. There are three basic types of testing:

1. as a condition of employment, also known as preemployment testing
2. for cause when an employer has objective reasons to suspect substance abuse, including postaccident testing, because the accident itself is seen as justification for the testing
3. random testing of employees as part of an ongoing program

Each type of testing raises distinct legal issues. Preemployment testing, for example, implicates the ADA. Testing job applicants for illegal drug use does not violate the ADA, because illegal users of drugs are not "individuals with disabilities" under the law. However, a test for the illegal use of drugs could also reveal the presence of a lawfully prescribed drug. Because legal prescription drug use is protected under the ADA, an employer would have to determine whether the applicant's use of the drug is in accordance with a lawful prescription before refusing to hire the individual. Under these circumstances only (when a job applicant has tested positive for illegal drug use), according to the EEOC, an employer may inquire about lawful drug use to validate the test results. Test results that indicate lawful drug use must be kept confidential, as they constitute a medical record. Individual state laws may prohibit inquiries regarding an employee's lawful drug use.

By far the most controversial type of employment-related drug testing is random testing of current employees. Several states have prohibited this type of testing by statute [*see, e.g.*, CONN. GEN. STAT. § 31-51x; IOWA CODE § 730.5; MINN. STAT. § 181.951(4)]. Random testing programs have been struck down on constitutional grounds in some states [*see, e.g., Hennessey v. Coastal Eagle Point Oil Co.*, 609 A.2d 11 (N.J. 1992)]. As a result, employers are more likely to only use random testing in conjunction with for-cause testing of employees. In other words, if an employee is involved in a workplace accident, and a for-cause test reveals substance abuse, an employer might require that the employee agree to unannounced testing for a specific period as part of a return-to-work agreement.

State Laws on Impaired Practitioners

In addition to laws that apply to employees generally, additional laws and regulations have been enacted to address the problem of substance abuse among health care professionals. Many state legislatures have addressed the need to protect patients who may be harmed by an impaired health care provider by establishing a medical board committee to investigate reports of practitioners unable to practice safely due to substance abuse or alcoholism. In New Mexico, for example, the "examining committee" may order a medical examination of the provider, hold a hearing, determine a provider's fitness to practice, impose restrictions on practice (if necessary), and report its findings to the medical board. The board may then formally proceed, suspend, or restrict the provider's license. A provider may avoid formal board action by voluntarily requesting a restricted license [N.M. STAT. ANN. §§ 61-7-3 through 61-7-12].

States also encourage the identification of impaired health care practitioners by providing immunity from liability to individuals who are members of impaired practitioner committees or who provide information to a committee [*see, e.g.*, N.M. STAT. ANN. § 61-7-11]. Other states require health care providers to report other providers who are impaired by substance abuse. In Maine, the board may discipline any PA who fails to report a physician or PA who is addicted to alcohol or drugs, or who is mentally ill, unless the other practitioner is a patient or is under treatment within guidelines set by a professional review committee [CODE ME. R. § 02-373-002].

PAs should also be aware that in some states suspension of clinical privileges due to impairment caused by drug or alcohol abuse may be reportable to the National Practitioner Data Bank (NPDB). Although federal regulations do not require health care entities to report actions against PA privileges, the regulations do permit reports on PAs. [Reporting requirements are discussed in detail in Chapter 8: Credentialing and Peer Review, at Reporting Adverse Credentialing Actions.] State law, however, may insulate impaired practitioners from disciplinary action, including peer review and medical board reporting, unless the impairment becomes habitual or poses a danger to patients. If an impaired practitioner has enrolled in a treatment program, but has not suffered any disciplinary or peer review action, the impairment is not reportable.

WRONGFUL DISCHARGE

The employment-at-will doctrine is a legal presumption that the employment relationship can be severed by either the employer or the employee for any reason at any time. Throughout the twentieth century, however, the government has adopted legislation aimed at distinguishing an employer's right to fire an employee without cause from firing or discriminating against an employee on an unlawful basis such as age, race, or gender. Numerous federal and state laws have placed limitations on an employer's right to discharge employees, including Title VII, the ADEA, the FLSA, and the ADA. In addition, courts are increasingly willing to entertain wrongful discharge cases, adopting a variety of rationales to conclude that employment relationships are not indefinite and that employees may sue employers for wrongfully terminating the relationship. Grounds on which courts have permitted employees to sue for wrongful discharge by creating an exception to the at-will employment rule include the implied contract exception and the public policy exception.

Implied Contract

In suits by employees against employers for wrongful discharge, courts will generally look for evidence that an employment relationship was for a definite time period or was "permanent," in order to overcome the presumption that employment was at will and therefore could be terminated at any time. In this regard, courts will scrutinize promises of job "guarantees" found in employee manuals, handbooks, or other policy statements to determine whether they might have created enforceable contractual rights. In a well-known ruling by the Michigan Supreme Court, for example, the court found that an employee handbook stating that employees would only be fired for "just cause" and including specific procedural safeguards had vested employees with certain legal rights [*Toussaint v. Blue Cross and Blue Shield,* 292 N.W.2d 880 (Mich. 1980)]. The court emphasized that it was not creating a duty not to discharge an employee without just cause; it was simply recognizing and giving effect to a promise voluntarily issued by the employer. The court appeared to accept the argument that because a reasonable employee could be expected to rely on a promise not to be discharged without just cause, a reasonable employer should expect to be held to its promise.

Public Policy

The public policy exception to the at-will employment rule is a second way that a discharged employee can recover for wrongful discharge. Public policy causes of action are established by state law. Generally, to recover for wrongful discharge under this theory, the discharged employee must show that the employer's motives in firing the employee contravened an established public policy. To determine whether the discharge decision violated a public policy, courts examine whether the employer's conduct violated a constitutional, statutory, or regulatory provision. Courts have also relied on prior judicial decisions to establish a public policy. Specifically, courts have held that discharges violate public policy when an employee acted in furtherance of safety and health considerations, conformed to a code of professional conduct, lobbied against a piece of legislation favored by the employer, or publicly complained about unlawful employer activity. Because the health care industry is heavily regulated by both public and private standards that could be classified as public policies, health care employees should be sensitive to possible causes of action for wrongful discharge under the public policy exception.

A Missouri appeals court ruled, for example, that a hospital wrongfully discharged a nurse for complaining to other hospital employees about the level of care given by a physician to a hospital patient who subsequently died. The appeals court held that Missouri law recognized a public policy exception to the employment-at-will doctrine. Specifically, the court noted, the state's Nursing Practice Act imposes on nurses an obligation to serve the best interests of their patients. Although the nurse's superior told her to "stay out of it" after she complained about the physician's level of care, to do so would have violated public policy as enunciated in the Act, the court concluded [*Kirk v. Mercy Hosp. Tri-County,* 851 S.W.2d 617 (Mo. Ct. App. 1993)].

Whistleblowers

A subset of wrongful discharge suits based on a violation of public policy are what are known as whistleblower suits. This exception to the common law employment-at-will doctrine protects the right of an employee to protest publicly what the employee perceives as improper or unlawful business activities on the part of the employer. These cases usually involve an employee who objects to work assignments, who alleges that the use of certain materials is wasteful or dangerous, or who contends that certain business practices violate either state or federal law. The employee protests to management or a supervisor, finds a "deaf ear," and ultimately denounces the practice outside the workplace. The employee is subsequently discharged, often for an allegedly contrived or misleading reason (e.g., lack of cooperation, poor attitude), then later sues for wrongful discharge. An Oregon appeals court, for example, ruled that a nursing home violated public policy by terminating an employee who threatened to report possible patient abuse. The employee, the inservice director of nurse training, was concerned about the treatment of her aunt who was a patient at the facility. When the employee informed the nursing home administrator that she intended to report the nursing home for violating her aunt's rights under the Nursing Home Patient's Bill of Rights, she was fired. The court ruled that, regardless of whether abuse actually occurred, the employee could sue for wrongful discharge based on the good faith belief that she had an obligation to report the nursing home [*McQuary v. Bel Air Convalescent Home*, 684 P.2d 21 (Or Ct. App. 1984)].

CHAPTER 10

Third-Party Reimbursement

INTRODUCTION

Most third-party payment programs recognize PAs as covered providers and provide reimbursement for their services. Coverage and reimbursement policies differ, however, between the various programs that provide coverage for medical services furnished by PAs. This chapter gives PAs a basic understanding of reimbursement policy so that their employers can obtain appropriate reimbursement for their services. The chapter provides a general overview of the major third-party payment programs, summarizes their PA coverage policies, and provides guidance on avoiding and resolving reimbursement issues.

MEDICARE

Medicare is the federal program of health insurance for the aged (age 65 and older), the disabled, and persons with End Stage Renal Disease (ESRD). Medicare provides basic health insurance coverage for most Americans at age 65 if they are entitled to Social Security or Railroad Retirement benefits [42 C.F.R. § 406.6]. Individuals under 65 are also covered by Medicare at their 25th month of eligibility for Social Security or Railroad Retirement benefits due to disability [42 C.F.R. § 406.12]. In addition, if a Medicare applicant suffers from ESRD, the applicant can qualify for Medicare as early as the month that a physician determines that the applicant suffers from ESRD, as long as the applicant has worked long enough to be insured under Social Security or is the spouse or dependent of a fully insured individual [42 C.F.R. § 406.13].

Administration

Medicare is administered at the federal level by the Health Care Financing Administration (HCFA), which is a part of the Department of Health and Human Services (HHS). The Social Security Administration also is involved in the program, mostly to assist in eligibility determinations. Local administration of the Medicare program is provided by private insurance companies under contract with HCFA, which deal directly with hospitals and other providers. These companies are known as "intermediaries" under Medicare Part A and "carriers" under Medicare Part B. Medicare intermediaries and carriers process claims and provide support services such as professional relations, financial accounting, and statistical activities.

HCFA has quasi-legislative and quasi-judicial functions in administering the Medicare program. HCFA issues interpretive guidelines to carriers and intermediaries, which are contained in various Medicare manuals such as the *Medicare Carrier's Manual* (MCM). The administrative interpretations contained in these manuals are ". . . ordinarily entitled to considerable deference unless it is plainly inconsistent with the clear meaning of the statute and regulations or unreasonable" [*Downtown Med. Ctr./Comprehensive Health Clinic v. Bowen,* 944 F.2d 756 (10th Cir. 1991)]. HCFA also has the power to decide how interpretive guidelines, as well as federal statutes and regulations, apply to specific situations.

Covered Services

The Medicare program is composed of two parts—Part A and Part B. Persons who qualify for Medicare benefits automatically receive coverage under Part A. Medicare Part A pays primarily for inpatient services provided by institutions such as hospitals, skilled nursing facilities, home health agencies, and rural health clinics [42 U.S.C. § 1395d]. Medicare beneficiaries are entitled to coverage for a hospitalization of up to 90 days during a "spell of illness" plus up to 60 lifetime reserve days, limited extended care services, limited hospice care, and unlimited home health services [42 U.S.C. §§ 1395d and 1395x]. Part B is a voluntary program, available only to persons who enroll and pay the premium for these services. Individuals age 65 or older can enroll in Part B even if they are not receiving Part A benefits [42 C.F.R. § 407.10]. For Medicare beneficiaries who are also eligible for Medicaid, state Medicaid agencies are required to pay Medicare premiums, deductibles, and coinsurance [42 U.S.C. §§ 1396a(a)(10)(E) and 1396d(p)]. Benefits under Part B supplement the services offered under Part A and include coverage for the costs of services provided by physicians and some other providers, medically necessary treatments, home health care, and other medical and health services [42 U.S.C. §§ 1395j through 1395m].

Beneficiary Cost-Sharing

Most Medicare beneficiaries are required to pay for part of their medical care. Under Part A, beneficiaries are responsible for paying a deductible, as well as coinsurance for hospital stays after 60 days and up to 90 days [42 U.S.C. § 1395e]. Beneficiaries are also responsible for payment of a deductible under Part B before Medicare will begin paying its share of costs. After the deductible is satisfied, Medicare pays 80 percent of the reasonable costs as reflected in its fee schedule, while the beneficiary pays 20 percent of the reasonable charges [42 U.S.C. §§ 1395e and 1395l(b)].

Provider and Supplier Payment Policies

Most Medicare providers and suppliers are paid a prospectively determined amount rather than an amount based on the institution's or provider's charges. Medicare Part A uses a prospectively determined amount based on the patient's condition and factors affecting the hospital's cost of providing care to pay for most inpatient hospital services [42 C.F.R. §§ 412.25 through 412.32]. On January 1, 1992, Medicare modified its payment methodology for some Part B suppliers. Medicare began using a fee schedule based on a resource-based relative value scale (RBRVS) to reimburse physicians and other providers, such as PAs, whose payment is based on the physician's fee schedule amount. Payment for physician services is the lesser of the actual charge or the fee schedule amount [42 C.F.R. §§ 414.22 and 414.26].

Participation Requirements

Some Part B suppliers must meet federally determined requirements before they are eligible to receive payment from Medicare. Rural health clinics, for example, must enter into contracts with Medicare known as participation agreements [42 U.S.C. § 1395x(aa)]. They must agree not to charge Medicare beneficiaries for services, except for the amount of any applicable deductible or copayment.

Although physicians and other eligible providers are not required to sign participation agreements, Medicare payment differs depending on whether the provider is a participating or nonparticipating provider. Providers who agree to accept assignment receive payment from Medicare directly and agree to accept the Medicare reimbursement amount as payment in full. Once a provider accepts assignment, the patient cannot be charged anything beyond the applicable deductible or copayment for the service in question. Participating providers, who agree to accept assignment, are reimbursed five percent more than nonparticipating providers [42 U.S.C. § 1395u(h)].

Nonparticipating providers are not required to accept Medicare as payment in full for services, except if the patient is eligible for both Medicare and Medicaid or state law provides otherwise [42 U.S.C. § 1395w-4(g)(3)]. The beneficiary is expected to make up the difference between the provider's charges and the Medicare payment. However, nonparticipating providers are limited in what they can charge for their services by a new upper charge limit called the "limiting charge." As of January 1, 1993, the limiting charge became 115 percent of the fee schedule amount for nonparticipating physicians [42 U.S.C. § 1395w-4].

Secondary Payer Requirements

In situations where a Medicare beneficiary is covered by other insurance, Medicare is the secondary payer. The Medicare Act provides that the program's liability for covered services is secondary to coverage provided by workers' compensation, an automobile or liability insurance policy, or an employer group health plan [42 U.S.C. § 1395y(b)(2)]. The Medicare secondary payer statute precludes payment for services to the extent that payment has been made or can reasonably be expected to be made "promptly" by workers' compensation, liability insurance, or no-fault insurance [42 U.S.C. § 1395y(b)(2)(A)(ii)]. If payment has been made or can reasonably be expected to be made—promptly or not—by an employer group health plan, Medicare also will not pay [42 U.S.C. § 1395y(b)(2)(A)(i)]. Medicare will, however, make a conditional payment under certain circumstances where the beneficiary has filed an insurance claim [42 U.S.C. § 1395y(b)(B)].

Reimbursement for PA-Provided Medical Services

Medicare provides reimbursement for a wide range of services provided by PAs, including those furnished in hospitals, nursing and skilled nursing facilities, physician offices, clinics, or rural health clinics, and for first-assisting at surgery. [See Appendix 10-A, Medicare Policy for Physician Assistants.] Generally, a PA can perform the same services that physicians can provide to Medicare beneficiaries as long as the PA is legally allowed under state law to provide the service. [See Chapter 3: Licensure and Scope of Practice.] PAs use the same Current Procedural Terminology (CPT) codes as physicians to describe the medical services that they perform. Medicare pays the PA's employer, not the PA, for his or her services.

A PA's employer must accept assignment, that is, accept the Medicare rate as payment in full when a PA treats beneficiaries in hospitals, nursing facilities, rural health professional shortage areas, and when the PA provides first-assistant surgical services. However, when PAs provide services "incident to" the services of a nonparticipating provider, the physician can decide if the services provided by the PA will be billed on an assigned basis.

"Incident to" Services

Medicare covers services provided by PAs in physician's offices or clinics if they are "incident to" covered physician's services. Under the "incident to" provision, such services are reimbursed at 100 percent of the physician's fee schedule. A service is considered "incident to" a physician's service if it is:

- an integral, though incidental, part of the physician's care
- commonly either performed without charge or included in the physician's bill
- commonly furnished in a physician's office or clinic
- provided under the physician's direct personal supervision
- rendered by the physician or an individual who qualifies as an employee of the physician

[MCM § 2050].

Services eligible for reimbursement under the "incident to" provision include medical services ordinarily performed by a member of the physician's staff such as taking blood pressures and temperatures, as well as services such as minor surgery, setting casts or simple fractures, and other evaluation or treatment procedures that are ordinarily performed by the physician himself or herself. Services provided incident to an excluded service, such as the services of a podiatrist, are not covered.

Direct personal supervision does not require the physician to be in the same room with the PA every time the PA treats a patient. The physician must, however, be physically present in the same office suite and be immediately available if the PA requires the physician's assistance. In a large clinic or group practice with departments, more than one physician may have the responsibility of supervising a PA, depending on the particular department providing the service, rather than the physician ordering the service [MCM § 2050.2].

Although the treatment provided by a PA must be "incident to" the physician's services, this does not mean that every time a PA treats a patient the physician must also see the patient. Rather, the services furnished by the PA must be an incidental part of a course of treatment initiated by a physician. In addition, the physician must demonstrate his or her active involvement in and management of the patient's treatment by rendering subsequent services of a frequency that reflects participation in managing the patient's condition [MCM § 2050.3].

Physicians can only bill under the "incident to" provision for services performed by an individual who qualifies as the physician's employee. Although the direct employment requirement is not contained in the Medicare statute or regulations, it is contained in the *Medicare Carrier's Manual* and was upheld in the only federal court decision to address this issue [*Downtown Med. Ctr./Comprehensive Health Clinic v. Bowen*, 944 F.2d 756 (10th Cir. 1991)]. A nonphysician performing an "incident to" service is considered an employee if he or she is a part-time, full-time, or leased employee of the supervising physician, group practice, or the legal entity that employs the physician [MCM § 2050.1]. A leased employee is a nonphysician working under a written employee leasing agreement. The agreement must specify that the nonphysician, although employed by the leasing company, provides services as the leased employee of the physician, practice, or other entity, and the physician, practice, or other entity exercises the same amount of control over the leased employee regarding the provision of medical services as they would exercise over a directly employed individual. To determine whether a nonphysician practitioner, either leased or directly employed, is considered an employee of the physician, practice, or entity, HCFA uses the common law test of an employer-employee relationship [20 C.F.R. § 404.1007; for a more detailed discussion of the employer-employee relationship, see Chapter 9: Employment Laws, at Determining Employee Status].

Hospital Services

Medicare covers services performed by PAs in a hospital, including inpatient, outpatient, and emergency department services, with the exception of assisting at surgery, at 75 percent of the physician fee schedule amount for the same services [42 C.F.R. § 414.52(b)]. Physicians can delegate tasks to PAs to the extent recognized under state law [42 C.F.R. § 482.12; see also Chapter 3: Licensure and Scope of Practice]. The physician is not required to be physically present when a PA performs a service, unless state law provides otherwise. When a physician is not physically present, the physician must immediately be available to the PA by telephone [MCM § 16001; see Chapter 3: Licensure and Scope of Practice, at Physician Supervision].

First-Assisting at Surgery

Medicare will cover PAs for the same surgical first-assistant services as a physician first-assistant. Reimbursement for PAs assisting at surgery may not exceed 65 percent of the amount a physician would be paid to assist at surgery [42 C.F.R. § 414.52(a)]. Because the physician fee schedule amount for assisting at surgery is 16 percent of the surgeon's fee, a practice cannot be reimbursed for the PA-provided first-assistant services at more than 65 percent of the 16 percent fee schedule amount, which is 10.4 percent of the surgeon's fee. Medicare will pay on a reasonable charge basis if that amount results in a lower payment than a percentage based on the physician's fee schedule [MCM § 16001]. Payment is not permitted for surgical procedures where an assistant at surgery is used in fewer than five percent of cases. Medicare lists by CPT codes the services provided by PAs or physicians that will not be covered as assistant-at-surgery services. The list can be obtained from the PA's local Medicare carrier [*see* MCM § 5039].

With a few exceptions, Medicare reimbursement is not allowed for the services of an assistant at surgery furnished in a teaching hospital that has a training program related to the medical specialty required for the surgical procedure and a qualified resident is available to provide the service. When qualified residents are not available, the Medicare carrier may require that the HCFA 1500 claim form [see Appendix 10-B] be accompanied by the following signed statement from the primary surgeon:

> I understand that § 1842(b)(7)(D) of the Social Security Act generally prohibits Medicare Part B reasonable charge payment for the services of assistants at surgery in teaching hospitals when qualified residents are available to furnish such services. I certify that the services for which payment is claimed were medically necessary, and that no qualified resident was available to perform the services. I further understand that these services are subject to post-payment review by the Medicare carrier [MCM § 15016D].

Exceptional medical circumstances, such as an emergency requiring immediate treatment, may justify the use of a PA as an assistant at surgery even though a qualified resident is available. In addition, payment may be made for surgical assistants, including PAs, in teaching hospitals if the primary surgeon has a policy of never involving a resident in any aspect of the care of his or her patients. This exception is generally applied to physicians in the community who are not involved in the hospital's graduate medical education program [MCM § 15016D].

Nursing Facilities

Medicare reimburses employers at 85 percent of the physician's fee schedule for services performed by PAs in long-term care facilities, both nursing facilities and skilled nursing facilities [42 C.F.R. § 414.52(c)]. After a patient is admitted to a nursing facility, Medicare regulations require that a physician see a resident every 30 days in the 90 days following admission and once every 60 days thereafter [42 C.F.R. § 483.40(c)(1)]. In skilled nursing facilities, the initial visit must be made by a physician, but a PA and physician may alternate the subsequent required visits [42 C.F.R. § 483.40(c)(4)]. A physician may delegate tasks in skilled nursing facilities to a PA as long as the PA is acting in accordance with the scope of practice as defined by state law, is under the supervision of the physician, is in conformance with the facility's policies, and is not delivering a service that Medicare regulations specify a physician must perform [42 C.F.R. § 483.40(e)]. At the option of the state, a physician may delegate tasks in a nursing facility, including tasks that Medicare regulations state must be performed by a physician, to a PA who is not an employee of the physician but is working in collaboration with a physician [42 C.F.R. § 483.40(f)].

Medicare will pay for one visit by a physician or PA to the same patient in a nursing facility per calendar month as long as the visit is medically necessary. Payment for additional visits will be made if documentation establishes the need for these visits. For nursing home residents who receive visits from a member of a team of providers, which can include PAs, Medicare will pay for 1.5 visits per month per resident. Medicare will pay for additional visits if the need for the visits is substantiated. A PA can make the extra visits without affecting the alternating schedule for the required visits.

When a PA visits a patient at a nursing facility, the PA is allowed to write, sign, and date all progress notes without a physician's countersignature unless state law provides otherwise. The physician supervisor is always responsible for the medical care delivered by the PA. [See Chapter 3: Licensure and Scope of Practice, at Physician Liability.] However, unless state law provides otherwise, Medicare does not require that the physician be physically present when a PA provides medical services as long as the physician is immediately available by telephone [42 C.F.R. § 483.40; MCM § 16001].

Home Health Care

Physician assistants are covered when they provide home health care to Medicare beneficiaries. Except for two circumstances, however, a physician must be physically present when services are provided [MCM § 16001]. In unusual circumstances when a PA provides home health services in the presence of a physician, the services provided by the PA are billed as "incident to" the physician's services and reimbursement is at 100 percent of the physician's fee schedule.

A physician's physical presence is not required when PAs provide services in rural health professional shortage areas or if there is no federally qualified home health agency available to provide services to the Medicare beneficiary. Billing is under the physician's name and number when PAs treat Medicare beneficiaries in areas where there is no federally qualified home health agency. In rural health professional areas, coverage is at 85 percent of the physician's fee schedule [*see* MCM §§ 2051, 2051.1, and 16001].

Rural Health Professional Shortage Areas

Medicare will provide reimbursement at 85 percent of the physician's fee schedule for services supervised by a physician that are delivered by PAs in a federally designated rural health professional shortage area, regardless of the site of the services [42 U.S.C. § 1395x(s)(2)(K)(i); 42 C.F.R. § 414.52(c)]. The medical services provided by the PA must be services that the PA is legally able to perform under state law [42 U.S.C. § 1395x(aa)(5)]. Unless state law provides otherwise, Medicare does not require the on-site presence of a physician supervisor, even if services are provided in a office or clinic. If the physician supervisor is not physically present, Medicare guidelines require the physician to be immediately available by telephone [MCM § 16001].

To improve access to medical care in rural medically underserved areas, Congress enacted the Rural Health Clinic Services Act in 1977 [Pub. L. No. 95-210]. Rural health clinics can obtain reimbursement for medical services provided by PAs from both the Medicare and Medicaid programs. [For a detailed discussion of rural health clinics, see Rural Health Clinics.]

Medicare Managed Care

Medicare beneficiaries may elect to receive health benefits through a federally qualified health maintenance organization (HMO), competitive medical plan, or health care prepayment plan that has contracted with the government to provide care for Medicare recipients. These plans must meet certain federal requirements relating to areas such as administration and management, range of services, furnishing of services, quality assurance, and marketing activities. The government limits what managed care organizations may charge beneficiaries beyond the Part B premium. The beneficiary must go to the health plan for all care, except in an emergency, and the health plan must provide all Medicare-covered services. Many managed care organizations actually provide richer coverage than Medicare requires by covering prescription drugs or preventive care services. Medicare beneficiaries are free to disenroll from the managed care plan at any time and receive Medicare services on a fee-for-service basis.

Medicare managed care plans are paid on a capitated basis. Individual plans decide whether to include PAs as part of their provider panel. If PAs are part of a plan's provider panel, a visit with a PA would be considered a covered service. PAs are authorized to provide all services specified in the managed care organization's contract with HCFA, assuming the services are within the PA's scope of practice. Finally, PA supervision requirements may vary from managed care plan to managed care plan. Although state law establishes the legal parameters under which a PA may practice, the managed care plan may establish a more stringent supervision requirement. [See Chapter 8: Credentialing and Peer Review, at Clinical Privileges.]

MEDICAID

Medicaid is a cooperative state-federal program that provides certain medical and health services to the financially needy. The Medicaid program is state operated under a specific set of federal requirements established by Title XIX of the

Social Security Act [42 U.S.C. § 1396 *et seq.*]. This statute, and the federal regulations implementing it, set forth a number of fairly specific minimum requirements and provide the basis for federal matching of a portion of the state funds paid in the program. This state-federal share varies according to a formula based on the state's per capita income, and can range from 50–50 sharing to an almost 80–20 federal-state ratio in the poorer states. Each state government designates the single state agency responsible for the administration of the Medicaid program. Each state is permitted to determine its own Medicaid benefits and its own eligibility requirements as long as the state requirements remain consistent with federal law.

Medicaid is a means-tested entitlement program. States must provide medical coverage to the categorically needy—those individuals who qualify based on a particular category of need such as receipt of Aid to Families with Dependent Children or Supplemental Security Income, and certain categories of pregnant women and children. At their option, states may cover the medically needy, defined as persons who would qualify in the mandatory coverage group but whose income exceeds the income limits for these programs but is still not sufficient [42 U.S.C. § 1396a(a)(10)(A)(ii)]. States that choose to cover the medically needy will qualify for federal matching funds for that part of their Medicaid program.

States have great discretion in setting reimbursement rates for both health care facilities and providers under Medicaid. Three general requirements govern reimbursement of health care facilities. First, the state reimbursement rate must be reasonable and adequate to meet the necessary costs of an efficiently and economically operated facility. Second, the state must ensure that Medicaid patients have reasonable access to inpatient hospital care. Finally, the state must consider the situation of those hospitals serving a disproportionate share of low-income patients [*see Temple Univ. v. White,* 941 F.2d 201 (3d Cir. 1991), *cert. denied sub nom., Snider v. Temple Univ.,* 502 U.S. 1032 (1992)]. As a result of the Boren Amendment which allowed states to experiment with reimbursement methods for health care facilities, most states now pay hospitals and other institutional providers under a prospective payment system rather than a cost-based reimbursement system [42 U.S.C. § 1396(a)(13)].

States also have great flexibility in setting physician payment rates. The federal government only mandates that the state rates must be sufficient to enlist enough providers so that services are available to Medicaid beneficiaries to the same extent that they are available to the general public [42 U.S.C. § 1396a(a)(30)(A)]. In general, Medicaid rates are lower than Medicare rates.

Most states use a fiscal agent to process Medicaid claims, although a few states use a government agency. Providers must submit Medicaid claims within 12 months of furnishing services. Medicaid generally only makes payments to providers [42 C.F.R. § 447.10]. The only exception to this rule is that direct payment can be made to medically needy recipients for physicians' or dentists' services [42 C.F.R. § 447.25]. Providers must accept Medicaid rates as payment in full, except for spend-down amounts or any deductible or coinsurance amounts required under the state's plan [42 C.F.R. § 447.15]. Finally, Medicaid, like Medicare, is a secondary payer [42 C.F.R. § 433.138].

Reimbursement for PA-Provided Medical Services

With the exception of federally certified rural health clinics where Medicaid law mandates coverage of services provided by PAs, states have the option of including PAs as part of their Medicaid program. In states covering medical services provided by PAs, coverage can vary from all settings to specified services. Some states do not cover PAs for all the services that PAs can legally perform in that state. The reimbursement rate may also be different depending upon the state; some states reimburse at the physician's rate of reimbursement while others use a discounted fee basis. Presently, PAs are eligible providers in 42 states and their services are reimbursed at either the same or a lower rate than physicians. [See Appendix 10-C for a list of state medical programs that provide PA coverage.] In some states, including Hawaii, New Mexico, and Pennsylvania, PAs are not allowed to provide surgical first-assistant duties even though Medicaid will cover services provided by PAs in all other settings.

Depending on the state, PAs bill for their services under the physician's name, are required to use a modifier code, or must use a specific fee schedule. A few states allow PAs to bill directly for the services they provide to Medicaid patients. Physician assistants should check with their individual Medicaid offices to ascertain the proper billing procedures in their state of practice.

State Health Reform Initiatives

In an attempt to stem rapidly increasing Medicaid costs, states are requesting waivers from federal Medicaid requirements to implement state health reforms. States must request waivers from HCFA in order to experiment with ways to expand coverage, finance care, and provide health care to Medicaid recipients [42 U.S.C. § 1396n]. The two most common waiver categories are known as 1115 waivers and 1915 waivers, which refer to the sections of the Social Security Act that states are requesting HCFA to waive. Section 1115 waivers are research and demonstration waivers that allow states to make large-scale changes in their Medicaid program for a five-year period. States can use this waiver to make managed care mandatory, change the benefit package provided to Medicaid recipients, or change the population eligible for Medicaid coverage. HCFA requires that Medicaid enrollees' access to care is not diminished under a proposed 1115 waiver program [42 U.S.C. § 1396n(b)(1)]. Section 1915 waivers, known as program waivers, allow more limited modifications and can be used to provide particular services, such as at-home or community-based services for individuals who might have to be institutionalized.

The Medicaid waiver process can make it difficult for PAs to treat Medicaid patients. Many Medicaid managed care programs require patients to select a primary care provider (PCP), but may only authorize physicians to be PCPs. Even if the state Medicaid plan allows PAs to be assigned patients, the state might assign PAs fewer patients than physicians. An additional problem for PAs posed by Medicaid waivers is the threat that they could eliminate the federal requirement to reimburse rural health clinics at the clinic's cost-based payment rate for treating Medicaid patients. Part of the rural health clinic's patient population could be reduced if the clinic's reimbursement rate changes.

RURAL HEALTH CLINICS

In 1977, Congress enacted the Rural Health Clinic Services Act [Pub. L. No. 95-210] in order to increase the availability of primary health care services in rural areas with a shortage of health care professionals. Congress extended Medicare and Medicaid coverage to PAs, nurse practitioners (NPs), and, in 1989, to certified nurse midwives who work at rural health clinics [*see* 42 U.S.C. § 1395b-1]. Certification as a rural health clinic under Medicare and Medicaid requires that the clinic be located in a rural or nonurban area certified by the federal government as a health professional shortage area or a medically underserved area [42 U.S.C. § 1395x(aa)].

A rural health clinic must be under the medical direction of a physician, and an NP or PA must be available to furnish patient care at least 60 percent of the time the clinic is open [42 C.F.R. §§ 491.7 and 491.8]. The clinic may be owned by either a PA, NP, or physician [42 C.F.R. § 491.8; see also Chapter 3: Licensure and Scope of Practice, at Physician Supervision]. Although the clinic is not required to have full-time on-site supervision by a physician, state laws regarding PA supervision must be met [42 C.F.R. § 491.8]. A physician must be present at the clinic for sufficient periods of time, at least once every two weeks under ordinary circumstances, to provide medical direction, medical care services, consultation, and supervision. In addition, the physician must be available through direct telecommunication for consultation, assistance with medical emergencies, or patient referral [42 C.F.R. § 491.8(b)(2)].

If a rural health clinic is located in an area where HHS has determined there is a shortage of home health agencies, the clinic may provide visiting nurse services to homebound individuals. These services are generally furnished by a registered nurse, licensed practical nurse, or licensed vocational nurse employed by or compensated by the rural health clinic. A PA is one of the practitioners who may establish and sign the required written plan of treatment. A supervising physician must review the treatment plan every 60 days [42 C.F.R. § 405.2416].

Medicare and Medicaid cover medical services performed by a PA and services incident to a PA's services in certified rural health clinics [42 C.F.R. §§ 405.2460 and 410.45]. In addition, rural health clinic services are eligible for reimbursement when furnished to a patient at a hospital, another medical facility, or the patient's residence, in addition to services furnished at the clinic [42 C.F.R. § 405.2411(b)]. All reimbursement is paid to the clinic.

State Medicaid programs are required to provide coverage to the categorically needy for services performed by a PA in a rural health clinic, and may extend coverage to the medically needy in accordance with the state's plan [42 U.S.C. §§ 1396a and 1396d]. Provider-based clinics, clinics that are an integral part of a hospital, skilled nursing facility, or home health agency, are reimbursed at the lower of reasonable costs or the provider's customary charges [42 C.F.R. §§ 447.371, 405.2462, and 413.1]. Under Medicaid, independently owned clinics are reimbursed 100 percent of the reasonable cost rate per visit as determined by the Medicare carrier [42 C.F.R. § 447.371].

Medicare pays independent clinics based on the all-inclusive rate for each beneficiary visit for covered services as determined by the intermediary. Medicare will pay 80 percent of the all-inclusive rate if the beneficiary has fully met the deductible and the Medicare patient is responsible for paying the clinic the remaining 20 percent [42 C.F.R. § 405.2462].

MILITARY HEALTH PROGRAMS

The Civilian Health and Medical Program of the Uniformed Services (CHAMPUS) pays for health services provided by nonmilitary health care institutions and health care providers, including PAs, to dependents, current and former spouses, widows, and widowers of active duty service members, as well as military retirees [32 C.F.R. § 199.3]. By 1997, a new program, known as TRICARE, will be implemented throughout the United States. TRICARE covers active duty service members and offers managed care options in addition to the standard CHAMPUS benefit [32 C.F.R. § 199.17].

TRICARE offers three options with differing benefits, deductibles, copayments, and cost-sharing:

1. TRICARE Prime is a health maintenance organization that uses military treatment facilities and designated civilian provider networks.
2. Under the TRICARE Extra plan, beneficiaries must use a preferred provider network for treatment and will also be eligible for military treatment facilities on a space-available basis.
3. TRICARE Standard is similar to the standard CHAMPUS benefit which allows beneficiaries a broad freedom of choice of civilian providers and access to military medical treatment facilities on a space-available basis.

[32 C.F.R. § 199.17].

Payment Policies

Payment under the standard CHAMPUS benefit, which will be called TRICARE Prime, closely resembles Medicare's payment system. Like Medicare, CHAMPUS uses a prospective payment system to pay for most inpatient hospital care. Most individual health care professionals and noninstitutional providers are reimbursed at the lesser of the billed charge or a fee schedule amount called the local CHAMPUS Maximum Allowable Charge (CMAC) [32 C.F.R. § 199.14].

Participation Requirements

Individual health care providers can agree to participate in the CHAMPUS program on a claim-by-claim basis [32 C.F.R. § 199.6(a)(8)(iv)]. Individual and institutional providers who have agreed to become CHAMPUS participating providers must accept the CHAMPUS fee schedule amount, as well as any applicable deductibles or cost-sharing amounts, as payment in full. Payment is made directly to participating providers [32 C.F.R. § 199.6(5)]. Nonparticipating providers are only paid 95 percent of the CMAC and may not charge more than 115 percent of the CHAMPUS allowable charge [32 C.F.R. § 199.14(g)].

Coordination of Benefits

In most situations where a CHAMPUS beneficiary is covered by another insurance program in addition to CHAMPUS, CHAMPUS is the last payer. If Medicare is involved, CHAMPUS is always the secondary payer. However, if a beneficiary is eligible for Medicaid, CHAMPUS is the primary payer [32 C.F.R. § 199.8].

Reimbursement for PA-Provided Medical Services

In its fee-for-service program, CHAMPUS covers all medically necessary services provided by a PA. A physician must supervise the PA in accordance with state law and be an authorized CHAMPUS provider. In addition, a PA must meet state licensure requirements.

The PA's employer bills and receives reimbursement for the medical care delivered by the PA. Exclusive of surgical assistant services, the PA reimbursement rate is up to 85 percent of the allowable charge for a comparable service performed by a physician in a similar location. CHAMPUS covers PAs up to 65 percent of the rate paid a physician first-assistant if the procedure is an authorized procedure. CHAMPUS restricts the procedures for which it will reimburse a physician and PA surgical first-assistant [42 C.F.R. §§ 199.4 and199.14(g)(1)].

FEDERAL EMPLOYEES HEALTH BENEFITS PROGRAM

The Federal Employees Health Benefits Program (FEHB) is the health insurance plan administered by the Office of Personnel Management (OPM) that provides health insurance coverage for federal employees, retirees, and dependents. More than 300 private health insurance plans contract with OPM to provide health insurance coverage through the FEHB. All health insurance plans offered through the FEHB must meet certain minimum standards [5 C.F.R. §§ 890.202 and 890.201]. It is up to the individual plan to determine whether it will cover PAs and the circumstances under which that coverage occurs. [A list of insurance companies that participate in the FEHB and their coverage policies for PA-provided medical services is provided in AAPA, *Physician Assistant Third-Party Coverage,* at 34 (Apr. 1996).]

WORKERS' COMPENSATION

Workers' compensation provides insurance coverage for medical care and compensation for wage loss or survivorship benefits for workers who are killed or injured at work. All states have a workers' compensation system. Although workers' compensation is primarily a state-run program, certain employees are covered by federal statutes. The major federal workers' compensation statutes include the Longshore and Harbor Workers' Compensation Act [33 U.S.C. § 901]; the Federal Coal Mine Health and Safety Act of 1969, as amended [30 U.S.C. § 801]; the Federal Employer's Compensation Act (covers federal civilian employees) [5 U.S.C. § 8101]; and the Federal Employer's Liability Act (covers interstate railroad employees) [45 U.S.C. § 51].

Employers pay for the cost of providing benefits under workers' compensation either by purchasing insurance coverage from an insurance company or by self-insuring. All state workers' compensation statutes provide for all medically necessary care and treatment for injuries related to employment. Individual states, however, determine the practitioners who may assess a worker's condition, certify a disability, treat an injured worker, and certify when a worker may return to work. Physician assistants need to check with the workers' compensation office in their state to obtain more information about the extent to which they may provide services under the workers' compensation program. [For a state-by-state list of workers' compensation programs and their coverage policies for PA-provided medical services, see Appendix 10-D.]

PRIVATE INSURANCE COMPANIES

Most private insurance companies and self-insured businesses cover PA-provided medical services. These insurance companies, however, may differ in PA coverage and claims submission policies, which can make it confusing for practices to obtain reimbursement for medical services provided by PAs. Some states, such as Oregon, Iowa, and Connecticut, require private health insurance policies to cover medical services provided by PAs [OR. REV. STAT. § 743.724; IOWA CODE § 514C.11; CONN. GEN. STAT. § 38a-526]. Even in those states, however, companies that self-insure are exempt from state law requirements by the Employee Retirement Income Security Act (ERISA) [29 U.S.C. §§ 1001 through 1461].

Most insurance policies do not specifically list each type of provider that can provide services under the health plan. However, most plans do have language indicating that they cover medically necessary services provided by doctors of medicine and osteopathy. Nearly all private insurance companies will cover services delegated to a PA by a physician if they are within the scope of the PA's training and expertise and in accordance with state law [see Chapter 3: Licensure and Scope of Practice]. Most insurers require the physician, and not the PA, to bill for these services. However, a few insurance companies require the claim to be filed under the PA's name, so PAs should check with the insurance company's claims department, or provider or professional relations department for specific billing requirements.

Practices may encounter difficulties in obtaining reimbursement for PA surgical first-assistant duties. Some insurance companies do not want to pay a separate fee for first-assistant duties. Many insurance companies, however, will cover services provided by PAs if they are part of a global fee for surgery, and expect the first-assistant fee to be built into the surgical fee. Under a global fee schedule, a surgeon can determine both who will assist and the fee for that person's duties.

BILLING AND CODING ISSUES

Physician assistants should pay careful attention to billing issues to ensure that their employers receive appropriate reimbursement for medical services, and to ensure that violations of fraud and abuse laws do not occur. Careful billing includes the proper use of CPT and modifier codes, as well as understanding what services are eligible for reimbursement. Fraud concerns can be raised by inadvertent administrative billing errors, not just deliberate attempts to file false claims.

Coding

Developed by the American Medical Association (AMA) in 1966, the CPT coding system is a compilation of terms and codes used to describe medical procedures. HCFA has made the CPT system part of its Common Procedure Coding System, which must be used for all Medicare Part B services and outpatient surgical procedures, and by state Medicaid agencies. In addition, the CPT coding system is used by most private insurance companies.

Improper coding can deprive a medical practice of earned revenue or subject the practice to fraud and abuse penalties. *Downcoding* means using a code that is lower than the proper code and results in depriving the medical practice of earned income. *Upcoding* means classifying a procedure into a higher code than the procedure warrants, which can subject the medical practice to fraud and abuse charges.

HCFA has issued voluntary guidelines developed in conjunction with the AMA for Evaluation and Management (E&M) Services. The purpose of these guidelines is to help providers document their services more accurately. The guidelines cover seven components of E&M services: history, examination, medical decision making, counseling, coordination of care, nature of presenting problem, and time. If a medical practice is audited, the local Medicare carrier uses the guidelines during the audit; these guidelines, in conjunction with the CPT manual, therefore can provide an understanding of the logic used by Medicare claims reviewers during the audit process. In the future, private third-party payers may adopt similar parameters.

Completing the HCFA 1500 Form

Medicare requires providers, including PAs, to use a particular claim form, known alternatively as the HCFA 1500, the Medicare 1500 claim form, and the Uniform Health Insurance Claim Form, to bill for services provided to Medicare beneficiaries. [A copy of the form appears at Appendix 10-B.] Some military health programs and private insurance companies also use this form. Physician assistants must use modifier codes when bills are submitted to Medicare for services provided in hospitals, nursing facilities, rural health professional shortage areas when the physician is not on-site, and as a first-assistant at surgery. PAs use the following modifier codes for Medicare claims:

- AN—services performed in the hospital, including emergency department services but not surgical assistant services
- AS—assisting at surgery in any location
- AU—used for services provided in nursing homes and skilled nursing facilities when PA and physician use a team approach
- QB—used for services provided in rural health professional shortage areas when a physician is not on site

Because Medicare carriers have some discretion to determine specific modifier codes to describe medical services provided by PAs, PAs should check with their local Medicare carrier. No modifier code is used for services that are "incident to" physician services.

Medicare will only make payment to a PA's employer. An employer may be a physician, medical group, professional corporation, hospital, or nursing facility. A group of PAs is not permitted to incorporate and bill Medicare for their services. To satisfy Medicare's employment requirement, the PA (either leased or directly employed) must be considered an employee of a supervising physician or other legal entity under the common law test of an employer-employee relationship [MCM § 2050.1C; for a discussion of employee status, see Chapter 9: Employment Laws].

The HCFA 1500 contains several sections that PAs should be aware of when completing the form.

- The CPT code for the procedure should be placed on line 24, followed by the appropriate modifier code in the space indicated on this line.
- The actual charges are recorded on line 24 (section F). The charge for services provided by PAs in nursing facilities, rural health professional shortage areas, hospitals, or assisting at surgery should not be discounted. The Medicare carrier will discount the fees.
- Line 25, which asks for a tax identification number, should be completed with the tax identification number of the PA's employer.
- The form asks for additional insurance information if the patient has insurance other than Medicare on lines 9 and 11.
- Lines 31 and 33 must be completed with the PA's signature, and the PA's name, address, zip code, phone number, and provider number, if applicable.

The military health program CHAMPUS requires PAs to include specific information on the HCFA 1500 claim form. Services provided by PAs should be billed as a separately identified line item accompanied by the PA's provider number. Physician assistants do not need to use a modifier code if they provide services in an office or clinic. The "80" modifier code should be used by PAs when they first-assist at surgery. CHAMPUS does not use "incident to" billing.

Because Medicare carriers have some discretion to determine specific billing practices, PAs should always check with their local carrier for more specific information. Local carriers may be able to determine the Medicare codes that should be used to describe medical services provided by PAs. Although some carriers issue provider numbers to PAs, these PAs do not have the authority to bill independently for their medical services; payment continues to go to the PA's employer.

Fraud and Abuse Concerns

Fraud and abuse can take a number of forms, ranging from the deliberate submission of false claims to inadvertent billing errors. Civil and criminal laws address health care fraud committed by a wide range of health care providers. The Medicare-Medicaid Antifraud and Abuse Amendments to the Social Security Act are designed to detect and prevent fraud or abuse in those programs [42 U.S.C. § 1395u *et seq.*]. The Health Insurance Portability and Accountability Act of 1996 [Pub. L. No. 104-191] extended the fraud and abuse prohibitions contained in the Medicare-Medicaid Antifraud and Abuse Laws to all health care systems regardless of the payer.

Under these laws, fraud is defined as knowing and willful deception or misrepresentation, or a reckless disregard of the facts, with the intent to receive an unauthorized benefit; abuse is a manner of operation that results in excessive or unreasonable costs to Medicare or Medicaid. One of the primary targets of federal health care fraud enforcement activities is false claims and other fraudulent billing practices. Fraud and abuse violations can result in civil and criminal penalties, including denial of payment, the refund of wrongfully obtained payments, civil monetary penalties, program exclusion, fines, or prison sentences.

A fraud and abuse case settled by the Office of Inspector General (OIG), an independent unit within HHS, emphasizes the need for midlevel practitioners, including PAs, to pay attention to their billing practices. While conducting an audit at Philadelphia's Clinical Practices of the University of Pennsylvania (CPUP), the OIG and HCFA uncovered many billing errors, including inappropriate billing for the services of midlevel practitioners, residents, and interns. The CPUP eventually settled the case for $30 million [Settlement Agreement between the U.S. Department of Justice, the U.S. Attorney for the Eastern District of Pennsylvania, the Office of Inspector General of the U.S. Department of Health and Human Services, and the Clinical Practices of the University of Pennsylvania, Dec. 12, 1995].

CONTESTING REIMBURSEMENT DECISIONS

Payers deny providers' reimbursement claims for a variety of reasons. In the PA context, typical reasons for a denial include that a PA is not a covered provider, the service performed by the provider was not a covered service, or the provider incorrectly coded the insurance claim form. In investigating a denied claim, it is imperative to demand from the payer a clear explanation of the reason for the denial, preferably in writing. It is important to confirm that the denial did not occur because of a simple clerical error, such as a coding mistake or an incorrectly completed claim form. If the matter is not easily resolved and the conclusion is that the claim was unfairly denied, the physician or PA may want to contest the denial.

At the outset, the PA pursuing this course of action should make sure not to miss any deadlines. Most government payment programs and many private insurance companies have a deadline after which the claimant can no longer pursue a formal appeal process. Many times the deadline will be noted in the coverage denial letter, and the PA should keep this date in mind. Before initiating a formal appeals process, however, the PA might want to consider less formal methods of contesting the denial, such as attempting to resolve the issue via telephone.

Physician assistants should pay attention to their terminology when inquiring about an insurer's PA coverage policy; in particular, PAs should be careful not to ask whether PAs are reimbursed for a service or covered by the policy. Because PAs legally act under the supervision of a physician, the insurer may state that PAs are not covered providers under the policy. Likewise, because most insurance companies do not directly reimburse PAs, a question about reimbursement may elicit a negative response. However, asking whether physician services performed by a PA in the physician's office are covered when the physician submits the bill will usually generate a positive response.

The PA has several options in fighting a claim denial. First, the PA should contact the individual who has the power to change a coverage decision; in some cases, the matter is resolved simply by providing the insurer with more information. Insurers, however, do not always have the authority to change a coverage decision. Many employers self-insure their group health insurance plans and hire a traditional insurance company only to administer the plan benefits. Under these circumstances, many issues, such as whether a PA is a covered provider, are decided by the business, not the insurance company. If the plan is self-insured, the PA should discuss denied claims with the employee or health benefits manager at the business that provides the patient's health insurance benefits.

Second, the PA and/or the supervising physician should consider writing a letter to the insurance company or business administering the plan to explain why the claim should not be denied. Businesses that have purchased insurance for their employees may also be willing to advocate on behalf of the patient because it is in the employer's interest to make sure that employees receive the health coverage agreed on under the insurance plan. Patients can also assist in this process, particularly with respect to self-insured plans, by explaining why the medical services provided by the PA should be covered.

Finally, the PA or supervising physician may decide to formally contest a claim denial through (1) a private insurance company's internal appeals process, (2) the administrative process that is available to contest coverage denials in government payment programs, or (3) a judicial proceeding. Many insurance companies have an internal appeals process to contest coverage decisions, and the PA pursuing this route must find out about the procedures for contesting a coverage decision from the insurance company. The appeal procedures for some common government payment programs are discussed in the following sections.

Medicare

If a health care provider or rural health clinic is not satisfied with the amount of reimbursement determined by a Medicare carrier, the provider or clinic may contest this decision. A party affected by the carrier's decision, such as the patient or health care provider, may request a new, full review by another carrier employee [42 C.F.R. § 405.807]. After this review, if the amount in controversy exceeds $100, a beneficiary, a physician, or other provider accepting assignment of the beneficiary's claim for reimbursement is entitled to a proceeding before a hearing officer appointed by the Part B carrier [42 C.F.R. § 405.815]. Providers may aggregate claims to meet the threshold levels of appeal [42 C.F.R. § 405.817].

At the proceeding, the claimant or a representative has the opportunity to review evidence relied upon by the carrier in making the determination and may present witnesses in testimony [42 C.F.R. § 405.830]. However, the beneficiary need not appear at the session.

Prior to 1986, there was no provision for judicial review of disputes pertaining to Part B. As of 1986, however, if the amount in dispute is $500 or more, the provider is entitled to a hearing before an administrative law judge (ALJ) [42 C.F.R. § 405.815]. If $1,000 or more remains in controversy after the ALJ hearing and Appeals Council review, the provider may obtain judicial review [42 C.F.R. § 405.815].

Medicare HMOs

Medicare HMOs are required to establish a grievance and appeals process [42 C.F.R. §§ 417.600 through 417.636]. In addition to the Medicare beneficiary, a provider, such as a PA, who has provided a service to the beneficiary and formally agreed to waive payment from the beneficiary for that service may contest the HMO's decision [42 C.F.R. § 417.610]. Physician assistants who render emergency and out-of-area services may need to pursue an appeal if the HMO denies payment for the services because it claims the services should have been obtained from the HMO. The HMO must have procedures to reconsider the initial determination.

If the claim is for $100 or more, the Medicare beneficiary can request a hearing before an ALJ [42 C.F.R. § 417.630]. A dissatisfied party may request the Appeals

Council to review an ALJ's decision [42 C.F.R. § 417.634]. Finally, judicial review of the Appeals Council decision can be requested if the amount in controversy is $1,000 or more [42 C.F.R. § 417.636].

Medicaid

Federal Medicaid law provides limited appeal rights for providers, although providers accepting assignment may take advantage of the Medicaid recipient's fair hearing system as a beneficiary representative. Medicaid law requires that whenever a state agency takes an action affecting an individual's claim to Medicaid, it must provide notice of the proposed action and of the availability of an administrative hearing, except for certain federal or state laws requiring an automatic change affecting some or all Medicaid recipients [42 C.F.R. §§ 431.220 and 431.221]. Medicaid law does not provide for a separate appeal process for provider reimbursement disputes, except for very limited review of issues the state Medicaid agency deems appropriate regarding payment rates for hospitals and long-term care facilities [42 C.F.R. § 447.253(e)]. Providers may, however, have greater remedies under specific state law provisions, including state Medicaid or administrative procedure statutes.

Providers also have the option of bringing lawsuits in state or federal court. Generally, administrative remedies must be exhausted before providers may bring a judicial action. Claims based on state constitutions, statutes, regulations, or federal law may be brought in state court. Alternatively, under certain conditions, providers may challenge the way states reimburse health care providers and the reasonableness and adequacy of the rates in a suit against state officials either in state or federal court [42 U.S.C. §§ 13200-2 and 1983; *see, e.g., Arkansas Med. Soc'y v. Reynolds,* 6 F.3d 519 (8th Cir. 1993)].

CHAMPUS

CHAMPUS provides an administrative review procedure for appealing decisions that adversely affect providers. CHAMPUS peer review organizations will notify providers and fiscal intermediaries if a claim is denied, and this decision, known as an initial determination, will include a statement of the provider's right to appeal the determination and instructions for filing the appeal. A nonparticipating provider and a third party, such as an insurance company, are not considered a party to the initial determination and may not appeal.

The sequence and procedures of an appeal under CHAMPUS vary, depending upon who made the initial determination. The determination will undergo further review, known as either reconsideration or formal review, where the aggrieved party may submit further written evidence to support his or her claim. In some circumstances, reconsideration or formal review will be a final decision that is not eligible for further appeal.

If the decision is not final, the dissatisfied party may request a hearing, an administrative proceeding where the party and his or her representative have a chance to present facts relevant to the issues in the case. The hearing officer issues a recommended decision, which becomes final upon review and agreement of the Office of the Civilian Health and Medical Program of the Uniformed Services (OCHAMPUS) [32 C.F.R. § 199.10(d)(12)].

Federal Employees Health Benefits Program

Under the FEHB, each health insurance company resolves claims filed under its plan. Claims must be filed by a covered individual or other individuals or entities who are acting on the behalf of a covered individual and have the covered individual's specific written consent to pursue payment of the disputed claim. Claims must be submitted initially to the health insurance company.

If the company denies the claim, the covered individual has six months from the date of the notice denying the claim to submit a written request asking the insurance company to reconsider its denial. If the company affirms its denial or fails to respond, the covered individual may ask the OPM to review the claim.

The request to OPM must be made within 90 days after the date of the insurance company's notice to the covered individual that the denial was affirmed. If the insurance company failed to respond to the covered individual, he or she must request review by OPM within 120 days after the date of the request for reconsideration or the date the carrier requested additional information. A covered individual must exhaust both the health insurance company's and OPM's review procedures before seeking judicial review [5 C.F.R. § 890.105].

A covered individual may seek judicial review of OPM's final action. The lawsuit must be brought against OPM and not the health insurance company or any of the company's subcontractors. The lawsuit may not be filed later than December 31 of the third year in which the care or service was provided. Finally, judicial review is limited to the record that was before OPM [5 C.F.R. § 890.107].

Appendix 10-A

Medicare Policy for Physician Assistants

Setting	Supervision	Reimbursement Rate	Services
Office/clinic not located in rural health professional shortage area (rHPSA)	Physician must be in the building or suite of offices	100 percent of physician's fee schedule[1]	All services PA is legally authorized to provide that would have been covered if provided personally by a physician
Home visit	Both PA and physician must be present at house call[2]	100 percent of physician's fee schedule	Same as above
Skilled nursing facility and nursing facility	State law	85 percent of physician's fee schedule	Same as above

continues

[1]Using carrier guidelines for "incident to" services

[2] PA may provide care without the on-site presence of a physician in areas without participating home health agencies

[3] i.e., 65 percent × 16 percent = 10.4 percent of surgeon's fee

Source: Reprinted with permission from American Academy of Physician Assistants, *Medicare Policy for Physician Assistants* (October 1996) (fact sheet), © 1996.

Setting	*Supervision*	*Reimbursement Rate*	*Services*
Office or home visit if rHPSA	State law	85 percent of physician's fee schedule	Same as above
Hospitals including the emergency department	State law	75 percent of physician's fee schedule	Same as above
First assisting at surgery in all settings	State law	65 percent of physician's first assist fee schedule[3]	Same as above
Federally certified rural health clinics	State law	Cost-based reimbursement	Same as above
HMO	State law	Reimbursement is on capitation basis	All services contracted for as part of an HMO contract

Appendix 10-B

HCFA 1500 Form

PICA **HEALTH INSURANCE CLAIM FORM** PICA

1. MEDICARE (Medicare #) MEDICAID (Medicaid #) CHAMPUS (Sponsor's SSN) CHAMPVA (VA File #) GROUP HEALTH PLAN (SSN or ID) FECA BLK LUNG (SSN) OTHER (ID)

1a. INSURED'S I.D. NUMBER (FOR PROGRAM IN ITEM 1)

2. PATIENT'S NAME (Last Name, First Name, Middle Initial)

3. PATIENT'S BIRTH DATE MM DD YY SEX M F

4. INSURED'S NAME (Last Name, First Name, Middle Initial)

5. PATIENT'S ADDRESS (No., Street)

6. PATIENT RELATIONSHIP TO INSURED Self Spouse Child Other

7. INSURED'S ADDRESS (No., Street)

CITY STATE

8. PATIENT STATUS Single Married Other

CITY STATE

ZIP CODE TELEPHONE (Include Area Code) ( )

Employed Full-Time Student Part-Time Student

ZIP CODE TELEPHONE (INCLUDE AREA CODE) ( )

9. OTHER INSURED'S NAME (Last Name, First Name, Middle Initial)

10. IS PATIENT'S CONDITION RELATED TO:

11. INSURED'S POLICY GROUP OR FECA NUMBER

a. OTHER INSURED'S POLICY OR GROUP NUMBER

a. EMPLOYMENT? (CURRENT OR PREVIOUS) YES NO

a. INSURED'S DATE OF BIRTH MM DD YY SEX M F

b. OTHER INSURED'S DATE OF BIRTH MM DD YY SEX M F

b. AUTO ACCIDENT? YES NO PLACE (State)

b. EMPLOYER'S NAME OR SCHOOL NAME

c. EMPLOYER'S NAME OR SCHOOL NAME

c. OTHER ACCIDENT? YES NO

c. INSURANCE PLAN NAME OR PROGRAM NAME

d. INSURANCE PLAN NAME OR PROGRAM NAME

10d. RESERVED FOR LOCAL USE

d. IS THERE ANOTHER HEALTH BENEFIT PLAN? YES NO *If yes*, return to and complete item 9 a-d.

READ BACK OF FORM BEFORE COMPLETING & SIGNING THIS FORM.

12. PATIENT'S OR AUTHORIZED PERSON'S SIGNATURE I authorize the release of any medical or other information necessary to process this claim. I also request payment of government benefits either to myself or to the party who accepts assignment below.

SIGNED DATE

13. INSURED'S OR AUTHORIZED PERSON'S SIGNATURE I authorize payment of medical benefits to the undersigned physician or supplier for services described below.

SIGNED

PATIENT AND INSURED INFORMATION

14. DATE OF CURRENT: MM DD YY ILLNESS (First symptom) OR INJURY (Accident) OR PREGNANCY(LMP)

15. IF PATIENT HAS HAD SAME OR SIMILAR ILLNESS. GIVE FIRST DATE MM DD YY

16. DATES PATIENT UNABLE TO WORK IN CURRENT OCCUPATION FROM MM DD YY TO MM DD YY

17. NAME OF REFERRING PHYSICIAN OR OTHER SOURCE

17a. I.D. NUMBER OF REFERRING PHYSICIAN

18. HOSPITALIZATION DATES RELATED TO CURRENT SERVICES FROM MM DD YY TO MM DD YY

19. RESERVED FOR LOCAL USE

20. OUTSIDE LAB? YES NO $ CHARGES

21. DIAGNOSIS OR NATURE OF ILLNESS OR INJURY. (RELATE ITEMS 1,2,3 OR 4 TO ITEM 24E BY LINE)

1. ___ . __ 3. ___ . __

2. ___ . __ 4. ___ . __

22. MEDICAID RESUBMISSION CODE ORIGINAL REF. NO.

23. PRIOR AUTHORIZATION NUMBER

24. A DATE(S) OF SERVICE From MM DD YY To MM DD YY	B Place of Service	C Type of Service	D PROCEDURES, SERVICES, OR SUPPLIES (Explain Unusual Circumstances) CPT/HCPCS MODIFIER	E DIAGNOSIS CODE	F $ CHARGES	G DAYS OR UNITS	H EPSDT Family Plan	I EMG	J COB	K RESERVED FOR LOCAL USE
1										
2										
3										
4										
5										
6										

25. FEDERAL TAX I.D. NUMBER SSN EIN

26. PATIENT'S ACCOUNT NO.

27. ACCEPT ASSIGNMENT? (For govt. claims, see back) YES NO

28. TOTAL CHARGE $

29. AMOUNT PAID $

30. BALANCE DUE $

31. SIGNATURE OF PHYSICIAN OR SUPPLIER INCLUDING DEGREES OR CREDENTIALS (I certify that the statements on the reverse apply to this bill and are made a part thereof.)

SIGNED DATE

32. NAME AND ADDRESS OF FACILITY WHERE SERVICES WERE RENDERED (If other than home or office)

33. PHYSICIAN'S, SUPPLIER'S BILLING NAME, ADDRESS, ZIP CODE & PHONE #

PIN# GRP#

PHYSICIAN OR SUPPLIER INFORMATION

(APPROVED BY AMA COUNCIL ON MEDICAL SERVICE 8/88) **PLEASE PRINT OR TYPE** FORM HCFA-1500 (12-90) FORM OWCP-1500 FORM RRB-1500

Source: Reprinted from U.S. Department of Health and Human Services/Health Care Financing Administration, Washington, D.C.

APPENDIX 10-C

State Medicaid Programs Coverage for Physician Assistants

State	PA Covered Provider	Reimbursement Rate (% Physician Fee)	Physician Supervision Requirements[2]	Services Covered
ALABAMA	Yes	100%	Physician on site	All medical services cited in PA law except assisting at surgery
ALASKA	Yes	100%	Physician on site except in RHCs and FQHCs	
ARIZONA [1]	Yes	100%		
ARKANSAS	Yes	100%	Physician on site 50%	All medical services cited in PA law
CALIFORNIA	Yes	100%	Same as PA law	All medical primary care, incl. home care
COLORADO	Yes	100%	Physician on site[2]	All medical services cited in PA law
CONNECTICUT	Yes	100%	Physician present except in free-standing clinic	All except nonsupervised inpatient services; only "incident to" in physician office

continues

[1] Arizona Health Care Cost Containment System (AHCCCS)

[2] In the case of federally certified Rural Health Clinics (RHCs), the state Medicaid program cannot establish supervisory requirements more stringent than those found in the state PA law. Consequently, the "physician on site" requirement does not apply to Medicaid reimbursement in RHCs unless it is a requirement of the Medical Practice Act.

[3]Reimbursement based on PA assigned Relative Value Unit

Source: Reprinted with permission from American Academy of Physician Assistants, *State Medicaid Programs: Coverage for Physician Assistants* (Feb. 1997) (fact sheet), © 1997.

State	*PA Covered Provider*	*Reimbursement Rate (% Physician Fee)*	*Physician Supervision Requirements*[2]	*Services Covered*
DELAWARE	Yes	100%		All medical services cited in PA law
D.C.	No			
FLORIDA	Yes	80%		All medical services cited in PA law
GEORGIA	Yes	90%	Same as PA law	All medical services cited in PA law
HAWAII	Yes	100%	Same as PA law	All medical services except assisting at surgery
IDAHO	Yes	85%	Same as PA law	All medical services cited in PA law
ILLINOIS	Yes	100%	Same as PA law	Services within physician's scope of practice
INDIANA	Yes	100%	Same as PA law	All medical services cited in PA law
IOWA	Yes	100%	Same as PA law	All medical services cited in PA law
KANSAS	Yes	75%	Same as PA law	Office visits & H&Ps, home visits, nursing home visits, H&Ps, recerts, subsequent hospital visits
KENTUCKY	No			
LOUISIANA	No			
MAINE	Yes	100%	Same as PA law	All medical services cited in PA law. Limits on settings in which services are covered (i.e., no birthing centers)
MARYLAND	Yes	100%	Physician on site[2]	All medical services cited in PA law

MASSACHUSETTS	Yes			Routine well-care services to beneficiaries under age 21 and obstetric care
MICHIGAN	Yes	100%	Same as PA law	All medical services cited in PA law
MINNESOTA	Yes	90%	Physician on site 50% of time	All delegated tasks
MISSISSIPPI	No			
MISSOURI	No			
MONTANA	Yes	80%	Same as PA law	All medical services cited in PA law
NEBRASKA	Yes	100%	Same as PA law	All medical services cited in PA law
NEVADA	Yes	PA rate[3]	Same as PA law	All medical services cited in PA law
NEW HAMPSHIRE	Yes	100%	Same as PA law	All medical services cited in PA law
NEW JERSEY	No			
NEW MEXICO	Yes	100%	Same as PA law	All medical services except assisting surgery
NEW YORK	Yes	100%	Same as PA law	All medical services cited in PA law
NORTH CAROLINA	Yes	100%	Same as PA law	Only "incident to" services
NORTH DAKOTA	Yes	75%	Same as PA law	All medical services cited in PA law
OHIO	Yes	85–100%	Same as PA law	All medical services
OKLAHOMA	Yes - Fee for Service	75% for Outpatient Fee for Service		10.4% for first-assisting (Fee for Service)
	Yes - Managed Care	EPSDT, Lab, X-rays at 100%	areas	Primary Care Provider status in rural

continues

State	*PA Covered Provider*	*Reimbursement Rate (% Physician Fee)*	*Physician Supervision Requirements[2]*	*Services Covered*
OREGON	Yes	100%	Same as PA law	All medical services cited in PA law
PENNSYLVANIA	Yes	100%	Same as PA law	All medical services cited in PA law except assisting at surgery
RHODE ISLAND	Yes			
SOUTH CAROLINA	Yes	100%	Physician on site	All medical services cited in PA law
SOUTH DAKOTA	Yes	90%	Same as PA law	All medical services cited in PA law
TENNESSEE	Yes	100%	Same as PA law	All medical services cited in PA law
TEXAS	Yes	100%	Same as PA law	All medical services cited in PA law
UTAH	Yes	100%	Same as PA law	All medical services cited in PA law
VERMONT	Yes	90%	Same as PA law	All medical services cited in PA law
VIRGINIA	No			
WASHINGTON	Yes	100%	Same as PA law	All medical services cited in PA law
WEST VIRGINIA	Yes	100%	Same as PA law	All medical services cited in PA law
WISCONSIN	Yes	90%	Same as PA law	All medical services cited in PA law
WYOMING	Yes	100%	Same as PA law	All medical services cited in PA law

Appendix 10-D

State Workers' Compensation Programs

State	PA Covered Provider	Reimbursement Rate (% Physician Fee)	Physician Supervision Requirements	Services Covered
ALABAMA	No			
ALASKA	Yes	100%		
ARIZONA	*		Physician signs all paperwork	
ARKANSAS	Yes	100%	Same as PA law	
CALIFORNIA	Yes	% depends on service provided	Physician signs all paperwork	Insurer authorizes PA services, first-assist 10%
COLORADO	Yes	75%	Physician must evaluate patient	Same as PA law
CONNECTICUT	Yes	% depends on service provided		
D.C.	No			

continues

* Individual workers' compensation insurance carriers determine coverage policy. The state has no specific policy regarding medical services provided by PAs.

This chart is based on information gathered from phone calls made to workers' compensation offices throughout the country. Blank spaces indicate incomplete information provided by state agencies. It is best to call the state workers' compensation offices for specific information about their policies regarding coverage of medical services provided by physician assistants. In most cases (except when the reimbursement rate is less than 100%) services provided by PAs are billed under the physician's name and provider number.

Source: Reprinted with permission from *Physician Assistant Third-Party Coverage,* pp. 36–37, © 1996, American Academy of Physician Assistants.

State	PA Covered Provider	Reimbursement Rate (% Physician Fee)	Physician Supervision Requirements	Services Covered
DELAWARE	No			
FLORIDA	Yes	100%	Same as PA law	PA cannot assist at surgery
GEORGIA	Yes	100%	Physician signs all paperwork	Same as PA law
HAWAII	Yes	60%	Physician signs all paperwork	
IDAHO	*			Determined by supervising physician & insurer
ILLINOIS*				Determination made by insurance carrier(s)
INDIANA*				Determination made by insurance carrier(s)
IOWA	Yes	100%	Same as PA law	
KANSASYes	% depends on	Same as PA law service provided		
KENTUCKY	Yes	100%	Same as PA law	20% reimbursement rate for first-assisting
LOUISIANA	No			
MAINE	Yes	100%	Same as PA law	
MARYLAND	No			
MASSACHUSETTS	No			Determination made by insurance carrier(s)
MICHIGAN	Yes	85%	Same as PA law	13% reimbursement rate for first-assisting
MINNESOTA	Yes	% depends on service provided	Physician signs all paperwork	Same as PA law

MISSISSIPPI	No			
MISSOURI	Yes	% depends on service provided	Same as PA law	
MONTANA	Yes	80%	Physician signs all paperwork	
NEBRASKA	Yes	100%	Same as PA law	
NEVADA	Yes	100%	Physician signs all paperwork	Rural PA contacts physician daily when treating wc patient
NEW HAMPSHIRE	Yes	% depends on service provided	Same as PA law	
NEW JERSEY	*			Determination made by insurance carrier(s)
NEW MEXICO	Yes	100%	Physician signs all paperwork	Same as PA law
NEW YORK	No			
NORTH CAROLINA	Yes	100%	Physician on premises, signs all paperwork	PA cannot assist at surgery
NORTH DAKOTA	Yes	100%	Physician signs all paperwork	
OHIO	Yes	100%		
OKLAHOMA	Yes			10% reimbursement rate for first-assisting
OREGON	Yes	100%	Same as PA law	
PENNSYLVANIA	Yes	% depends on service provided	Same as PA law	
RHODE ISLAND	Yes	80%	Same as PA law	16% reimbursement rate for first-assisting
SOUTH CAROLINA	*			

continues

State	*PA Covered Provider*	*Reimbursement Rate (% Physician Fee)*	*Physician Supervision Requirements*	*Services Covered*
SOUTH DAKOTA	Yes	100%	Same as PA law	10% reimbursement rate for first-assisting
TENNESSEE	No			
TEXAS	Yes	100%	Physician signs all paperwork	Same as PA law
UTAH	Yes	65%	Physician must see patient on initial visit	PA cannot take anyone off work
VERMONT	Yes	100%	Same as PA law	
VIRGINIA	Yes	100%	Same as PA law	PA and physician determine PA role
WASHINGTON	Yes	100%	PA can write reports, but physician signs	18% reimbursement rate for first-assisting
WEST VIRGINIA	Yes	% depends on service provided	Same as PA law	
WISCONSIN	*			Determination made by insurance carrier(s)
WYOMING	Yes	100%	Physician signs all paperwork	

CHAPTER 11

Participation in Government Affairs

INTRODUCTION

Many factors influence the implementation of legislation and regulations, and in each state, PA practice laws are derived from a separate and distinct process of negotiation between competing interests. This chapter provides information on how and why a PA, and the PA profession in general, should participate in the political process. Physician assistants can play an active and useful role in the formulation of laws regulating PA practice, and this chapter explains some of the steps leading to greater involvement in government affairs.

AAPA AND STATE PA ASSOCIATIONS

At the headquarters of the American Academy of Physician Assistants (AAPA) in Alexandria, Virginia, a full-time staff works to advocate for PAs and their profession on a national level. Along with public education, research, data collection, and a host of other member services, AAPA representatives speak for the profession before the Congress and federal agencies. Lobbying is done daily by the AAPA's professional staff; for example, activities commonly undertaken by an AAPA staff member include attending congressional hearings or meeting informally with members of Congress or their staff. Sometimes the AAPA staff member will bring along practicing PAs or PA educators who have special expertise, have been elected as officers of the Academy, or have an established relationship with legislators.

The AAPA also carries out significant networking and information campaigns on a regular basis, using legislative alerts and other AAPA publications to inform member PAs and the larger PA community about important government affairs issues. [For a list of issues briefs and other publications available from the

AAPA, see Appendix 11-A.] Requesting that AAPA members contact their congressional representative, state assemblyperson, and federal or state agencies about a particular subject is one strategy employed by the AAPA to achieve national and state legislative reforms for the purpose of maximizing PAs' ability to practice and to deliver high-quality, cost-effective patient care. Another effective lobbying activity organized by the AAPA has been the annual gathering of more than 100 PAs from across the country who visit Congress for a day to discuss health issues, as well as legislation that affects the profession, with their senators and representatives.

Although the AAPA's involvement in lobbying the federal government is essential to voicing the PA profession's views on federal legislation and regulations, state PA associations may have a more direct impact on the individual PA's practice environment. State PA associations (which are chartered constituent chapters of the AAPA, and sometimes referred to as state academies), work toward advancing the interests of the PA profession before the state legislature, the state licensing board, and other state agencies. Most of these associations lack the financial resources to employ a full-time staff, and government affairs work is frequently undertaken by practicing PAs who are members of the state PA associations.

In assisting its state chapters, the AAPA provides information, technical and financial resources, and consultation services. The AAPA's government affairs division, for example, recently published a state government affairs handbook to guide state PA association members in their lobbying efforts [*see* AAPA, *Taking Charge: A State Government Affairs Handbook* (Sept. 1996) (hereinafter "*AAPA Government Affairs Handbook*")]. As part of its goal to promote uniformity in state PA laws, the AAPA also will provide, on request, copies of state PA laws, model state PA legislation, sample fact sheets, and an analysis of proposed rules and legislation.

STATE CHAPTER'S GOVERNMENT AFFAIRS COMMITTEE

Because every PA's ability to practice is determined by state law (excluding PAs who work for the federal government), the practicing PA and the PA educator should be concerned about and aware of new developments in laws or regulations affecting PA practice and patient care in their state. Monitoring such activity and participating in the legislative and regulatory process are central functions of state PA associations, and contacting the association's government affairs committee should be the individual PA's first step in seeking to become more involved in this process.

As discussed in greater detail later, the primary activities of a government affairs committee within a state PA association include:

- networking with state government, other professional organizations, and consumer groups
- monitoring legislation, regulations, and policy changes
- advocating the state academy's position in meetings with the regulatory board governing PAs
- strategic planning and coordination of efforts to accomplish changes in PA legislation and regulations for the purpose of maximizing PAs' ability to practice and provide high quality patient care
- responding to inquiries about PA practice and the profession from state legislators and regulators
- undertaking other lobbying, education, or research tasks as defined by the board of directors

A government affairs committee within a state PA association typically has five to seven members; the PA association president usually appoints the committee chairperson who then appoints other committee members. Ideally, a government affairs committee should include PA association members from different regions of the state and, if possible, different types of practice settings. Also, in the "ideal" committee, the chairperson or cochairperson resides in the state capital.

In addition, other aspects of the committee may contribute to its effectiveness. For example, the committee should have an active agenda and should not view itself as a group appointed simply for the purpose of handling legislative or regulatory "crisis" situations. Accordingly, the committee should hold regular meetings, especially in advance of state chapter board of directors meetings. In addition, sufficient funding is crucial to the success of the committee's agenda, which may include activities such as travel to meetings and/or legislative and regulatory hearings, phone networking, printing of legislative alerts and other public education materials, organizing and putting on a legislative "event," and obtaining services and advice from professional lobbyists or an attorney.

Although a government affairs committee should be granted sufficient authority by the board of directors to proceed on an independent basis in carrying out most of its agenda, including autonomy in making decisions with respect to implementing legislative activities, the committee should keep in mind that its policy goals are subject to board approval. If a substantive policy decision needs to be made in the context of what legislative action or language to pursue, the committee should make a recommendation to the board for its consideration and ultimate determination as to the appropriate course of action.

In addition to obtaining board approval for its actions, the government affairs committee often may turn to the state PA association's legal counsel for advice on dealing with legislative and regulatory issues. Generally, state PA associations do not routinely retain expensive law firms nor do they necessarily seek daily legal advice. Nonetheless, every state PA chapter needs to have access to an attorney to address any of several legal problems that may arise, including issues related to the association's corporate affairs, or to legislative and regulatory affairs requiring legal analysis and effective communication with state legislatures, licensing boards, or other state agencies [*see AAPA Government Affairs Handbook,* at 13].

The government affairs committee will likely encounter many situations where an attorney's assistance is particularly useful; some of the examples outlined in the AAPA handbook are:

- review and legal analysis of whether conflict exists between the medical board's proposed rules and the PA practice statute, or whether rules exceed the board's authority under an enabling statute
- attendance at meetings to ensure compliance with administrative law or other legal requirements of due process such as bringing the association's lawyer to a meeting between the committee members and the medical board to safeguard against suspected noncompliance with the state's open meeting law
- assistance in drafting potential regulatory or legislative changes and legal review to ensure that no provision conflicts with existing state law
- correspondence with medical or pharmacy boards regarding interpretation of PA scope of practice, including PA prescribing, to steer boards away from placing limitations on services that PAs are authorized to perform under PA practice statutes

[*AAPA Government Affairs Handbook,* at 13].

The handbook also provides advice on how to select an attorney for the state PA association and includes a sample "Request for Proposal for Legal Services" for use in seeking to retain an attorney [*see AAPA Government Affairs Handbook,* Appendix B].

Research and Monitoring Activities

To deal effectively with a state government, a PA advocate must be informed. An important part of gathering information is monitoring legislative activities and the activities of departments that regulate health care. The PA member of a government affairs committee should keep track of not only PA legislation and regulations, but also other areas that may influence PA practice, including state health care reform issues, insurance law, the state Medicaid program, workers' compensation policies and regulations, pharmacy law, corporations law, and nursing law.

An initial step toward setting up a monitoring system involves communicating with people who know what is going on and maintaining this network of contacts so that the committee will be alerted as to potentially important legislative or regulatory changes. [See Networking.] State legislators or their staff, the medical board or PA advisory committee to that board, attorneys, and other state government employees can be consulted to see what, if any, health care initiatives impacting PAs are forthcoming. Colleagues or members of professional associations and organizations with a similar interest in health care issues (e.g., state medical society, family physicians' association, nurses' association) also can be excellent sources of information.

In addition to developing an informal monitoring system, the government affairs committee can, if desired, obtain early warning of pending legislation from lobbying firms that specialize in monitoring and who, for a fee, will provide periodic reports on specific subjects of interest. [See Contracting Out Lobbying Activities.] Also, according to the AAPA, at least five firms operating in all 50 states will provide online information on all bills introduced in a particular state legislature. Moreover, each state has a local system for tracking legislative bills and usually can provide a for-fee service of alerting subscribers to pending bills that may impact any subject area specified. If the government affairs committee determines that it needs to obtain the full text of pending legislation, that can usually be accomplished free by placing a request with a state legislature's "bill room" or legislative document office. [For a state-by-state list of the addresses and phone numbers of House and Senate legislative document offices, see Appendix 11-B.]

Networking

Networking is the exchange of information or services among individuals, groups, or institutions, and developing a networking system is an essential part of any state PA chapter's government affairs program. A good starting point for developing a network for government affairs purposes is to determine the connections and contacts already established by the state chapter as a whole (including member PAs who are not necessarily active in chapter activities) [*see AAPA Government Affairs Handbook,* at 7]. The objective of forming a network is to maintain connections with various groups and individuals who can band together and exert collective influence in support of projects on the government affairs committee's agenda.

The state medical society, according to the AAPA, is the most important group in the network organized by the government affairs committee of many state PA chapters. Although the PA profession has gained increasing recognition on the national level and more consistent support of the American Medical Association (AMA), there are certainly groups of physician-members in state medical societies who remain unfamiliar with the PA profession or are even opposed to the concept of medical services provided by nonphysician providers. Thus, it is very important that state chapters work to gain the support of state medical societies. In the AAPA's words, "[h]aving an educated and supportive medical society is critical to the success of any state government affairs program." [*AAPA Government Affairs Handbook,* at 8]. Other groups recommended by the AAPA for inclusion in a state chapter's government affairs network include:

- senior citizens organizations such as the American Association of Retired Persons (AARP)
- allied health professional organizations
- hospitals and hospital groups, health maintenance organizations (HMOs), and nursing home organizations
- primary care associations
- rural health care advocates
- legislative staff and regulatory boards
- PA educational programs
- medical school staff

To effectively create and then maintain a network requires consistent and active attention involving phone calls, letters, and meetings with the persons and groups in the network. Networks are usually operated in an informal manner; somewhat formal procedures, however, such as making it a regular practice to follow up phone conversations with letters to the appropriate parties, are an excellent way to increase the effectiveness of networking efforts. Also, to avoid duplicative efforts or unclear lines of communication, one PA member of the government affairs committee (in many state chapters, the committee chairperson), should be the committee's network coordinator.

Contracting Out Lobbying Activities

Lobbying is known by names such as government relations and legislative representation, but, in essence, it is communicating, exchanging ideas, building relationships, processing information, influencing, and advocating. On the level of the individual PA, lobbying is the chance to have a voice in government and is accomplished in many different ways. When a PA writes to an elected official, calls an agency asking for changes in regulation, asks an assemblyperson to vote on a particular bill, talks one-on-one to a legislator about legislative concerns—these are all examples of lobbying.

It is not uncommon, however, for the government affairs committee of a state PA association to enhance the effectiveness of individual lobbying activities by hiring a professional lobbyist. [For a more detailed discussion, see Hiring a Lobbyist.] Regardless of whether a contract lobbyist is obtained, it is important for members of the government affairs committee to become familiar with their state's lobbying registration and reporting laws before initiating any lobbying effort. Some states have significant penalties, including fines, for failure to register and report certain lobbying activities.

Legal counsel should be consulted to ensure compliance with state lobbying laws, but some common state law provisions require that

- professional lobbyists register with the state in order to lobby before either the legislative branch or the executive branch; although this requirement exists in all 50 states, the registration requirements vary, as do the criteria for determining who is a professional lobbyist (e.g., amount of time spent, money earned or money spent in lobbying, or officials or staff being lobbied)
- organizations registering their lobbying activities disclose who is advocating before the legislative or administrative branch of government, what that person's compensation is and, frequently, what expenditures have been made for dining, tickets to events, and other gifts by a lobbyist to government officials; some states require only contract lobbyists or other employees whose jobs require lobbying on a regular basis to register, while others require registration of any citizen talking to a legislator
- registering persons fill out forms that typically ask for the name of the business or group advocating a position, the name of the person or persons who will be speaking to government officials, pertinent information about these businesses or individuals, and information about the subject matter on which the lobbying will occur; other requirements include periodic reporting, at intervals determined by state law, as to compensation for rendering lobbying services, and all expenditures incurred in the lobbying effort (e.g., mailings, printings, salaries, and money spent on legislators)

[*see generally* Council of State Governments, *The Book of The States 1994–95,* vol. 3D (1994)].

Moreover, PA members of a state PA association's government affairs committee should be aware of the federal requirements related to money spent for lobbying applicable to nonprofit associations such as state PA chapters. [See Nonprofit Associations and Federal Lobbying Law.]

Is a Contract Lobbyist Necessary?

Whether to hire a contract lobbyist is a decision that each state PA association must assess independently. Many state chapters have been very successful in state legislatures without paid professional representation, while other chapters point to the persuasive clout of a professional lobbyist as the key to success in some legislative reform campaigns. The following items should be considered by the government affairs committee in evaluating whether hiring a contract lobbyist may be the most effective strategy toward achieving a legislative or regulatory objective:

- *Budget considerations*—For a state PA association with limited funds, inadequate financial resources for employing a contract lobbyist is a primary concern. If funds are insufficient, the members of the government affairs committee must seek other ways to influence the system.
- *Coalitions*—Often a contract lobbyist is very helpful in bringing together a coalition if needed on a particular issue. The lobbyist acts as a liaison with the other members of the coalition while watching out for the individual client's interests.
- *Contacts, expertise, and time*—The professional lobbyist has established contacts with legislators and their staff, and with legislative attorneys. Moreover, he or she is paid not only to be completely familiar with the legislative process and the political maneuvers that may be used for or against the legislative recommendations of the PA association's government affairs committee, but also for spending as much time on site as may be necessary to ensure that the committee's position is voiced at legislative or regulatory hearings and meetings (if a contract lobbyist is employed on a yearly basis, the lobbyist can be expected to monitor both legislative and regulatory activities).
- *Professional clout*—If there is a major problem or a need for constant involvement in the political process, a contract lobbyist can add clout to the message and put a professional face on lobbying efforts.
- *Proactive legislation*—If legislation is needed to enact a new law or add provisions to an existing law, a contract lobbyist can be very helpful in drafting language, obtaining sponsors, and seeing the bill through the legislative process. If a proactive measure is undertaken, it is advisable to hire a contract lobbyist.

Hiring a Lobbyist

Hiring a contract lobbyist serves merely to formalize the process of lobbying. As indicated earlier, the advantage in employing a contract lobbyist is having a representative who has a place in the system and, therefore, can be both effective and cost-effective. It is important, however, to be very careful when selecting someone to represent the government affairs' positions of the state PA association in the legislative and regulatory arenas. Issues such as compatibility in philosophies, trust, legal skills, reputation, style, and price are important considerations.

Potential contract lobbyists can be found through word of mouth, other professional associations, or health care organizations. Also, if a legislator is known, that legislator should be asked for recommendations. While there are excellent contract lobbyists in every state, it is best to hire a lobbyist who meets the PA association's needs. The following are some general tips on selecting a contract lobbyist:

- *Review the contract lobbyist's client list.* Most contract lobbyists will be receptive to providing such a list, and if not, it can be obtained as a public record through the appropriate state government office. In hiring a lobbyist, it is important to be comfortable with the other clients the lobbyist represents; moreover, a client list can disclose potential competition for the time and attention expected from the lobbyist.
- *Assess whether the contract lobbyist's client list causes conflicts of interest.* It is important to avoid potential conflicts of interest (e.g., the lobbyist's representation of the pharmacy profession whose position directly opposes legislative objectives related to PA prescribing).
- *Evaluate the value of an attorney-lobbyist.* A good attorney-lobbyist often brings skills and knowledge of the law to the process, which is an extra benefit to be considered in searching for a contract lobbyist.

A good advocate at a good value is desirable; however, what to pay a contract lobbyist varies from state to state. There are many factors that contribute to overall cost. For example, does the state have a 30-day session or is it a year-round legislature? What is the going market rate? Geographical considerations are important; for example, there is probably a higher fee for a contract lobbyist in a large capital city such as Boston than in Montpelier, the capital city of Vermont. Another prime consideration is the function the contract lobbyist will perform; will it be a short-term relationship or a continuing relationship? Are there proactive issues or will the lobbyist be trying to defeat legislation? All of these factors affect price.

Perhaps the most important element of the client-lobbyist relationship is the written contract. It is important that both parties know what is expected. The contract should spell out the particulars of the work to be undertaken and the compensation to be paid. It should set forth who the client's contact person is, how communications are to flow, and how much authority is delegated to the lobbyist.

If a contract lobbyist is used, members of the government affairs committee are the individuals to whom that lobbyist should report, and the committee should designate one contact person (and an alternate). The AAPA recommends ways to locate and decide on a professional lobbyist in its state government affairs handbook, and also recommends steps to take in negotiating for lobbyist services that will likely result in the most effective use of those services, including educating the lobbyist about the PA profession, clearly delineating the state association's legislative goals and priorities, and signing a contract that outlines the responsibilities and duties of the lobbyist. [For other recommendations and a sample lobbyist contract, *see AAPA Government Affairs Handbook,* at 28–29 and Appendix G.]

Nonprofit Associations and Federal Lobbying Law

Members of the government affairs committee should also be aware of the federal requirements related to money spent for lobbying that may or may not apply to a state PA association. This section provides a brief overview of these requirements, but as the reader may recognize in the subtle distinctions that separate activities considered nonlobbying from those deemed to be lobbying, compliance with the federal tax laws in this area can be quite complex and an attorney or the AAPA's contact person for finance and administration should be consulted if there is uncertainty as to a state chapter's compliance with these laws.

If a state chapter has tax exempt status under Section 501(c)(6) of the Internal Revenue Code (IRC), then any lobbying expenses must be recorded and members must be told what percentage of their dues is spent on legislative efforts. Federal legislation enacted in August 1993 amended the federal tax code by disallowing, in many circumstances, business deductions for lobbying expenses, including direct and grassroots lobbying at the federal and state level [Omnibus Reconciliation Act of 1993, Pub. L. No. 103-66]. Of particular importance to most state PA associations and their members is a provision specifying that lobbying expenditures of IRC § 501(c)(6) noncharitable exempt organizations (state and federal) are to be treated as lobbying expenses of the dues-paying members of those organizations. Accordingly, a percentage of the members' dues will be nondeductible.

Under IRC § 4911, lobbying is defined broadly, and includes: influencing legislation through contact with (1) any member or employee of a legislative body or (2) any government official or employee who may participate in the legislative process; participating in, or intervening in, any political campaign; attempting to influence the general public with respect to an election, or any legislative matter or referendum; and any direct communication with a "covered executive branch official" in an attempt to influence official action. Moreover, business deductions are disallowed for lobbying expenses other than direct communications with legislators and government officials; any research, planning, or preparation of a lobbying activity would be included in the costs of influencing legislation and therefore disallowed. In addition, indirect costs associated with lobbying fall under nondeductible expenses; for example, business deductions for expenses paid for printing and mailing letters to urge association members to contact their legislators regarding a particular issue are disallowed. Monitoring expenses, however, are not considered part of lobbying expenses, but activities designed to monitor legislation may be treated as nondeductible lobbying costs if there are subsequent attempts to influence the enactment of legislation that was previously monitored by the association [*see AAPA Government Affairs Handbook,* at 15–16].

While most state PA chapters fall under the requirements of IRC § 501(c)(6), it is possible that some PA associations qualify for an exemption from the disallowance rules pertaining to that section. For example, if the association's direct lobbying expenses (not including overhead) are less than $2,000 for the tax year, the lobbying law is not applicable to that association [*see AAPA Government Affairs Handbook,* at 16].

Also not covered under these disallowance rules are organizations recognized as tax-exempt charities under IRC § 501(c)(3); these organizations have separate lobbying restrictions [*see, e.g.,* Treas. Reg. §§ 1.501(c)(3)-1(c)(3) and 56.4911-1]. Moreover, the disallowance provisions applicable to organizations categorized under IRC § 501(c)(6) would not apply to an association receiving 90 percent or more of its dues from IRC § 501(c)(3) tax-exempt organizations that are not entitled to take a tax deduction for the payments.

This background information on tax-exempt charitable organizations is significant to the IRC § 501(c)(6) noncharitable exempt organization, such as the state PA association, because the "90 percent rule" also exempts from the disallowance rules organizations that receive 90 percent or more of their dues income from individuals who cannot deduct the dues because of the 2 percent limitation for itemized miscellaneous deductions (which usually applies to professional associations whose members pay moderate dues and are not self-employed). To qualify for this status, however, a state PA association would have to request a private letter ruling from the Internal Revenue Service, and in presenting the case, would have to prove that more than 90 percent of membership dues are not deductible. Although such evidence may be gathered through a member survey, successful completion of this task, as well as obtaining a full response, may be a difficult undertaking for the PA association.

In addition to broad provisions disallowing business deductions for lobbying expenses of IRC § 501(c)(6) organizations, federal tax law also requires maintenance of a recordkeeping system that identifies lobbying activities and properly estimates related expenses, and reporting of total lobbying expenses on the organization's Form 990 Tax Return. Also, the association is required to notify its dues-paying members, in appropriate advance of their payment and in a conspicuous format, of the estimated portion of the dues that will be spent on lobbying activities and of the legal requirement that this percentage of the dues is nondeductible by association members. In its state government affairs handbook, the AAPA provides an example of an association's calculation of the nondeductible portion of its dues and other pertinent information regarding ways to ensure compliance with federal tax law related to the lobbying activities of organizations with IRC § 501(c)(6) tax-exempt status [*see AAPA Government Affairs Handbook,* at 15–18].

Building a Grassroots Network

In addition to professional lobbying, either by a contract lobbyist or the association itself, grassroots lobbying by PAs in a legislator's district can have a significant impact on the legislative process. "Grassroots" is a political or public relations term whose meaning has been expanded to cover a multitude of situations. In its most basic sense, grassroots refers to the effort to raise the consciousness of those who do not normally participate in political activity so as to enlist their help in influencing legislators by writing letters, attending meetings, contacting media, and promoting common interests. In the state legislative process, grassroots efforts can be used by PAs, especially PA members of a government affairs committee, to influence health care providers, employers, patients, and their friends and families to contact legislators, write letters to the media, and attend functions en masse to show support or opposition to a given policy, bill, or regulation.

To begin a simple grassroots network, a list of targeted participants should be compiled, along with the legislative district for each potential participant, and a list of the state representatives for each district [see Networking]. Network participants should be encouraged to contact their legislators before issues arise; establishing a relationship with a legislator is important so that when there is a problem, communication lines are already in place. When contacted, the network participants can send postcards, make telephone calls, or visit legislators. It is far easier to respond to a call for action if the preliminary grassroots have been planted. [For recommendations on developing in-the-district contacts, *see AAPA Government Affairs Handbook,* at 33 and Appendix H.]

Many state PA associations have found the use of legislative alerts to be a valuable tool in promoting support among PA members. Such alerts should provide information about pending legislative activity, including specific instructions to members and other supporters on the action that is needed. The AAPA puts out its own legislative alert, and a sample alert appears as an appendix to the AAPA's state government affairs handbook [*see AAPA Government Affairs Handbook,* Appendix I].

Forming a Political Action Committee

Aside from the aforementioned direct lobbying activities, another option for influencing legislative activity is the formation of a political action committee

(PAC). A PAC is a committee formed for the purpose of accepting contributions from like-minded persons for distribution to political candidates. The committee can serve broad educational functions or it may be limited in scope to collecting and distributing campaign contributions. PACs can give aggregate funds collected from many contributors to campaigns, and thus a PAC donation has a significantly greater impact than small individual donations.

PA members of a government affairs committee should consider the benefits and disadvantages of forming a PAC for the state PA chapter. One benefit of forming a PAC is that such an entity usually allows for the state PA association to participate more fully in the political process through well-targeted donations to certain incumbent legislators or candidate legislators. A PAC, for example, can donate funds to incumbents or candidate legislators friendly to PA issues or to a candidate who is running against a legislator known to be unsupportive of pro-PA legislation. Also, more focused attention on an issue of importance to the PA profession may be accomplished if a legislator receives a donation from a PAC that is clearly identified as a state "PA PAC."

On the negative side, creation of a PAC can put a significant drain on the PA association's limited funds because once a donation has been made to a particular legislator, the future will likely hold more contribution requests from that legislator's office. Thus, in considering whether to set up a PAC, it would be prudent for members of the government affairs committee to determine whether the state PA association will be able to fund ongoing PAC activities; a one-time contribution from a PAC does little to ensure a legislator's consistent support of the PA association's position on legislative issues. Nonetheless, even if a state PA association opts not to establish a PAC, members of the government affairs committee should take advantage of disclosure requirements under most state laws regulating PAC activity to determine what interest groups have contributed to particular legislators.

On deciding to establish a PAC, a designated person (usually a member of the government affairs committee) should obtain copies of all state laws and regulations relating to PACs and PAC activity (i.e., formation of the PAC, disclosure requirements, solicitation of contributions, and PAC expenditures). Requirements for forming a PAC vary from state to state; in most states, however, the laws are similar, and specific rules and regulations regarding PACs can be obtained from the state election office or the attorney general's office. In setting up a PAC, state PA associations should consult an attorney familiar with lobbying laws. Moreover, a state PA association may want to seek more information as to forming a PAC from other organizations in the state that have sponsored or created PACs, such as the state medical society or state chamber of commerce. [For a more detailed discussion of PACs and guidelines for establishing a state PA chapter PAC, *see AAPA Government Affairs Handbook,* at 19–20 and Appendix C.]

PARTICIPATING IN STATE LEGISLATIVE PROCESS*

For PA members of a government affairs committee to be most effective in their legislative efforts, familiarity with state legislatures and their process is essential. A state legislative body may be called the legislature, the general assembly, the general court, or the legislative assembly [*see* Council of State Governments, *The Book of States, 1994–95,* vol. 30, at 108 (1994)]. State legislatures are generally based on one model; except for the state of Nebraska, all state legislatures are bicameral. Nebraska has only one chamber, called the Legislature, and all legislators are called senators. The upper house in a state legislature is called the Senate in every state, and all legislators in the upper house go by the title of senator.

In all states except Arkansas, Kentucky, Montana, Nevada, North Dakota, Oregon, and Texas, legislatures meet on an annual basis. Virginia holds a 30-day session in odd years and a 60-day session in even years, while California meets virtually year-round [*see* Council of State Governments, *The Book of States, 1994–95,* vol. 30, at 109ff (1994)]. All states have provisions for special sessions to be called.

Most states elect legislators to four-year terms although there are several states that provide for a term of two years. The size of legislatures varies considerably from the smallest 49-member unicameral Nebraska legislature to the 424-member legislature in New Hampshire [*see* Council of State Governments, *The Book of States, 1994–95,* vol. 30, at 113 (1994)]. Interestingly, the country's most populous state, California, with 120 legislators is significantly smaller than the New Hampshire legislature.

There is also great variety in the type of staff, including secretaries, legislative assistants, and administrative assistants, a legislator may employ in a given state. An individual legislator may be given no personal staff, may share staff, or may have personal staff members. Committees of the legislature may also have assigned staff. While the number of staff grew dramatically nationwide in the 1970s and 1980s, the focus on less government in the 1990s has resulted in the reevaluation of staff size with an emphasis on efficiency [*see* Council of State Governments, *The Book of States, 1994–95,* vol. 30, at 103 (1994)]. In addition to paid staff, a legislator may often be provided services by interns, who may be college students earning credits for such internships. Other legislators may use volunteer help from those constituents who have worked for the political campaign.

**Source:* Sections on state legislative process are adapted from M. Adler, "Legislative Activity and Lobbying for the Home Health Provider," in *Home Health Care Law Manual,* M. Nathenson, ed., pp. 4:22–29, © 1996, Aspen Publishers, Inc.

In state legislatures, as opposed to the federal government, PA advocates may have an opportunity to talk directly to a legislator. In large states with large staffs, the chance of a one-on-one meeting with the legislator seems to diminish in proportion to the size of the staff. Whether a PA speaks to the legislator or not, however, it is vital to a lobbying effort to know who the staff are, what their functions are, and who are the closest to the legislator. Above all, learn to treat the staff with the deference that is expected, and also be cognizant of office protocol. There is a pecking order, and one is advised to know it; one of the advantages of using contract lobbyists is their familiarity with staff protocol.

In some legislative offices, the legislative agenda may be staff driven. Legislators often rely on their staffs in terms of public opinion, political realities, and legislative information. Often, depending on the circumstances, it is vital to have a staff person buy into a position, especially if there is a close relationship between that staff person and the legislator.

The Committee System

Legislative bodies are committee driven and, therefore, effective lobbying should concentrate on the committee to which a bill is assigned. While it is important to have broad contacts among legislators and leadership, lobbying resources are limited both in terms of money and time, and a PA advocate's concern should be with the committee that considers the particular PA-specific issue. The business of most state legislatures is conducted in standing committees. Standing committees handle the substantive work of the body and are assigned bills in certain jurisdictional issues. For example, standing committees will have jurisdiction over health issues, including health policy issues, health insurance issues, Medicaid issues, and Medicaid funding issues. Depending on the state, these health issues may be assigned to one or more standing committees.

The committee system may be very strong. If it is, decisions made by a committee, while certainly subject to floor amendments and vote, will be given weight in floor deliberations. Committee courtesy, more evident in some states than in others, dictates that members defer to the committee in its particular area of expertise. Therefore, if lobbying is successful in the standing committee to which a bill is assigned, there is more likelihood that the successful product will survive.

Nonetheless, if a bill comes out of a committee in an untenable form, an effort should be made to amend or kill the bill on the floor of the house of origin. Failing that, there is a chance (except in Nebraska) to influence the form or passage of the bill in the opposite chamber. In a bicameral legislature, a bill must pass both houses in the same form, and so opportunity does begin again when a bill goes from the chamber of origin to the other chamber. Again, in the second chamber, the greatest impact may be achieved during committee deliberations.

How Legislation Is Enacted

The process of passing a bill follows basic principles in each state, except for Nebraska, which has a unicameral legislature. For the other 49 states, the following discussion provides an overall picture of the steps to enacting legislation.

First, legislation stems from an idea offered by an individual or group, which must have a sponsor to introduce that idea in bill form. The idea must be drafted into legislative language; some states even require that a bill be drafted in its final form for introduction by a drafter employed by the legislature. The bill then goes through a first reading in the chamber of origin, which consists simply of a reading of the title of the bill by the clerk and assignment of the bill to the legislative committee that will consider it.

Although each legislature has varying rules and procedures governing the work of committees, bills are generally assigned to what is known as a standing committee, that is, a permanent committee of the chamber organized to consider bills in defined subject areas. The bulk of work done on a bill, and thus the most important time for lobbying, is during the committee process. The committee may hold a public hearing (many states require one, others hold public hearings as a matter of policy, and, in some states, a bill may go through a committee without a public hearing). The committee then votes on the bill, often amending it from its original version. During this time, communicating with members of the committee should occur to ensure passage, defeat, or amendment, as the case may be.

The second reading of a bill on the floor of the chamber of origin is a report given by the standing committee. The bill is thus "reported out to the floor." On second reading, the committee's report may be accepted, amended, or rejected. If the bill passes second reading, with or without amendments, it is then held over for a third reading. In a few states, bills may get only two readings. It is during the second reading phase that most of the work takes place on a bill and that the final form of a bill is generally determined.

State legislatures vary with respect to the form of the bill when it comes to the body for a third reading. In some states, the original bill and its amendments are voted on together, and in other states the bill is reprinted for a third reading. In any case, it is at the time of the third reading when debate and the final vote on a bill take place. Passage of a bill depends on the constitutional requirements of each state. Generally, the vote of a majority of the elected members is necessary to pass a bill. There are, however, extraordinary majorities necessary for the passage of certain legislation such as an emergency bill.

The bill then moves to the second chamber for consideration and goes through a similar process of first, second, and third readings. If passed, the bill is sent back to the chamber of origin either in its original form or with amendments from the other chamber. The chamber of origin may concur in the amendments or put the bill into a conference committee composed of conferees from the two chambers.

The conference committee can be an open process or its activities can occur behind closed doors, depending on the state's procedures. When the conference committee does finally decide on a bill, the bill is sent back to each chamber. It must then be passed by each chamber of the two chambers in the same form in order to be sent to the governor, who may sign a bill or veto it. In some states, a bill will be automatically vetoed if not signed by the governor within a particular time period (a "pocket veto"). In other states, a bill will become law without the governor's signature. If the bill is vetoed by the governor, it goes back to the legislature, which may either sustain or override the veto.

Testifying Before a Legislative Committee

It is during the standing committee deliberations that the fate of a piece of legislation is often determined. Mailings and telephone calls to legislators, visits from constituents, and visits from lobbyists occur during these deliberations. A formal legislative hearing is generally a part of this legislative process. Testimony at the hearing can be presented by a contract lobbyist, an association lobbyist, or an individual PA (whether or not a member of a state PA association's government affairs committee). Hearing from an affected individual or representative of the PA profession can be very illuminating for a legislator, and often the affected party can answer specific questions on the substance of the bill.

Certain simple guidelines apply to testifying before a legislative committee:

- *Be brief.* Most committees have time limits on testimony. Even if such time limits are not enforced, the brevity of a message can be its biggest asset. Legislators hear hundreds of people on hundreds of bills, and a short, succinct presentation is more likely to be remembered.
- *Know the facts.* Be prepared to back up a position with facts. Accurate statistics are much more effective than anecdotal evidence; the AAPA is a good source for such information.
- *Never lie.* If a question is asked for which an answer is not known, it is best to be candid. Tell the committee the answer is not known but that the information will be forthcoming. If the answer to a question will be detrimental to the cause, present the answer in the most favorable light, but be truthful.
- *Bring written testimony.* In addition to the oral testimony to the committee, bring a prepared statement and enough copies to distribute to the entire committee.
- *Avoid reading testimony.* Try to address the committee without reading straight from a prepared script; some committees do not even permit reading testimony.
- *Use visual aids.* Visual aids in the form of videotape presentations, charts, and graphs are useful when testifying before a legislative committee; but

keep in mind that any presentation must be cleared with legislative staff and must remain within established time limits.

For further information on testifying before the legislature or undertaking some other form of legislative project, including proposing legislation to various legislators or working to influence committee meetings, an excellent source is the AAPA's guide for state PA associations' government affairs committee [*see AAPA Government Affairs Handbook* (Sept. 1996)].

PARTICIPATING IN STATE REGULATORY PROCESS

Every state has rule-making procedures that permit citizen input, and when a law is enacted, it is important to be aware that the process of implementing that law is just beginning. For PAs, paying attention to the regulatory process is particularly important because in most states it is the state medical board that has the statutory power to promulgate rules to implement PA practice statutes. Past experience in several states has shown that the medical board may attempt to adopt rules contrary to the legislative intent of a particular provision in a PA practice act for the purpose of restricting PAs' scope of practice or otherwise limiting PA-provided health care services. [For a discussion of the scope of the agency's legal authority to adopt regulations, see Chapter 3: Licensure and Scope of Practice, at Regulatory Boards and Their Powers.]

All states outline procedures for the adoption of rules by their regulatory agencies that allow for input by interested parties. [See Appendix 11-C: Summary of State Model Administrative Procedures Act.] Physician assistants primarily deal with the state medical board, which, in most states, is the regulatory agency that adopts and administers rules pertaining to PA practice. In many states, PAs have been granted the privilege of direct, formal input in the regulatory process through PA representation on medical boards [see PA Representation on Regulatory Boards], but also practicing PAs, PA educators, and especially PA members of a state chapter's government affairs committee can play an important informal participatory role, for example, by testifying at public hearings and maintaining regulatory board contacts.

Involvement in Regulatory Affairs

As with the legislative process, an important initial step in participating in the regulatory process is monitoring. Maintaining dialogues with the regulating agency provides valuable information on regulations that are about to be promulgated. In many instances, depending on state policies, the department will contact interested parties for input prior to preparing the first draft of regulations. If the state has a process for disseminating proposed regulations, this information should be accessible either through the library, a subscription, or a computer if the regulatory bulletin is on-line. [For tips on developing relations with regulatory board members and staff, *see AAPA Government Affairs Handbook,* at 55.]

When legislation creates new duties, licensing requirements, or changes the regulation of a profession in any way, it is likely that such legislation will be implemented by regulations. For those who have followed the legislation from its inception, the transition to participation in the promulgation of regulations is easy. It is important to understand who the players are in the regulatory process and how rules are adopted or changed. The composition of regulatory boards responsible for administering state PA statutes, as well as the specific steps in the regulatory process, varies from state to state. Nonetheless, the following sections provide a general description of state regulatory boards and the processes they use in promulgating rules. Since most states follow some version of the Model State Administrative Procedure Act (MSAPA), which sets out certain rule-making procedures (including public notification and public comment), there are common elements to each state's regulatory process [*see AAPA Government Affairs Handbook,* at 51; see also Appendix 11-C: Summary of State Model Administrative Procedures Act].

Generally, medical licensing boards are staffed by three groups of state employees:

1. board members, who are usually appointed by the governor, serve limited terms, and are the persons authorized to vote on adoption of new rules and amendments (typically some or all of these members are physicians and PAs
2. board members' staff, who handle the administrative tasks of the board members and facilitate the board's daily agenda (including coordination of meetings and public hearings)
3. attorneys, who advise the board on legal issues and rule-making procedures and are typically assigned to a board from the state attorney general's office

In a majority of states, the medical or PA regulatory board has a PA board member with full voting privileges or otherwise receives formal input from PAs (i.e., through the PA advisory committee to the medical board). [See PA Representation on Regulatory Boards.]

The regulatory agency is charged with developing regulations necessary to implement a newly enacted law or an amendment to an existing law. The legislator who sponsored a bill that has been enacted usually knows the regulatory board members who will oversee the drafting of regulations to implement the new law. Typically, the task of writing the regulations is left to board staff or the board's attorneys.

Because it is usually easier to influence the initial writing of a regulation than it is to persuade changes in already written draft regulations, a PA with contacts at the regulatory board should consider the strategic value of contacting board staff and attorneys at this drafting stage. In making these initial contacts, the primary goal is a valuable exchange of information; the PA should inform the regulator of PA concerns regarding the language and substance of the new regulation, while also attempting to find out when the board intends to promulgate the regulations and whether any other special interest groups are influencing development of the regulations [*see* K. Sadler Sparkes and N. Gara, "PAs and the Political Process," in R. Ballweg, S. Stolberg, and E. Sullivan, eds., *Physician Assistant: A Guide to Clinical Practice,* 31 (1994)].

Once the initial regulations are written, they are reviewed by the full board and then made available for public comment. Among other requirements, most state administrative procedure statutes require that interested parties be notified of proposed regulations. [See Appendix 11-C: Summary of State Model Administrative Procedures Act.] The notification process differs from state to state, but is generally accomplished through one of three means:

1. publication in a state register, which contains the text of all proposed regulations issued by state agencies (similar to the Federal Register containing government agencies' proposed regulations on the federal level); this is often the means of notification in larger states
2. publication in a statewide-circulated newspaper, and thus an appropriate means of notification only in smaller states
3. publication within a state agency's notice of all proposed regulations to those persons or groups who have made previous written requests to the agency for advance notice of all rule-making proceedings

[*See* K. Sadler Sparkes and N. Gara, "PAs and the Political Process," in R. Ballweg, S. Stolberg, and E. Sullivan, eds., *Physician Assistant: A Guide to Clinical Practice* 31 (1994).]

During a specified time after notification of a proposed regulation, individuals or groups interested in the rule may submit written comments to the agency and/or request a public hearing. [In some states, public hearings are required for specified types of regulation; *see* K. Sadler Sparkes and N. Gara, "PAs and the Political Process," in R. Ballweg, S. Stolberg, and E. Sullivan, eds., *Physician Assistant: A Guide to Clinical Practice* 32 (1994)]. For PA advocates, including members of the state PA chapter's governmental affairs committee, participation in this comment process is particularly important because it is an excellent opportunity to put forth position statements on how and why a proposed regulation might be improved. Either in writing or at a public hearing, comments on a regulation should be concise. Testimony before a regulatory board at a hearing, for example, is frequently limited to 5 or 10 minutes per individual. Also, it is important to remember that comments should be persuasive, but not argumentative; thorough research of the particular issue usually facilitates a well-articulated written or spoken presentation. [For strategies in presenting testimony before a regulatory hearing, *see AAPA Government Affairs Handbook,* at 63; see also Testifying Before a Legislative Committee.]

After considering both written comments and those presented at a public hearing, the regulatory agency will decide whether or not to adopt the regulation. The agency can make modifications to the proposed rule to incorporate comment suggestions or may decide to adopt the original version of the proposed regulation. The agreed-upon version of the regulation is then filed and published as required by the state administrative procedure statute. Each state may have specific requirements for final adoption of a rule. For example, some states require that proposed regulations be adopted (or made final) within a certain time period of second publication; other states require that certain regulations undergo legislative or judicial review before they become final [*see AAPA Government Affairs Handbook,* at 61; see also Appendix 11-C: Summary of State Model Administrative Procedures Act].

While understanding the regulatory process is important for PAs who participate on an informal level through contacting regulators and speaking at public hearings, it is absolutely essential knowledge for PAs who are appointed to serve as regulators. Often, appointed PAs are former leaders of state PA chapters, and once they take on a role as a regulator, their primary responsibility shifts from advocating for the interests of the PA profession to protecting the health and welfare interests of the state and its citizens. It is important for active members of the state chapter to remember that a PA regulator must avoid conflict-of-interest concerns and should not be asked to be a member of the chapter's board of directors or any of its committees that interact with the regulatory board, particularly the government affairs committee. [For a more detailed discussion of the role of the PA regulator, *see AAPA Government Affairs Handbook,* at 57.]

PA Representation on Regulatory Boards

Physician assistants act in a formal capacity on state regulatory boards under three different approaches. In most states, PAs are either members of the state medical board, which is the regulatory agency responsible for administering PA practice statutes, or members of a PA advisory committee to such board. PA advisory committees may be mandated by the legislature or by formal action of the medical board (as provided in regulations promulgated by the board). The third approach is creating a separate PA licensing board charged with the regulation of PAs, which is generally comprised of board members who are physicians and PAs. This section provides some examples of various state regulatory systems under each approach. [For a full state-by-state listing of agencies and/or PA committees responsible for regulating PAs, see Appendix B: State Regulation of Physician Assistants]. Additional sources containing summaries of the specific text of state PA law provisions in this area can be obtained from the AAPA [*see* AAPA, *Physician Assistants: A Role in Regulation* (Dec. 1996) (pamphlet containing summary of regulatory board/advisory committee provisions in state PA practice statutes)].

Several states recognize the need for PA participation in the regulatory process solely by designating a PA seat on their state medical licensing boards. In Connecticut, for example, there are 11 seats on the medical licensing board for members appointed by the governor: 6 physicians (including 1 physician who supervises a PA), 4 public members, and 1 PA [CONN. GEN. STAT. § 20-8a]. Other states following this approach include Montana [MONT. CODE ANN. § 2-15-1841 (1 PA seat, and PA may vote only on issues that affect licensure and regulation of PAs)], New York [N.Y. EDUC. LAW § 6523 (2 PA seats)], North Carolina [N.C. GEN. STAT. § 90-2 (1 seat rotated between PAs and nurse practitioners)], Vermont [VT. STAT. ANN. tit. 26, § 1351(e) (1 PA seat)], West Virginia [W. VA. CODE § 30-3-5 (1 PA seat)], and Washington [WASH. REV. CODE § 18.71.015 (2 PA seats on the Medical Quality Assurance Commission; PAs may vote only on matters directly related to PAs or PA disciplinary matters)].

In a few states, the medical licensing board designates a seat for the PA and also receives advice from a PA advisory committee. The Georgia Composite State Board of Medical Examiners, for example, designates one seat for a representative from a board-appointed PA advisory committee consisting of two physician-board members, two other physicians, and four PAs; the board member from that committee does not have voting privileges and serves only in an advisory capacity in matters relating to PAs [GA. CODE ANN. § 43-34-21]. Other states designating a PA seat on the medical board in conjunction with establishing a PA advisory committee include New Hampshire [N.H. REV. STAT. ANN. § 329:2 (board of registration in medicine receives recommendations on PA issues from a four-member PA advisory committee existing of two physicians and two PAs, while reserving one of seven seats on the board for a PA, an occupational therapist, or a physical therapist, to be appointed by the governor on a rotating basis)], and New Jersey [N.J. REV. STAT. § 45:9 (one PA seat on medical board and a five-member advisory committee consisting of three PAs, one physician, and one public member)]. A slight variant of this approach is employed in Michigan [MICH. COMP. LAWS §§ 333.17021, .17025, and .17521], where there is a separate PA regulatory board that sends a PA member to serve on the medical and osteopathic boards. (Other states with independent PA licensing boards are discussed later.)

Several states establish a PA advisory committee to the medical board without reserving a seat for a PA member. The composition of advisory committees varies from state to state, as do the committees' regulatory powers. Most PA advisory committees are comprised of PAs, physicians (some of whom are usually either medical board members, have experience supervising PAs, or both), and other public members. The committee members may be appointed by the governor, a state official, or the medical board.

In some states, the role of the committee may be limited to an advisory capacity, while in other states the advisory committee has significant responsibilities, including rule making, disciplinary decision making and procedure, and review of applications for approval or denial of license determinations. In Kansas and Kentucky, for example, the PA advisory committees serve to advise or aid the state medical board in carrying out provisions of the state PA practice statutes and regulations [Kan. Stat. Ann. § 65-2896 and Ky. Rev. Stat. Ann. § 311.565; *see also* Del. Code. Ann. tit. 24, § 1703; 2125; Ill. Comp. Stat. 95/11; Neb. Rev. Stat. § 71–1,107.25; Ohio Rev. Code Ann. §§ 4730.05-.06].

In California, however, the advisory committee, called the Physician Assistant Examining Committee, essentially functions as the regulatory authority, although it must have the cooperation of the medical board in rule-making functions [Cal. Bus. & Prof. Code § 354 (committee's responsibilities include establishing standards and approval of PA education programs, advising the medical board on PA scope-of-practice issues, and considering and approving PA applications); *see also* N.J. Rev. Stat. § 45.9; Ind. Code § 25-27.5; Md. Code Ann., Health Occ. §§ 15-202, -203, and -205; Tenn. Code Ann. § 63-19-104, and Tex. Rev. Civ. Stat. art. 4495, § 5.02].

Separate PA licensing boards exist in a small, but growing, number of states. In these states, PAs and physicians comprise the board, and PAs are full voting members. For example, the Utah Physician Assistant Licensing Board consists of four physicians (at least two of whom are or have been PA supervisors, and one of whom may be a medical board member), one PA, one PA program administrator, and one public member. The board members are authorized to adopt rules defining the scope of practice of PAs in that state [Utah Code Ann. §§ 58-1-202 and -203, 58-70-201]. In Iowa, the Board of Physician Assistant Examiners registers and licenses PAs, investigates and disciplines PAs, and develops rules relating to PA scope of practice (which must pass scrutiny of a separate rules review group). The board consists of three PAs, two supervising physicians, and two public members [Iowa Code §§ 147.14(12) and 148C.7]. Other states that have established PA licensing boards with substantial regulatory responsibilities and some PA membership are Arizona [ARIZ. REV. STAT. ANN. § 32-2502 (two PAs of nine-member board)], Massachusetts [MASS. GEN. LAWS ANN. ch. 13, § 10B (two PAs and one PA educator of nine-member board)], Michigan [MICH. COMP. LAWS § 333.17025 (five PAs of nine-member board)], and Rhode Island [R.I. GEN. LAWS § 5-54-5 (two PAs of seven-member board)].

Appendix 11-A

Legislative Efforts: How the AAPA Can Help

Model language, including "replacement part" (standard and customized). The AAPA has researched and prepared model language on a variety of topics. Many chapters have avoided reinventing the wheel by consulting and adopting the AAPA's model language.

Rapid response consultation. The AAPA is generally able to give suggestions or advice on very short notice; the AAPA recognizes that many issues arrive without warning and AAPA staff makes every attempt to provide prompt assistance.

Site visits. Upon request, AAPA staff persons will make a site visit to a state chapter to meet with members, testify at a hearing, or assist in planning a strategy at a board meeting.

Draft testimony, letters, alerts, etc. The AAPA can draft testimony, background documents, letters, alerts, and a wide variety of documents for a legislative or public education project, or can provide examples of documents used by other state chapters.

Decision memoranda. Some state chapters have found that they needed additional information to make an important decision; AAPA staff can prepare decision memoranda to give you a framework for making your decision.

Networking. AAPA staff and elected leadership network with groups from the AMA to the National Conference of State Legislatures, and can provide state chapters with relevant contacts for a particular issue.

Legal language review. The AAPA can review draft legislative language and point out concepts that have worked in other states in an effort to prevent a state chapter from legal obstacles.

Ghostwriting. AAPA staff is available to assist in preparing, or even to ghostwrite, a draft of testimony or an important letter.

Source: Reprinted with permission from *Taking Charge: State Government Affairs Handbook,* p. 67, © 1996, American Academy of Physician Assistants.

Research and background information. The AAPA has a wealth of facts at its offices, and can provide a state chapter with background information on PA-specific and general health care issues.

Summary information. The AAPA has materials containing summaries in the following areas:

- Prescribing and Dispensing Laws
- State PA Laws
- State Laws on Temporary PA Licensure
- State PA Law Provisions on Supervision Requirements
- Supervising Physician to PA Ratios
- PA Roles in Regulation
- States Granting Licensure, Certification, and Registration
- Legal Opinions on PA Orders

Fact Sheets on State Health Reform Issues. The AAPA has fact sheets in the following areas:

- Medical Savings Accounts
- Medicaid Waivers
- Medical Liability Reform
- Work Force Reform
- Anti-Managed Care Proposals
- Insurance Reform
- Medicaid Managed Care
- Utilization Review Regulation
- Mandated Length of Stay, Post-Delivery

Issue Briefs. The AAPA has short factual summaries of information in the following areas:

- PAs and Anesthesiologist Assistants: The Distinctions
- Antitrust Implications of Negotiating with Third-Party Payers
- PAs and Orthopedic PAs: The Distinctions
- PAs in Hospital Practice
- PA Educational Preparation for Prescribing
- Medicare's Final Rule on Billing Requirements for Teaching Physicians
- Meeting Rural America's Needs: PA Presence Remains Strong
- Standardization of Regulatory Terms: Licensure for PAs

State Legislative Assistance Grants. The AAPA Board of Directors budgets each year to fund a grant program for chapters with government affairs projects. For more information on grants, contact the director of state government affairs at the AAPA.

APPENDIX 11-B

State Legislative Document Offices

The following list contains the addresses and phone numbers of state legislative document offices (including the District of Columbia) from which House and Senate bills may be obtained.

ALABAMA
Senate Bill Room
State House
Montgomery, AL 36130
(334) 242-7824

House Bill Room
State House
Montgomery, AL 36130
(334) 242-7637

ALASKA
Documents Room
State Capitol
P.O. Box Y
Juneau, AK 99811
(907) 465-3737

ARIZONA
Bill Room
Arizona Legislature
Capitol Complex, House Wing
1700 W. Washington St.
Phoenix, AZ 85007
(602) 542-4379

ARKANSAS
Bill Room
Bureau of Legislative Research
State Capitol, Rm. 315
Little Rock, AR 72201
(501) 682-1937

CALIFORNIA
Bill Room
State Capitol Bldg.
Sacramento, CA 95814
(916) 445-2323

Source: Adapted from "State Health Officials," *1996 National Health Directory,* pp. 200–279, © 1996, Aspen Publishers, Inc.

COLORADO
Bill Room
State Capitol
Denver, CO 80203
(303) 866-2340

CONNECTICUT
Bill Room
Legislative Ofc. Bldg.
300 Capital Ave.
Hartford, CT 06106
(860) 240-0333

DELAWARE
Bill Room
Office of Legislative Council
Legislative Hall
Dover, DE 19903
(302) 739-4114

DISTRICT OF COLUMBIA
Bill Room
Office of Legislative Services
City Council, District Bldg.
1350 Pennsylvania Ave., N.W.
Washington, D.C. 20004
(202) 724-8050

FLORIDA
Bill Room
Senate Documents
303 State Capitol
Tallahassee, FL 32399
(904) 487-5285

Documents Division
House Documents
513 State Capitol
Tallahassee, FL 32399
(904) 488-7475

GEORGIA
Clerk's Office
House of Representatives
309 State Capitol Bldg.
Atlanta, GA 30334
(404) 656-5015

HAWAII
Senate Bill Room
Chief Clerk's Office
State Office Tower
235 S. Beretania St.
Honolulu, HI 96813
(808) 586-6755

House Bill Room
Chief Clerk's Office
State Capitol Bldg.
Honolulu, HI 96813
(808) 586-6400

IDAHO
Documents Room
Legislative Information Center
State Capitol Bldg.
Boise, ID 83720
(208) 334-3012

ILLINOIS
Senate Bill Room
State House
Springfield, IL 62706
(217) 782-9778

House Bill Room
State House
Springfield, IL 62706
(217) 782-5799

INDIANA
Bill Status
Office of Legislative Information
State House
Indianapolis, IN 46204
(317) 232-9856

IOWA
Legislative Information
State Capitol
Des Moines, IA 50319
(515) 281-5129

KANSAS
Document Room
Statehouse, 1st Fl.
300 S.W. 10th Ave.
Topeka, KS 66612
(913) 296-4096

KENTUCKY
Public Bill Room
State Capitol Bldg.
Frankfort, KY 40601
(502) 564-8100

LOUISIANA
Bill Room
State Capitol Bldg.
Baton Rouge, LA 70804
(504) 342-2192

MAINE
Document Room
Law & Legislative Library
State House
Augusta, ME 04333
(207) 287-6330

MARYLAND
Bill Room
90 State Circle
Legislative Services Bldg.
Annapolis, MD 21401
(410) 841-3840

MASSACHUSETTS
Document Room
State House
Boston, MA 02133
(617) 722-2860

MICHIGAN
Document Office
Legislative Services Bureau
P.O. Box 30036
Lansing, MI 48909
(517) 373-0169

MINNESOTA
Senate Documents
117 University Ave.
St. Paul, MN 55155
(612) 296-2343

House Documents
117 University Ave.
St. Paul, MN 55155
(612) 296-2314

MISSISSIPPI
House Docket Room
New Capitol
P.O. Box 1018
Jackson, MS 39201
(601) 359-3358

Senate Docket Room
New Capitol
P.O. Box 1018
Jackson, MS 39201
(601) 359-3229

MISSOURI
Senate Bill Room
State Capitol Bldg.
Jefferson City, MO 65101
(573) 751-2966

House Bill Room
State Capitol Bldg.
Jefferson City, MO 65101
(573) 751-3968

MONTANA
Bill Room
State Capitol
Helena, MT 59620
(406) 444-4853

NEBRASKA
Bill Room
Clerk of the Legislature
2018 State Capitol
Lincoln, NE 68509
(402) 471-2609

NEVADA
Publication Officer
Legislative Counsel Bureau
401 S. Carson St.
Carson City, NV 89710
(702) 687-6835

NEW HAMPSHIRE
Sargeant at Arms
State House
Concord, NH 03301
(603) 271-3315

NEW JERSEY
Bill Room
Office of Legislative Services
State House Annex
Trenton, NJ 08625
(609) 292-6395

NEW MEXICO
Bill Room
State Capitol, Rm. 363
Santa Fe, NM 87502
(505) 827-4600

NEW YORK
Bill Room
State Capitol
Albany, NY 12224
(518) 455-2311

NORTH CAROLINA
Bill Room
1430 State Legislative Bldg.
Raleigh, NC 27601
(919) 733-5648

NORTH DAKOTA
Legislative Council
State Capitol
600 E. Boulevard Ave.
Bismark, ND 58505
(701) 328-2916

OHIO
Bill Room
State House
Columbus, OH 43266
(614) 466-8842

OKLAHOMA
Bill Distribution Office
State Capitol
Oklahoma City, OK 73105
(405) 521-5515

OREGON
Bill Room
State Capitol
Salem, OR 97310
(503) 986-1180

PENNSYLVANIA
Senate Bill Room
Capitol Bldg.
Harrisburg, PA 17120
(717) 787-6732

House Bill Room
Capitol Bldg.
Harrisburg, PA 17120
(717) 787-5320

RHODE ISLAND
Legislative Library
State House
Providence, RI 02903
(401) 277-2473

SOUTH CAROLINA
Bill Room
State House
P.O. Box 11489
Columbia, SC 29211
(803) 734-2056

SOUTH DAKOTA
Bill Room
State Capitol
500 E. Capitol
Pierre, SD 57501
(605) 773-3835

TENNESSEE
Bill Room
Legislative Plaza
Nashville, TN 37243
(615) 741-0927

TEXAS
Bill Distribution Room
State Capitol
Austin, TX 78701
(512) 463-1155

UTAH
Bill Room
436 State Capitol
Salt Lake City, UT 84114
(801) 538-1588

VERMONT
Legislative Council
State House
Montpelier, VT 05633
(802) 828-2231

VIRGINIA
Bill Room
General Assembly Bldg.
Richmond, VA 23219
(804) 786-6984

WASHINGTON
Bill Room
Legislative Bldg.
Olympia, WA 98504
(360) 786-7573

WEST VIRGINIA
Senate Journal Room
Legislative Services
State Capitol
Charleston, WV 25305
(304) 357-7947

House Journal Room
Legislative Services
State Capitol
Charleston, WV 25305
(304) 340-3200

WISCONSIN
Documents Room
1 East Main St.
Madison, WI 53703
(608) 266-2400

WYOMING
Bill Room
State Capitol
Cheyenne, WY 82002
(307) 777-7648

APPENDIX 11-C

Summary of State Model Administrative Procedures Act

In 1981, the National Conference of Commissioners on Uniform State Law revised its 1961 Model State Administrative Procedures Act. Most states have adopted some form of the 1961 or 1981 models, the requirements of which are explained in the summary below.

PUBLIC NOTICE

Agencies must give notice to interested parties when contemplating rule making. The model act requires that at least 30 days' notice be given before any action is taken by the agency. The notice must include the text to the proposed action and invite interested parties to submit written data in response to the proposed action. Many states require the notice of proposed action be published in a newspaper with statewide circulation. Persons or groups who might be interested in board actions must make a written request to be listed with the agency as an interested party in order to receive timely notice. [MODEL STATE ADMIN. PROCEDURE ACT § 3-103 (1981)].

HEARINGS

If an agency is attempting to promulgate substantive rules that interested parties feel would have an adverse effect, an oral hearing may be requested. The request must come by petition of 25 or more persons or from an association with

---

Source: Reprinted with permission from *Taking Charge: State Government Affairs Handbook,* pp. 51–53 (citation to 1981 Model Act added), © 1996, American Academy of Physician Assistants.

25 or more members. Governmental subdivisions, including legislative committees, may also request an oral hearing on an issue. [Model State Admin. Procedure Act § 3-104 (1981)].

EXPLANATION OF REASONS FOR ADOPTION

If the rules have gone through the process described above and, despite overwhelming opposition received through written comment and testimony, the board persists in promulgating the rules, the next step is to request an official explanation of why the agency chose to adopt the rule. Most state administrative procedure statutes give any interested party the right to request a written explanation either prior to adoption or up to 30 days following adoption. The agency must issue a concise statement of all the reasons for and against adoption and its reasons for overruling these considerations. Should the agency choose to adopt its proposal, even though there is significant opposition to the rule, this written explanation can be used as evidence in any subsequent judicial review of the rule. [Model State Admin. Procedure Act §§ 3-105 and 3-110 (1981)].

SANCTIONS

Most state administrative procedure statutes require substantial compliance with the rule-making process, and if the agency fails to follow required procedure and its noncompliance is discovered within two years following implementation of the rule, then any interested party can file for an injunction against the agency and have the disputed rule(s) declared invalid. [Model State Admin. Procedure Act § 3-113(b) (1981)].

JUDICIAL REVIEW

Upon an agency's decision to promulgate objectionable rules (assuming proper rule-making procedures have been followed), there is still an opportunity under many state administrative procedure statutes to prevent implementation via judicial review. For PAs, deciding to pursue this final step of judicial review must be weighed against the impact of the agency's decision in terms of ability to function as PAs.

If all negotiations with the regulatory board have failed, and all administrative remedies have been exhausted, a person or group objecting to promulgation of a rule can, with the assistance of legal counsel, seek a judicial review of the validity of the rule. [Model State Admin. Procedure Act § 5-107 (1981)]. It should be noted, however, that courts accord extreme deference to decisions made by an administrative agency. Unless the agency has exceeded its authority or violated required procedures, the court will defer to the expertise of the agency. The most valid arguments used by attorneys in opposing an agency's action are that promulgation of a particular rule: (i) exceeds the authority conferred to the agency, (ii) extends or modifies the statute, (iii) has no relationship to statutory purpose, (iv) is unconstitutional, arbitrary, or unreasonable, and (v) is in conflict with the governing statute. [Model State Admin. Procedure Act § 5-116 (1981)].

LEGISLATIVE REVIEW

Although not reflected in the model act, many states have included some type of legislative review of proposed agency rules in their administrative procedure statutes. During the notice period, the medical board may be required to send its proposed rule changes to a particular committee of the state legislature. The committee that reviews the proposed rules will vary from state to state, but usually it is the House or Senate committee that deals with health issues. Some states have a special rules committee that meets periodically and does nothing but review agency rules.

What happens after the legislative review also varies from state to state. The legislative committee(s) can formally object to implementation. The agency, if it chooses, then can proceed with promulgation, but the legislature can sustain the committee's objection through passage of a resolution in either the House or the Senate. Other states allow legislative committees actual veto power over the agency or require ratification by the legislative committee before the agency can implement new rules.

APPENDIX A

Physician Assistant National and Specialty Organizations

This appendix contains a list of the major national and specialty organizations representing PAs or PA education programs. The list is not exhaustive, and the AAPA should be consulted for the most current and comprehensive information about these organizations. Also, where address information contained in this list changes frequently, no address appears for the organization, but can be obtained on request from the AAPA or from the following online address: http://www.aapa.org/special.htm.

American Academy of Physician Assistants (AAPA)
950 North Washington Street
Alexandria, VA 22314
703-836-2272

The AAPA is the national professional society for PAs; its members comprise approximately 80 percent of all practicing PAs. Founded in 1968, the Academy has chapters in all 50 states, the District of Columbia, and Guam. There also are chapters that represent PAs working for the Public Health Service, the Department of Veterans Affairs, and all branches of the military. The AAPA's mission is to "promote the professional and personal development of PAs," which the Academy strives to achieve through activities such as government relations, public education, research and data collection, and professional development.

Association of Physician Assistant Programs (APAP)
950 North Washington Street
Alexandria, VA 22314
703-548-5538

In contrast to the AAPA's membership of student and practicing PAs, members of APAP are PA education programs and their faculty. Founded in 1972, APAP shares its national headquarters with the AAPA; both organizations are located in

Alexandria, Virginia. APAP's central objective is to help maintain the high quality of PA education, and thus its main activities include encouraging communication among programs and serving as a national information center on PA education.

National Commission on Certification of Physician Assistants (NCCPA)
6849-B2 Peachtree Dunwoody Road
Atlanta, GA 30328
770-399-9971

The NCCPA is an independent organization established to ensure the competency of PAs; it was formed in 1975 by AAPA and other health professional associations to administer a national certifying examination to graduates of accredited PA programs. NCCPA certification obtained on passing the exam is a requirement of state licensure in a majority of states.

The following specialty organizations, recognized by the AAPA Board of Directors, are comprised of PA members practicing in the particular specialized field of medicine identified in the organization's name:

American Academy of Physician Assistants in Occupational Medicine (AAPA-OM)
American Association of Surgeon Assistants (AASA)
Association of Neurosurgical Physician Assistants (ANSPA)
Association of Physician Assistants in Cardiovascular Surgery (APACVS)
Association of Physician Assistants in Obstetrics and Gynecology (APAOG)
Association of Physician Assistants in Oncology (APAO)
Physician Assistants in Family Practice (PAFP)
Physician Assistants in Orthopedic Surgery (PAOS)
Society of Dermatology Physician Assistants
Society of Emergency Medicine Physician Assistants (SEMPA)
Society of Physician Assistants in Addiction Medicine (SPAAM)
Society of Physician Assistants in Otorhinolaryngology/Head and Neck Surgery
Society of Physician Assistants in Pediatrics
Society of Physician Assistants in Physical Medicine and Rehabilitation

APPENDIX B

State Regulation of Physician Assistants

This appendix contains a list of state regulatory agencies governing physician assistants, followed by a list of the state statutory and regulatory provisions concerning PAs. Since state legislatures and regulatory agencies revise statutes and regulations frequently, the regulatory agency or the AAPA should be consulted for actual statutory language and to ensure that references herein remain up-to-date. This appendix should be used only as a general guide to PA laws in the various states.

ALABAMA

Regulatory Body
Alabama Board of Medical Examiners
P.O. Box 946
Montgomery, AL 36101
(334) 242-4116
Applicable Statute
ALA. CODE §§ 34-24-290 through -294
Applicable Regulation
ALA. ADMIN. CODE r. 540-X-7-.01 through -.16, 540-X-.18 through -.33 and Board of Medical Examiners Guidelines Governing the Prescription Privileges of Assistants to Physicians

ALASKA

Regulatory Body
Alaska Medical Licensing Board
Division of Occupational Licensing
3601 C Street, Suite 722
Anchorage, AK 99503
(907) 269-8163

Applicable Statute
ALASKA STAT. §§ 08.64.010 through -.64.380.
Applicable Regulation
ALASKA ADMIN. CODE tit. 12, §§ 40.400 through -.490, 40.960 through -.990

ARIZONA

Regulatory Body
Joint Board on the Regulation of Physician Assistants
1651 East Morten Avenue, Suite 210
Phoenix, AZ 85020
(602) 255-3751
Applicable Statute
ARIZ. REV. STAT. ANN. §§ 32-1502, 32-2501 through -2506, 32-2521 through -2534, 2551.
Applicable Regulation
ARIZ. ADMIN. CODE R4-17-101 through R4-17-504.

ARKANSAS

Regulatory Body
Arkansas Medical Board
2100 Riverfront Drive, Suite 200
Little Rock, AR 72202
(501) 296-1802
Applicable Statute
ARK. CODE ANN. §§ 17-94-101 through -113
Applicable Regulation
Medical Board Regulations Governing Physician's Trained Assistants, Regulation 4(1) through (17)

CALIFORNIA

Regulatory Body
Physician Assistant Examining Committee (PAEC)
Medical Board of California
1424 Howe Avenue, # 35
Sacramento, CA 95825
(916) 263-2670
Applicable Statute
CAL. BUS. & PROF. CODE §§ 3513 through 3519, and 3500 through 3546; *see also* CAL. BUS. & PROF. CODE § 3535 (osteopathic PAs)
Applicable Regulation
CAL. CODE REGS. tit. 16, §§ 1399.500 through -.574

COLORADO

Regulatory Body
Colorado Board of Medical Examiners
1560 Broadway Street, Suite 1300
Denver, CO 80202
(303) 894-7690
Applicable Statute
Colo. Rev. Stat. §§ 12-36-106 (5) & -106.5
Applicable Regulation
Colorado State Board of Medical Examiners Rules and Regulations for Certification of and Practice by Physician Assistants §§ 1 through 6

CONNECTICUT

Regulatory Body
Division of Medical Quality Assurance
Department of Public Health—PA Licensing
410 Capitol Avenue MS#12APP
P.O. Box 340308
Hartford, CT 06134
(203) 509-7566
Applicable Statute
Conn. Gen. Stat. §§ 20-8a, 20-12a through -12g
Applicable Regulation
none issued

DELAWARE

Regulatory Body
Delaware Board of Medical Practice
(PA Regulatory Council)
Cannon Building
P.O. Box 1401
Dover, DE 19903
(302) 739-4522
Applicable Statute
Del. Code Ann. tit. 24, § 1770A
Applicable Regulation
Delaware Board of Medical Practice Regulation 23 (controlled substances), and Regulation 25 (PA scope of practice, license renewal, and prescriptive authority).

DISTRICT OF COLUMBIA

Regulatory Body
District of Columbia Board of Medicine
Department of Consumer and Regulatory Affairs
(PA Advisory Committee)
614 H Street, N.W., Rm. 904
Washington, DC 20001
(202) 727-5365
Applicable Statute
D.C. CODE ANN. §§ 2-3301.2 & 2-3302.3
Applicable Regulation
D.C. MUN. REGS. tit. 17, §§ 4900 through 4916; 4999.1 (definition of PA)

FLORIDA

Regulatory Body
Florida Board of Medicine &
Board of Osteopathic Medical Examiner
(Council of PAs)
Department of Professional Regulation
[both boards are located at the same address]:
1940 N. Monroe Street, #60
Tallahassee, FL 32399-0770
(904) 488-0595
(904) 922-6725 (osteopathic PAs)
Applicable Statute
FLA. STAT. § 458.347; *see also* FLA. STAT. § 459.022 (osteopathic PAs)
Applicable Regulation
FLA. ADMIN. CODE ANN. r. 59R-3.001 through 3.010 (application, fees, and renewal); 59R-30.001 through 30.017 (PA scope of practice; prescriptive authority); see also FLA. ADMIN. CODE ANN. r. 59W-6.001 through .-005 & 6.010 through .-013 (osteopathic PAs)

GEORGIA

Regulatory Body
Georgia Composite State Board of Medical Examiners
(PA Advisory Committee)
166 Pryor Street, S.W.
Atlanta, GA 30303
(404) 656-3913
Applicable Statute
GA. CODE ANN. §§ 43-34-100 through -108

Applicable Regulation
GA. COMP. R. & REGS. r. 360-1-.01; 360-5.01-.12; 480-30-.01 (dispensing)

HAWAII

Regulatory Body
Hawaii Board of Medical Examiners
Department of Commerce and Consumer Affairs
Division of Professional Licensing
(PA Advisory Committee)
P.O. Box. 3469
Honolulu, HI 96801
(808) 586-3000
Applicable Statute
HAW. REV. STAT. § 453-2 & -5.3
Applicable Regulation
Haw. Admin. Rules §§ 16-85-44 through -52 (proposed)

IDAHO

Regulatory Body
Idaho Board of Medicine
(PA Advisory Committee)
P.O. Box 83720
Boise, ID 83720-0058
(208) 334-2822
Applicable Statute
IDAHO CODE §§ 54-1803 through -1814
Applicable Regulation
Board of Medicine Rules for the Registration of Physician's Assistants, IDAPA 22.01.03.010 through .-054

ILLINOIS

Regulatory Body
Illinois Department of Professional Regulation
(PA Advisory Committee to Board of Medicine)
100 W. Randolph Street, #9-300
Chicago, IL 60601
(312) 814-4500
or
320 W. Washington Street
Springfield, IL 62786
(217) 785-0820

Applicable Statute
225 ILL. COMP. STAT. 95/1 through 95/24
Applicable Regulation
ILL. ADMIN. CODE, tit. 68, §§ 1350.10 through -.120

INDIANA

Regulatory Body
Indiana Health Professions Service Bureau
Medical Licensing Board
(PA Advisory Committee)
402 W. Washington Street, Suite 041
Indianapolis, IN 46204
(317) 232-2960
Applicable Statute
IND. CODE §§ 25-27.5-1-1 through -.5-7-3
Applicable Regulation
IND. ADMIN. CODE tit. 844, r. 2.1-1-1 through -.1-1-10

IOWA

Regulatory Body
Iowa Board of Physician Assistant Examiners
Department of Public Health
Professional Licensing Division
Lucas Office Building, Capitol Complex
Des Moines, IA 50319
(515) 242-5937
Applicable Statute
IOWA CODE §§ 148C.1 through -.11; IOWA CODE § 147.107 (prescriptive authority)
Applicable Regulation
IOWA ADMIN. CODE r. 645-325.1 through -.17; IOWA ADMIN. CODE r. 653-21.2 (physician eligibility for PA supervision)

KANSAS

Regulatory Body
Kansas Board of Healing Arts
(PA Council)
235 S.W. Topeka Blvd.
Topeka, KS 66603
(913) 296-7413
Applicable Statute
Kan. Stat. Ann. §§ 65-2896 through -2897b

Applicable Regulation
KAN. ADMIN. REGS. 100-60-1 through -60-15

KENTUCKY

Regulatory Body
Kentucky Board of Medical Licensure
(PA Advisory Committee)
310 Whittington Pkwy, Suite 1B
Louisville, KY 40222
(502) 429-8046
Applicable Statute
KY. REV. STAT. ANN. § 311.565 (board powers)
Applicable Regulation
201 KY. ADMIN. REGS. 9:175 §§ 1 through 9

LOUISIANA

Regulatory Body
Louisiana Board of Medical Examiners
(PA Advisory Committee)
630 Camp Street
New Orleans, LA 70130
(504) 524-6763
Applicable Statute
LA. REV. STAT. ANN. §§ 37:1360.21 through -.38
Applicable Regulation
LA. ADMIN. CODE tit. 46, §§ 1500 through 1517; 4501 through 4513 (physician(s) responsibility over PA)

MAINE

Regulatory Body
Maine Board of Registration in Medicine
(PA Advisory Committee)
137 State House Station
Augusta, ME 04333
(207) 287-3601
or
Maine Board of Osteopathic Examiners
142 State House Station
Augusta, ME 04333
(207) 287-2480

Applicable Statute
ME. REV. STAT. ANN. tit. 32, §§ 3270-B and C; ME. REV. STAT. ANN. tit. 32, §§ 2594-B through D (osteopathic PAs)
Applicable Regulation
CODE ME. R. §§ 02-373-002 through -003; 02-383-001 through -002 (osteopathic PAs)

MARYLAND

Regulatory Body
Maryland Board of Physician Quality Assurance
Department of Health and Mental Hygiene
(PA Advisory Committee)
P.O. Box 2571
Baltimore, MD 21215
(410) 764-4777; (800) 492-6836
Applicable Statute
MD. CODE ANN., HEALTH OCC. §§ 15-101 through -102; 15-201 through -206 (role of board and advisory committee); 15-301 through -315 (scope of practice); 15-401 through -403 (prohibited acts and penalties)
Applicable Regulation
MD. REGS. CODE tit. 10, § 10.32.03 *et seq.*

MASSACHUSETTS

Regulatory Body
Board of Registration of Physician Assistants
Department of Consumer Affairs and Business Registration
Division of Registration
100 Cambridge Street, Rm. 1516
Boston, MA 02202
(617) 727-3069
Applicable Statute
MASS. GEN. L. ch. 112, § 9C-K; ch. 13, §§ 10B & 11C (role of board); ch. 94C, §§ 7 & 9 (prescribing and dispensing)
Applicable Regulation
MASS. REGS. CODE tit. 263, §§ 2.01 through -.04; 3.01 through -.06; 4.01 through -.06; 5.01 through -.08; 6.01 through -.02; tit. 105, §§ 700.001 through -.020 (prescribing); 721.030 (prescription blanks); tit. 243, § 2.08 (physician supervision)

MICHIGAN

Regulatory Body
Task Force on Physician Assistants

Health Professions Division
P.O. Box 30018
Lansing, MI 48909
(517) 373-6650
Applicable Statute
MICH. COMP. LAWS §§ 333.17001 through -.17088, -.17501 through -.17556 (osteopathic PAs), .17745 (dispensing requirements for authorized prescribers)
Applicable Regulation
MICH. ADMIN. CODE r. 338.6101, 6301, 6305, 6308

MINNESOTA

Regulatory Body
Minnesota Board of Medical Examiners
(PA Advisory Council)
2700 University Ave. West, Ste. 106
St. Paul, MN 55114
(612) 642-0538
Applicable Statute
MINN. STAT. §§ 147A.01 through -.26
Applicable Regulation
MINN. R. 5600.2600 through -.2665

MISSOURI

Regulatory Body
Missouri Board of Registration for the Healing Arts
(Advisory Commission for Registered PAs)
P.O. Box 4
Jefferson City, MO 65102
(314) 751-0098
Applicable Statute
MO. REV. STAT. §§ 334.100 through -.749
Applicable Regulation
MO. CODE REGS. ANN. tit. 4, § 150-7.010 *et seq.*

MONTANA

Regulatory Body
Montana Board of Medical Examiners
(PA Advisory Committee)
111 N. Jackson
P.O. Box 200513
Helena, MT 59620

(406) 444-4284
Applicable Statute
MONT. CODE ANN. §§ 37-20-201 through -203; -301 through -303; -401 through -409
Applicable Regulation
MONT. ADMIN. R. 8.28.1501 through -.1520

NEBRASKA

Regulatory Body
Nebraska Board of Examiners in Medicine and Surgery
(PA Committee)
P.O. Box 95007
Lincoln, NE 68509
(402) 471-2115
Applicable Statute
NEB. REV. STAT. §§ 71-1,107.15 through -1,107.30
Applicable Regulation
Neb. Dept. of Health, Professional and Occupational Licenses Regulations, tit. 172, ch. 90, Rules and Regulations for Certification and Supervision of Physician Assistants §§ .001 through -.015

NEVADA

Regulatory Body
Nevada Board of Medical Examiners
(PA Advisory Committee)
P.O. Box 7238
Reno, NV 89510
(702) 688-2559
Applicable Statute
NEV. REV. STAT. §§ 630.010 through -.415; NEV. REV. STAT. §§ 453.377, 454.215, & 639.1373 (prescribing and dispensing)
Applicable Regulation
NEV. ADMIN. CODE ch. 630, §§ 630.010 through -.415 (scattered sections); ch. 633, §§ 633.290 & -.330 (osteopathic PAs); ch. 639, §§ 639.270 through -.295 (prescribing and dispensing)

NEW HAMPSHIRE

Regulatory Body
New Hampshire Board of Registration in Medicine
(PA Advisory Committee)
2 Industrial Park Drive, Ste. 8

Concord, NH 03301
(603) 271-1203
Applicable Statute
N.H. Rev. Stat. Ann. §§ 328-D:1 through :13
Applicable Regulation
N.H. Code Admin. R. Ann. Med 601 through 608

NEW JERSEY

Regulatory Body
New Jersey Division of Consumer Affairs
(PA Advisory Committee)
P.O. Box 45035
Newark, NJ 07101
(201) 504-6328
or
New Jersey Board of Medical Examiners
140 East Front St., 2nd Fl.
Trenton, NJ 08608
(609) 826-7100
Applicable Statute
N.J. Stat. Ann. §§ 45:9-27.10 through -27.28
Applicable Regulation
N.J. Admin. Code tit. 13 §§ 13:35-2B.1 through -2B.16; 6.13 through -.15

NEW MEXICO

Regulatory Body
New Mexico Board of Medical Examiners
(PA Advisory Committee)
491 Old Santa Fe Trail, 2nd Fi.
Santa Fe, NM 87501
(505) 827-7363
or
Board of Osteopathic Medical Examiners
P.O. Box 25101
Santa Fe, NM 87504
(505) 827-7171
Applicable Statute
N.M. Stat. Ann. §§ 61-6-7 through -10; N.M. Stat. Ann. §§ 61-10A-1 through -7 (osteopathic PAs)

Applicable Regulation
Board of Medical Examiners Rules and Regulations (Physician Assistant), Rules 1-9; N.M. Admin. Code §§ 18.1.1 through -.9.1 (osteopathic PAs)

NEW YORK

Regulatory Body
Medical Unit, Division of Professional Licensing Services
State Education Department
Cultural Education Center
Albany, NY 12230
(518) 474-3817
Applicable Statute
N.Y. Educ. Law §§ 6540 through 6548; N.Y. Pub. Health Law §§ 3701 through 3702
Applicable Regulation
N.Y. Comp. Codes R. & Regs. tit. 8, §§ 60.1-.8; N.Y. Comp. Codes R. & Regs. tit. 10, §§ 94.1-.2 (prescribing); 707.1-.3 (hospitals employing PAs).

NORTH CAROLINA

Regulatory Body
North Carolina Board of Medical Examiners
(PA Advisory Committee)
P.O. Box 20007
Raleigh, NC 27619
(919) 828-1212
Applicable Statute
N.C. Gen. Stat. § 90-18.1
Applicable Regulation
N.C. Admin. Code tit. 21, r. 32O.0001 through -.0021; N.C. Admin. Code tit. 21, r. 32Q.0101 through -.0207 (rehabilitative programs for impaired physician assistants)

NORTH DAKOTA

Regulatory Body
North Dakota Board of Medical Examiners
418 East Broadway, Ste. 12
Bismarck, ND 58501
(701) 328-6500

Applicable Statute
N.D. Cent. Code §§ 43-17-02.1 through -02.2
Applicable Regulation
N.D. Admin. Code §§ 50-02-05; 50-03-01 through -03-15

OHIO

Regulatory Body
Ohio Medical Board
(PA Policy Committee)
77 South High Street, 17th Fl.
Columbus, OH 43266
(614) 466-3934
Applicable Statute
Ohio Rev. Code Ann. §§ 4730.01 through -.34; 4730.99 (penalties)
Applicable Regulation
Ohio Admin. Code §§ 4731-4-01 through -04

OKLAHOMA

Regulatory Body
Oklahoma Board of Medical Licensure and Supervision
(PA Committee)
P.O. Box 18256
Oklahoma City, OK 73154
(405) 848-2189
Applicable Statute
Okla. Stat. Ann. tit. 59, §§ 519.1 through -.11, 521
Applicable Regulation
Okla. Admin. Code r. 435:15-1-1 through -13-3

OREGON

Regulatory Body
Oregon Board of Medical Examiners
(PA Committee)
1500 S.W. First Avenue, Ste. 620
Portland, OR 97201
(503) 229-5770
Applicable Statute
Or. Rev. Stat. §§ 677.495 through -.550
Applicable Regulation
Or. Admin. R. 847-50-005 through -065

PENNSYLVANIA

Regulatory Body
Pennsylvania Board of Medicine & Board of Osteopathic Medicine
(both boards are located at the same address)
P.O. Box 2649
Harrisburg, PA 17105
(717) 787-2381
(717) 783-4858 (osteopathic PAs)
Applicable Statute
63 PA. CONS. STAT. §§ 422.2 through -.3; 422.13 and 13b; 422.36; 271.2 through -.10 (osteopathic PAs)
Applicable Regulation
49 PA. CODE §§ 18.121 through .183

RHODE ISLAND

Regulatory Body
Board of Registration for PAs
Division of Professional Regulation
Health Department
3 Capitol Hill, Rm. 104
Providence, RI 02908
(401) 277-2827
Applicable Statute
R.I. GEN. LAWS §§ 5-54-1 through -21
Applicable Regulation
Department of Health Rules and Regulations for the Registration of Physician Assistants, R5-54-PA, §§ 1-10

SOUTH CAROLINA

Regulatory Body
South Carolina Board of Medical Examiners
P.O. Box 11289
Columbia, SC 29211
(803) 737-9300
Applicable Statute
S.C. CODE ANN. §§ 40-47-20 and -47-25 (PA representation on board)
Applicable Regulation
S.C. CODE ANN. REGS. 81-100(A) through (S); 81-110

SOUTH DAKOTA

Regulatory Body
South Dakota Board of Medical and Osteopathic Examiners

(PA Advisory Committee)
1323 South Minnesota Ave.
Sioux Falls, SD 57105
(605) 336-1965
Applicable Statute
S.D. Codified Laws §§ 36-4A-1 through -48
Applicable Regulation
S.D. Admin. R. 20:52:01 (certificate as PA)

TENNESSEE

Regulatory Body
Committee on PAs
Tennessee Board of Medical Examiners
Cordell Hull Bldg, 1st Fl.
426 5th Avenue North
Nashville, TN 37247
(615) 367-6243
Applicable Statute
Tenn. Code Ann. §§ 63-19-101 through -114
Applicable Regulation
Tenn. Comp. R. & Regs. tit. 63, ch. 0880-3-.01 through -.22

TEXAS

Regulatory Body
Texas Board of Physician Assistant Examiners
Texas Board of Medical Examiners
P.O. Box 2018
Austin, TX 78768
(512) 305-7010
Applicable Statute
Tex. Rev. Civ. Stat. Ann. art. 4495b-1, §§ 1 through 28 (PA licensing)
Applicable Regulation
22 Tex. Admin. Code §§ 185.1 through -.29; 186.1 through -.3 (supervision of student PAs); 193.2 through -.8 (standing orders for prescribing)

UTAH

Regulatory Body
PA Licensing Board
Division of Occupational and Professional Licensing
P.O. Box 45805
Salt Lake City, UT 84145
(801) 530-6623

Applicable Statute
UTAH CODE ANN. §§ 58-70-101 through -102, -201, -301 through -304, -401, -501 through -502
Applicable Regulation
UTAH ADMIN. CODE R156-70-101 through -104, -302 through -314, -502; R156-37-301 (prescribing authority)

VERMONT

Regulatory Body
Vermont Board of Medical Practice
109 State Street
Montpelier, VT 05609
(802) 828-2673
Applicable Statute
VT. STAT. ANN. tit. 26, §§ 1731 through 1743
Applicable Regulation
VT. CODE 04-050-001, § 3.1; 04-057-001, § 3.710 (prescribing authority)

VIRGINIA

Regulatory Body
Virginia Board of Medicine
(Advisory Committee on PAs)
6606 West Broad Street, 4th Fl.
Richmond, VA 23230
(804) 662-9908
Applicable Statute
VA. CODE ANN. §§ 54.1-2949 through -2953
Applicable Regulation
VA. ADMIN. CODE tit. 18, §§ 85-50-10 through -170, and part VII (forms)

WASHINGTON

Regulatory Body
Washington Medical Quality Assurance Commission
P.O. Box 47866
Olympia, WA 98504
(360) 586-8934
Applicable Statute
WASH. REV. CODE ANN. §§ 18.71A.005-.085; 18.57A.005-.070 (osteopathic PAs)
Applicable Regulation
WASH. ADMIN. CODE §§ 246-918-005 through -310; 246-918-990 (fees)

WEST VIRGINIA

Regulatory Body
West Virginia Board of Medicine
101 Dee Drive
Charleston, WV 25311
(304) 558-2921
or
West Virginia Board of Osteopathy
334 Penco Road
Weirton, WV 26062
(304) 723-4638
Applicable Statute
W. VA. CODE §§ 30-3-1; 30-3-16(a)-(q); 30-14A-1 through -4 (osteopathic PAs)
Applicable Regulation
West Virginia Board of Medicine, Legislative Rules, tit. 11, §§ 11-1B-1 through 11-2B-3

WISCONSIN

Regulatory Body
Wisconsin Medical Examining Board
Department of Regulation and Licensing
(Council on PAs)
P.O. Box 8935
Madison, WI 53708
(608) 266-2811
Applicable Statute
WIS. STAT. §§ 15.407 (composition of board); 448.01 through -.21
Applicable Regulation
WIS. ADMIN. CODE §§ Med 8.01 through -.11; Med 17.01 through -.06 (prescribing and dispensing)

WYOMING

Regulatory Body
Wyoming Board of Medical Examiners
(Advisory Committee on PAs)
Colonial Bldg, 2nd Fl.
211 W. 19th Street
Cheyenne, WY 82002
(307) 778-7053

Applicable Statute
WYO. STAT. ANN. §§ 33-26-501 through -511
Applicable Regulation
Board of Medicine Rules and Regulations for Physicians and Physician Assistants ch. 5, §§ 1 through 18; Code of Wyoming Rules 024-052-001, § 8 (fees); and 024-052-005, § 10 (locum tenens)

Table of Cases

E

F

G

H

K

T

U

V

W

Y

Index

B

C

D

E

F

G

H

M

N

O

About the Authors

Patricia Younger, JD, Cynthia Conner, LL.L, Kara Kinney Cartwright, JD, Susan M. Kole, JD, and **Jennifer C. Forsyth, JD, MPH,** are Health Law Center staff members at Aspen Publishers, Inc., where they are involved in extensive research and writing on health law issues. Among the publications these attorneys write for are the *Hospital Law Manual,* a multivolume, looseleaf treatise (now available on CD-ROM), on a full range of health law issues, such as medical records, medical staff, pharmacy, consents, reproductive issues, tax, and financial management; the *Health Care Labor Manual,* a three-volume, looseleaf treatise on labor and employment issues of concern to health care providers; the *Managed Care Law Manual,* a two-volume, looseleaf treatise on legal issues of concern in the managed care environment, such as antitrust, utilization management, taxation, and fraud and abuse; and *Physician Organizations and Medical Staff,* a two-volume, looseleaf treatise on contracts, rights, and liabilities associated with the wide array of affiliations and contractual relationships through which physicians currently render medical care. They also have authored three legal answer books: the *Physician Credentialing and Peer Review Answer Book,* the *Legal Answer Book for Managed Care,* and the *Pharmacy Law Answer Book* and collaborated with William H. Roach, Jr., in writing the second edition of *Medical Records and the Law.* In addition, these attorneys work with outside authors in producing the *Laboratory Regulation Manual,* a four-volume, looseleaf treatise addressing legal issues of concern to clinical laboratories written by the law firm of O'Connor and Hannon; the *Hospital Contracts Manual,* a three-volume treatise covering contract issues relevant to health care providers; and the *Managed Care Contracts Manual,* a treatise on managed care contracting, both edited by the law firm of Baker and Hostetler.